Early Experience
and
Human Development

Early Experience
and
Human Development

Theodore D. Wachs and Gerald E. Gruen
Purdue University, West Lafayette, Indiana

Plenum Press - New York and London

Library of Congress Cataloging in Publication Data

Wachs, Theodore D., 1941-
   Early experience and human development.

   Includes bibliographical references and index.
   1. Cognition. 2. Experience. 3. Developmental psychology. I. Gruen, Gerald E.,
1937-   . II. Title.
BF713.W32   155.4'22   82-5273
ISBN 0-306-40685-3

© 1982 Plenum Press, New York
A Division of Plenum Publishing Corporation
233 Spring Street, New York, N.Y. 10013

Printed in the United States of America

To our parents, who provided us with our unique
early experiences

Preface

Our goal in writing this book was to fill a perceived gap in the early experience literature. Most existing volumes on early experience and development can be dichotomized on a basic versus an applied dimension. Volumes falling on the basic side are designed for researchers and theoreticians in the biomedical and behavioral sciences. Most existing basic volumes are either primarily based on infrahuman data or are based on single major human studies. In going over these volumes, we are not convinced of the generality of infrahuman data to the human level; in addition, we were concerned about the replicability of findings from single studies, however well designed these studies were. As a result, the relevance of data from these volumes to applied human problems is quite limited. In contrast, volumes falling on the applied side are designed primarily for those involved in intervention work with infants and young children. These applied books generally tend to be vague and nonempirical compilations of the views of experts and the collective "wisdom of the ages." Rarely in applied volumes do we find conclusions based on solid, consistent, empirical findings. Nowhere could we find a volume in which an attempt was made to summarize systematically all available research on early experience as it relates to critical human developmental parameters and to use these findings not only as a means of understanding the nature of development and the nature of early environmental action, but also as a means of transmitting empirically validated conclusions to those interested in the applied uses of early experience. Our goal became the production of a volume on early experience based on empirical studies but having relevance for the practitioner as well as for the scientist. We envisioned a volume which would be useful not only for the basic researcher interested in the nature of early environmental action, but also for those workers in the field who are doing intervention with high-risk or developmentally disabled babies and who are constantly faced with the question, "What do I do next?" Our interest in producing such a volume came from our own "early experience," in that one of us (Wachs) was trained as a child clinical psychologist but with a strong background in developmental psychology while the other (Gruen) was trained as a developmental psychologist but with postdoctoral training in child clinical psychology. The fact that one of us (Wachs) was interested primarily in cognitive-intellectual development while the other (Gruen) was interested primarily in social development led to the major focus of the book on these two specific developmental parameters.

In reading this book, the reader may become aware of differences not only in style but in orientation. This results from the fact that each of us took primary responsibility for certain sections of the book (with the exception of Chapter 10). Specifically, Wachs was primarily responsible for Chapters 1 through 5 and Chapter 9 and Gruen was responsible for Chapters 6 through 8. Chapter 10 was jointly written. However, each of us went over the other's chapters and made suggestions both in orientation and content. Thus, at least to that extent, all chapters are a joint product. Chapter divisions were not arbitrary, but rather reflected our differing interests. Despite our monitoring of each other's chapters, the reader may be aware of major differences in orientation. This is a function not only of individual differences in style but also of the nature of the field. The fact that one of us (Wachs) is by nature (or nurture) basically empirical and atheoretical while the other (Gruen) is basically theoretical in orientation obviously meant that we would approach our respective chapters in different ways. These initial differences were reinforced (or reinstated) by the fact that there is simply much more available evidence on the relationship of early experience to cognitive development, and therefore these chapters tend to be empirically oriented. In contrast, the social area, while rich in theory, has comparatively less data. Chapter 8 represents Gruen's current interests while Chapter 9 was a painful exercise for Wachs in terms of attempting to develop some kind of theoretical model from empirical data. Overall, for those individuals interested in scientific aspects of early experience Chapters 2 through 9 will be most relevant; for those interested in applied aspects Chapter 10 will obviously be most relevant, but we hope that the applied reader will also look at Chapters 3 through 7 to get an idea of how the conclusions developed in Chapter 10 have arisen.

In the writing of this book we would like to acknowledge the help of Professor Alan Clarke (University of Hull) for his exchange of letters on the topic of early versus later experience. Neither one of us convinced the other, but it was a highly stimulating interchange. We are also grateful for the comments of Professor Pat Gallagher in the Department of Special Education at Purdue University for his reading and comments on our applications chapter. The comments of Professor Robert Bradley (University of Arkansas at Little Rock) were of great help in terms of scope, organization, and the translation of empirical data into intervention applications. Our secretary, Debbie Sweeney, not only typed flawlessly and corrected our grammar but most importantly, cheerfully put up with cut-and-paste rewrites and badly garbled inserts; for this, special thanks. Finally, we would like to acknowledge the pervasive influence of our intellectual father (in the case of Gruen) and intellectual grandfather (in the case of Wachs), Professor J. McV. Hunt, whose theorizing and research in the area of early experience not only helped usher in the modern age of early experience research but has also been an inspiration to those of us who continue to be interested in the topic.

T. D. WACHS
G. E. GRUEN

Contents

CHAPTER 1

Introduction

The potential influence of the early years upon later behavior has always fascinated observers of human development.

> And the first step, as you know, is always what matters most, particularly when we are dealing with those who are young and tender. That is the time when they are taking shape and when any impression we choose to make leaves a permanent mark. (Plato, *The Republic*)

While there have been continual references to the role of early experience in development at least from the time of the Greek philosophers, as Hunt (1979) has pointed out, these scattered references never became "socially or politically dominant" until after 1945. A number of factors appeared to coalesce at that time to form a *zeitgeist* centering around the importance of early experience for later behavior. Thompson and Grusec (1970) suggest that three influences were of particular importance in this process. First was the influence of psychoanalytic theory with its emphasis on the primacy of the first six years of life for later personality development. From Freudian theory came infrahuman research on the effects of infantile stress on physiological and emotional development and human research on the effects of maternal deprivation in orphanage and crisis situations. A second influence came from the field of neuropsychology. Sparked by Hebb's classic work *Organization of Behavior* (1949), a large number of studies were developed relating the early experience of the organism to both morphological and biochemical central nervous system development. A third influence was the ethological tradition which became quite prominent after 1945. The idea that a relatively brief early exposure could insure lifelong bonding had a major influence on socialization studies at both the human and infrahuman level.

Beyond these three factors, we should also point to a fourth influence, namely the educational tradition. Starting with Rousseau and carrying on through Itard, Seguin, and Montessori, there has been a long tradition of intervention with the young child for the purpose of promoting cognitive gains. This tradition was tied to the area of early experience, at least in part,

1

by publication of Hunt's seminal volume *Intelligence and Experience* (1961). In this volume Hunt brought together current infrahuman and human research on early experience effects and related this research to the theorizing of both Hebb and Piaget; as a result of this integration, the idea of early intervention as a means of promoting cognitive growth was firmly established. Also influential was the volume *Stability and Change in Human Characteristics* by Bloom (1964). Hypothesizing that environmental variation was most salient for a trait during the trait's most rapid growth period, Bloom presented a good deal of evidence which suggested that both intelligence and personality had their most rapid growth periods during the early years of life. The obvious conclusion was that environmental influences should be directed at development primarily during this age period. As a corollary to Bloom, Ausubel (1964) suggested that once development is channeled into a specific area early in life the individual becomes less responsive to stimulation later in life.

    As a result of these disparate influences, there was a tremendous upsurge of research on early experience during the 1950s and thereafter. Hunt (1979) has reported that from 1954 to the present the number of reported studies on early experience went from fewer than 300 to over 1,500. Reviews of this research on both the infrahuman (Ambrose, 1969; Hunt, 1979; Reisen, 1975; Scott, 1968) and human (Freeberg & Payne, 1967; Haywood & Tapp, 1966; Hunt, 1979; Streisguth & Bee, 1972) levels clearly showed the relevance of early experience to a variety of physiological, cognitive, social, and motivational parameters. Much of this research was translated directly into practice, as witnessed by the tremendous proliferation of infant and preschool intervention programs.

THE COUNTERREVOLUTION: EARLY VERSUS LATER EXPERIENCE

    As is well known, when a pendulum swings, at some point it reaches its apex and thereafter starts to return to a middle point. The same phenomenon appears to hold as well for ideas as for clocks. Following the almost unbridled enthusiasm for early experience during the 1960s, doubts began to set in during the 1970s as to how relevant early experience actually was. This was in part the expected reaction following the reported failure of intervention projects such as Head Start. However, part of the chorus of doubt was founded on basic scientific and methodological grounds.

    The increasingly powerful body of evidence running counter to the predictions of Freudian analytic theory attacked one of the foundation stones of the early experience movement. Methodological articles (King, 1958) pointed out that many of the infrahuman studies supporting the importance of early experience used enrichment or deprivation experiences only during early life periods; few systematic comparisons are available on the magnitude or duration of effects occurring when early and later experiences are compared. That evidence which is available on this point is highly complex and suggests differential effects on development as a function of age at intervention rather than a waning of experiential effects as they are applied later in life. The developmental position of Bloom has recently been reviewed in critical papers by McCall (1977) and Clarke (1978). Both authors point out that many of Bloom's conclusions are based on correlational data. As McCall notes, while correlations between two time points may be highly stable there may also exist significant mean gains between these time points indicating continuing change. Further, even statistically significant correlations over time may be accounting for little common variance; that is, a correlation of .5 between infant and adult performance leaves only 25% common variance between the two measurements (Clarke, 1978). Finally, there has been little empirical evidence to support the channeling concept of Ausubel; indeed, a contrary position, that of developmental canalization (Waddington, 1962) appears to have received more empirical support.

The increasing number of attacks on the primacy of early experience culminated in the work of Clarke and Clarke (1976, 1979). Clarke and Clarke do not deny the relevance of early experience for development; rather, they suggest that there is nothing special about the early years *per se* and that they must be viewed as simply one more link in the developmental chain. According to the Clarkes, early influences will fade unless supported by later experiences, and later experiences can have as dramatic effects upon development as early experiences:

> There is certainly no implication that infancy and early childhood are unimportant, only that their long-term role by itself is very limited. (1979, p. 147)

Clarke and Clarke support this conclusion by presenting both case and scientific studies in which the effects of extreme early deprivation fade, at least in part, with the passage of time. While one can criticize both their reliance on case reports and the methodology of many of their cited studies (reliance on retrospective data, ceiling effects with older, nondeprived comparison groups), the sheer amount of documentation cited by the Clarkes must lend at least some weight to the conclusion that later experiences may be as important as earlier ones. A similar conclusion based on cross-cultural (Kagan & Klein, 1973) and intervention (Kagan, Kearsley, & Zelazo, 1978) studies has also been formulated by Kagan.[1]

Based on the above, the Clarkes and Kagan conclude that there has been an overemphasis on early experience to the detriment of consideration of the

---

[1]It is worth noting, however, that in a more recent study Kagan, Klein, Finley, Rogoff, and Nolan (1979) report data indicating that the lack of cognitive differences among adolescents from urbanized and primitive cultures reported in their earlier work (Kagan & Klein, 1973) was most likely due to ceiling effects. When more difficult tasks are used, cognitive differences appear across cultures. This clearly contradicts their earlier conclusion that deprived early rearing will have few potential long-term consequences.

later experiences of the organism. With this point we would certainly agree. It seems almost a truism to suggest that over the lifespan of the organism later experience will modify and alter the effects of earlier experiences. This point has been most eloquently expressed by Susan Gray in her criticism of the so-called inoculation model of intervention:

> The most effective intervention program for pre-school children that could possibly be conceived cannot be considered a form of inoculation whereby the child forever after is immune to the effects of a low-income home and of a school inappropriate to its needs. Certainly, the evidence on human performance is overwhelming in indicating that such performance results from the continued interaction of the organism with its environment. (Gray & Klaus, 1970, p. 923)

Although agreeing with the Clarkes and Kagan that later experiences should be considered as well as earlier experiences, we strongly disagree with their formulation that *equivalent* effects may come from later as well as earlier experiences. Rather, we would stress that early experiences have a greater *probability* of having a more dramatic and longer lasting impact upon the organism than later experiences. To paraphrase both the Clarkes and George Orwell: There is certainly no implication that middle and late childhood or even adulthood are unimportant, only that while all developmental periods are equal in importance some may be more equal than others. Our emphasis on the salience of the early period over later ones is based on empirical, developmental, and theoretical grounds.

Empirically, on the basis of a sketchy review of the intervention literature, Clarke and Clarke suggest that there is little evidence for the postulate that the earlier the intervention, the more dramatic the effect. However, evidence presented even within their first volume (Tizard & Rees, 1976) contradicts their contention. Looking at the effects of age of adoption upon intellectual development, Tizard and Rees point out that the IQ of children adopted from institutions after the age of 4½ is notably lower than the IQ of children adopted between 2 and 4 years; according to Tizard and Rees, differential adoption rates for brighter children do not seem to be a factor. A more recent study on transracial adoptions (Scarr & Weinberg, 1976) reports much the same type of finding. Consistent with this evidence is data from the preschool intervention literature. Although there are some inconsistencies within the literature (see Williams, 1977), in general the available evidence suggests that the earlier effective intervention is instituted, the more dramatic and longer lasting the intervention gains will be (Robinson & Robinson, 1968; Bronfenbrenner, 1974). A recent review on maternal deprivation by Rutter (1979), although pointing out the limited amount of evidence available, comes to a similar conclusion, namely that environmental impairment early in life probably has a greater effect than similar impairment later in life.

Developmentally, we would also disagree with the contention that age of experience is irrelevant. Available infrahuman evidence suggests considerable plasticity of central nervous system development which is influenced by the early experiences encountered by the organism (Bekoff & Fox, 1972; Greenough & Juraska, 1979; Haywood & Tapp, 1966; Rosenzweig & Bennett, 1977). Although for obvious ethical reasons similar experiments have not been done on the human level, there is certainly ample evidence for the plasticity of the human central nervous system. There appears to be no reason why early experience should not also affect human central nervous system development. Indeed, this position is consistent with a major human developmental theory, namely that of Hebb (1949).

On the basis of this model, a number of researchers have attempted to specify the major biochemical and physiological growth periods of the human central nervous system. Underlying their work is the assumption that only during major growth periods will the central nervous system be sensitive to experiential effects (ignoring major traumas) (Epstein, 1974a; Winick, 1968). Although different regions of the central nervous system mature at different rates (Yakovlev & RochLecours, 1967), with evidence suggesting continued growth into adolescence (Epstein, 1974b) and adulthood (Yakovlev & Rochlecours, 1967), most available evidence suggests that the maximum growth of the central nervous system occurs prior to 5 years of age (Yakovlev & Rochlecours, 1967; Epstein, 1974b). Some evidence is available indicating that changes in DNA content level off at about 5 months of age (Winick, 1968), whereas changes in brain RNA protein may level off by the age of 3 years (Epstein, 1974b).

On the strength of the above pattern of evidence, we would suggest that a second reason for the critical nature of early experience lies in the interface between experience and central nervous system development. If experience is relevant for development of the human central nervous system, then it appears clear that early experience will be more critical than later experience on the basis of central nervous system growth rates. It may well be that one reason for the critical nature of human early experience is that experience during the first 5 years affects both central nervous system and behavioral development, whereas experience after age 5 primarily affects behavioral development.

Theoretically, there are two reasons that we emphasize the effects of early experience. First, as Thompson and Grusec (1970) have noted, the young organism is less differentiated and less organized than the older organism. As a result, one would predict that early experience should have a more dramatic and global immediate effect on behavior than would later experience. A. D. Clarke (personal communication) has graphically described this greater earlier plasticity in terms of a "wedge theory" wherein responsivity to change is a wedge-shaped phenomenon, broadest in the early years and tapering to a point in the later years. Thus, less powerful input is needed to affect behavior significantly in the early years than in the later years. Along the same lines, Wohlwill (1974) has pointed out that early experience may be more potent for the younger child than the older child because of the fact that the older child, by reason of its greater mobility, is better able to escape specific types of noxious experiences. The younger child, by reason of its lessened mobility and greater dependency upon adults, often has less chance to escape stress experiences which may be detrimental to growth. More critically, we would also hypothesize that one major reason for the primacy of early experience is that experiences during this period may well set up environment–child behavioral transactions that in and of themselves continue to maintain the effects of the early experience. This hypothesis derives from the transactional position of Sameroff and Chandler (1975), who postulate a "continual and progressive interplay" between the child and his environment. In this view, the child and the environment tend to alter and affect each other.

Given this state of affairs, we would contend that early experiences, by setting in motion these types of transactional situations, can be maintained over the course of time. Clarke and Clarke (1976, 1979) recognize this point to some extent in their discussion of the classic early experience studies of Skeels (1966), wherein infants were raised in stimulating versus nonstimulating orphanages. We would agree with the Clarkes that without the differential adoption rates between the two groups the long-term group differences reported by Skeels would undoubtedly have been greatly lessened. However, the critical question here is what was the source of the differential adoption rates that maintained the early gains for the enriched groups. The source can only be the initial early intervention that made the experimental infants brighter, more alert, and more adoptable. Direct evidence on this point comes from the Teheran orphanage interventions instituted by Hunt (1977), wherein there was a direct relationship between adoption rates and the quality of intervention experience the orphanage infants received. Clarke and Clarke dismiss the initial intervention by Skeels as unimportant and thus fail to recognize that without the specific early intervention the probability of differential adoption would also have been greatly lessened, leading to consistently lower development for all infants. The data by Skeels and Hunt present a clear demonstration of how early interventions may act not only in terms of having immediate effects but also in terms of developing setting conditions which in and of themselves may maintain the initial effects of the intervention. The follow-up on early intervention effects by Darlington, Royce, Snipper, Murray, and Lazar (1980) also appears to fit this model. Integrating results from eleven early intervention projects, Darlington *et al.* report that effect of intervention upon IQ fades within three to four years after intervention ceases. However, facilitative effects of early intervention on school success are still seen when the children have reached the fourth and sixth grades. The initial effects of the intervention upon IQ may have given the children enough early school success to maintain their motivation and efforts in the later grades when the direct effect of early intervention upon IQ begins to fade.

A similar formulation has been developed by Bronfenbrenner (1974) in his discussion of why home-based early intervention is superior to group-based intervention. By having the mother become involved in her infant's development, the initial intervention sets the stage for later systematic transactions between mother and child which will maintain the initial gains. One could argue that later interventions could also set positive transactions in motion. We would agree with this point, but, on the basis of the literature on age of interaction reviewed earlier, we would suggest that later interactions may first have to overcome the negative effects of earlier inadequate environments. Put in a learning framework, for later experience, previous negative experiences may have to be unlearned before positive learning experiences can be learned. Again, this is not to say that later experiences are irrelevant to development, only that more effort and resources may have to be committed to have a comparable effect at the later age (Clarke & Clarke, 1979).

Overall, it appears clear that the major disagreement between advocates of early experience and those of later experience is the impact weight we should assign to the experience. Later experience proponents such as the Clarkes would say that all age periods are *equally* important. On the basis of evidence and theory cited above, we would say that all age periods are important but, in terms of impact, the early period of life is most critical.

The Problem of Definition

Although the term *early experience* has been mentioned a number of times in this chapter, up to the present we have made no attempt to define it. Unfortunately, previous writings are of little help in this matter. Earlier definitions of experience have traditionally been either vague or all-encompassing. Our attempts at definition are not intended to be definitive, but we do wish to approach this issue at least briefly in order to give the reader an idea of the nature of the variables that will be discussed.

In the definition of the term, one is faced with two problems: the definition of *early* and the definition of *experience*. The concept *early* has typically been defined by some type of agreed-upon *a priori* boundaries with little consideration for the validity of these boundaries. Thus, for infrahuman populations many early experience studies define the early period as any time period up to the point at which the animal is weaned. Unfortunately, for humans, no equivalent boundary point exists. As a result, for humans, early experience studies encompass a wide range of age points (Thompson & Grusec, 1970).

The definition of *early* to be utilized in the present paper will be no less arbitrary than those utilized before. For purposes of the present volume, we will define the early period for humans as that time period between birth and 5 years of age. In adopting this time span we were guided by two considerations. First, as noted earlier, by age 5 much human central nervous system development has occurred and experiences after this time will probably have their effect primarily on behavioral or storage mechanisms rather than on central processes. Second, it is clear from a look at infrahuman definitions that the age at which the animal is weaned is in a sense the time at which the animal becomes independent and can leave the nest. Similarly, for humans in our culture, the age period around 5 years is the point at which the child begins his long trip from the family situation into the world around him in terms of encountering such new demands as kindergarten or equivalent school-related activities. Thus, both biologically and sociologically, the period at and around 5 years of age is a likely terminal point for the end of the so-called early experience period. We admit that our definition is still arbitrary. However, we hope to make up for this deficiency by specifying age-related effects of experience so that we may begin to talk about experiences occurring during a specific developmental period rather than using less precise terms like "early" and "later."

As for a definition of *experience*, again, if we were working within an infrahuman context, our task of definition would be much easier. In infrahuman studies early experience is usually defined on the basis of either adding or subtracting stimulation to that normally encountered during the preweaning period (i.e., handling, isolation). On the human level, however, such a distinction is not so easily made. First, as White (1969) has noted, little is known about the "normal" environment for human infants in a given culture; as a result, it is extremely difficult to know whether we are adding or taking away anything that is normally encountered in the environment. Further, ethical reasons often forbid the addition or subtraction of experiences such as those utilized with infrahuman organisms. As a result, most human early experience studies are correlational in nature, attempting to relate variability in environments sampled to subsequent development.

Traditionally, most definitions of experience refer to environmental factors encountered by the individual: "conditions, forces and external stimuli which impinge on the individual . . . a network of forces which surround, engulf and play on the individual" (Bloom, 1964, p. 187). Within this framework, Wohlwill (1973) has suggested that human early experience may be described on a stimulus–response continuum. That is, experiences may be conceived primarily in terms of the influence of either antecedent stimulus conditions (the hospital bed model), previous responses or practice (the swim meet model), or combinations of these two dimensions (amusement park or tennis match models). On a theoretical level, these distinctions between stimulus and response dimensions correspond to the influences of Hebb (sensory) and Piaget (actions). As Wohlwill suggests, the dominant experiential dimension may prove to be age-related. Thus, the young infant is more likely to have an experiential space that is predominantly sensory than an older infant who can influence his environment or selectively attend to specific features of the environment.

Wohlwill (1973) notes that most definitions of early experience typically involve both the stimulus and response dimensions. He criticizes this approach as "fence straddling" and suggests that this straddling leads to overinclusive definitions and poorly conceived early experience studies. Although we would agree with Wohlwill on these two points, we do not feel that the time is yet right for a choice among any of the four models suggested by Wohlwill. It may well be that either the stimulus or response conceptualization is more correct. More likely, stimulus and response aspects of the environment may have differential effects upon early development. Such a possibility clearly fits the hypothesis of *environmental specificity* to be described later in this volume. Further, there may well be a systematic age shift in the nature of environment–development relationships as the child develops (i.e., the hypothesis of *age specificity*). For purposes of the present volume, experience will be defined both on the basis of stimulus parameters passively or actively encountered by the organism and by response parameters involving either reactivity or practice. Operationally, stimulus dimensions will be defined on the basis of any type of measureable experience that is encountered by the child in his day-to-day activities. Response definitions will include exercise or practice; they will not include child behaviors such as those defined by White and Watts (1973) which do not appear to involve practice or exercise components (i.e., staring into space).

In defining experience purely on the basis of encountered stimulus and response parameters we are not overlooking the distinction between environment and experience. Most available definitions of experience are based on environment (Bloom, 1964). In contrast, a number of theorists (Thomas & Chess, 1976; Uzgiris, 1980; Wachs, in press) have pointed out that an environment encountered by the individual is not *necessarily* effective in influencing the individual's behavior. Thus, Thomas and Chess (1976) note that antigens in the environment are relevant only for those individuals who are allergic to those particular antigens. What we have done in the present volume is to utilize an operational rather than a phenomenological definition of experience. The distinction between environment and experience is maintained in our concept of *organismic specificity*, wherein the impact of the environment is mediated by the individual organismic characteristics of the infant. One of our goals in the present volume will be to suggest the types of organismic characteristics that can act as mediators of the impact of the environment.

THE NATURE OF NURTURE

Although much evidence implicates the importance of early experience in subsequent development, it is less clear which of the specific parameters of the early environment are most relevant. Reviews of factors predicting developmental differences among children (Fowler, 1962) tend to become vague, at best, when discussing what specific environmental parameters are relevant to accelerated or retarded development. Approaches to this question based on existing theories (Rohwer, Ammons, & Cramer, 1974) also tend to avoid specifics in favor of vague general statements. Concepts such as maternal deprivation, which at least in terms of face validity look promising, also show alarming degrees of vagueness when one asks what specifically is meant by maternal deprivation (Clarke & Clarke, 1976). Summaries of intervention research (Bronfenbrenner, 1974), when scrutinized in the light of the critical question of what aspects of the intervention lead to observable gains, provide only such vague concepts as "cognitively stimulating activities." Even in the most successful interventions (i.e., Skeels, 1966) little is known about what environmental parameters or what aspects of the intervention are important in leading to developmental changes.

The problem becomes even more acute when one considers the possibility that the time of experience may be as critical as the experience itself (Sigel, 1972) or that there may be individual differences in reactivity to early experiences (Wachs, 1977). Unfortunately timing and individual differences have received even less study than attempts to define what specific environmental parameters are relevant.

Perhaps the state of our knowledge on the relationship of early experience to subsequent development can best be summed up by two earlier reviews:

> The answer to a parent who asks specifically "what can I do during my child's pre-school years to improve his learning ability or intelligence" would have to be couched in fairly broad and guarded generalizations.... Perhaps, little more than a generalization to provide "maximum environmental enrichment" could at best be supported with confidence. (Freeberg & Payne, 1967, p. 65)

> We are appallingly ignorant of... (1) what infants are like, (2) what their worlds are like, or (3) how environmental circumstances and resulting experiences affect the development of an infant's abilities. (White, 1969, p. 53)

More recent reviews have also expressed a concern about the emphasis on early intervention when we know so little about the relevant specific parameters of early experience (Fowler, 1969; Hunt, 1975; Williams, 1977; Wohlwill, 1974). This emphasis may be due to the fact that once the importance of early experience was accepted, social pressure forced an immediate application of the concept. This pressure left little time to investigate what specific parameters might be most useful in the developmental process. It is as if the principle of immunization had been accepted and put into practice without evidence for which diseases could be immunized against or what the specific immunizing substances were.

However, within the past seven or eight years a number of researchers have become interested in specifying the relevant early experience parameters for a given child at a given age. Specifically, the question which has become increasingly addressed is: *For a given child at a given age, what specific parameters of the environment will promote a given effect?* It is the aim of the present volume to summarize the available evidence on this question and to suggest implications for intervention which are empirically based rather than founded upon vague theories, models, or the idea that experience is good.

Plan of the Volume

To approach the above goals, the present volume can be conceived of as being divided into approximately five sections. The first will consist of a chapter on methodology (Chapter 2); although a reading of it is not critical for an understanding of later sections, we feel that knowledge of the strengths and weaknesses of the various approaches used to study early experience will allow a greater appreciation of the validity or lack of validity of the data to be cited. The second section will be a review of the relationship of the physical, social, and interpersonal environment to intellectual development (Chapters 3, 4, and 5) and social development (Chapters 6 and 7). Although we are dealing with cognitive and social development in different chapters, recent reviews (Sroufe, 1979) have emphasized the potential interrelationship of supposedly distinct areas of development. To assess this possibility in more depth and to look at the possible implications of this interrelationship for research and practice in early experience, the third section (Chapter 8) will discuss the relationship between social and cognitive development in infancy and early childhood. The fourth section (Chapter 9) will look at the nature of early environmental action. Finally, the last section (Chapter 10) will derive implications from the preceding chapters in terms of potential applications of early experience.

The above tells the reader what the book will contain. It is perhaps incumbent upon the authors to specify also what the book will not contain. Thus, if the reader's favorite subject or point of view is missing, he will realize that it has been eliminated by intent and not through ignorance.

Of the topics not to be considered, the heredity–environment controversy is the first. It has become increasingly clear that this controversy is irrelevant, immaterial, and wasteful of scientific time. It is obvious that both heredity and environment play a part in the developmental process (Scarr-Salapatek, 1975) and the critical question is not so much which is more relevant but rather *how biology and environment interact to influence development* (Allen, 1961; Sameroff & Cavanaugh, 1979). We accept the relevance of hereditary factors to development and the transaction of heredity with environment and will attempt to present data, whenever relevant, on the interaction of these two factors. Unfortunately, the available data is extremely limited, as the reader will see.

Second, infrahuman evidence will not be considered to any great extent. In part, this decision is based on a desire to keep the size of the present volume within reasonable bounds. However, it is also based in part on recent evidence (Sackett, Holm, Ruppenthal, & Fahrenbruch, 1976) suggesting highly limited generalization of early experience effects across different species. Given this caution, we would not feel on firm ground recommending conclusions for humans based on infrahuman data. Therefore, except for use in model-testing, infrahuman evidence on early experience effects will not be reviewed. Excellent reviews of the infrahuman early experience literature can be found in a number of sources (Ambrose, 1969; Reisen, 1975; Thompson & Grusec, 1970).

Third, except for certain specific studies, infant and preschool intervention data will not be considered further here. This is based primarily on the fact that we are interested in the relation of specific environmental factors to development; most infant intervention programs are a "blunderbuss" (Gray & Miller, 1967) of stimulus levels and modalities such that it is impossible to delineate what specific aspects of the intervention curriculum led to the observed effects (Riksen-Walraven, 1978). This conclusion holds even for those programs which approach intervention from a theoretical or conceptual perspective. Available evidence suggests that among programs having a similar conceptual basis, teachers may be doing different things with children; similarly, in programs having different conceptual orientations, teachers may be doing similar things (Miller & Dyer, 1975). Thus, intervention studies will be discussed in the present volume only when the interventions lend themselves to discussion of specific aspects of experience. Reviews of infant and preschool intervention studies *per se* can be found in a number of sources (Belsky & Steinberg, 1978; Bronfenbrenner, 1974; Caldwell, Bradley, & Elardo, 1973; Horowitz & Paden, 1975; Williams, 1977).

Fourth, although the early nutritional status of the child is undoubtedly a form of early experience, this type of experience is primarily biological rather than psychological. In contrast, the major emphasis in this volume is upon psychological rather than biological variables. Further, it is becoming increasingly clear that nutrition in and of itself may not have major effects upon development unless it interfaces with the child's specific experiential-ecological environment (Brozek, 1978). Therefore, nutritional studies by themselves will not be considered. For a recent review of this area see the excellent paper by Brozek.

Fifth, we will not be looking at the role of socioeconomic status or other demographic measures as these relate to development. Socioeconomic variables as an approach to early experience will be considered in more depth in Chapter 2. For the present, let it suffice to say that differences in development as a function of socioeconomic status or other demographic indexes tell us little about the specific proximal experiences encountered by a child in a given demographic class (Caldwell, 1970; Schoggen & Schoggen, 1971). Yet, it is the specific experiences and not the demographic indexes that are relevant to observed differences. Along the same lines, with a very few exceptions, institutional, cross-cultural, and extreme environment studies will also not be considered. This is because in most cases the delineation of the nature of the child's actual environment is vague and unclear. When these studies are considered, an attempt will be made to specify the environmental parameters which differ across specific settings and are most likely to be related to specific cultural differences. A review of institutional research can be found in Thompson & Grusec (1970); a review of recent cross-cultural research can be found in Leiderman, Tulkin, and Rosenfelt (1977); extreme environment studies can be found in Clarke and Clarke (1976).

We will also not be considering major ecological variables. Bronfenbrenner (1977) has made an eloquent plea for the consideration of these variables in the study of experiential effects. Among the major ecological variables which Bronfenbrenner specifies as critical are environmental setting, major environmental changes (grade change, birth of a new sibling, etc.) and major social variables such as mass media or government actions. We agree with Bronfenbrenner's concern with emphasizing settings and hope to delineate settings in our review as they relate to differences in development. As for the other variables, however, we hold that major ecological variables such as environmental changes or social actions ultimately will have primary impact upon a child's development only insofar as they are reflected in the *specific experiences* encountered by the child. We contend that those changes in the environment or those social actions which do not directly impact upon the child's experiences will have little effect on development.[2] Thus, an increasing amount of television violence will have little influence on the child who does not watch television; in contrast, disruptions in the lives of parents (divorce, unemployment) will have an impact upon the child primarily because they are reflected in changes in child–parent transactions. Ecological factors which have an effect upon development will thus be reflected in changes in the child's experience and should be measurable. Unfortunately, most macroecological studies do not attempt to measure the effects of changes in ecological variables such as the birth of a sib or the loss of a job as these are reflected in the child's immediate experience. Therefore, at present these studies contribute little to our understanding of the nature of the *specific* effects of early experience.

Although we are in sympathy with the transactional position espoused by a number of authors (Lewis & Lee-Painter, 1974; Sameroff & Chandler,

[2]One could argue that ecological changes which have a minor impact upon the child's direct environment could still have a major impact upon development through altering a child's expectancies. We would argue, first, that there must be some measurable environmental change to cause expectancy changes in the child. We would further point out that the problem of measuring expectancies in the infant (or even the preoperational child, to a lesser extent) is one that has no easy solution at present.

1975), most of the research presented in the present volume will be nontrans-actional in nature. The reason for this is simple and lies in the nature of the available evidence. Sameroff and Chandler (1975) delineate three types of developmental research: main effect research (the study of the effects of the environment upon development), interactional models (the interaction of in-dividual differences and environment as these relate to development), and transactional models. As will be seen in the review section of this volume, the overwhelming majority of early experience research is done primarily using a main effects model. Some research is available using an interactional framework, looking mainly at age and/or sex effects as these mediate experi-ence. However, with the exception of a few studies investigating changes in mothers as a function of the infant's participation in early intervention pro-grams (Falender & Heber, 1975; Farran, Ramey, & Campbell, 1977; Zeskind & Ramey, 1978), the recent work of Clarke-Stewart (1977) on interactional changes among family triads over time, and data on high-risk babies (Beckwith & Cohen, 1978), there is virtually no available early experience research done within a transactional framework.

A similar lack of data is seen on the role of the family as a general experiential system. Most available evidence is centered in one of two areas. There are a number of studies looking at the role of specific family constella-tion factors (i.e., number of sibs, spacing of sibs) as these relate to develop-ment. This literature will be discussed in this volume, particularly in terms of mechanisms underlying observed relationships. There is also a large litera-ture on the relationship of family trauma (i.e., divorce, father's absence, or single-parent rearing) to development. However, in general, this literature has been primarily descriptive and thus is of little help in delineating the specific experiential effects associated with divorce or father's absence. Thus, with some exceptions, this literature will not be considered in great detail. What is most clearly missing is evidence concerning the way in which spe-cific family constellations affect the quality of experience received by the infant or young child. Only a few studies are available here (Pedersen, 1975; Clarke-Stewart, 1977) and by themselves they cannot be considered conclu-sive. Thus, we would agree with Parke (1979) on the existence of "second order effects" in family interactions (i.e., the nature of the mother–infant interaction will differ depending on whether or not the father is present). However, what is not known is whether these second-order effects dif-ferentially influence development; for example, does the relationship of amount of contact to early development change when studied in a single-parent versus a nuclear family situation? Pedersen (Pedersen, Yarrow, An-derson, & Cain, 1979) has speculated that the presence of the father sharpens the infant's discriminative and cognitive skills through providing the infant with a set of experiences which are noticeably different from those provided during mother–infant interaction. Pedersen *et al.* have also suggested the relevance of family interaction for providing the infant with interpersonal expectations different from those which the infant would obtain in a relationship with a single parent. Intriguing as these speculations are, at present there is little evidence available either to confirm or to deny their validity. Only when it can be shown that there is a unique relationship between development and stimulation provided by mother versus father, or single parent versus dyad (controlling for the amount of experience under study, as well as the amount of other potentially relevant stimulation sources) can one truly make a case for the greater relevance of second-order effects over main effects.[3] One hopes that future early experience research will approach this area using a more specific family-transactional framework. For the present, however, our review and conclusions must be based primarily on child-centered main effect and interaction research models.

Finally, a word should be said about our use of the phrase *human development*. In spite of the grandiosity of the title, not all aspects of human development will be covered in this volume; specifically, we will be concentrating on cognitive and social parameters. The choice of these two areas of development as our focus was made on a variety of grounds. For some areas of development (i.e., language, exploration, learning) little if any literature was available on experiential determinants.[4] As a result, we did not feel that detailed analysis was justified. Where they are relevant, we have noted the few existing studies in these areas so as to provide complete coverage. For other areas, a body of literature existed, but the quality or orientation of studies did not fit the goals of this volume. One such area is psychopathology, where a rich theoretical tradition has pointed to the child's experience as a critical determinant of development. However, much of the psychopathology literature is based on case reports, from authors with obvious theoretical axes to grind (i.e., Freud, 1966; Tinbergen, 1974). These data are not considered. Other experiential psychopathology studies are based on global rearing situations, such as institutionalization (i.e., Tizard & Hodges, 1978), in which specific experiential parameters are difficult to identify. Still others (i.e., kibbutz-reared children: Kaffman & Elizar, 1977) are based on situations with highly restricted environmental ranges. Reviewers have concluded that we are unable, at this point, to isolate specific environmental components which are relevant for the development of specific forms of

---

[3]In a recent study, Belsky (1980) reported a relationship between parental restriction and infant competence which appeared only when the family was studied as a unit. Belsky interprets these results as evidence for a unique family influence upon development. However, a closer inspection of these data suggests that these results may be more parsimoniously interpreted as a threshold phenomenon, that is, a low frequency experience that has an impact upon development only when its frequency reaches a certain point, as when mother and father scores are considered together.

[4]For a very recent review regarding what evidence is available on environmental factors associated with individual differences in young children's language characteristics, see Nelson (1981).

psychopathology (Jacob, 1975). Since the focus of this book is on *specific aspects* of the environment, we did not feel justified in including the study of psychopathology as a content area. Institutional and kibbutz studies in this area are noted when they are specifically relevant to a particular point. A similar problem can be seen with the areas of personality and emotional development. Personality traits are typically *inferred* characteristics of individuals presumed to be fairly constant across situations. They are not empirical realities but instead are summary variables which are global and derive from theory. Further, there appears to be a fixed quality to the above notion of personality "traits" suggesting that they may be impervious to environmental factors and relatively static (cf. Hunt, 1961). Since we are focusing on early environmental parameters as they relate to specific behaviors, coverage of personality characteristics of this sort was not consistent with our goals.

Finally, emotional development was not reviewed as a separate entity in itself. Affective aspects of cognitive and social development are frequently referred to, especially in infancy. Conceptually, emotion has not been very clearly defined in the literature and the authors were not able to improve on this state of affairs. It is difficult, for example, to distinguish conceptually between emotion and motivation (cf. Endler, Boulter, & Osser, 1968); yet most authors do not perceive them as identical, nor do they explain how these differ from temperament. On an empirical level there are all kinds of problems in measuring or even reliably identifying emotions in young children. The empirical problem is, of course, related to our conceptual confusion. With only a few exceptions, (in infants, the positive affect associated with the smile, separation anxiety and fear of strangers), we have chosen, therefore, not to treat emotional development as a separate dependent variable in this volume. Rather, we have chosen to bring it in as a concomitant of both cognitive and social development whenever relevant. Thus, we have brought emotion into our review when we have discussed interest, curiosity, and motivation as phenomena associated with the child's interaction with his physical and social world.

CHAPTER 2

The Study of Early Experience

In analyzing methodological statements in the area of early experience, one finds two approaches prevalent in the literature. One approach concentrates on the analysis problem (i.e., different types of correlational techniques, ANOVA versus MANOVA). The other approach concentrates on the design aspect (how one studies the phenomena under scrutiny regardless of how the data will be subsequently analyzed). Our emphasis in the present chapter will be on the design aspects of early experience. In part, this decision is based on reviews suggesting that too much emphasis is placed on data analysis with too little emphasis placed on problems in data collection (Wachs & Mariotto, 1978). Badly collected data will yield little of value regardless of how elegant are the statistical approaches used (that is to say, garbage in, garbage out, regardless of how expensive a compactor one has). Our decision is also based on the existence of an excellent volume, *The Study of Behavioral Development* (Wohlwill, 1973b), which surveys many of the available statistical approaches for individuals interested in developmental problems including the study of early experience. In contrast to Wohlwill, we will be concentrating mainly on design problems. Suggestions for data analysis will be made only when specifically relevant.

In studies of the relationship of early experience to subsequent development a number of approaches have been utilized. It is our aim to highlight the strengths and weaknesses of these various approaches, both to give the reader a way of evaluating the validity of the data to be described later on in this volume and to encourage the reader to take advantage of the more appropriate designs to be discussed. Obviously, not all design issues can be discussed in detail in a single chapter. At best we can only raise issues and suggest possible solutions. Readers who would wish a more detailed discussion of design problems should consult the volume on this question by Sackett (1978).

Methods of Studying Early Experience

The Use of Labeled (Distal) Environments

One of the earliest approaches to the study of early experience has been to study children living in different environmental situations that are thought to represent distinct types of stimulation. The case of Victor, the Wild Boy of Aveyron, studied by Itard (1962), is one of the earliest examples of a labeled environment study. More recently the emphasis has shifted away from feral children to the study of children from different social classes or children reared in institutions. These divergent approaches are placed under the heading of labeled environments since common to all of them is the assumption that the particular label (be it low social class or institutionalization) reflects a different type of rearing experience from that normally encountered in our society. For the overwhelming majority of these studies the major comparison is between the developmental level of a child reared in a particular labeled environment with a child reared in a "normal" environment. Differences in development for children living in the labeled environment are thought to be due to the influence of the environmental variables supposedly nested under the particular label utilized.

In terms of labeled environmental variables, social class or some variant of this such as parental educational level has had the most productive history. Many of the early studies described by Hunt (1961) on IQ level in canal boat children or among Appalachian children were examples of labeled environment studies. During the 1930s and 1940s many of the classic longitudinal studies such as those developed at Fels (i.e., Kagan & Freeman, 1963) and Berkeley (i.e., Bayley & Schaefer, 1964) often looked at social class or educational level as these variables were related to development. More recently genetically based twin studies (i.e., Wilson, 1972) have utilized social class as an index of environmental adequacy for nature versus nurture comparisons; other biologically oriented studies have also used socioeconomic status (SES) in a similar way (Broman, Nichols, & Kennedy, 1975; Jordan & Daner, 1970; Jordan & Spooner, 1972). One of the major virtues of demographic labeled environmental studies is the speed at which data can be gathered. A measure of parental educational level can be taken from existing records or a measure of parental social class can be taken from one short interview within the home. Once collected, these data can be used immediately for analysis.

However, in spite of their long history and in spite of the virtue of easily obtained data, in recent years the use of labeled environments has come under increasing criticism centered around three points (Wachs, 1972). First, research indicates that the range of environments within a given socioeconomic level is so great as to render impossible any generalizations about the types of experiences infants are actually having. There are studies reporting significant differences between the social classes, particularly in terms of maternal/attitudinal factors (Hess & Shipman, 1967; Streisguth & Bee, 1972; Tulkin & Cohler, 1973). However, other available evidence indicates either that there are no differences between social class groups on directly measured environmental parameters (Laosa, 1978; Roberts & Rowley, 1972; Wulbert, Ingles, Kriegsmann, & Mills, 1975), that parental social-class differences are primarily a result of different behavior patterns of lower- and middle-class children (Farran & Haskins, 1980), or that differences exist only for a minority of environmental measures (Ninio, 1979; Williams & Scott, 1975) at certain age levels (Farran & Ramey, 1980). These inconsistencies may be due to the fact that intraclass differences in rearing patterns appear to be as large as interclass differences (Williams, 1977). They may also be due to the fact that social class indexes themselves are, at best, only moderately intercorrelated (Shipman, 1977) and may have different meanings across different cultural groups (Laosa, 1978).

Second, comparisons of the predictive power of labeled environmental measures such as social class with those based on more detailed observations of the child's actual proximal environment clearly favor the latter. Typically, multiple regressions are computed between a criterion of developmental level and predictors such as ratings of the home environment, parental teaching styles, and social class. In all cases, significant predictive variance is associated only with directly measured environmental parameters (Beckwith, 1981; Bradley, Caldwell, & Elardo, 1977; Hess & Shipman, 1967, 1968; Radin, 1972a). Along the same lines, evidence is also available suggesting that nonsignificant relationships between social class and developmental level do not mean that environmental variables are irrelevant to development; rather, when direct measurements of the environment are taken, significant relationships appear (Kennedy & Wachs, 1975).

Finally, even when differences exist as a function of social class, these differences tell us nothing about the specific experiences encountered by a particular child. This point has been stressed repeatedly by behavioral ecologists (Caldwell, 1970; Deutsch, 1973; Schoggen & Schoggen, 1971). As Yarrow, Rubenstein, and Pedersen (1975) note: "Social class membership *per se* does not effect the infant's development; rather, it is the proximal variables, the kind of stimulation and pattern of care-giving that are important."

On the basis of evidence cited above, it must be concluded that social class studies were undoubtedly a necessary step in developing the concept that environment is important to development. Unfortunately, social class studies do not take us beyond this generalization. Since the focus of interest in recent years has swung to the question of what specific aspects of the environment are relevant for development, it seems clear that social class studies of early experience variables have little to offer at present. The variability among social classes and the lack of predictive power of social class when compared to more direct measures clearly suggest that alternative approaches to data-gathering are needed.

Other labeled environmental studies share many of the same disadvantages as social class. Because extreme environment studies are often retrospective, we can often only infer what specific experiences were encountered by the young child while being reared by wolves or while locked in an attic closet. Given the dangers inherent in retrospective reports (see below), such inferences are often highly suspect. Further, causality in extreme environment studies is often difficult to establish. Did being reared by wolves cause the child to become socially and cognitively retarded or was a retarded child simply abandoned to the wolves by its parents? Institutional versus noninstitutional comparisons may tell us that environment is important. However, unless one believes that all institutions are identical in nature, these studies tell us nothing about the specific environmental variables relevant to development. Available evidence clearly suggests that it is not the institution *per se* that produces the decrement in IQ so often associated with institutional rearing, but rather the experiences encountered by the child in a specific institution (Blank, 1964; Tizard & Rees, 1976). Like social class studies, too often institutional comparisons simply report differences in development without attempting to look at what specific aspects of the institutional experience are relevant for development. Again, like social class, institutional and extreme environment studies seem to have been a necessary precursor of current research which have since become outmoded.

Although not really a labeled environment design, cross-cultural studies also appear to suffer from may of the defects noted above. A general description of cultural approaches to child-rearing tells us nothing about the specific experiences encountered by an individual child in a particular culture. As Stevenson (Stevenson, Parker, Wilkinson, Bonnevaux, & Gonzalez, 1978) has pointed out, cultural group differences are related to development only insofar as group membership is associated with specific, unique environmental conditions. Similarly, Greenbaum (1979) has suggested that prior to assuming that developmental differences are culturally based, it is first necessary to observe actual parent–child interactions across cultures and to relate culturally associated interaction patterns to developmental differences. Few if any cross-cultural studies have met this criterion (Greenbaum, 1979). The criterion may be necessary, for some evidence (Antonovsky & Feitelson, 1973; Greenbaum, 1979) suggests that there may be more similarities than differences in rearing patterns among diverse cultural groups particularly when parental educational level is equated (Laosa, 1980). Other evidence indicates tremendous variability in child–parent interaction patterns even within a given culture (Landau, 1976). Clearly, cross-cultural studies do have the potential to yield valuable environmental data if direct environmental measures are taken across cultures, as suggested by Greenbaum. Too often, however, this is not done, and we are simply left with cultural differences plus anecdotal, subjective inferences on why these differences occurred.

Interview Methods

Use of interview methods is typically based on questioning the parent about the type of experience provided for the child, about child–parent transactions, or about parent attitudes about the child. Interviews may concern themselves either with events that happened in the child's past (*retrospective method*) or events currently happening to the child (*concurrent method*).

So far as predicting the long-term effects of early experience is concerned, the retrospective method is clearly the most economical approach since one is dealing with a population of already developed individuals. Thus, it is only necessary to ask what early environmental variables are correlated with variations in current development. This approach has been tried perhaps most often in the area of abnormal development, where "follow-back" studies are quite common. In these studies one looks at the past history of deviant populations such as adult alcoholics or psychopaths. Unfortunately, the retrospective method, although economical, clearly has limited validity. A number of critiques have been made of retrospective data (Robbins, 1963; Yarrow, Campbell, & Burton, 1970). In general, the problem appears to be similar across studies; parental retrospective reports of children's experiences simply are not accurate representations of what was actually going on while the child was developing. Even when as short a time interval as a month is used, the mean correlation between maternal recollections and actual occurrence was only .40; for longer periods the mean correlation between recollection and actual occurrence drops to between .2 and .3 (M. R. Yarrow *et al.*, 1970). Parental inaccuracy occurs whether one interviews for specific aspects of rearing (duration of weaning) or more judgmental aspects (attitudes). Overall it seems clear that retrospective interviews, while an economical data source, clearly are not an accurate representation of the child's actual environment.

For concurrent interview studies the issue of validity is somewhat more complex. By assessing only current behavior or current transactions the distortion of events occurring in retrospective studies is minimized. Although not as economical as retrospective studies, use of concurrent interviews still is a highly economical approach to data collection because a good deal of predictive data can be obtained in a relatively short period of time. However, on the basis of evidence from three sources we must again question the validity of the data obtained.

First, most interview data is based on one informant, usually the child's mother. As Landau (1976) has noted, particularly for children over 12 months of age, the mother is not the main source of environmental stimulation for the child. Other critical sources of experience also exist (fathers, sibs, peers), and their input to the child may be missed by questioning only one member of the family. As M. R. Yarrow (1963) has pointed out, when the same questions concerning the child's environment were asked of father and mother, agreement between parents occurred for only 61% of the questions.

Second, as Kagan (1967) has pointed out, interactions characterized in one way by the parent may not be construed in the same way at all by the child (relativism). Kagan suggests, for example, that what the parent may see as stern discipline the child may see as harshness. It is of interest to note here that data reported by M. R. Yarrow (1963) indicate that in only 48% of questions do the mother and child agree and in only 51% of questions do the father and child agree. These data suggest that a parent's perception of an event may be quite different from the child's perception; in terms of the impact of the experience, it is the child's perception that may be more critical. Clearly, of course, one could cross-validate by having interviews with both parents and children, but for studies of early experience this seems impractical. The use of interview techniques with children who are pre-verbal is impossible, and even for children with a developed verbal system (4- and 5-year-olds) the types of cognitive operations required in verbally oriented interviews may be difficult, if not impossible, for a child in the preoperational stage.

A final problem with concurrent interviewing centers around the possibility of social responding by the individual being interviewed. As McCord and McCord (1961) have noted, significant differences occur when one compares environmental data obtained by observation to that obtained by interviewing. Similarly, Lytton (1971) has noted that the correlation between interview and observational data ranges from between −.2 to +.9, suggesting at best only partial isomorphism between these two data sources. Interview data typically indicate less rejection of the child, more role differentiation in the family, more esteem among parents, and less punitive discipline (McCord & McCord, 1961). This clearly suggests the influence of social responding in interview situations. In many cases parents' responses to interviewers are based either on popular social stereotypes (i.e., boys are more aggressive; M. R. Yarrow, 1963) or by what child guidance experts suggest is the correct thing to be done (Robbins, 1963). In part this may be due to the fact that the interviewer typically asks for modal behavior from the parent leading to a loss of less frequent nonmodal behaviors which, by themselves, may be as critical as the more frequent behaviors (M. R. Yarrow, 1963). Also relevant here is temporal sequence. Too often in interviews parents describe their actions as affecting the child when in fact it may be the child's behavior influencing the parents' actions. This problem is not unique to interview methods, but it may be more difficult with the interview method to separate child effects from parent effects.

One alternative approach that has been used in place of formal interviews is parental self-ratings of behaviors. However, comparisons of self-ratings to actual observations indicate many of the same problems with self-ratings as with concurrent interviews (Crandall & Preston, 1955). In spite of the economy of interview data, the potential problems listed above lead us to question the utility of this approach in the study of early experience effects with humans.

Parental Attitude Measures

Many of the major longitudinal studies relating early experience to subsequent development are based on the use of parental attitudes about children or about children's development as a measure of the child's early experience. Typically, measures of parental attitude are taken either through use of parental self-report, as in the Parental Attitude Research Instrument (PARI), or by means of synopsis of narrative observation. The former approach has many of the same problems discussed above in the interview section.

For the latter method, an observer typically spends a certain amount of time in a child's home taking field notes of parent–child interactions. These notes are later coded on the basis of observer judgment into previously established superordinate attitudinal categories (hostility, affection, rejection, acceleration, democracy). In some cases the attitudinal measures are done without benefit of field notes, but distortions inherent in this approach make it less popular. Use of observer-derived attitudinal measures of early experience have several advantages over previously discussed approaches. This approach avoids the vagaries of demographic methods and the opportunities for distortion found in interview approaches. By reducing the observer-derived data into superordinate codes, data-processing time is reduced substantially; as a result, one can obtain a highly detailed description of certain aspects of the child's environment at little cost beyond observer time.

Although use of observer-derived parental attitude measures of early experience has a number of advantages, there are also a number of specific disadvantages inherent in the use of this method. Some of these are based on the use of observation *per se* and these will be covered in the following section. Others are unique to attitudinal measures *per se*. In general, there appear to be four specific objections to the use of attitudinal measures as indexes of early experience. First, in most cases attitudinal measures are derived from observations of mother–child interaction. As we have noted previously (Landau, 1976), particularly as children get older the mother represents a decreasing influence on the child's development. More use of paternal and sib/peer data would minimize this problem.

More critical are three other faults. First, there is the problem of the relationship between the parental attitude and the child's perception of the attitude. This problem of relativism has been discussed for interview methods. The same problem holds for attitudes. As Kagan (1967) has noted, too often we assume a one-to-one correspondence between observer perception of parental attitudes and the child's perception. Yet what the observer may see as hostility or rejection may not be perceived as such by the child.

Observers (Gewirtz, 1969; Kagan, 1967) have reported instances in which typical cultural or social patterns, not at all descriptive of actual parental attitudes, were defined incorrectly by observers. Again, the use of child perceptions as a cross-validation device appears to be impossible for infants and young children.

Even if child perceptions were not a factor, two other problems lead to serious questions about the validity of attitudinal reports. First, questions have been raised about the construct validity of attitudinal measures *per se;* that is, the degree to which parental attitudes actually reflect parent–child interactions. Given the widespread use of attitudinal measures, it is surprising that so little research has been done on this point. In general, available studies relating parental attitude measures to objectively derived measures of parent–child interaction indicate either that there is no significant relationship between attitude and interaction (Zunich, 1962, 1966) or that relationships are weak and inconsistent at best (Brody, 1965). One flaw in the available research is that parental attitudes are derived from attitude scales such as the PARI rather than from direct observation. The question of whether observationally based studies would relate to actual child–parent transactions still appears to be unanswered.

Even if a significant relationship were found between observationally based parental attitudinal measures and parent–child interactions, a final problem exists. As Gewirtz (1969) has pointed out, attitudinal measures by their nature are global summary variables. As a result, one gets only an average, modal picture of the child's environment. The possibility that specific aspects of the predictor (attitudinal) variable may enter into specific forms of functional relationship with criterion variables is simply not assessable to attitudinal studies. Yet, as will be shown later, environmental specificity may be characteristic of early experience effects. Similarly, Lytton (1971) has pointed out that attitudinal variables, being by nature superordinate, are less amenable to precise definition. As a result, if there are complex relationships between development and specific parental attitudes, small differences between studies in definition of attitudes may lead to major discrepancies in results.

Overall then, while observationally based attitudinal studies of the child's early experience have a number of distinct advantages over previous methods, they also have a number of distinct disadvantages. Particularly compelling are validity problems. In general, it seems clear that attitudinally based measures may be useful as supplemental information, but taken by themselves they seem clearly inadequate as a total measure of early experience.

Observational Methodology

Observational approaches are traditionally defined as the recording and encoding of behaviors displayed by an organism in a specific setting (Weick,

1968). Traditionally, observations are based on naturally occurring organism–environment relationships with no direct attempt to manipulate the behavior of the organism. However, the setting in which the behavior occurs may be initially structured in certain ways. Observational methodology can be used as a data collection device when manipulation occurs, but this approach, for purposes of the present volume, will be considered in the experimental methodology section. For the present, only nonmanipulated observational approaches will be considered. In contrast to many other areas of scientific investigation, human early experience studies have relied heavily on observational methodology. This is in part due to problems of subject cooperation in manipulated studies.

All too often, unfortunately, observational research is considered to be "second class" or "unscientific" in spite of the fact that a number of highly respected scientific disciplines such as astronomy are completely observational in nature. In part, this disdain for observational research is based on certain misconceptions about the validity of the observational method. Among the misconceptions that have been developed are the following: Observational research is not reliable; observational research is too sensitive to the biases of the observer; observational research is never a true picture of the child's environment due to distortions inherent in the presence of an observer in a natural situation; observational research is by its nature nonreplicable; observational research is subjective and inferential. However, recent evidence suggests that these biases in fact have little relationship to reality.

So far as the reliability question is concerned, reliability can be defined in one of two ways: either between persons or over time (*stability*). As in all other studies, including experimental ones, stability of measures is essentially an empirical question. Reliability between observers would appear to be easy to assess, but recent research on this question has specified a number of problems. It seems clear that covert reliability measures tend to be significantly lower than overt reliability measures (Lytton, 1971; Reid, 1970; Wildman, Erickson, & Kent, 1975). Further, reliability taken later in the course of a study tends to be higher than reliability taken earlier (Wildman *et al.*, 1975). However, even with these constraints most published observational studies reach significant levels of interobserver reliability (Weick, 1968; Hutt & Hutt, 1970). (An excellent discussion of statistical approaches to estimating observer reliability can be found in the chapter by Hollenbeck, 1978.)

In the matter of observer bias, available data clearly suggest that, with proper training, bias becomes a problem only if there is a long delay between observation and actual recording (Weick, 1968). In general, as with any other method, the more training observers receive the greater the validity of the observations (Wildman *et al.*, 1975). Further, the greater the unpredictability in material used during training the greater the validity of observations (Mash & McElwee, 1974). This, of course, suggests the value of training under field conditions.

As for the distortions induced by the presence of an observer, available evidence clearly suggests initial distortion, particularly in an increased incidence of positive behavior sequences (Zegiob, Arnold, & Forehand, 1975). These distortions may be related to the lack of replicability of findings occurring when short-term, nonextensive observations are made (Clarke-Stewart, Vanderstoep, & Killian, 1979). However, available evidence also suggests that with repeated observations the bias introduced by the presence of an observer is minimized (M. R. Yarrow, 1963; Weick, 1968). This is particularly true if infants or young children are used as subjects (Wright, 1967; Lytton, 1973). One cue to the sensitive observer that his presence is no longer a major factor is the occurrence of negative parent–child interactions. The occurrence of these (yelling, spanking) suggests that the observer has become familiar enough to allow "real" behavior sequences to occur (Lytton, 1973). The conclusion that must be drawn from these data is that observational approaches to the study of early experience are valid only to the extent that care is taken to minimize initial distortion effects (as in the use of repeated observations).

So far as the replicability question is concerned, one must make a clear distinction between replicability of methods and replicability of results. If one describes subjects, settings, methods of training, and codes utilized, observations can clearly be replicated. The results may not be replicable, but this is a problem for experimental studies as well as for purely observational studies.

Finally, as to the question of whether observational studies are subjective or inferential, while the preponderance of the early observational data was subjective, more recent observational studies primarily utilize specific behaviors and frequencies of specific responses. These data cannot, by any standard, be considered as inferential or subjective (Hutt & Hutt, 1970).

Although the above factors do not appear to lend major weight to the bias against observational studies, there are other more relevant problems associated with the observational method. Some of these are minor or are inherent in other methodologies. These include the problem of obtaining representative observations of the child's environment and the loss of rare but still significant child–parent interactions, since observations cannot be carried out continuously. Representative sampling can be assured by having observations made at a variety of times when people other than the mother will be at home. The problem of the loss of rare but relevant occurrences is one faced by all methods and is not unique to observational study.

Representativeness may also be a problem if subjects are followed longitudinally. Selective attrition (Clarke, 1978) which occurs when one class of subjects is more likely to drop out of the study can cause highly misleading results. Simply assessing whether there are significant differences in initial assessment scores between subjects who dropped out and those who stayed on may be misleading since differences may occur after the initial assessment

(Clarke, 1978). Cross-sectional designs are not a satisfactory answer to this problem. Problems associated with cross-sectional designs, including statistical inefficiency and the necessity to ensure comparable samples, have been discussed elsewhere (Wohlwill, 1973a). Generational-cohort effects are rarely a problem in cross-sectional early experience research because of the brief duration of the age span, unless one is attempting to compare data from cross-sectional studies done in different eras. If one assumes a lack of generational effects in early experience cross-sectional studies, the use of a series of superimposed short-term overlapping, longitudinal followups (the convergence method: Wohlwill, 1973a) may be one satisfactory compromise between pure cross-sectional and longitudinal observational designs.

A more troublesome problem is that of coding complexity. In general, the available evidence suggests that the greater the complexity of the code utilized the greater the probability of inaccurate recording (Mash & McElwee, 1974; Mash & Makohonuk, 1975; Taplin & Reid, 1973). This may be partially solved by training observers in coding using field situations, but even then one cannot guarantee highly accurate responding. Unfortunately, this problem strikes at one of the major advantages of observational methodology, namely its potential to gather and code highly complex behavioral sequences. The use of recordings which can be coded later may mimimize the problem, but these methods are tremendously time consuming.

The confounding of environmental and genetic variance when observations are done in natural family groupings may also lead to problems in interpretation (Plomin & DeFries, 1980). Designs are available which disentangle confounded sources of variance (Plomin & DeFries, 1980; Wachs & Mariotto, 1978), although these have not been used as often as they could be.

Furthermore, there is the question of generalizability. It is not surprising that parent–child interaction will vary as a function of the child's sex (Jacobs & Moss, 1976), of birth order (Cohen & Beckwith, 1977), or of what parent–child combinations are being observed (Pedersen, 1975; Lamb, 1977); these factors can be quantified and their effects studied. Less amenable to quantification are certain hidden mediators, such as whether the child is attending day-care (Farran, Ramey, & Campbell, 1977; Ramey, Farran, & Campbell, 1979) or the child's level of sociability during testing (Stevenson & Lamb, 1979). These hidden mediators may alter either patterns of parent–child relationships or the relationship between environment and development and thus lead to inconsistent results across studies. Most critical, however, is evidence that interaction patterns may vary in a complex manner across settings (Beckwith *et al.*, 1973; Clarke-Stewart, 1977; Rose, Blank, & Spattler, 1975). Although settings can be specified and even quantified, conclusions may have to be limited to the specific settings in which they were made.

A few words should also be said about the statistics used in observational studies. Although some observational studies analyze for differences between children encountering different, naturally occurring circumstances (i.e., preschool children whose nurseries are close to or far from noisy subways; Hambrick-Dixon, 1980), the majority use correlational statistics as their major mode of analysis. As has been repeatedly pointed out (Weizmann, 1971; Clarke, 1978), correlational analysis is insensitive to changes in mean level. Correlation levels may well stay constant even when major mean changes in developmental level have occurred. Thus, when correlations are used, particularly over time, it is critical to present means and variances as well as correlations. Too often this is not done. Further, when correlations are used care must also be taken to note the amount of variance accounted for by the correlation (r^2) (Clarke, 1978). This enables the researcher to guard against making major generalizations on the basis of statistically significant correlations which account for less than 10% of the variance.

In spite of the above limitations, direct observational strategies have been a mainstay of human early experience research because these approaches have a number of virtues which override many of the above problems. For example, generalizability of observational data may be limited to a specific setting; however, this is still a step beyond laboratory-based studies which must eventually be tested in the "real world" to establish validity (Bronfenbrenner, 1977; Willems & Raush, 1969).

A second advantage is the type of problem that can be investigated using observational studies. It seems obvious that for certain subject populations, particularly infants, direct observation appears to be the only way to obtain certain types of data. For example, we have found (Wachs, 1980) that noise–confusion in the home is related to lowered levels of cognitive development. Clearly there is no way in which one could obtain this kind of data using manipulative methods since experimentally exposing infants to high noise levels would be illegal and unethical. A similar problem is seen in studies of maternal deprivation. Essentially, all one can do in these studies is to observe already existing situations.

Another favorable point for observational studies is that of construct validity. In all previous approaches (demographic measures, interviews, questionnaires) the validity of the predictor variable was always in question. In contrast, with direct observation of child–parent interactions and recording of specific behaviors there seems to be no question of validity. Validity is built into the methodology since the observation is isomorphic with the interaction. As a result, for observationally based studies we know specifically what our predictor variables are, in contrast to other methods where we can only infer indirectly what the predictors are (Weick, 1968).

It should be noted that in the past observational studies were criticized for a lack of causal inference; that is, since most observational studies are correlational, one cannot determine whether there is an actual causal relationship between the specific predictor and criterion variables. However, recent innovations in statistics have made it possible to infer causality from a correlationally based observational design. Through use of such techniques as cross-lag correlation or time lag path analysis (Kenny, 1979) one can begin to infer whether an observed correlational relationship is causative or is the result of extraneous factors.[1] It is worth noting that in these designs there may be the problem of repeated testing effects, but available evidence (Haskins, Ramey, Stedman, Dixon, & Pierce, 1978; McCall, 1977) suggests that these effects are mainly operative on the first retesting.

Given the advantages noted above, particularly generalizability and construct validity, it seems clear that for human early experience studies, observationally derived methodology may be the method of choice. Although there are a number of problems inherent in observational methodology, these appear to be outweighed by the obvious advantages of this method. However, once the researcher decides to use observational methodology there are still a number of specific approaches to observation that are available. Each approach has its own advantages and disadvantages, and it is pertinent to specify these so that the researcher can make an informed choice of methods.

Time-Sampling

Time-sampling essentially involves the recording of preselected behavioral categories at regular time intervals (Hutt & Hutt, 1970). Thus, in a typical time-sampling situation, over a 90-second time cycle the observer would observe parent–child interactions for 60 seconds and record observations made for 30 seconds. The 60–30 cycle would then be repeated. Recording is almost always done by means of checklist. The major advantage of time-sampling is the speed with which data can be analyzed (Hutt & Hutt, 1970). In contrast to free observation, time-sampling data can typically be gathered and put on computer cards on the same day. Unfortunately, in obtaining this information so rapidly there is a difficulty. Typically in the time-sampling situation there is a loss of patterning, duration, and tempo of interactions (McDowell, 1973) as well as a loss of all data occurring while recording goes on (Moss, 1965). In addition, in time-sampling it is often difficult to distinguish between repeated and continuing acts. Here the duration of observe–record cycles used may well govern the type of information obtained; for example, greater frequencies of a specific behavior may be counted with short cycles than with long cycles. Further, since codes must be derived ahead of time, unexpected but nonetheless potentially relevant interactions are completely lost (Lytton, 1971). In many of the early time-

---

[1]A recent review by Rogosa (1980), however, suggests major problems in the use of cross-lag correlational designs to infer causality.

sampling studies interactions were also impossible to obtain, but more recent time-sampling studies have built-in interaction codes (L. J. Yarrow *et al.*, 1975).

Event-Sampling

In contrast to time-sampling, for event-sampling the occurrence of behaviors is recorded regardless of when they occur (Hutt & Hutt, 1970). Typically, events are recorded on some sort of electronic device, such as a Rustrak Event Recorder, which is specifically designed for this purpose. In contrast to time-sampling, when electronic recording devices are used for event-sampling, duration of behavior can easily be obtained. In general, event-sampling shows the same strengths and weaknesses as time-sampling, with the additional caution that for event-sampling it helps to have some idea of the general frequency of the behavior studied; without this frequency the behavior may occur too rapidly to be recorded accurately or too rarely to be efficiently studied.

Free Observation (Specimen Records)

In the typical free observation situation, the observer attempts to record the occurrence of all behaviors and interactions occurring across a specific time period. Recording is continuous and goes on as the behavior continues. Behavior may be recorded by a checklist, by writing down actions as they occur, or through videotaping; but in general it is agreed that observer-dictated audio recordings may perhaps be the most satisfactory method at present (Hutt & Hutt, 1970).

Use of checklists implies preselected categories which lose some of the flexibility of the free observational method. Writing down material tends to lead to loss of information, particularly for fast-paced behavior (Lytton, 1973); abbreviations may be used, but there is a danger of distortion (Hutt & Hutt, 1970). Unless one is specifically interested in microanalysis, for which video recordings are indispensible, video recording tends to be unecomical because of the time required to analyze the data. Data loss obtained by live audio as opposed to video recording appears to be negligible (Sackett, Ruppenthal, & Gluck, 1978).

Thus, at present, the most useful method appears to be an observer who follows the child around dictating all child interactions into a portable tape recorder. Once this data is obtained, it is transcribed, corrected, and then coded into preselected categories. The major advantage of the free observation technique is that, unlike other approaches, it allows the observer to go back to the raw data and look for unsuspected relations or interaction patterns that were not originally considered. The process is also invaluable for learning about the phenomena under study and for generating further hypotheses.

Free observation also allows for analysis of interaction patterns as well as time sequences and durations.

These advantages must be considered, however, in the light of potential disadvantages. The major disadvantage of free observation is the tremendous amount of time needed to transcribe and code the available information (with a risk of inaccuracy at each transcription-coding point). The authors' own experience shows that it may take a period of years to process available tape-recorded data to the point at which it can be analyzed. This disadvantage may be compensated for to some extent by the use of electronic recording devices, such as the Datamyte, which allow free observation data to be translated directly onto computer tape. However, electronic recording devices of this sort are essentially nothing more than automated checklists, and as a result one loses the flexibility of going back and reanalyzing data not originally coded. In addition to the above factors, there is also the problem of behavior sequences occurring too rapidly to be recorded accurately (Hutt & Hutt, 1970) and the problem of obtaining large concentrations of scores in categories that are essentially irrelevant to the purposes of the study (Lytton, 1971).

Overall, in evaluating the worth of free observation it seems clear that no one method of observation is clearly superior to any other. Each has its own strong and weak points, and the choice of method may in part depend on the purposes of the research. When there is a lack of previous data, which would allow one to develop specific criterion codes for hypothesis-testing purposes, or when there are a large number of categories that must be obtained, free observation clearly seems the method of choice (Lytton, 1971; McDowell, 1973). However, if the number of categories needed is small and if the researcher can specify, based on previous data, what the relevant categories are, then time- or event-sampling may be more appropriate.

Observation in a Structured Setting

Up to the present we have assumed that observation will take place in the child's natural environment such as home or preschool. However, use of observational methodology is also possible in a structured situation such as a laboratory setting. The standard situation here is one wherein the mother and child are brought into a laboratory setting and asked either to solve a task jointly or to play together in a natural way. Observations of the interaction are coded using either observers or videotape procedures. In general, the same benefits and problems found for natural observation also occur for structured observation. However, there is some agreement that one can get better observer reliability in a structured setting (Lytton, 1973). Structured settings also avoid the effects which different background settings can have on results.

For these benefits there is a definite negative result. Specifically, the

question has been asked whether the same characteristic interactional sequences between parent and child that occur in a natural setting also occur at
the same frequency in a structured setting. Infrahuman evidence clearly
indicates radically different behavior patterns by primates observed in the
laboratory and in the wild (Menzel, 1969). At the human level evidence is
mixed. Stewart and Burgess (1980) report no significant differences in interaction patterns when parents and children were observed in their home or in a
home-like laboratory setting. However, their sample size was quite small
($n = 4$). In contrast, distinctly different patterns of infant cognitive (Durham &
Black, 1978) and spatial performance (Acredolo, 1979) have been reported
when infants are tested in a structured laboratory setting rather than in the
home. Available evidence also suggests a more limited range of behavior
occurring in the structured laboratory setting than in the home (Lytton,
1971). For certain questions (i.e., the child's reaction to separation from the
mother in a strange environment) the lack of a natural setting may not be
critical (Weinraub & Lewis, 1977). However, when one is interested in "typical" parent–child interactions the constraints found in a nonnatural setting
may be quite serious.

Part of the problem with structured observations may not be so much
the setting *per se*, but rather the highly overt nature of observations done in
the structured setting. The problems of nonrepresentative, "social" responding discussed earlier under interview data appears also to occur when observations are highly overt (Randall, 1975). Although knowledge of observer
presence clearly exists in home observations, the problem appears to be
magnified when mother and infant are brought into a strange setting and
asked either to perform or told they are going to be "on camera." Interestingly, Lytton (1973) has reported greater parental behavioral constraints
when recording was done by camera than when recording was done by a
observer dictating into a tape recorder. This may reflect the fact that parents
are used to interacting with their children in the presence of others but are
not used to being filmed in these interactions.

Given this difficulty, one obvious way to minimize the bias inherent in
structured observations would be to do repeated observations of parent–child
interaction over a period of time in the structured situation until both parent
and child appear comfortable with the situation. The same distortion criteria
noted earlier in the section on natural observation could also be applied in
the structured situation. Only data obtained after a series of repeated warm-
up sessions would be used. Unfortunately, the great majority of structured
observation studies still use only a single short-term observation session and
result in potentially nonrepresentative interactional sequences. This is most
clearly seen in the low frequency of occurrence of anything other than positive behaviors. It is this situation that is most likely to produce findings
which will later prove nonreplicable (Clarke-Stewart *et al.*, 1979).

Although parents may be reluctant to return to the laboratory for repeated sessions, such a control may well be necessary if one is to obtain valid observational sequences. Failing this, an alternative approach is to make the structured observation as covert as possible. An example would be to ask the parent and child to wait in the test room prior to the start of the "actual study" and to observe their interaction either by hidden observer or hidden camera. Such a situation, although of questionable ethical value, may minimize some of the problems found with highly overt single structured observations.

MANIPULATIVE RESEARCH

Unlike procedures in many other areas, in human early experience research a remarkably small proportion of studies can be described as manipulative. Manipulative studies are those which investigate the effects of systematically varying, subtracting, or adding different experiences on the child's level of development. In part, this paucity of evidence is due to ethical or legal constraints on early experience research with humans. Where fewer constraints are operative, as in the infrahuman early experience area, many more manipulative studies are found.

There has been a certain amount of conflict between proponents of manipulative research and nonmanipulative research (Hutt & Hutt, 1970). Although such conflict is not unique to the early experience field, it may be more visible here because of the large amount of nonmanipulative research in this field in contrast to other areas of study. Rather than attempting to take sides in this continuing battle, we will concentrate on both the strengths and weaknesses of manipulative early experience research with humans so that readers can make an informed choice as to what research strategy is best for a particular problem. In discussing the weaknesses of manipulative methods we will avoid more or less common problems such as lack of adequate control groups or tester bias and concentrate on those problems which are particularly germane to the human early experience area.

Particularly for the study of cognitive development much of the available research seems to be either intervention research or quasi-intervention research; that is, the research is usually conducted in a field setting with one experimental group and one control group. Rarely does one find research being done under controlled laboratory conditions where a number of parameters are systematically varied and compared, though a few such studies do exist (Korner & Thoman, 1970).

One occasionally finds reports of the effects of naturally occurring manipulations which avoid the legal and ethical problems. For example, the study by Friedman, Maarten, Streisel, and Sinnamon (1968) was based on the unique hypothesis that many existing human medical interventions are analogous to infrahuman deprivation procedures. To test this hypothesis, the authors studied the developmental level of children with phenylketonuria (PKU) as a function of the amount of medically ordered isolation experiences the children encountered. Unfortunately, too often in these studies other confounding factors exist, limiting the conclusions that can be drawn. For example, in the Friedman *et al.* (1968) paper one could ask whether the lowered intelligence in the PKU children with medically ordered isolation was due to the isolation or due to the fact that these children were sicker and hence isolated more. In the latter case, it would be the extent of illness rather than the isolation that caused the lowered IQ.

In analyzing the utility of manipulative research in the human early experience area, one can point to a number of strengths of this method. In contrast to nonmanipulative research, manipulative studies tend to be highly efficient. Rather than waiting for specific events to occur, with a consequent loss of observer time, in a manipulative study one can schedule events to suit the convenience of the experimenter. As a result, one can get by with many fewer observers and much less irrelevant data. Related to this is the fact that in manipulative studies one can more readily test specific hypotheses than one can in nonmanipulative research. This is because in nonmanipulative research one must depend on the actual occurrence of the variables one is looking for; in manipulative research one can simply program these variables into the study.

A third factor supporting the utility of manipulative research is the problem of background variables. Particularly in observational research done in natural settings there exist many background variables which can confound results or add unwanted error variance. In contrast, in manipulative studies, particularly those done in a laboratory, there can be more precise control of exactly which experiences impinge on the organism. Obviously, of course, it is easier to specify causality in manipulative research than it is in observational research. Even if one uses special designs such as cross lag or path approaches one can, at best, only imply causality in nonmanipulative studies. In contrast, by means of precise control, manipulative research can more easily specify the relevant causal factors.

In addition, manipulative research may often avoid many of the problems associated with nonmanipulative observationally based research, such as observer bias and problems in estimating observer reliability. Of course, if one wishes to be highly practical, there is also the fact that manipulative research is more scientifically "respectable" (Hutt & Hutt, 1970) and thus more publishable.

In spite of the above advantages, there are also a number of specific problems associated with manipulative early experience research. Certain problems relate to manipulative early experience human research in general, while others are specifically relevant to intervention studies. Before looking at more general questions, we will first look at problems unique to intervention studies. First, there is the question of causality. Too often in intervention studies, when all relevant variables may not be under the control of the experimenter, causality may be attributed to the manipulation utilized when it in fact may be due to some naturally occurring, uncontrolled variable that is confounded with the manipulation. Examples of these include: (1) nonspecific motivational factors associated with intervention rather than the intervention *per se* (Zigler & Butterfield, 1968) and (2) previous intervention experiences which, when combined with current intervention, may alter the pattern of parent–child relationships leading to effects independent of the latter intervention (Farran, Ramey, & Campbell, 1977; Macrae & Jackson, 1976). The use of pretests has also been suggested as a possible confounding factor (Cornell & Gottfried, 1976), but the data on which these arguments are based have come under severe criticism (Wohlwill, 1973a). A related problem occurs when manipulations given to the experimental group are also inadvertently presented to the controls, leading to a loss of significance (Sayegh & Dennis, 1965; Gray & Klaus, 1968).

Also, for intervention research a relevant problem is individual differences in response to intervention. In many intervention projects significant effects of intervention are shown as a main affect. However, when one looks at individual gains or losses, it is typically found that some children show major benefits from intervention while others show virtually no effect (Levenstein, 1970; Engleman, 1970; Williams, 1977). Obviously there are individual differences in reaction to intervention, but rarely, if ever, are these individual difference factors considered in intervention studies (Wachs, 1977).

The first general problem associated with manipulative studies is the question of generalizability of the causal statements obtained. In several recent papers (Wohlwill, 1973a; McCall, 1977) the point has been raised that manipulations in a laboratory may well cause a developmental change; however, this tells us nothing about whether these manipulations actually exist in the real world and, if they do, whether they cause the same change in the real world. The classic example here lies in attempts to apply SR reinforcement models to language development. Clearly, one can influence the rate of verbal production in a laboratory by means of appropriate reinforcers. However, available evidence clearly suggests that these reinforcers do not exist to a great extent in the real world and that language apparently does not develop primarily by means of shaping or reinforcing of the child's vocalizations (Nelson, 1973). Specifically, for early experiences Wohlwill (1973a) points to a number of examples, including the development of discrimination abilities and conservation training, wherein causal statements based on laboratory manipulations proved to be irrelevant when the same problem was investigated in the real world. As Epstein (1962) so aptly points out:

> The experimental method is necessarily an artificial one. Herein lies both its strength and weakness. Because of its artificiality experimentation is able to establish causal relationships under highly controlled conditions which makes it emi-

nently suitable for testing theory. However, where an attempt is made to understand events in the natural world which all theory must eventually do if it is to be more than an intellectual exercise, it is necessary to bridge the gap between the natural event and the experimental situation. It is here that experimentation in psychology has been at its weakest. Because an event can be produced in the laboratory does not mean that the event is so produced in the natural world. Because a child can be shown to learn by trial and error in the laboratory does not mean that this is the way he learns in every day life. I can produce a light by pressing a button on a flashlight but this does not prove the sun is a giant flashlight which someone turns on and off on a twelve hour schedule. Such thinking is obviously magical rather than scientific. (pp. 269–270)

It appears clear, as McCall (1977) notes, that causal statements derived in the laboratory must be tested in the natural habitat of the child before one can accept the generalizability of the original causal statement.

A second problem centers around the ecological validity of manipulative studies. Even in infrahuman research it is becoming increasingly clear that laboratory-based behavioral studies have at best only a limited value in explaining the behavior of organisms in their natural habitat for such parameters as rearing patterns, exploration (Hutt & Hutt, 1970), and the maintenance of leadership (Willems, 1969). On the human level, similar conclusions have been drawn. In many cases phenomena such as frustration which are studied in the laboratory exist, if at all, only in a limited sense in the outside world (Fawl, 1963). Too often, dimensions are placed together in ways that would never occur outside a manipulated laboratory setting. For example, in the Gump and Kounin (1960) study the game-playing behavior of children was investigated as a function of the skill of the child and the power position of the child in the game. Laboratory-based studies indicated that poorly skilled boys were more successful in high power than low power positions. However, when the same phenomenon was studied in a nonmanipulative, natural situation, it was reported that poorly skilled boys rarely allowed themselves to be put in the high power position. If by some chance they found themselves in this position, the game situation very quickly deteriorated. Clearly, if manipulative studies are to be relevant to early experience research, more attention must be paid to the ecological validity of the manipulations utilized by determining whether the laboratory manipulations are isomorphic with naturally occurring manipulations affecting the child in the real world. As Bronfenbrenner (1977) so aptly puts it: "Contemporary developmental psychology is the science of the strange behavior of children in strange situations with strange adults for the briefest possible period of time."

This is not to say that ecological validity must be the major criterion for judging the adequacy of manipulative research. Clarke-Stewart (1979) argues that researchers taking up the ecological banner today are running the risk of making the study of social behavior "the study of the natural behavior of children in familiar situations with familiar adults and the fewest possible constraints." Thus, naturalistic observation can be just as narrow and selective as laboratory research. As with types of observational research, Clarke-Stewart argues that the choice of method should be governed by the questions asked:

> Generalization from naturalistic observation is challenged by the extreme variability between children's natural settings. And even worse for assessment of social development, interpretation of naturalistic observation of children's social behavior is restricted to partner-specific patterns, since social interaction, by definition, is reciprocal, and the child's contribution cannot, naturally, be separated from the partner's. When the subject of interest is the dyad, this limitation is inconsequential, but if we want to find out about children's social qualities more generally, about individual differences in these qualities or about variations in children's interactions with different kinds of partners, some systematic constraint or manipulation seems unavoidable. (Clarke-Stewart, 1979, p. 1)

Further, Clarke-Stewart points out that if we are interested in social cognition or social competence, as distinct from spontaneous performance in naturally occurring social situations, we must rely on experimental procedures. That is, manipulative, probing procedures enable us to study the child's potential for social thought or action. Clarke-Stewart thus argues that it is the combination of manipulative approaches with naturalistic observation that provides the most fruitful and informative manner in which to study social development.

Overall, when it comes to choosing between observational and manipulative approaches, it must be stressed that there is no right way to do early experience research; the choice of method will depend on the problem studied and the availability of background data. In problems for which there is little background data or where ethical constraints are operative, observationally based nonmanipulative studies may be most useful. Where ethical constraints are not a problem and the background data are such that a specific hypothesis can be generated for testing, manipulative research may be the method of choice. For situations intermediate between these extremes nonmanipulative observational research using special techniques that allow one to infer causality may be most appropriate. Ideally, a combination of both naturalistic and manipulative research would be used to promote maximal generation of information.

INTERACTIONAL APPROACHES TO THE STUDY OF EARLY EXPERIENCE

Interactional approaches cut across both manipulative and observational data strategies. Thus, issues pertinent to this approach would seem to deserve a separate section. This is particularly true if one is interested in social development because the study of the effects of early experiences on later social development is somewhat more complicated than the study of the effects of these same experiences on cognitive development. Social behavior has to be studied in the interactional contexts in which it occurs. Research designs purportedly directed at the study of social development must preserve the essential nature of social interchange phenomena by including observations of two or more individuals interacting at the same points in time and noting their influence on each other. The problem is one of determining how specific social interchanges early in life are translated over time and space to influence later social interactions. Thus, both the independent and dependent variables require the study of interactional behavior. It is a step forward that it has been recognized in recent years (R. Q. Bell, 1968, 1971; Sameroff & Chandler, 1975) that children can influence their parents as much as their parents influence them. However, the view that the child controls the parent has as many potential pitfalls as did the long-held view that the parent controls the child. Studying child effects in isolation may be as narrow an approach as studying parent effects. It is the interaction, the reciprocity of influence, the mutural control that one member of a relationship provides over another's actions in any interchange that must be the focus of study.

It should be emphasized that because this interactional approach requires the investigator to study acts within the relational or social contexts in which they occur does not mean that only natural or "field" observations are appropriate to this method. Ideally, the question asked will dictate whether a phenomenon is best studied in the field or in the laboratory (Weinraub & Lewis, 1977). Laboratory analyses of attachment or of affiliative or aggressive interchanges are indeed possible and often done. Cairns (1979, p. 16) has suggested that this procedure is suitable for use in any setting where the relationship itself may be the determining factor of the behavior of the individual or individuals. Ainsworth's finding (1967) that the security of the mother–infant attachment is related to the child's exploratory and other behavior is an example of this.

Cairns (1979) pointed out another essential difference in making comparisons across social (interactional) and nonsocial behaviors: that the evidence for persistence of individual differences is considerably less in the case of social behavior characteristics than in the case of cognitive and motor ones. This is important when one attempts to separate the effects of experience from individual difference factors which presumably continue throughout development. He suggests three possible reasons for this apparent lack of continuity in social development that serve to clarify the different methodological problems inherent in studying social as opposed to nonsocial behaviors:

1) The goal of most tests of cognitive and motor development is to measure the child's *optimal performance*, while the goal of social interchange and personality assessments is to measure *representative* performance.... To obtain truly representative samples of social behavior, it is necessary to use unobtrusive yet sensitive

measures that apply to a variety of circumstances. One negative by-product of this state of affairs is that measures of social behavior and personality have typically been less reliable and more vulnerable to error in both the early and later tests.

2) There is a higher level of specificity—situational, relational, and time—in the interactional patterns of children than in the noninteractional ones. . . . This view is . . . consonant with speculations about why rating measures tend to yield more consistent results with regard to interindividual differences than do more precise behavioral assessment techniques: ratings tend, in general, to explicitly eliminate situational sources of variance.

3) Social interactions are more likely affected and reorganized by the transactions that occur during the course of development than are nonsocial patterns. . . . Absolute changes (intraindividual) may be required to maintain relative continuity (interindividual) because the reference group in society is undergoing change. (p. 389)

For all of these reasons, the persistence of individual differences (or what Cairns calls "interindividual consistency") is more difficult to document in the area of social development than that of cognitive development. Whenever we try to predict on the basis of an individual's initial status on some characteristic what his later status on that characteristic will be, we run into difficulties. We agree with Cairns's observation that the child's early status should be only one component in the prediction equation. Other components, such as the nature of the social network in which development occurs and, especially for early development, the consistency of the behavior of parents (and probably siblings) across time, must be considered in making predictions. This point is reinforced by the findings of Green (1977), who reported that mother–infant dyads in which relatively large numbers of social initiations occurred at 6 months were observed to have relatively more social initiations at 8 months. Green concluded that the consistencies were supported principally by the actions of the mothers—whose talking, initiations, and so forth, remained stable—rather than by the actions of the infants. Thus, what may initially appear to be individual differences inherent in the child may, on closer examination, turn out to be reflections of a stable environment. A similar conclusion in the cognitive area has been reached by Ramey, Campbell, and Nicholson (1973). Thus, the stability of the total social network and the behavior of persons within that network must be assessed in order for the effects of early experiences on later behavior to be divorced from the effects of the current environment on the same behavior. This applies to both cognitive and social development but seems particularly important when the dependent variable (later behavior) is itself a part of an interactional system, as is the case with social behavior.

Manipulative studies in which the effects of differing environments, for example, stability or instability in the mother's behavior, are studied could help to determine the degree to which experiential differences can be used to predict differences in social development. In practice, studies of groups exhibiting such differences are usually selected rather than directly manipulated, which results in further complications in analyzing and interpreting them. For example, mothers who are more stable in their initiation behavior across time may differ from other mothers on a variety of other parameters as well—socioeconomic status, responsiveness, and sensitivity, for example. But these differences can sometimes be corrected for statistically, rather than by experimental design. Thus, at least some reliable estimates of experiential effects can be achieved through such semimanipulative investigations.

Summary

Early experience research directed at studying either cognitive or social early experience interactional effects must address many of the same problems. Questions of causality, generalizability, representative measurements, and individual differences are pertinent to both areas whether naturalistic or manipulative approaches are employed. Choice of strategy clearly appears to be a function of what specific questions are being asked and what background data are available. What is most critical is to keep in mind the strengths and weaknesses associated with each method.

CHAPTER 3

The Physical Environment and Its Relationship to Cognitive-Intellectual Development

In contrast to research on the relationship of animate, interpersonal, or mother–child interaction variables upon early cognitive development, there has been relatively little evidence on the relationship of the physical, inanimate environment to early cognitive-intellectual development.[1] In part, this paucity of data on the inanimate environment may be due to the contention by certain authors (Provence & Lipton, 1962; Clarke-Stewart, 1973) that the physical environment can have little effect upon development unless mediated by social variables. However, both correlational data (L. J. Yarrow *et al.*, 1975) and experimental evidence (Brossard & Decarie, 1971) clearly do not support this contention. Similarly White (1975) has contended that only after the first year of life, when children can locomote and process language, do the stimulus characteristics of the home become critical for development. However, in contrast, Schaffer and Emerson (1968) have argued that it is the very young infant, lacking self-stimulation capacities, who is most dependent upon physical stimulation.

Although some may object that the distinction between the physical and interpersonal environment is an arbitrary one since interpersonal figures help structure the physical environment, empirical evidence shows little relation-

---

[1]Throughout the next three chapters we will be using the term *cognitive-intellectual development* to refer to our criterion variable. Though some may find the term redundant, we have chosen to use it for a specific reason: We wish to look at the role of early experience across a wide variety of adaptive and problem-solving parameters, not just Piagetian or laboratory tasks (cognitive) or performance on psychometric scales (intellectual). Hence the term *cognitive-intellectual* as a means of calling the reader's attention to the wide scope of the criterion variables under consideration.

ship between dimensions of the physical and social environment (L. J. Yarrow *et al.*, 1975). Furthermore, there are clearly certain distinctions between these two classes of experience (Wohlwill, 1974). One obvious distinction is the population of the social environment. The social environment is populated by people or other animate objects such as pets; in contrast, the physical environment is populated by inanimate objects. As a consequence, while the social stimulation a child receives is multidimensional, including perceptual, interactional, and emotional stimuli, in the physical environment the stimuli received by the child are mainly perceptual, deriving primarily from the physical or sensory attributes (loudness, brightness, color) of the objects *per se*. Further, in general, the social environment is characterized by feedback loops from child to parent to child or parent to child to parent (Clarke-Stewart, 1978). In contrast, the physical environment is primarily passive and nonreactive. The child reacts upon the physical environment; only in a limited and very special sense does the physical environment react upon the child. Finally, while the social environment can be extrinsically rewarding to the child by providing the child with various kinds of emotional or physical reinforcers, the reinforcement value of the physical environment lies mainly in the intrinsic reinforcement value of the physical properties of objects themselves.

Accepting the distinction between the physical and social environments, we aim in the present chapter to review the available evidence on the relationship between *specific* aspects of the physical environment and the child's early cognitive-intellectual development. This evidence can be divided into a number of areas depending on the type of physical stimulation involved. Although in some cases there may be overlap, we have utilized the authors' description of the environmental parameter involved as a basis for categorizing the physical environment.

AVAILABILITY OF STIMULUS MATERIAL

Both cross-cultural (Geber, 1961) and institutional studies (Sayegh & Dennis, 1965) tend to implicate availability of stimulus material as a critical factor in early cognitive growth. However, confounding by other environmental variables makes it difficult to attribute developmental gains solely to the presence of available toys or objects. This caution appears more than warranted when one looks at current evidence relating availability of stimulus material to early cognitive development. Prior to 9 months of age, existing evidence does suggest that availability of stimulus material is positively related to early cognitive development. Thus, Brossard and Decarie (1971) note that providing a decorative mobile plus distinctive sounds to 2½-month-old institutionalized infants arrests the decline in measured intelligence normally found for institutionalized babies. Direct observational studies relating availability of toys and playthings in the home report significant correlations between 5-month availability of objects and 5-month Bayley performance (Riksen-Walraven, 1974) and between 8-month availability of objects and 8-month Griffiths Infant Scale Scores (Ainsworth & Bell, 1974).

In contrast to this early data, after 9 months of age the evidence becomes less consistent, particularly for correlational studies. Positive results are shown by Ainsworth and Bell (1974) who, repeating their 8-month procedures at 11 months, again report a significant relationship between availability of toys and Griffiths performance. Utilizing interview and observational measures, Van Alstyne (1929) correlated various home environmental measures obtained at 3 years to the child's Kuhlman–Binet performance. Several items apparently tapping availability (opportunities for constructive play materials; number of children's books a child sees) were positively and significantly related to mental age. These results are particularly impressive in view of the homogenous nature of Van Alstyne's sample. However, Van Alstyne further reported that the above variables were also significantly related to maternal IQ and may therefore reflect the action of Type I organism–environment covariance[2] (Wachs & Mariotto, 1978), rather than a direct environmental effect.

Inconsistent data on the relationship of availability of stimulus material to development are most evident in the data by Clarke-Stewart (1973) and Moore (1968). On the basis of a series of home observations between 9 and 18 months, Clarke-Stewart reports that both the number of available toys and the number of toys and objects actually used by the child are correlated with a composite factor defining infant competence across a variety of tasks between 9 and 18 months of age. However, when these two variables are related to specific tasks, the results are less clear-cut; number of toys available is unrelated to performance on either the Piaget-based Infant Psychological Development Scale (IPDS) (Uzgiris & Hunt, 1975) obtained between 12 and 14 months or on the Bayley Mental Scale obtained at 10 and 18 months; number of toys actually played with by the child is related to 17-month Bayley but not to 10-month Bayley or the IPDS.

Moore (1968) reports that home observations indicating the availability of toys and books at 2½ years of age were significantly related to males' Stanford–Binet IQ at age 3 years when socioeconomic class was held constant. When socioeconomic class was allowed to vary, the relationship was not significant. In addition, the relationship for females between availability of books and toys at 2½ years and IQ at 3 years was not significant.

Evidence directly contrary to the importance of availability of stimulus material is most clearly shown by Riksen-Walraven (1974). Repeating her earlier observations at 11 months, she reports no significant correlations

[2]Type I organism–environment correlation refers to parents transmitting not only genes but also rearing environments to their offspring.

between availability of material and Bayley performance. Further cautionary evidence on the relevance of availability of stimulus material to development is seen in the case report of a child born without limbs (Kopp & Shaperman, 1973). In spite of the fact that all of the child's interactions with the environment were nonmotor (since the child was unable to manipulate objects), the child's performance on Binet items given between 33 and 40 months of age was clearly at age level. This suggests that distance receptors may alone be sufficient and the availability of objects for manipulative purposes may not be critical for development.

The above data are studies of short-term relationships. However, the few long-term correlational prediction studies are just as inconsistent. Moore (1968) reports that for both males and females a 2½-year measure of availability of toys and books predicts 8-year Binet IQ. In contrast, Tulkin and Covitz (1975), using two hours of home observation at 6 months of age, report no relationship between measures of object availability and 6-year-old Peabody Picture Vocabulary Test (PPVT) or reflectivity–impulsivity scores. They do indicate a significant relationship between their 6-month environmental assessment and 6-year performance on the Illinois Test of Psycholinguistic Abilities (ITPA). Because of age measurement differences, it is difficult to explain directly inconsistencies between these two studies. Experimental studies, where additional stimulus material is directly provided to the child, show little relationship between availability and development. Williams and Scarr (1971), as part of an enrichment project for premature infants between 1 and 4 years of age, utilized a control group who received additional age appropriate toys over the course of a year. No effects of this manipulation were found on Gesell, PPVT, or ITPA scores. Similarly, as a control for other conditions, Levinstein (1970) reports that 24 visits by a home worker who simply provided educational toys to the child over a 7-month period led to a nonsignificant 1-point gain in general IQ and a significant 4-point loss of PPVT performance. In an unusually well-designed study, Busse, Ree, Gutride, Alexander, and Powell (1972) reported that the addition to classrooms of extra educational material designed to stimulate verbal and performance abilities, visual auditory perception, and social interaction did not increase Binet, Wechsler Pre-school and Primary Scale of Intelligence (WPPSI), or ITPA performance of the children receiving this material as compared to a nonenriched control group—this in spite of the fact that observations during the course of the study indicated use of the material by the children.

Summary: Availability

For availability of stimulus material, *it appears clear that if this variable has any effect upon development this effect will be mainly restricted to the first nine months of life.* After this time, the inconsistent correlational data plus the nonsignificant results from experimental studies do not support the relevance of availability of stimulus material to later development.

As to why differences occur before 9 months but not thereafter, there are several possibilities. One could postulate a critical period hypothesis suggesting that the availability of material may be relevant at some ages but not at others. However, this is simply a description of an empirical result. A more likely possibility is the onset of standing and walking after 9 months of age. This developmental milestone may have two effects. First, it may lessen the child's interest in available objects while the child is learning to stand and then to walk. Second, once the child has achieved mobility, he is less dependent upon the presence of objects in the immediate environment. Unlike the infant, the toddler has the capability to go outside the immediate environment to obtain the relevant stimulus material. To assess the validity of this hypothesis, it would be of interest to note whether the child's opportunities for exploration after 9 months of age are related to development. This possibility will be taken up in a later portion of this chapter.

Variety of Stimulus Material

J. McV. Hunt (1976) has suggested that while disadvantaged children received the same amount of stimulation as advantaged children, this stimulation is quite monotonous and lacking in variety for lower-class children. Hunt postulates that it is this monotomy of stimulation that lowers the cognitive-intellectual functioning of these children. On the basis of this hypothesis, one would therefore predict that variety of stimulation should be positively related to infants' cognitive-intellectual development. While there have been a number of approaches to the definition of variety of stimulation, in general the available evidence bears out this prediction.

The majority of evidence has been centered on short-term within-session variety: that is, the number of different objects, toys, or stimulus characteristics available to the infant at a single point in time. In one of the most comprehensive studies, Yarrow, Rubenstein, and Pedersen (1975), with a sample of black infants across different socioeconomic groups, assessed the 5-month home environments of these children using time-sampling observational techniques. The observations obtained were then related to the infants' performances on the Bayley Mental Scale, item clusters derived from Bayley items, object permanence, and exploratory behavior. The results indicate that variety, defined as the number of different objects available to the infant during observations, was positively and significantly related not only to Bayley Mental Development scores but also to object permanence, problem-solving, and exploratory behavior. The variety–exploratory relationship appears to be of particular theoretical significance in that it supports not only Hunt's (1965) intrinsic motivation concept (the more a child has seen and heard, the more he wishes to see and hear) but also an adaptation level concept: that is, a child exposed to varied stimulation is more likely to explore novel stimulation.

For older infants, supportive results are reported by Clarke-Stewart (1973). Clarke-Stewart reports that variety of toys available at 17 months of age is positively and significantly related to the child's overall competence and to 17-month Bayley Mental Score. The data by Clarke-Stewart were less than clear, however, in that the author's measure encompasses not only variety but also age-appropriateness of toys. The importance of age-appropriate physical stimulation will be discussed subsequently in the section on "match."

Significant but somewhat less consistent findings are also reported by Piper and Ramsay (1980), using a sample of Down's syndrome infants between 2 and 28 months. These authors report that infants in homes categorized as having high variety showed significantly less decline over a six-month period on the personal-social subscales of the Griffiths Infant Test than infants from less varied homes. Variety scores were unrelated to level of decline on other Griffiths subscales or to total Griffiths performance. These data suggest that variety may relate only to certain aspects of cognitive-intellectual development. Evidence is also available indicating that only certain aspects of variety may be relevant for development. In the previously described study by Riksen-Walraven (1974), tactual variety, as defined by differences in material of toys available for the infant, was positively and significantly related to Bayley Mental performance at both 5 and 11 months of age. Variety as defined by differences in colors or shapes was not related to Bayley performance. The lack of relationship of the color dimension is echoed in the report by Wohlwill and Heft (1975), who note that measures of variety of color in the home are unrelated to preschool children's performance on a variety of tasks tapping selective attention. The fact that a unitary dimension such as color is unrelated to a variety of developmental parameters at 5, 11, and 53 months suggests that variety should be defined primarily as a multivariate stimulus dimension and not as a function of any single dimension.

The most inconsistent findings for the variety hypothesis are reported by Elardo, Bradley, and Caldwell (1975) using the Caldwell HOME Inventory to measure the environment at 6, 12, and 24 months. HOME scores at those ages were correlated with Bayley Mental Scale performance at 6 and 12 months plus the Binet at 36 months. The results obtained by Elardo *et al.* indicated a delayed environmental effect. Specifically, the 6 months inventory of home stimulation subscale "opportunity for variety in daily stimulation" was not related to Bayley performance at 6 or 12 months but was significantly related to the Binet at 36 months. Similarly, the 12-month variety score was not related to 12-month Bayley but was related to the 36-month Binet. The lack of concurrent predictions for early HOME variety scores has also been shown by Field (Field, Hallock, Ting, Dempsey, Dabira, and Schumann, 1978), Plomin and DeFries (1980), and Stevenson and Lamb (1979), in the first year of life. At least for Stevenson and Lamb, a restricted subject sample and low HOME score reliability may account for the negative results; low variability associated with a restricted sample is also found in the Plomin and DeFries study.

Whereas delayed effects of variety of stimulation are consistent with previous results, the above nonsignificant results for variety of stimulation are inconsistent with data reported earlier. Elardo *et al.* (1975) suggest that early abilities, as measured by the Bayley, may not be as sensitive to effects of variety as abilities measured by the Binet. However, given the fact that both L. J. Yarrow *et al.* and Clarke-Stewart have used the Bayley, this interpretation does not appear to be valid. More intriguing is the possibility that the discrepancy between studies may lie in the definition of variety utilized. The data used by L. J. Yarrow *et al.* (1975), Riksen-Walraven (1974), and Clarke-Stewart (1973) were primarily measures of the variety of the child's play objects. The HOME variety scale used by Elardo and others measures mainly the variety of people available to the child. It may well be that the child's early cognitive-intellectual development is facilitated more by object variety than by person variety, while later cognitive development is facilitated more by person variety. Certainly developmental shifts in the nature of early intelligence are congruent with the above hypothesis. McCall, Hogarty, and Hurlburt (1972) report that manipulative exploration of objects is a major intellectual factor in the first 6 months of life, whereas after 12 months social-verbal factors become more characteristic of the child's early cognitive intellectual functioning. It would be logical to postulate that early object exploration will be facilitated more by interaction with a variety of objects, whereas social-verbal intelligence would be affected more by interaction with a variety of people.

The previously noted data by Piper and Ramsay (1980), indicating a relationship between HOME variety scores and level of decline in the Griffiths personal-social subscale, is not incongruent with the above hypothesis. Support for this hypothesis is also found in longitudinal studies. Following up their original sample using the Binet at 54 months, Bradley and Caldwell (1976a) again report significant predictions from 6- and 24-month HOME variety scores. Similarly, Bradley and Caldwell (1976b) report that increases in IQ between 6 (Bayley) and 36 (Binet) months are associated with opportunities for variety in the home; decreases in IQ between 6 and 36 months are associated with a lack of opportunity for variety. Similar long-term prediction from 12 months HOME Variety Scores to 36 months Binet and to language comprehension and expressiveness at 30 and 36 months have also been reported by Siegel (1979).

The only inconsistent longitudinal evidence comes in data by Farran, Ramey, and Campbell (1977), who report that Caldwell HOME Variety scores at 6 and 18 months do not predict 36-month Binet when entered in a multiple regression equation. Differences between these studies may well lie in differences in the statistical techniques utilized. A significant univariate correlation may not appear as a multivariate predictor due to a number of factors including the degree of interrelationship with other predictors.

The fact that different aspects of development may be affected by different aspects of the environment at different ages (i.e., early object orientation by variety of objects, later social orientation by variety of people) is an example of what we will later describe as age by environmental specificity. A detailed discussion of specificity will be explored at length in a subsequent chapter.

Taken as a whole, the above data do suggest that the presence of a variety of available persons or play objects is positively related to early cognitive-intellectual development and may well have long-term consequences. At first glance, these results would seem to support the variety hypothesis expounded by Hunt. Unfortunately, the above data are not conclusive because the variety measured in the above studies is within-session rather than between sessions. Hunt's hypothesis clearly involves a time dimension; namely, it is the change in available stimulation over time which is relevant for development. A child may have a large number of play objects at a given time (within-session or short-term variety); unless the child gets new and different play objects as he develops (between-session or long-term variety), development will not be facilitated. Clearly, what is needed are longitudinal measures of variety.

Two recent studies by Wachs (1978, 1979) have investigated this question of long-term variety. In the original study (Wachs, 1979), home observations done between 12 and 24 months included two measures of long-term variety: changes in room decoration and presence of new toys each month. Results indicated that changes in room decoration between 15 and 24 months were significantly related to female performance on one of the IPDS subscales—foresight—while the presence of new toys between 12 and 20 months was significantly related to male level of scheme development on the IPDS.

When 12–24 month measures of variety were related to the child's Binet performance at 31 months, even more consistent results were found (Wachs, 1978). For females, both changes in room decoration and presence of new toys were highly and significantly related to level of Binet performance; the data for males were nonsignificant. These sex differences are particularly reminiscent of the data obtained by Weizmann, Cohen, and Pratt (1971), who reported that the female infant's visual attention to a novel stimulus was facilitated by being placed in an unfamiliar rather than a familiar environment; the reverse held true for males. The possibility that sex of infant will mediate the role of environmental stimulation upon development is an example of what we have called organismic specificity. A detailed discussion of this concept is presented in Chapter 9. At least for females, therefore, the above data are clearly supportive of Hunt's variety hypothesis in suggesting the relevance of long-term variety to development. These findings parallel the results for exploratory behavior which suggest that exploration is facilitated by short-term novelty (within-session) as well as by long term novelty (between-session) (Hutt, 1970).

Taking the above data pattern as a whole, one could suggest that although a large selection of play objects would initially facilitate a young child's development (short-term variety), unless there were adequate replacements or changes in the child's set of play objects (long-term variety) the initial gains would be lost. This concept of long-term variety would appear to be especially important for older infants because of their earlier exposure to a varied number of toys with the possibility of habituating to once-novel toys. Long-term variety may also be important for the development of older infants, with novel objects being discrepant from previously established schemes and thus leading to increased attention (Appleton, Clifton, & Goldberg, 1975).

The above findings have been based on a series of short- and long-term studies of the effect of within-home variety. An alternative approach to the question of stimulus variety would measure the degree to which the child is exposed to stimuli other than those existing in his immediate home environment. In general, data on this particular question are mixed, particularly for younger infants.

Using adopted infants, Beckwith (1971) reports a significant relationship between a measure of the number of places an infant visits and the child's 10-month Cattell score. Unfortunately, this measure of out-of-home variety is also confounded by the number of people visiting in the home, and therefore it is unclear whether Beckwith's results are due to variety or social stimulation. Wachs, Uzgiris, and Hunt (1971) report that visits out of the home several times a week to neighbors are positively related to levels of IPDS development at 7 months, while occasional trips outside of the neighborhood or family trips are positively related to various IPDS indexes at 18 and 22 months. The authors also report that continual variety may be detrimental to development since visits outside of the home or neighborhood every day are negatively related to IPDS level at 15 and 18 months. For older, institutionalized children, Tizard and Rees (1976) report that two measures of variety–routine variety (shopping) and special variety (trips) are significantly and positively related to 4½-year-old WPPSI IQs.

Negative results are reported in two studies. Wachs (1979) reports no relationship between IPDS performance and number of visits outside the home or out of the neighborhood in the second year of life. For prediction of 31-month Binet, only out-of-home variety for males between 15 and 17 months is significant (Wachs, 1978).

Because of the paucity of studies available in this area it is difficult to integrate results across studies, particularly since different ages and, in most cases, different criterion variables were used. However, the latter data by Wachs and the fact that the correlations obtained by Tizard and Rees, though significant, were quite low (.21, .26) suggest that the importance of out-of-home variety may be less relevant to the development of infants and young children.

Summary: Variety

Overall, in terms of variety of stimulation, the data clearly suggest, particularly for young infants, that exposure to a wide variety of toys or objects is positively related to cognitive intellectual development. As a child gets older, long-term changes in object variety may become more important than the number of different objects available at a given time. The relationship of out-of-home variety to development appears nowhere to be as consistent or as relevant as within-home variety parameters.

OTHER STIMULUS CHARACTERISTICS

Studies of stimulus variables other than variety are rarely found in the literature. L. J. Yarrow *et al.* (1975) did look at complexity of available objects and reported many fewer correlations between complexity and development than for variety. Specifically, complexity was related only to certain Bayley clusters but was not related to the overall Bayley Mental Development Index or to object permanence performance. Riksen-Walraven (1974) reports a significant correlation between 5-month object complexity score and 5-month Bayley; by 11 months this relationship had vanished. White and Watts (1973), looking at the relationship of various environmental parameters to children's competence between 12 and 36 months of age, report that there are no consistent differences between competent and incompetent children in the physical characteristics of objects used in play. Physical characteristics involved such factors as personal toys as opposed to household objects, and size of toys. The general lack of results for object characteristics other than variety clearly is no news to parents who have brought home expensive toys to their children and watched the children spend most of their time playing with the wrappings of the box in which the toy was presented.

RESPONSIVITY OF THE PHYSICAL ENVIRONMENT

Several authors have suggested that, even for young infants, the responsivity of the environment may be an important variable in promoting cognitive intellectual development. Although much of the available evidence is based on responsivity of persons in the environment to the infant (Clarke-Stewart, 1973), laboratory evidence (Watson & Ramey, 1972) suggests the importance of nonsocial contingencies for development as well. The available evidence on nonsocial responsivity to the infant, while sparse, is quite consistent. L. J. Yarrow *et al.* (1975), in a previously noted study, reported that the responsiveness of the environment (defined in terms of the extent to which objects change in sensory properties as the result of the infant's interaction) was significantly and positively related to the 5-month-old infant's Bayley mental performance, level of goal directed behaviors, secondary circular reactions, and exploration. At least from a Piagetian point of view, the relationship between responsivity and secondary circular reactions is particularly interesting, since these reactions are, in part, developed by the feedback the infant receives from the environment (Piaget, 1952). Similar data are also shown by Riksen-Walraven (1974), who reports that the responsivity of objects in the child's environment is related to 5-month and 11-month Bayley performance.

The above data are correlational. Experimental evidence on the relationship of inanimate responsivity to development is seen in the study by Hunt, Mohandessi, Ghodssi, and Akizama (1976). In this study, infants residing in an Iranian orphange were exposed to one of four rearing conditions. One of these conditions involved conjugate reinforcement[3] from weeks 6 to 14 by means of the Friedlander play-test apparatus plus mobiles mounted on springs. For the responsive environment group, results indicate significantly higher development across all IPDS subscales than for untreated controls.

The above findings are restricted to infants below 12 months of age. Until recently no evidence was available for infants above 12 months of age, but two recent studies (Wachs, 1978, 1979) have suggested the relevance of inanimate responsivity of objects to development through the second and third years of life as well. In the 1979 study, results indicate that one measure of a physically responsive environment (the number of audiovisually responsive toys available to the child) is the physical environmental parameter most relevant for subsequent cognitive intellectual development between 12 and 24 months of age. Specifically, for six out of seven IPDS subscales, level of performance was significantly and positively related to number of audiovisually responsive toys. Only on the verbal imitation scale was no relationship found. The follow-up of this parameter into the third year of life (Wachs, 1978) again confirms the earlier relationship. At all age levels between 12 and 24 months, the number of audiovisually responsive toys was significantly and positively correlated with 31-month Binet.

Summary: Responsivity

Taken as a whole, the studies noted above clearly suggest the importance of nonsocial inanimate responsivity for cognitive intellectual development at least during the first 2½ years of life.

---

[3]The child's acting toward the environment leads to visual, auditory, or tactile stimulation of the child; it is the stimulation from the environment that acts as a reinforcer for the child's actions.

The importance of nonsocial responsivity may well lie in the fact, based upon naturalistic observation (Provence & Lipton, 1962) and experimental evidence (Watson & Ramey, 1972) that infants deprived of a responsive environment stop responding to the environment. This tuning-out of the environment not only reduces the infant's intake of environmental stimulation but also minimizes the infant's willingness to display adaptive behaviors (Provence & Lipton, 1962). In addition, nonresponsive infants are also more likely to promote further nonresponsivity from those around them (Osofsky & Danzger, 1974); thus a vicious circle may develop. While much of the environmental responsivity to infants comes from the infant's parents or other caretakers, the present pattern of results suggests the relevance of non-social inanimate responsivity to development as well. These results may have definite implications for institutional or residential settings where there is a lack of adult interaction. The general pattern of data suggests that in those institutions where a socially responsive environment is missing efforts should be made to provide a physically responsive environment for the infant in order to avoid detrimental effects associated with living in a totally non-responsive environment. While Provence and Lipton (1962) suggest that sufficient social interaction may be necessary before the infant can respond to nonsocial contingencies, the data by Hunt et al. (1976) do not support this contention.

AMOUNT OF STIMULATION

Prior to the late 1960s, most evidence on the effects of intensity of stimulation was based on infrahuman data, which suggested a linear model relating intensity of stimulation to cognitive intellectual development. That is, the less the available stimulation, the slower development occurs; the greater the amount of stimulation, the faster development would occur. The available human data, based primarily on orphanage populations (stimulus deprivation) tended to support this model (Das, 1973; Rutter, 1979). Unfortunately, as we noted earlier, in most orphanage studies factors such as the amount of stimulation are hopelessly confounded with other variables, making it difficult if not impossible to isolate specific components of relevant stimulation from orphanage data. Indeed, what parametric evidence was available, although limited in scope, suggested little effect of *short-term* stimulus deprivation *per se* upon infants' cognitive development (Schaffer & Emerson, 1968).

Because of the popularity of the linear model, a number of enrichment programs were devised in the 1960s for "stimulus-deprived" children. However, it was soon obvious to observers who actually went into homes of disadvantaged children that these children were not living in the human analogue of a sensory deprivation chamber, but rather were living in noisy, confused environments (Deutsch, 1964; Klaus & Gray, 1968). As a result, observers began to suggest that disadvantaged children may in fact be receiving too much rather than too little stimulation.

In addition to this observational evidence, the little experimental evidence that was then available also suggested the possibility that too much stimulation can be as detrimental to development as too little stimulation. Thus, White and Held (1966), attempting to accelerate the attentional development of orphanage-reared infants, placed the infants in cribs surrounded by a large stimulus array including mobiles, crib liners and distinctive clothes. The results indicated that rather than accelerating attentional development this procedure slowed it. White and Held interpret their results as the stimulus array providing too much stimulation for the infant to assimilate. As a result, in recent years most theoreticians in the area of early experience have tended to utilize a curvilinear (too much or too little can be detrimental) rather than a linear model (Wohlwill, 1974). If the relationship of environment to development is curvilinear, suggesting that too much stimulation may be detrimental, it is legitimate to ask what is meant by too much stimulation.[4] On the basis of observations of disadvantaged children, Gray and Klaus (1968) suggest at least two relevant dimensions: noise and confusion and spatial-temporal irregularity. Based on infrahuman data (Calhoun, 1962), we would add a third factor, namely overcrowding. It could be argued that these three constructs, noise–confusion, overcrowding, and temporal-spatial irregularity, are simply aspects of one general overstimulation dimension. However, a recent factor analytic study of the physical environment of infants (Wachs, Francis, & McQuiston, 1979) indicates that these three dimensions are in fact orthogonal. Therefore, under the heading of amount of stimulation we will review available evidence on the relationship to infants' cognitive development of noise–confusion, overcrowding, and temporal and spatial irregularity.

Noise–Confusion in the Home

Although there were a number of earlier suggestions on the possible relationship of noise–confusion in the home to early developmental level (Deutsch, 1964), the first systematic evidence on this concept was provided by Wachs, Uzgiris, and Hunt (1971). These authors measured the home environment of infants at five different age levels and correlated home en-

---

[4]This is not to slight stimulus deprivation as a relevant factor. However, a review of the literature suggests that much of what we call stimulus deprivation is a function of other specific parameters—that is, a lack of responsivity or verbal stimulation from the environment. In contrast, hyperstimulation appears to involve stimulus parameters differing from those discussed elsewhere in this volume. Thus, this section will concentrate primarily on the overstimulation aspects of the hypothesized inverted U-shaped curve between environment and development.

vironmental measures with the child's IPDS performance. Results indicated
that at all five age levels the items most consistently and negatively related to
cognitive functioning were those tapping the presence of high noise and
confusion levels in the home. Support for these findings in the first year of
life are seen in the Riksen-Walraven results. Using measures derived from
the Wachs *et al.* (1971) paper, Riksen-Walraven (1974) reports that there is a
20-point Bayley Mental Development Index difference between 5-month-old
infants from noisy homes and those from quiet homes, with the higher scores
being obtained by infants in the quieter homes. Surprisingly, the data for
11-month-olds were nonsignificant.

These findings have been replicated and expanded in a more recent
study by the senior author (Wachs, 1979). Looking at infant IPDS development longitudinally across the second year of life, Wachs reported that a
rating of the amount of noise–confusion in the home was negatively and
significantly related to male IPDS performance across all IPDS scales except
schemes. The data for females tended either to be positive and nonsignificant
or, in the case of causality, positive and significant. The strong sex differences noted here appear to provide further evidence for what we have
labeled organismic specificity: namely the interface of individual differences
with experience. The possibility of organismic specificity for noise–
confusion parameters is also suggested by the recent data of Wachs and
Gandour (1981). Looking at the interrelationship of early temperament, environment, and sensorimotor development at six months, these authors report
that temperamentally "difficult" infants are significantly more sensitive to
noise–confusion parameters, in terms of a relationship with sensorimotor
development, than are temperamentally "easy" infants. Similarly, data by
Finkelstein, Gallagher, and Farran (1980) suggest that infants at risk for mild
mental retardation may be more sensitive to noise–confusion than nonrisk
infants.

Supportive data for the negative effects of noise–confusion with older
children come from four studies. Hambrick-Dixon (1980) reports that ambient subway noise negatively affects preschool children's psychomotor performance but is unrelated to their memory skills. Using preschoolers between 4 and 6 Wohlwill and Heft (1975) measured a number of home environmental variables including a rating of background noise–confusion in
the home. They report that preschool children living in noisy homes are
poorer in information-processing and attentional skills than matched children
living in less noisy homes. Of particular interest are the data reported by
Cohen, Glass, and Singer (1973). In an ingeniously designed, naturally
occurring experiment, the authors measured the decibel level in apartments of a high-rise apartment house built over a freeway. Decibel level
in individual apartments was related to resident children's auditory discrimination. In general, results indicated that the higher the intensity of decibel
level, the poorer the child's level of auditory discrimination. Similar findings

have been reported by Glenn, Nerbonne, and Tolhurst (1978), who measured ambient noise levels in an institution for the retarded and related these measurements to speech perception in a sample including preschool-age retarded children.

Data on the long-term effects of noise–confusion are less consistent. In the only data available, Wachs (1978) reported that whereas noise–confusion ratings for males at 12–14 months predict 31-month Binet, ratings between 15 and 24 months do not. Wohlwill (1974) suggests that older children have more control over stimulation than younger children by virtue of their greater ability to move away from sources of intense stimulation and thus lessen the effects. However, the home-based data showing significant relationships for preschool children (Cohen et al., 1973; Wohlwill & Heft, 1975) tend to minimize the relevance of this suggestion. A more likely hypothesis, although untested, is that noise–confusion may have effects only when the child is directly exposed to the hyperstimulation and is forced to develop defensive responses to shield himself from hyperstimulation. In this case, unlike responsivity wherein the effects of a nonresponsive environment became incorporated into the child's approach to the world, the effects of noise–confusion would be environment-specific and one would predict less long-term carry-over.

The only study reporting evidence contrary to the hypothesis that noise confusion is negatively related to early cognitive intellectual development is that by Clarke-Stewart (1973). She reports essentially no significant relationship between the amount of time that the television or radio was on and the child's cognitive intellectual performance. There are two difficulties with this finding, however. First, Clarke-Stewart's measurement concerned only the amount of time the television or radio was on and did not measure the intensity of the television or radio sound. All previous studies reporting significant results obtained ratings not only of the amount of time but also the intensity. Second, Clarke-Stewart's sample was almost exclusively urban lower class. Evidence indicates that it is within this group that noise sources like television and radio are most likely to be on continuously (Lewis & Wilson, 1972; Tulkin & Kagan, 1972). This suggests, for the noise–confusion dimension, that Clarke-Stewart had a restricted range of environments. As has been pointed out (Weizmann, 1971), a restricted range of environment is likely to reduce the magnitude of the correlation coefficient and thus lessen the probability of significant results.

Summary: Noise Confusion

In general, it appears that there is a negative relationship between indexes of noise–confusion in the home and measures of cognitive intellectual development between 5 months and 5 years of age. This relationship appears to be particularly strong for males and difficult or at-risk infants; further, input mechanisms (perception, attention) appear to be more sensitive to noise–confusion than storage mechanisms such as memory.

There appear to be a number of potential reasons why intense or complex noise levels in the home could have an adverse effect on cognitive intellectual development. Most of these are tied in with some type of defensive reaction to the noise–confusion which disrupts the functioning of other critical cognitive systems. Thus, high noise levels could cause recurrent physiological defense reactions leading to an inhibition of stimulus-processing (Lacey, 1967). High noise levels could also cause habituation to auditory input, thus depriving the child of a major source of information (Deutsch, 1964; Glenn et al., 1978). Alternatively, high levels of noise–confusion could lead to direct interference either with information-processing (Wohlwill, 1974; Wohlwill & Heft, 1975) or with learning by classical conditioning (Thompson, 1972). There are some indications that noise–confusion may also relate to the use of more primitive modes of exploratory behavior (McQuiston & Wachs, 1979). Studies comparing the development of such phenomena as degree of cardiac acceleration, habituation rate, and ability to form classically conditioned associations by infants from homes having intense or adequate noise levels would undoubtedly help in isolating the mechanism responsible for the noise–confusion effect noted.

Overcrowding in the Home

A second major component of overstimulation appears to involve some measure of overcrowding. Based on available evidence, the most useful definition of overcrowding appears to be the number of sibs in the young child's environment. Definitions based on family size (Jordan, 1978; Madden et al., 1976), number of rooms (Jordan, 1978; Lawson & Ingleby, 1974), or on ratios of furniture or decorations to room size (Wohlwill & Heft, 1975) tend to be either nonsignificant or inconsistent. For number of sibs, the available evidence indicates that the *continuous* presence of sibs or other children in the young child's environment is negatively related to the child's cognitive intellectual development (Belmont & Marolla, 1973; Bradshaw, 1969; Horton & Crump, 1962; Riksen-Walraven, 1974; Scott & Kobes, 1975; Van Alstyne, 1929). The children do not have to be biological relatives since the same negative relationships appear when foster sibs are counted (Rheingold, 1943). Interestingly, the continuous presence of sibs may also act as a barrier to intervention effects. Bronfenbrenner (1974) reports data suggesting that if three or more children are present in the home during intervention attempts the IQ gain of the target child is negatively related to the number of children present.

Given the consistent negative relationship between number of children residing in the home and cognitive intellectual level, it is interesting to speculate on the reasons for this relationship. There appear to be four major hypotheses available to explain this relationship. It is possible that homes that are crowded with children are more likely to have high levels of noise–confusion which could predispose to slower development. However, factorial data (Wachs *et al.*, 1979) indicate separate factors for noise–confusion and number of people in the home, suggesting independent effects of these variables. Stern (1974b) has speculated that the presence of sibs may lower the mother's ability to concentrate on infant reactions in an interaction situation. Although this is a logical hypothesis, no data are available to support it.

A third approach to the question of overcrowding is seen in the theory by Zajonc (1976), who suggests that rate of intellectual growth in children depends primarily on family configurations. That is, it is not the number of sibs *per se* but the age span between sibs that is most critical in the relationship to cognitive intellectual development. Closely spaced sibs dilute the "family intellectual environment" available to incoming children and thus predispose to lower developmental levels. Much of Zajonc's data is based on averaged retrospective studies with older children, and it is not clear from his theory exactly what specific environmental transactions are involved in different types of spacing. Further, prospective studies attempting to predict individual differences in intellectual development among children as a function of spacing of sibs report either inconsistent data (Moore, 1968) or data contrary to Zajonc's model (Grotevant, Scarr, & Weinberg, 1977; Belmont, Stein, & Zybert, 1978). Clearly Zajonc's model, although theoretically ambitious, does not explain the overcrowding effect noted above.

It is also possible that the presence of a large number of people in a small space makes it more probable that there will be increased interference with the child's ongoing actions leading to increased amounts of frustration or a lack of closure. Along these lines, Wachs (1979) has suggested the relevance of personal space to development. As defined, personal space involves not only the number of sibs but, more importantly, the ratio of rooms to people and the presence of a "stimulus shelter." Wachs suggests that even with a large number of sibs, if there is adequate personal space (i.e., a high rooms-to-people ratio), development may not be inhibited. As support for this hypothesis, Wachs (1979) reports both univariate and multivariate (canonical) correlations indicating better prediction of IPDS performance by a rooms-to-people ratio measure than by a measure of number of sibs. The relationship between personal space and cognitive development appears to be particularly strong for males. Interestingly, Aiello, Nicosia, and Thompson (1979), using a population of school-age children, report that negative physiological and behavioral effects of short-term overcrowding are restricted primarily to males. Wachs also suggests the importance of a "stimulus shelter." The stimulus shelter is defined as a room or area where the child can be by himself out of the range of noise or people if he so desires. The presence of a stimulus shelter has been found to be positively related to sensorimotor development during the second year of life.[5]

Summary: Overcrowding

Overcrowding, defined as the number of sibs, has been consistently found to be negatively related to cognitive-intellectual development in infancy and the preschool years. The evidence tends to lend support to Wachs's personal space hypothesis as a causative factor for the negative relationship between overcrowding and development.

REGULARITY OF TEMPORAL AND SPATIAL SCHEDULING

A number of observers of the home environment of disadvantaged children (Klaus & Gray, 1968; Pavenstadt, 1965) have commented on the disorganization and lack of order in these homes. As Klaus and Gray described this phenomenon: "There is no one place for any object in the home if that object is moveable . . . the day is not organized around such standing patterns as mealtimes and bedtimes" (p. 7). The implication is that the lack of order in the home is in some way related to the poor intellectual performance of disadvantaged children.

Theoretically, these observations may relate to the perceptual theory developed by Gibson (1963), in which one of the primary developmental tasks of young children is to learn to differentiate and isolate foreground factors from background stimuli. According to Gibson, much of the child's initial learning is based on this early differentiation. For a child living in an environment such as that described by Klaus and Gray it would be extremely difficult to learn to isolate stimulus from background since there would be few consistent stimulus patterns in the environment. As such, one would predict a negative relationship between temporal/spatial irregularity and development.

Although there is little evidence on this topic, the available evidence is consistent with the above hypothesis, particularly after the first year of life. In the first year, Riksen-Walraven (1974) reports positive and significant correlations between ratings of the home's orderliness and the child's Bayley performance at 5 months of age; differences between the groups at 11 months were not significant. Elardo *et al.* (1975) reported positive though nonsignificant correlations between the Caldwell HOME subscale "organization of

---

[5]Note that a stimulus shelter is defined by its physical properties and not by whether the child has its own room. The child may have its own room, but if this room is noisy or in a family traffic pattern, it will not serve as a stimulus shelter. For this reason, it is not surprising that the child's having its own room *per se* does not predict development (Van Alstyne, 1929).

physical and temporal environment" measured at 6 and 12 months and the child's Bayley mental score measured at the same age. Also using the HOME, nonsignificant results in the first year of life have been shown by Field *et al.* (1978), Stevenson and Lamb (1979), and Plomin and DeFries (1980). Early differences between studies using the HOME and the Riksen-Walraven study may reflect the measurements of the orderliness-predictability of the environment that were utilized. In the Elardo *et al.* study, the orderliness measure appeared to center around the predictability of the environment for the child. This may well have delayed effects if predictability is a cumulative phenomenon not affecting the child until later. In contrast, the Riksen-Walraven measure was concerned primarily with the visual orderliness of the home, which may have a more immediate effect. If correct, this hypothesis would predict long-term (cumulative) relationships between early HOME organization scores and later development (assuming a stable environment). As will be noted below, available evidence is supportive.

Support for the importance of environmental predictability after the first year of life comes from data by Wachs (1979), who reported that one measure of environmental regularity (regularity of mealtimes) predicts male object permanence between 12 and 18 months and male level of scheme development between 12 and 20 months; a second measure of environmental predictability (regularity of naptimes) between 12 and 18 months predicts 31-month Binet (Wachs, 1978). Similarly, Elardo *et al.* (1975) report that 24-month organization of physical and temporal environment is significantly related to the child's Binet performance at 36 months of age. Utilizing a sample of Down's syndrome infants between 2 and 28 months of age, Piper and Ramsay (1980) report significantly less decline in Griffiths total scores on the personal-social subscale for those infants living in organized home environments (HOME scale) than those not. For normal infants, Bradley and Caldwell (1976b) report that decreases in intellectual performance between 6 and 36 months were related to a lack of organization in the physical and temporal environment.

Evidence on the long-term predictive value of early environmental organization also generally supports the relevance of these dimensions for development. Elardo *et al.* (1975) report significant positive correlations between HOME organization scores at 6 and 12 months and the child's Binet performance at 36 months. These data have been replicated by Bradley and Caldwell (1976a), who report that 6-month and 24-month organization of physical and temporal environment significantly predicts 54-month Binet. Comparison of the 36-month prediction with that of 54 months suggests that organization may be more critical for children earlier in life, since predictions are lower at 54 months than at 36 months. Bradley and Caldwell (1976b) suggest that organization may be more critical for children earlier in life since once children are into the preoperational stage they may be better able to organize the environment for themselves. Also supporting a cumulative effect hypothesis Ramey, Farran, and Campbell (1979) report that the 18-month Caldwell HOME organization score significantly predicts 36-month Binet scores of day-care program children; the six month HOME organization score for the same children is nonpredictive. Interestingly, the predictions were nonsignificant for control children who were not in the day care program. The authors suggest that day care in some way alters the relationship between environmental variables and the child's status, but it is unclear exactly why this alteration occurs.

In terms of inconsistent findings, Siegel (1979) does report that 12-month HOME organization scores are unrelated to Binet scores or language comprehension at 30 and 36 months; HOME organization scores do predict language expression at 30 and 36 months. Elardo et al. (1977), in their study of the relationship of the Caldwell scale organization factor at 6 and 30 months to ITPA at 3 years, report generally nonsignificant correlations between organization of physical and temporal environment and ITPA. The lack of relationship of organization with the Binet in the Siegel (1979) data is hard to reconcile with earlier results. The generally nonsignificant language results in her study and that of Elardo et al. (1977) may be consistent with Gibson's theory in suggesting that perceptual motor development may be more affected by early regularity than is language development. Previous data reported by Wachs (1979) is congruent with this hypothesis; looking at the relationship between schemes and regularity, Wachs reports that the relationship between environmental regularity and schemes disappears after 20 months when schemes are defined primarily by verbal naming; prior to this time, schemes are characteristically defined in terms of the child's motoric action upon objects.

Summary: Organization/Regularity

In general, the degree of regularity/organization in the home is positively related to early cognitive-intellectual development. However, this relationship may be mediated by the age of the child and may be specific only to nonlanguage measures. Further, the relationship between organization/regularity and development may be cumulative in nature, implying the necessity for a stable environment for this relationship to become manifest. Again the possibility of specificity of environmental action is suggested.

MATCH BETWEEN ORGANISM AND ENVIRONMENT

One of the more popular developmental concepts in terms of early experience has been that of the "match" or optimal stimulation hypothesis. This hypothesis suggests that maximal developmental rate will be achieved if the individual is presented with stimulation optimally discrepant (pacer-match) from the individual's own cognitive level or stimulus-processing ability. The importance of a match or pacer-type process has been suggested not only for early education (Caldwell & Richmond, 1968; Elkind, 1969; Hunt, 1967; Kohlberg, 1968) but also for early mental development (Lichtenberg & Norton, 1970) and motor development (Pontius, 1973). For infants, match has typically been defined primarily in terms of the age appropriateness of stimuli available to the infant. In addition, a few experimental studies involving presentation of stimuli at different levels also exist.

In terms of experimental evidence, one interesting line is found in the data by Papousek (1969), who attempted to train young infants on a difficult discrimination-learning test. One group of infants started at 44 days of age took an average of 224 trials to reach criterion. In contrast, a second group of infants started on the first day of life took an average of 814 trials to reach criterion. This discrepancy was attributed to the neonates' being unable to process and deal with environmental stimulation which was too complex for the infants' existing cognitive capabilities (Sameroff, 1971). Supportive evidence for this hypothesis is also found in the previously noted data by White and Held (1966) who reported that high levels of visual stimulation led to a decline in attentional development. In a second study, the authors (White & Held, 1966) removed some of the visual stimulation provided and reported that this reduction of stimulation led to an enhancement of infants' attentional development, indicating that a possible mismatch may have been converted into a match between organism and environment.

In terms of provision of age-appropriate stimulation, indirect evidence is seen in the report by Caldwell and Richmond (1968). In this paper the authors discuss an early intervention program which, as part of its curriculum, attempted to match stimulation to the child's level of development. Although this program did produce gains in the child's level of intellectual functioning, it is unclear from the report whether it was the match or other aspects of the enrichment program that were responsible for the gains. However, a number of other studies offer more direct evidence. Using 6-month-old infants, L. J. Yarrow (1963) reported that a home environment measure labeled stimulus adaptation ("the extent to which material experiences given to the infant were adapted to its individual capacity") was among the variables most highly correlated with the child's IQ (+.69). In a follow-up of this population at 10 years of age, L. J. Yarrow, Goodwin, Mannheimer, and Milowe (1973) reported a significant prediction between 6-month adaptation and 10-year Wechsler Intelligence Scale for Children (WISC) IQ for males (+.48) but not for females. Unfortunately, it is unclear from Yarrow's results exactly what specific criteria were used by parents to provide this match, and therefore these data can again only be considered as suggestive.

The importance of providing age-appropriate materials is also stressed in several papers by Caldwell and her associates. In the first study (Elardo et al.,

1975), provision of age-appropriate materials at 6, 12, and 24 months was significantly and positively related to 36-month Binet. In addition, 12-month provision of appropriate material was also related to 12-month Bayley, but 6-month scores were unrelated to 6-month or 12-month Bayley. In a second study (Bradley & Caldwell, 1976b), increases in intellectual functioning between 6 and 36 months were related to provision of age-appropriate play materials. Follow-up data (Bradley & Caldwell, 1976a) indicate that provision of age-appropriate play materials at 6 and 24 months is also related to 54-month Binet. Twelve-month HOME provision scores have also been found to be positively related to Binet scores, as well as measures of language comprehension and expression at 30 and 36 months (Siegel, 1979). In addition, Elardo, Bradley, and Caldwell (1977) reported that 6-month and 30-month measures of availability of age-appropriate play material are strongly related to the child's ITPA performance at 36 months. Looking at the question of causality, Bradley, Caldwell, and Elardo (1979) utilized a cross-lag design. In contrast to a match hypothesis, their results indicate that in the first year of life the child's cognitive level more strongly predicts subsequent provision of age-appropriate play materials than play materials predict cognitive level. After the first year a transactional pattern emerges such that brighter children receive more appropriate play material which further facilitates their development—this pattern suggests that match may not be unidirectional in nature as has been implicitly suggested in writings on this question.

The only other available, supportive, direct evidence is seen in data by Wachs (1977) using canonical correlations between physical environmental parameters measured between 12 and 24 months of age and the infant's performance on the IPDS. In terms of the relationship between physical environment and development, canonical correlations revealed that, at certain ages, a pattern emerged strongly resembling what one would predict from the optimal stimulation hypothesis. These data indicate that the 21-month-old child's level of cognitive intellectual development can be maximally predicted by a home environment between 12 and 14 months which is characterized by a predictability of environmental events, the presence of audiovisually responsive toys, regular changes of stimulus material, and an absence of intense noise and confusion. Taken as a whole, these results suggest that a physical environment characterized by the presence of adequate stimulation and the absence of hyperstimulation will maximize subsequent intellectual development. A similar pattern of results is also shown in the prediction of 24-month cognitive intellectual performance by the physical environment between 21 and 23 months. However, while these data suggest the operation of match, this pattern does not appear prior to 21 months nor does it appear for all measured environmental periods when development is assessed at 21 and 24 months. Finally, for children in the third year of life, Clarke-Stewart et al. (1979) report that maternal adaptation of her language level to the language of her child (language match), while unrelated to IQ performance, is positively related to measures of the child's language development.

Besides the age discrepancies noted in the Elardo *et al.* (1975) and Wachs (1977) reports, the question of causality raised by Bradley *et al.* (1979), and the specificity found by Clarke-Stewart (1979), evidence contrary to the match hypothesis is also seen in the report by Garms (1974). Garms visually stimulated infants either with initially preferred (match) checkerboard patterns or randomly selected checkerboard patterns (no match). Infants were subsequently tested on both Bayley performance and habituation rate. In terms of both habituation and Bayley performance, contrary to the match hypothesis, the differences between matched and nonmatched infants were nonsignificant. Garms's study might have yielded more successful results if the author had adopted Greenberg's (1971) procedure of changing stimulus levels after several weeks of exposure. Under the terms of the optimal stimulation hypothesis (Dember & Earl, 1957), with continued exposure to stimuli, subjects adaptation level changes. Negative evidence is also shown in the data by Farran *et al.* (1977) who related Caldwell HOME inventory scores at 6 and 18 months of age to the child's 36-month Binet performance. Results indicate no relationship between provision of age-appropriate materials at 6 months and 36-month Binet performance; at 18 months of age, provision of age-appropriate materials is related to development, but the relationship is negative rather than positive. Other nonsignificant results in the first two years of life using the HOME have been reported in four studies: Field *et al.* (1978), Piper and Ramsay (1980), Plomin and DeFries (1980), and Stevenson and Lamb (1979).

Summary: Match

Given the popularity of the optimal stimulation hypothesis, the inconsistency of results in this area is extremely disappointing. There have been a number of attempts to account for this inconsistency. Thomas (1971) argues that before one can unambiguously evaluate the optimal stimulation hypothesis, a number of as yet unspecified parameters must be specified. These would include a specification of differences between stimuli, a specification of subject placement on the stimulus curve, and evidence on the overall shape of the curve relating stimulus preference to development. Wachs (1977) notes further that most of the available *research* on the optimal stimulation hypothesis focuses solely on stimulus differences to the exclusion of subject parameters. In contrast, most *formulations* of the optimal stimulation hypothesis focus on both stimulus and subject (Dember & Earl, 1957; Hunt, 1961). In these theoretical statements, match is defined both as a function of the available stimulus and as a function of the individual's stimulus-processing capacity. Nowhere is there an indication that one can define optimal stimulation solely on stimulus characteristics such as age appropriateness. *It seems clear that unless more attention is paid to the subject's contribution to match little future progress will be made in this area* (Wachs, 1977).

RESTRICTION OF EXPLORATION

Like responsivity, restriction can either be a social (parents' interfering) or a nonsocial phenomenon (physical barriers, movement restricted to playpen). In terms of physical indexes, two major classes of studies are found: those measuring the amount of floor freedom available to the child and those measuring the presence of barriers or other obstacles to the child's exploration. The majority of evidence has dealt with floor freedom.

For floor freedom most available evidence deals with development in the first year of life. In a cross-cultural study, Ainsworth (1977) suggests that the acceleration on both Gesell and Griffiths performance for Ganda infants is a function, in part, of the extensive floor freedom which these infants receive. In a direct test of this hypothesis, Ainsworth and Bell (1974) related the amount of floor freedom available to the child at 8 and 11 months with the child's Griffiths IQ at 8 and 11 months. Results indicate highly significant relationships between amount of floor freedom at 8 and 11 months and Griffiths performance at both of these ages. When multiple regression techniques were used, floor freedom was the only physical environmental parameter that added significant variance to predictability of IQ. Possible specificity of the effects of floor freedom are reported by Beckwith, Cohen, Kopp, Parmelee, and Marcy (1976) using premature infants. Looking at regression analyses of various physical, social, and infant variables to Gesell developmental level at 8 months, these authors report that 8-month floor freedom is the primary environmental factor significantly associated with 9-month Gesell performance. In contrast, when the Piaget-based Casati–Lezine scale was employed, results indicated no relationship of floor freedom to Piagetian sensorimotor development.

Data in the second year of life are also consistent with the previous findings. White and Watts (1973) report that children rated as noncompetent are found to spend significantly more time in their playpen than children rated as competent. Wachs (1979) reports significant and positive correlations between the amount of floor freedom given to male children and the infants' levels of object permanence, foresight, and gestural imitation. The only clearly inconsistent concurrent data are those by Beckwith (1971), using adopted children. Beckwith reports a positive but nonsignificant correlation between floor freedom and 10-month Cattell performance.

In terms of follow-up, Wachs (1978) reports that second-year floor freedom was not found to predict 31-month Binet. Similar results in the first year are reported by Cohen and Beckwith (1979). Long-term predictability of floor freedom is, however, shown in the paper by Tulkin and Covitz (1975), who report a significant and negative correlation between time the child spends in the playpen at 10 months of age and middle-class children's PPVT IQ at age 6. The data for lower-class children, although in the predicted direction, were nonsignificant. This class difference may result from the greater stability of middle-class home environments as reported by Beckwith (1981).

In terms of physical restrictions such as barriers, gates, or covered windows, the data are fewer. Wachs (1979) reports significant and positive correlations between the degree to which the physical arrangement of the home allows exploration and the level of object permanence, foresight, and causality for males and the level of causality for females. At least short-term prediction is also shown by the fact that the degree to which the home allows exploration between 18 and 20 months is significantly related to the child's 31-month Binet (Wachs, 1978). In contrast, Tulkin and Covitz (1975) report that their 10-month measure, time with no barriers, is positively but nonsignificantly related to 6-year Peabody IQ for both middle-class and working-class children.

In addition to the above data, there are several studies reporting a relationship to development of a dimension labeled *restriction of freedom of movement*. In general, this dimension appears to be a combination of both floor freedom and barriers. Thus, Williams and Scott (1953) report that black infants in their first and second year of life who were not restricted in their freedom of movement had significantly higher Gesell developmental quotients than infants who were restricted. In contrast, using a Welsh sample, Roberts and Rowley (1972) report no relationship between degree of physical restriction and Griffiths score. Differences between the studies on definition of independent and criterion variables makes comparison of these two studies quite difficult.

Summary: Physical Restriction of Exploration

With a few exceptions, the available evidence suggests that physical restrictions of the child's attempts at exploration, defined primarily in terms of lack of floor freedom and possibly in terms of physical barriers, tends to be related to lowered cognitive-intellectual development. The rationale for this relationship may lie in Hunt's (1965) concept of intrinsic motivation. The intrinsic motivation concept postulates that one of the major developmental needs for infants and young children is the processing of stimulation or information. Environments which do not provide the child with adequate stimulation to process or which restrict the child's gathering of this information through limiting exploration would, in Hunt's formulation, be nonconducive to cognitive growth. The detrimental effects of stimulus-deprived environments such as orphanages have already been well documented (Hunt, 1961). Our current data support Hunt in suggesting that, when the stimulation is available, physically restricting the child's attempts to process stimulation can also have detrimental effects upon the child's cognitive intellectual development. Alternatively, as Appleton *et al.* (1975) have noted, freedom to explore allows the child to process stimulation at his own pace, thus producing a greater probability of match.

Conclusions

In general, the availabl evidence relating physical environment parameters to cognitive-intellectual development is sparse but consistent. The data suggests positive relationships between early cognitive intellectual development and short- and long-term variety of stimulation, environmental responsivity, and exploratory freedom. A negative relationship is found between early development and such parameters as noise–confusion, overcrowding, and a lack of temporal or physical organization in the home. Relationships between early development and such parameters as availability of material and match tend to be inconsistent.

Several caveats apply to the above conclusions. First, although there is evidence indicating the existence of time-lag effects, most of the available studies measure development at only one age or cross-sectionally. As a result, the potentially changing nature of the relationship between environment and development is lost. In too many cases we are forced to generalize without available evidence, saying that because an environmental parameter is related to development at time 1 it should also be related to development at time 2.

Second, the available evidence indicates that certain environmental parameters may be related to some indexes of development but not others (environmental specificity). The nature of the relationship between experience and development may also change as the child develops (age, and age by environmental specificity). Finally, there is the question of individual differences (organismic specificity) in response to environmental stimulation. Data from several studies have been presented which indicate that there may be sex or temperament differences in reactivity to environmental stimulation. Although it would be more convenient to have parsimonious results, such that development for all individuals is seen to be solely a function of several classes of environmental stimulation at all ages, there is no *a priori* reason why nature should necessarily follow Occam's razor. Whether such types of specificity occur only for physical environmental parameters or are also seen for social environmental parameters is a question that will receive special emphasis in the next chapter.

CHAPTER 4

The Social Environment and Its Relationship to Cognitive-Intellectual Development

As we noted previously, most of the available evidence relating early experience to cognitive development has involved the child's social-interpersonal environment—defined as specific parent–child interactions. In the present chapter, this evidence will be considered.

AMOUNT OF PARENT–CHILD INTERACTION

Historically, one of the classical approaches to the question of the role of amount of interaction upon cognitive development has been to look at situations in which one parent is unavailable for interaction. The most common group of studies here involves paternal absence. In a recent review on this topic, Radin (1976) notes that there is a trend for early paternal absence, prior to 5 years of age, to be associated with lowered cognitive-intellectual functioning. However, this is not a strong trend, for the literature also shows much evidence that is contradictory or inconsistent with this conclusion. In part, this inconsistency is due to the fact that the effects of paternal absence upon cognitive-intellectual development are mediated by a variety of factors including sex of the child, reason for paternal absence, and the father's degree of involvement with the family prior to his absence (Radin, 1976). If nothing else, this literature indicates the difficulties involved in studying in isolation such a complex parameter as paternal absence.

Another approach to the question of the relationship of amount of interaction with subsequent development is to look directly at studies which have attempted to measure the amount of parental involvement. In this area a large number of studies are found, many with divergent types of predictor variables. Some studies measure the total amount of interaction, regardless of type of interaction. Other studies utilize frequency of specific types of interactions (i.e., play plus vocalization). In spite of wide discrepancies in measures, the available data are surprisingly consistent in terms of finding relationships between amount of interaction and development, at least after 24 months of age.

In the first year of life, positive and significant concurrent correlations are reported between Griffiths Scale performance and measures of maternal contact (Roberts & Rowley, 1972) and maternal attentiveness (Blank, 1964). Also in the first year, L. J. Yarrow and his colleagues (1975) report significant correlations between a measure of level of social stimulation and the infants' Bayley and Piagetian performance.

In contrast, nonsignificant results are also reported for the first year. These include: (1) a lack of relationship between Bayley Scale performance and 6-months score on the Caldwell HOME maternal involvement subscale (Elardo et al., 1975); (2) a lack of relationship between amount of involvement during a twenty-minute mother–infant free play session at six months of age and Bayley performance at the same age (Burchinal & Farran, 1980); (3) a lack of relationship between 8-month HOME involvement scores and 12-month Bayley scores (Field et al., 1978); (4) a lack of relationship between Bayley scores and 10–12 month involvement scores based on observationally derived measures of social stimulation (Clarke-Stewart, 1973).

Cross-culturally, Goldberg (1977a) reports a nonsignificant relationship between observationally derived measures of maternal contact and 6-month and 9-month performance of Zambian infants on the Piaget-based Einstein scales. The Goldberg data could be a result of the use of a test instrument designed for North American babies with African children. However, other cross-cultural studies (Ainsworth, 1977; Geber, 1961; Konner, 1977; Leiderman & Leiderman, 1974) using African populations all indicate that the amount of mother–child contact is positively related to accelerated early development on a variety of infant tests including Bayley, Einstein, Gesell, and Griffiths scales.

Looking at reasons for inconsistencies in the first year, in general, the studies reporting significant results tend to utilize overall frequency rather than frequency of specific behaviors as a measure of parental involvement. However, at least one study utilizing a total frequency measure (Ainsworth & Bell, 1974) shows that the amount of maternal interaction is not significantly related to the child's Griffiths Scale performance at 8 months of age (although a significant relationship is reported at 11 months). The findings reported by Lewis and Coates (1980) do suggest that how amount is defined will influence both the level and direction of environment–development correlations. Beckwith et al. (1976) report that one-month social involvement with the infant is unrelated to 9-month Gesell performance but is significantly related to 8-month Casati–Lezine performance, suggesting the possibility of environmental specificity (i.e., amount is related only to specific developmental indexes). Similarly, Riksen-Walraven (1978) reports that training parents to give extra stimulation to their 9-month-old infants facilitated the infants' performance on a habituation task but was unrelated to gains on operant learning or exploration tasks. However, a review of the studies cited above does not yield any further consistent evidence for environmental specificity.

One possible hypothesis for the first year inconsistencies may lie in the interface between organism and environment. Escalona and Corman (1971) did an intensive observational follow-up of two infants over the first two years of life. These authors report that degree of maternal interaction had clear effects upon cognitive development; however, the effects were positive for one child but were negative for the second child. Unfortunately, these findings, while provocative, have not been followed up. Some evidence suggests that the infant's biomedical status may mediate the amount of parental contact. Unfortunately, directionality of relationships is unclear. Zeskind and Ramey (1978) report less interaction over time by mothers whose infants were fetally malnourished; in contrast, Beckwith and Cohen (1978) report more caretaking interactions by mothers of infants having problem pregnancies. Given the lack of data and inconsistent results, it is thus difficult to state precisely how individual difference factors may mediate the relationship of early contact to subsequent development.

For the second year of life, less evidence is available. Elardo et al. (1975), using the Caldwell Involvement Scale, and Clarke-Stewart (1973), using observationally based measures of mother–child interaction, report significant correlations between these variables and Bayley performance at 12 months of age (Elardo et al., 1975), object permanence between 12 and 14 months, and Bayley performance between 17 and 18 months (Clarke-Stewart, 1973). In contrast, Plomin and DeFries (1980) and Stevenson and Lamb (1979) report nonsignificant relationships between Caldwell Involvement scores and 12-month Bayley and IPDS scores. One could dismiss the latter results as a consequence of previously noted problems in these studies with low reliability and restricted ranges were it not for other existing nonsignificant results in the second year.

Piper and Ramsay (1980), using multiple discriminant analysis, report that HOME involvement scores add little discriminative power to that accounted for by other HOME scales in the prediction of developmental quotient (DQ) declines by Down's syndrome infants. Goldberg (1977a) reports a nonsignificant relationship between Caldwell Involvement scores and 12-month Einstein scores of Zambian infants; further, Klein, Lasky, Yarbrough, Habicht, and Seller (1977) report a nonsignificant relationship between amount of time Guatemalan children spent alone and a composite index of mental test items based on the Bayley, Cattell, Merrill–Palmer, and Gesell scales at 15 and 24 months. Again, one could question the relevance of these tests for foreign populations were it not for the report by Geber (1961) suggesting the relevance of significant amounts of maternal contact for second-year development of Bagandan infants on the Gesell. Thus, like the earlier data, the nature of second-year inconsistencies remains unclear.

For the third year of life the evidence is almost totally consistent. Measures of the amount of parental involvement or interaction based on the Caldwell Involvement Scale (Elardo *et al.*, 1975; Bradley & Caldwell, 1976b) are found to relate to Bayley performance, while observationally based measures of the amount of maternal contact are found to relate to a composite index of competence (White & Watts, 1973). Only one study (Clarke-Stewart *et al.*, 1979) reports nonsignificant results between 24 and 30 months. The Clarke-Stewart interaction measure was a composite one involving duration, quality, and responsivity; thus, it is difficult to know to what extent amount *per se* was represented in the interaction score.

From 36 months of age onward the evidence is again highly consistent. Involvement as measured by the Caldwell scale is found to relate to language development measured either by the ITPA (Elardo *et al.*, 1977) or by discrepancies between verbal and nonverbal performance (Wulbert *et al.*, 1975). Home ratings of maternal contact are found to correlate with Binet performance (Van Alstyne, 1929; Hanson, 1975), and total number of father–son interactions during an interview was found to relate to both Binet and PPVT scores (Radin, 1973). One cautionary note for older children is found in the study of Lawson and Ingleby (1974). These authors report that either too much or too little concentrated attention was related to lower Binet performance for 5-year-old children. Parental contact that was available but not concentrated was found to predict the highest levels of Binet performance.

All of the above data is concurrent. Some follow-up studies on the relationship of early degree of involvement to later development are also available. The Caldwell Involvement subscale taken at 6 and 12 months of age was found to predict significantly 36-month Binet (Elardo *et al.*, 1975); 6-month and 24-month Caldwell Involvement scores were also found to relate significantly to 54-month Binet (Bradley & Caldwell, 1976a). Somewhat less consistent are the data reported by Tulkin and Covitz (1975), who note that the time the mother is at a distance from the child at 10 months of age is negatively and significantly related to 6-year PPVT for middle-class children; the corresponding correlations for lower-class children, though in the same direction, are nonsignificant. As we noted in the previous chapter, differential stability of environments across classes (Beckwith, 1981) may be relevant here.

In contrast, Ramey, Farren, and Campbell (1979) report no significant relationship between 6-month Caldwell involvement score and 30-month Binet; 18- to 20-month involvement scores were predictive. Similarly, free play observations of 6-month mother–infant involvement were found to be unrelated to 18-month Bayley or 24- and 48-month Binet (Burchinal & Farran, 1980; Farran & Ramey, 1980); the 20-month Involvement score was found to predict 48-month Binet. The degree of decline in maternal involvement between 6 and 20 months was found to parallel the degree of drop in Bayley scores during this time period (Farran & Ramey, 1980). However, caution must be taken in using this last set of data, because the 20-month involvement score was a factorial composite, characterized primarily by vocal involvement. Since vocalization can have an independent effect on cognitive-intellectual development (as we will discuss later in this chapter), it is unclear whether the relationships found at 20 months are due to involvement or to vocal stimulation of the infant. Twelve-month Caldwell HOME involvement scores have also been shown to be unrelated to Binet performance at 30 and 36 months of age or indexes of language development at 30 months; 12-month involvement is related to 36-month language comprehension but not to language expression skills (Siegel, 1979). Age effects are also shown by Cohen and Beckwith (1979). These authors report that a 1-month multidimensional social interaction measure predicts 24-month Gesell, Casati-Lezine, receptive language and Bayley performance; the same measure taken at 3 and 8 months is nonpredictive.

Paralleling the concurrent data, the longitudinal results are also inconsistent, particularly for the first year of life. Part of this discrepancy may relate to the nature of the relationship between involvement and development. Using cross-lag analysis, Bradley *et al.* (1979) report that the child's cognitive level in the first year appears to predict maternal involvement rather than the reverse; in contrast, after 12 months the direction of prediction is from maternal involvement to child's cognitive level.

All of the above evidence is primarily correlational. For obvious ethical reasons less work has been done in varying the amount of interaction. However, there are some manipulative studies available, particularly with institutionalized populations. Hunt and his colleagues (Paraskevopoulos & Hunt, 1971; Hunt *et al.*, 1976) have reported significant accelerations in Uzgiris–Hunt scale performance for orphanage infants when the child–caretaker ratio was lowered from 10-to-1 to 3-to-1. In contrast, Rheingold (1956) notes no effect on Cattell performance when orphanage children were given 300 additional hours of adult interaction. Differences between the Hunt and Rheingold studies may reflect greater sensitivity of the IPDS to experiential effects. A more likely explanation, however, might lie in the fact that in the Rheingold study the child–caretaker ratio at best was 4-to-1. It may well be that for orphanage infants a 4-to-1 ratio is simply insufficient to allow for overcoming the effects of a severely restricted environment.

In terms of direct environmental stimulation, Schaffer and Emerson (1968) report that increased adult interaction for 2- and 3-day-old neonates leads to significant gains in developmental quotient. For 4- to 5-year-olds, Jacobsen, Berger, Bergman, Millham, and Greeson (1971) reported that the greater the degree of child–adult interaction (5 versus 10 versus 20 hours a week) in a day-care program, the greater the increment in Binet performance. Evidence supporting the concept of environmental specificity is reported in a short-term intervention study by Riksen-Walraven (1978). Comparing the impact of different interventions upon different outcome measures between 9 and 12 months, Riksen-Walraven reports that increasing the amount of parental stimulation facilitated infants' habituation but was unrelated to exploratory behavior. Somewhat inconsistent evidence is noted by Radin (1972b), who reports that degree of maternal involvement in a preschool program was unrelated to children's initial gains in PPVT or Binet but was related to IQ level one year after termination of the experience. Since all children were in the preschool program, Radin suggests that the relevance of increased maternal interaction may have been masked by the effects of the preschool program itself. Only when the program ceased to be a factor did differential amounts of maternal interaction become relevant.

Summary: Involvement

   Overall, it appears clear that when one talks of the relevance of amount of caretaker interaction to subsequent cognitive-intellectual development, a consistent and positive relationship does not appear until at least 24 months of age. Prior to that time a high degree of environmental specificity may exist in the relationship between amount of stimulation and cognitive-intellectual development. One rationale for the importance of parental involvement after 24 months of age comes from observational data by Honig, Caldwell, and Tannenbaum (1970). These authors looked at the amount of information-processing stimulation (showing, reading, informing, role-playing) given preschool children of different ages by adults and by peers. Honig *et al.* note that for 1- and 2-year-old children, 97% of all informational stimuli comes from adults rather than peers; even at 36 months 90% of all information comes from adults. Since the adult is a major source of information for the child, increased contact with adults would mean greater amounts of information transmitted to the child. However, these results do not explain the inconsistencies in results prior to 24 months.

   The answer here may lie in the interface between the child's capacities and the types of information being transmitted by adults. Much of the information transmission described by Honig *et al.* seems to rely heavily on language (reading, informing) or symbolic factors (role-playing). On the basis of studies of early cognitive development from a Piagetian (Uzgiris, 1976) or a psychometric perspective (McCall, Hogarty, & Hurlburt, 1972), language-symbolic capacities do not clearly appear in the child's repertoire until about 18 months of age. Thus, it may well be that the kind of adult contacts described by Honig *et al.* may not become important for development until the child has the capacity to utilize the type of information contained in these forms of adult interaction. The consistent relationship between amount of contact and language development after 36 months (Elardo *et al.*, 1977; Wulburt *et al.*, 1975) tends to support the above hypothesis. One critical implication of the above summation is that quality of contact may be more relevant for cognitive development than amount of contact *per se*. Thus, for children at a certain age, smaller amounts of contact A may be more beneficial than greater amounts of contact B, if contact A more closely matches the child's stage of development at that time.

Variety of Interactions

In addition to the total number of interactions between parent and child, one can also look at the number of different interactions in which parents and children engage. It could be hypothesized, for example, that parents who spend a great deal of time with their child but who continually repeat the same actions will be contributing little to development; in contrast, parents who spend less time with their children but who perhaps provide more varied interactions may be contributing more to their child's development. Unfortunately, little evidence is available on the relationship of variety of parental actions to development. What evidence is available, however, is consistent with the hypothesis that a variety of parent–infant interactions will be conducive to cognitive intellectual growth and development. Thus, in the first year of life, L. J. Yarrow *et al.* (1975) report that a summary score of variety of stimulation provided by parents to their 5–6-month-old infants significantly predicts not only overall Bayley performance but also performance in specific cognitive clusters such as goal directiveness and object permanence. In the second year of life, Gaiter (1976) reports that a summary score of the variety of play experiences encountered by a child during interaction with parents significantly predicts Bayley mental score, language development, and scores on perceptual discrimination tasks, as well as persistence in task behaviors. On the basis of scanty evidence, variety of social stimulation appears to bear some relationship to infant development. However, it seems clear that variety *per se* may not account for a high proportion of variance. In an interesting study involving the impact of infants' transition from foster to adoptive homes, L. J. Yarrow and Klein (1980) report that the degree of change in adult–child interaction is less critical than the direction of change; that is, the greater the improvement in quality of care, the less disturbance there was in infants' level of cognitive functioning. Clearly, more research is needed to attempt to look at the boundary parameters of variety of social stimulation.

Physical Contact Stimulation (Tactual, Vestibular Kinesthetic)

There is a rich infrahuman experimental literature indicating significant effects of early physical interactions (i.e., handling) upon a variety of developmental parameters including emotionality, exploration, learning (Thompson & Grusec, 1970), and physiological development (Denenberg & Zarrow,

1971). A number of attempts have been made to generalize this infrahuman data to the human level in terms of suggesting the importance of physical contact stimulation for human development (Prescott, 1971; White, 1971). Unfortunately, although the infrahuman data tend to show highly consistent effects for the role of physical contact stimulation, the human data are not nearly as consistent.

Looking at experimental studies, one sees at first glance that a high degree of consistency does appear to exist. Using either orphanage or new-born populations, the available experimental evidence indicates that infants receiving extra handling, rocking, rubbing, lifting, touching, or holding achieve higher developmental levels than nonphysically stimulated infants on a variety of infant measures including the Griffiths (Brossard & Decarie, 1971), Gesell (Casler, 1965a), Bayley (Solkoff, Sumner, Weintraub, & Blase, 1969; Lagerspetz, Nygard, & Strondvik, 1971), and Brazelton scales (Solkoff & Matuzsak, 1975), as well as tests of visual recognition memory (Rose, 1980). Unfortunately, a number of these experimental studies can be criticized on methodological grounds: Brossard and Decarie (1971) confounded physical contact with vocal stimulation, and both studies by Solkoff (Solkoff et al., 1969; Solkoff & Matuszak, 1975) employed very small samples of subjects and did not utilize statistical tests. Thus, of the five experimental studies showing significant results for physical contact stimulation, only three can be considered methodologically sound (Casler, 1965; Lagerspetz et al., 1971; Rose, 1980).

These three significant studies can be contrasted to two other experimental studies indicating nonsignificant effects of physical contact stimulation. White (1971) reports data indicating that 30 days of extra handling did not affect visual reaching or Gesell performance of orphanage infants as compared to nonhandled controls; significant differences were initially reported between the groups on visual attention, but a later reanalysis (White, 1971) indicates that the differences between handled and nonhandled infants failed to reach statistical significance. Similarly, Casler (1975) reports that six weeks of extra vestibular stimulation had no significant effects on the Gesell performance of orphanage infants as compared to untreated controls.

Similar inconsistencies are also found when observational measures of degree of physical contact between caretaker and child in the home are correlated with the infant's developmental level. The most consistent evidence supporting the importance of physical contact stimulation is found in data by L. J. Yarrow (L. J. Yarrow, 1963; L. J. Yarrow et al., 1975), who reports that measures of physical contact or kinesthetic stimulation are positively and significantly correlated with 5–6 month old infant's developmental level on both Bayley and Piagetian scales. In contrast, a large number of studies report no relationship between parental touching, holding, rocking, or other measures of physical contact and infant performance on the Bayley (Clarke-Stewart, 1973, 1977; Cohen & Beckwith, 1979; Hanks, 1972; Klein et al., 1977; Lusk & Lewis, 1972), Cattell (Beckwith, 1971), and Gesell- or

Piaget-based Casati–Lezine scales (Beckwith *et al.*, 1976; Cohen & Beckwith, 1979). Lewis and Goldberg (1969) report that maternal touching is significantly correlated with infant habituation but maternal holding is unrelated to performance on habituation tasks. A nonsignificant relationship between observed physical contact and habituation performance is also reported by Riksen-Walraven (1978).

Similar inconsistences are also found on follow-up data. Yarrow, Goodwin, Mannheimer, and Milowe (1973) report a significant correlation (+.68) between 6-month physical contact and 10-year WISC IQ for males; the relationship for females is essentially zero order (+.12). Similarly, Tulkin and Covitz (1975) report a significant correlation (+.48) between 10-month holding and 6-year PPVT for middle-class subjects but a negative (though nonsignificant) correlation (−.32) for lower-class subjects. Farran *et al.* (1977) observed mother–child interaction in a laboratory situation at 6 and 20 months. These interactions were related to 36 months Binet performance. Farran reports that 6-month maternal touching and holding predict later Binet performance, while the same measures taken at 20 months are not predictive. It should be noted that in a later study Ramey *et al.* (1979) report significant prediction of 36-month Binet from both 6 and 18–20 month physical contact indexes for infants who were not in day care; the predictive power of physical contact stimulation for day care infants was nonsignificant.

Cross-cultural research in general tends to implicate the importance of early physical contact for both Ganda (Ainsworth, 1977) and Kalahari (Konner, 1977) infants, but obviously contact is confounded with other culturally based rearing practices.

Given the above inconsistencies, one could well conclude that attempts to generalize handling results from the infrahuman level to the human level are simply incorrect. However, in reviewing the above studies one interesting fact seems to emerge. Particularly for correlational studies, reports indicating significant relationships typically used infants 6 months of age or younger; studies showing nonsignificant relationships either used infants older than 6 months of age or have heterogeneous samples including both younger and older infants. Thus, the pattern of correlational data suggests that physical contact stimulation may relate to development primarily for infants below 6 months of age. The experimental intervention study by Rose (1980) is also consistent with this hypothesis. However, this hypothesis is difficult to reconcile with other experimental evidence in that significant results were found with heterogeneous groups of infants (Lagerspetz *et al.*, 1971; Casler, 1965a), whereas nonsignificant results were found for very young institutionalized infants (White, 1971; Casler, 1975). However, evidence at least partially supportive of this hypothesis comes from two quasi-experimental cross-cultural studies.

Noting that Zambian babies receive a high level of kinesthetic tactual stimulation, Goldberg (1972) reports that at 6 months of age these babies are advanced in object permanance and spatial abilities; however, when tested at

9 months of age, the babies score below average in these abilities. In a more detailed study Goldberg (1977a) reports that at 6 months of age Zambian infants who received the greatest amount of carrying by their mothers showed advanced levels of object permanence; at 12 months of age those infants carried least by their mothers are the babies who show the most advanced levels of object permanence. Goldberg suggests that carrying (physical contact) may be appropriate for younger infants but not for older infants.

Summary: Physical Contact

Integrating the above correlational and experimental results suggests that for home-reared infants a relationship between physical contact stimulation and subsequent development occurs primarily between birth and 6 months of age. For home-reared babies after 6 months of age physical contact apparently is less relevant for development. The relationship of physical contact to development for institutionalized babies remains unclear.

Accepting the relevance of physical contact stimulation for younger home-reared babies, one can ask why this relationship occurs and what aspects of physical contact are most effective. In regard to the former question, a number of authors (Korner & Grobstein, 1966; L. J. Yarrow et al., 1975) hypothesize that early physical contact stimulation may activate the child's attentional capacities and thus alert the infant to objects or persons in the environment. L. J. Yarrow et al. also (1975) also note that vestibular stimulation may be particularly effective because the infant's vestibular system is myelinated early in development and is thus ready to act as a mediator for early physical contact stimulation.

In terms of the specific types of physical stimulation, the same authors (Korner, 1972; L. J. Yarrow et al., 1975) suggest that vestibular (movement) stimulation is most effective in bringing the child to an alert state; particularly effective appears to be movement of the child to the parent's shoulder. Data by Fredrickson and Brown (1975) appear particularly supportive of this hypothesis.

INDIRECT CONTACT: MATERNAL ORIENTATION

In our review of the literature only a few studies have related development to the amount of time during which the mother is directly oriented toward (i.e., looking at) the infant. Although little evidence is available, the results are fairly consistent. The relationship between infant cognitive performance and degree of maternal orientation toward the infant does not appear until after 12 months of age (Clarke-Stewart, 1973; Hanks, 1972; Riksen-Walraven, 1978; Stevenson & Lamb, 1979). After 12 months of age the degree of maternal orientation toward the infant is significantly and positively correlated with infant habituation performance (Lewis & Goldberg, 1969), with object permanence at 12 to 14 months (Clarke-Stewart, 1973), and with Bayley performance at 17 to 18 months (Clarke-Stewart 1973). Interestingly, degree of orientation is found to be significantly and negatively related to infant performance on the Uzgiris–Hunt Object Relations in Space scale at 12 to 14 months (Clarke-Stewart, 1973), suggesting some degree of specificity for this parameter.

Although there appears to be a consistent relationship between degree of maternal orientation toward the infant and infant performance after 12 months of age, the actual reason for this relationship remains unclear. Amount of maternal looking may reflect the degree of maternal stimulation given to the infant (i.e., mothers who are oriented toward their infants are more likely to stimulate their infants). Intercorrelations among maternal variables do not support this hypothesis in that looking is unrelated to measures of amount of stimulation given to the child by the mother (Clarke-Stewart, 1973). It could be hypothesized that amount of orientation may reflect some type of attitudinal variable such that mothers who are more frequently oriented toward their infants are more likely to be positive toward their infants in terms of attitudes. Again, however, the intercorrelations reported by Clarke-Stewart do not support this hypothesis. Indeed, a study of maternal behavior factors reported by Clarke-Stewart (1973) indicates that amount of maternal looking does not appear to relate systematically to any class of maternal behaviors. Thus, at present we are confronted by a relationship that, although consistent, remains unclear as to meaning.

RECIPROCAL INTERACTION

A line of research that has recently come into prominence refers to the degree of reciprocal interaction between parent and child. In a sense, this approach goes beyond the old "main effect" model of early experience in suggesting that reciprocal transactions between parent and infant may be more critical for development than one-way transactions (Sameroff & Chandler, 1975). In the area of early experience, three approaches to the study of the role of reciprocal interaction upon development have appeared; these include the degree of mutual interaction between parent and child, the contingency of these interactions, and the sensitivity of the mother to the infant's level and needs. All three approaches will be considered in the following section.

Mutual Interaction

The most general approach to the question of reciprocal interaction comes from studies looking at the degree of mutual play, gazing, or vocalization between parent and infant. In general, the available evidence suggests some degree of relationship between amount of mutual interaction and infant cognitive development, but the results are highly inconsistent both within and between studies. Thus, Clarke-Stewart (1973) reports that the degree of eye-to-eye contact or mutual playing between parent and child is unrelated to 10- to 12-month Bayley performance or 12- to 14-month Piaget scale performance but is related to 17- to 18-month Bayley performance. This could suggest that later mutual interactions are more relevant than early ones. However, Farran *et al.* (1977) report that while 6-month measures of mutual vocalizing between mother and baby predict 36-month Binet, the same measures obtained at 20 months do not predict. In contrast, Burchinal and Farran (1980) report that 6-month measures, of maternal play are unrelated to cognitive performance at 6, 18, and 24 months. Ramey *et al.* (1979) note significant prediction of 36-month Binet from mutual interaction measured at 6 and 18–20 months but only for infants enrolled in a day care program.

Beckwith *et al.* (1976) reported that measures of mutual gazing and social interaction at 1, 3, and 8 months are unrelated to 9-month Gesell performance; however, the 8-month measures do predict 8-month Casati–Lezine scores. In a later follow-up (Cohen & Beckwith, 1979), highly complex interactions were reported such that prediction of developmental level at 24 months was found to be a function of age of measurement of mutual interaction and type of cognitive measure used. In a further follow-up, Beckwith (1981) reports a positive and significant correlation between measures of reciprocal intervention at 2 years and child's performance at 5 years. In contrast, Bakeman and Brown (1980) report that detailed measures of mother–infant "dialogue" obtained during the first three months of life are unrelated to Bayley and Binet performance between 12 and 36 months. Tulkin and Covitz (1975) report that 10–month measures of reciprocal vocalization predict 6-year PPVT for middle-class children; the correlations for lower-class children, though in the same direction, are nonsignificant. In contrast to the above, Klein *et al.* (1977) report that measures of reciprocal vocalization between 8 to 16 months are totally unrelated to cognitive development through 24 months of age.

One approach to explaining these inconsistent results is the possibility that interaction, while reciprocal, may not necessarily be contingent (responsivity). For example, the parents' response to the infant may be delayed past the point when it is directly contingent upon the infant's behavior. Millar (1972) has noted that infants as old as 6 to 7 months are unable to learn an operant conditioning task if the reinforcement is delayed more than 2 seconds. A recent replication by Millar and Watson (1979) yielded similar results. As a result, one could hypothesize that timing of the parents' interaction may well be critical in determining whether the interaction is related or unrelated to development.

An alternative hypothesis would be that interaction, although contingent, may not be appropriate (sensitivity). Along these lines, Bronfenbrenner

(1974) has stressed the importance of *progressively more complex patterns* of contingent reciprocal interaction as a major factor influencing the child's level of development. Thus, one could also hypothesize that interaction, although mutual, may not necessarily have been appropriate to the child's level or needs.[1] Fortunately, there is literature available to allow us to determine the validity of these competing hypotheses.

Responsivity

For social responsivity, the majority of evidence is based on relationships between development and observationally based measures of contingencies, derived either in the laboratory or in the home. A few cross-cultural studies are also available. However, there is difficulty in interpreting the results of these studies because different interpretations of the same behavior occur. For example, the child's being constantly carried by the mother during the first year of life is considered to be an example of low contingency behavior by one author (Brazelton, 1972) and an example of high contingency behavior by a second author (Goldberg, 1972).

A few experimental-intervention studies are also available, but in most cases the contingency manipulations utilized are confounded with other variables. Thus, Siqueland (1973) reports that a combination of handling plus contingent stimulation given to hospitalized infants led to significant gains in learning ability as measured at 4 months of age. Unfortunately, it is difficult to know whether the results are due to the handling manipulation, the contingency manipulation, or an interaction of the two. Similarly, Hunt *et al.* (1976) reported that a group of orphanage infants receiving a reduction in infant–caretaker ratio plus the Badger stimulation program (which contains a high degree of contingent stimulation) showed significant gains in Uzgiris–Hunt scale performance over untreated controls and over a group that received simply a reduction in the infant–caretaker ratio; again, however, it is difficult to know whether these gains were due specifically to the contingency aspects of the Badger program or to other aspects of this particular stimulation program. Ramey, Starr, Pallas, Whitten, and Reed (1975) describe a program wherein half of a group of failure-to-thrive children were given extra food while the remainder were given food plus a once-a-week experience with response-contingent stimulation. Results indicated no differences between the groups on Bayley performance but better performance by the contingent group on a vocal conditioning task. However, even this result is suspect, since there was no attempt to control for differences between the groups on amount of stimulation *per se*, regardless of contingencies.

[1]Similarly, a recent review by Field (in press) suggests, for certain groups of high-risk infants, that only interactions within a very narrow range may be relevant for development, because of the narrow arousal range of these infants.

Other experimental studies also indicate an effect of environmental contingencies upon measures of early learning given immediately after the contingency experience; however, testing for delayed effects even over a two-week gap reveals little evidence for the stability of the contingency experience (Finkelstein & Ramey, 1977, Study I; Ramey & Finkelstein, 1978). In addition, some experiments again confound contingency with total amount of stimulation (Finkelstein & Ramey, 1977, Study III).

The prediction to only certain classes of cognitive-intellectual measures found in the Ramey *et al.* (1975) data is clearly echoed in the results reported by Riksen-Walraven (1978). She reports that training parents to be more responsive to their nine-month-old infants leads to significantly higher levels of infant exploration plus higher levels of performance in an operant task but is unrelated to infants' performance on a habituation task. Again, as with studies noted above, the responsivity manipulation in the Riksen-Walraven study appears to be confounded with amount of stimulation, particularly verbal interactions.

Overall, what the experimental data suggest is that any effects of parental responsivity that exist will be highly specific in terms of influencing only certain types of cognitive tasks (i.e., environmental specificity). Further, these experimentally induced effects may be of extremely short duration, suggesting the transitional nature of short-term environmental manipulations. The fading of early environmental effects associated with short-term stimulation illustrates what we have called the transitional nature of early experience. This topic will be considered at greater length in Chapter 9.

In terms of available observational data, several studies clearly show a consistent relationship between environmental contingencies and development. Interestingly, three studies showing consistent results deal with language development of children over 2½ years of age (Elardo *et al.*, 1977; Tizard, Copperman, Joseph, & Tizard, 1972; Wulbert *et al.*, 1975). All of these studies indicate a positive and significant relationship between verbal contingencies in the environment and the child's level of language development. Contingent responses to vocalization or distress relate to 12-month habituation performance (Lewis & Goldberg, 1969), while verbal contingencies at 24 months have also been found to predict 36-month (Elardo *et al.*, 1975) and 54-month (Bradley & Caldwell, 1976a) Binet performance. General or social contingencies predict 9-month exploration and operant performance (Riksen-Walraven, 1978), 12-month Bayley and IPDS performance (Stevenson & Lamb, 1979; Plomin & DeFries, 1980), 12–14 month object permanence and 17–18 month Bayley performance (Clarke-Stewart, 1973).

In contrast to the above results, a large number of studies report essentially no significant relationship between adult contingent responses and infant development (Beckwith, 1971; Bradley & Caldwell, 1976b; Clarke-Stewart *et al.*, 1979; Field *et al.*, 1978; Goldberg, 1977a; Hanks, 1972; Kierscht & Vietze, 1977; Piper & Ramsay, 1980; Siegel, 1979; L. J. Yarrow,

1963). Looking at this latter group of studies, one sees an interesting conclusion emerge. With the exception of the paper by Bradley & Caldwell, which looked at changes in developmental level between 6 and 36 months of age; that by Piper and Ramsay, who used Down's syndrome infants between 2 and 28 months; and that by Clarke-Stewart, which looked at children between 24 and 30 months, all other nonsignificant studies utilized infants at or below 12 months of age. On the basis only of the nonsignificant results, it could be suggested that environmental contingencies may be relevant only for older children. However, as shown above, several studies reporting significant results have used younger children.

A clearer picture emerges when one breaks down the contingency research into type of contingency. The available evidence indicates little direct relationship of observed contingencies to development below 12 months of age if general contingency scores (L. J. Yarrow, 1963) or contingencies to infant vocal responses are studied (Beckwith, 1971; Bradley & Caldwell, 1976a; Clarke-Stewart, 1973; Elardo et al., 1975; Field et al., 1978; Goldberg, 1977a; Kierscht & Vietze, 1977; Lewis & Coates, 1980). (The Caldwell subscale emotional and verbal responsivity utilized by Elardo, Bradley, Goldberg, and Field is defined primarily by responsivity to infant vocalizations; attempts to elicit causality with this subscale [Bradley et al., 1979] have yielded results that are essentially uninterpretable.) Intervention studies emphasizing verbal contingencies with young infants are typically confounded by other forms of stimulation (Riksen-Walraven, 1978). However, the data by Bakeman and Brown (1980) are congruent with a hypothesis of little relationship of contingencies to development below 12 months. Their results indicate that although there is no relationship between cognitive-intellectual development and 9-month Caldwell scale responsivity scores, a significant relationship does emerge at 20 months of age. Laboratory-based manipulative studies of vocal contingencies below 12 months yield, at best, short-term effects that soon wash out (Finkelstein & Ramey, 1977; Ramey & Finkelstein, 1978). Several studies do indicate that parental response to distress below 12 months of age predicts both short-term (L. J. Yarrow et al., 1975) and long-term (Tulkin & Covitz, 1975) cognitive development. However, two other studies (Kierscht & Vietze, 1977; Clarke-Stewart, 1973) report no relationship between distress contingencies and Bayley performance in the first year of life. A relationship between responsivity to infant smiles and Bayley performance has been reported in one study (Lewis & Coates, 1980).

All exceptions considered, the overall pattern of evidence appears to suggest that prior to 12 months of age the only type of contingent response possibly relevant to infant development is response to infant distress. Further, contingencies in the first year appear to be highly specific, both in the cognitive abilities they influence (Riksen-Walraven, 1978) and in the differential sensitivity of individual infants (Horowitz, Linn, Smith, & Buddin,

1981). Responses to infant vocalizations clearly do not appear to relate to cognitive development prior to 12 months of age but may be relevant after this time, particularly after 30 months.

Interestingly, a number of authors (Lewis & Wilson, 1972; Golden & Birns, 1976) have suggested that social class differences in maternal vocalization contingencies may be related to class differences in early cognitive performance. In contrast, the above evidence indicates that, at least prior to 12 months of age, class differences in maternal vocal contingencies cannot be related to class differences in cognitive skills since vocal contingencies apparently do not predict cognitive development in the first 12 months of life.

Given the fact that distress contingencies may be relevant to cognitive development prior to 12 months of age, and language contingencies clearly seem to predict language development after 30 months of age, one can ask: What of the period between 12 and 30 months? As noted previously, Lewis and Goldberg report that at 12 months of age both vocal and distress contingencies are related to infant habituation level. General or social contingencies concurrently predict object permanence measured at 12 to 14 months, Bayley performance measured at 17 to 18 months, and language competency level at 17 to 18 months. Verbal contingencies do predict 12-month psychometric and sensorimotor performance (Plomin & DeFries, 1980; Stevenson & Lamb, 1979). Longitudinally, 20-month vocal contingencies add significant variance to the prediction of 36-month Binet (Bakeman & Brown, 1980), while 24-month vocal responsiveness predicts 36-month and 54-month Binet (Bradley & Caldwell, 1976a).

From the above, one can hypothesize a developmental progression in the relationship between cognitive development and environmental contingencies. Specifically, up to 12 months of age, response contingencies involving distress may relate to development; after 12 months of age, general environmental contingencies, social contingencies, and verbal contingencies all appear to predict development. Finally, there appears to be a highly specific relationship after 2½ years of age between verbal contingencies in the environment and the level of the child's language development.

The fact that social contingencies, in a general sense, relate to development is consistent with the results for physical environmental contingencies noted in an earlier chapter. What may be unique for social response contingencies is the developmental progression. The reason for this progression may lie in the rationale suggested in an earlier chapter for the relationship of physical contingencies to development; namely, that contingencies create an expectancy in the child that he can effect his environment. This expectancy may well influence the child to interact more with the environment.

For the infant below 12 months of age, vocal behavior *per se* has limited communication value in alerting the parents to the infant's specific needs or wants. Rather, the infant's distress calls appear to be the primary means by which the infant can communicate with the parent. The often reported comment of mothers (Hetherington & Parke, 1979) that they can distinguish between infants' hunger versus wet diaper cries provides at least anecdotal support for this notion. Given the salience of distress as an early mode of communication, it is logical to hypothesize that contingent responses that meet the infant's immediate needs will be more noticeable to the infant than contingent responses that are unrelated to needs. Thus, early distress contingencies are more likely to create the expectancy, "I can influence my environment," than early vocal contingencies. After 12 months of age, when both language and social interaction behaviors become prepotent in the infant's repertoire, one would naturally expect that contingencies in these areas would become more and more relevant. As distress cries are replaced by vocalizations or gestures as a means of communication, contingent responses to these areas become more important in determining the degree to which the infant feels he can influence or affect his environment.

Parental Sensitivity

As we noted previously, a second hypothesis for the inconsistent results for mutual interaction may lie in the fact that studies looking at mutual interaction did not consider the appropriateness of the parental interaction. It may well be that a mutual interaction exists, but if the parent is misreading the child's signals, the interaction would not necessarily be beneficial for the child's development (Stern, 1974a).

One approach to this question of appropriateness lies in research on parental sensitivity. Unfortunately, unlike contingencies where there is a highly specific definition of the predictor variable, the few studies that have utilized measures of parental sensitivity have been fairly vague, idiosyncratic, and nonspecific in their definition. The impact of differing definitions is best seen in the study by Simons and McCluskey (1981). Their analysis at 2 months reveals that Bayley performance is positively related to indexes of maternal visual sensitivity, negatively related to indexes of maternal affective sensitivity, and unrelated to indexes of maternal vocal and social sensitivity.

Perhaps the most well-known definition is found in the work of Ainsworth (Ainsworth & Bell, 1974). On the basis of direct observation, Ainsworth and Bell rated maternal sensitivity according to the degree to which the mother can interpret and respond appropriately to the infant's signals. Using this approach to sensitivity, they report significant correlations between measures of sensitivity and the infant's Griffiths performance between 9 and 12 months of age. Comparing the predictive power of sensitivity to that of other social variables by means of multiple regression, Ainsworth and Bell report that a high proportion of environmental variance can be accounted for by sensitivity alone.

Along the same lines, Donovan and Leavitt (1978), using both physiological and behavioral measures of maternal sensitivity in the first year, report that infants who score high on the Piaget-based IPDS at 15 months of age have mothers who score high on both physiological and behavioral sensitivity. A high dropout rate of subjects in this study suggests that some caution in interpreting results may be necessary. Blank (1964) reports that a measure of maternal flexibility in dealing with the infant is significantly correlated with Griffiths performance between 20 to 28 and 40 to 46 weeks. In two studies L. J. Yarrow reports that a measure of 6-month maternal individualization (seeing the child as a unique person) is significantly related to 6-month IQ (L. J. Yarrow, 1963) and to 10-year WISC for males (though not for females) (L. J. Yarrow et al., 1973).

Early bonding manipulations, which have been shown to increase early maternal sensitivity, have also been shown to predict maternal verbal interactions with the child at 2 years; these verbal interactions, in turn, have been found to predict 5-year language and intelligence level (Ringle, Trause, Klaus, & Kennell, 1978). The early bonding/sensitivity manipulation per se was unrelated to 5-year performance, suggesting that sensitivity may be relevant to cognitive development only insofar as it serves as a mediator for other more salient variables.

Attempts to increase sensitivity by having mothers view their infants being tested on the Brazelton scale have had mixed results. Widmayer and Field (1980) report that this procedure led to subsequent gains in high-risk infants' Brazelton, whereas Peters (1979), using normal babies, reports nonsignificant effects of this intervention.

Using a rating of maternal empathy (understanding of the infant), Seegmiller and King (1975) report significant correlations in the second year of life between empathy and Bayley performance at 18 and 22 months but not at 14 months. Matas, Arend, and Sroufe (1978) report a positive relationship between maternal sensitivity and infant competence.

In contrast to the above, Wenar (1976) reports that mothers who are temperamentally out of phase with their infants have infants with higher levels of persistance (perhaps as a response to the mother's insensitivity). There are unfortunately some methodological problems with the Wenar study. Maternal ratings were often based on scores obtained during the first observation, and the representiveness of these scores may be questioned. Thus, the Wenar results must be interpreted with some caution. However, in a more well-controlled study, Burchinal and Farran (1980) report that degree of 6-month maternal sensitivity (degree to which mothers modify their own behavior in response to infant activity state) is unrelated to measures of infant intellectual development at 6, 18, and 24 months.

Overall, it appears clear that there is at least some relationship between maternal sensitivity and development. However, differing definitions of this phenomenon make it difficult to place sensitivity in a clear developmental framework or to account for discrepant results.

Summary: Reciprocal Interaction

In general, studies looking at the relationship to development of degree of mother–infant mutual interaction have yielded highly inconsistent results. It was suggested that interaction measures, while reciprocal, may not be measuring the degree of maternal contingency or sensitivity. *The data for contingencies suggest a developmental progression in the types of contingencies that influence early cognitive development. The data for sensitivity indicate that sensitivity is generally related to development but also suggest a greater need for definitional tightness of this concept.* Comparing responsivity to sensitivity, one cannot easily make a clear-cut choice. The available data for sensitivity is more consistent, but the construct is less well operationalized than contingencies. Perhaps the only way to determine which is more important is a longitudinal study investigating both contingency and sensitivity of parental response to infants' behavior. As yet, such a study has not been reported.

VERBAL STIMULATION

In terms of early experience and development, no environmental factor has received greater emphasis than the verbal or language environment of the child. A number of reviews have consistently implicated the language environment of the child as critical for subsequent cognitive-intellectual development (Lichtenberg & Norton, 1970; Bronfenbrenner, 1974; White, 1975). Unfortunately, the available evidence does not provide the degree of consistent support for this parameter that one would expect given its emphasis.

There are a number of studies supporting the relevance of verbal stimulation for subsequent development. The majority of these projects used older children, above 3 years of age. In general, these data indicate that the intellectual level of children from ages 3 to 5 years is positively and significantly related to various measures of parent–child language interaction, such as the amount of time the parent has read to the child (Van Alstyne, 1929; Tizard & Rees, 1976), the degree to which the parents act as language models (Hanson, 1975), and the degree to which mothers can accurately communicate information and meaning to the child (Dickson, Hess, Miyake, & Azuma, 1979). Similarly, older children's use of complex language sequences in problem-solving tasks is directly related to their parents' use of complex language sequences (Hess & Shipman, 1965). For children below 3 years of age, evidence is available indicating the relevance of parental verbal stimulation to cognitive development between 12 and 30 months (Clarke-Stewart, 1977) and to language level and IQ between 24 and 30 months (Clarke-Stewart *et al.*, 1979); there is also evidence indicating a relationship between amount of parental talking to infants and Cattell (Ball, 1969) and Bayley (Riksen-Walraven, 1974) performance in the first year of life. Finally, two out of four measures of parental verbal stimulation showed significant but low level (−.22, −.28) correlations with habituation rate at 9 months (Riksen-Walraven, 1978).

In contrast to the above findings, there is a large body of literature indicating essentially nonsignificant relationships between language environments and cognitive development. Interestingly, the overwhelming majority of nonsignificant evidence is for the first year of life. These data indicate essentially no significant relationship between amount of parental vocalization and infant Bayley performance (Cohen & Beckwith, 1979; Hanks, 1972; Lusk & Lewis, 1972; Stevenson & Lamb, 1979; L. J. Yarrow *et al.*, 1975), Griffiths performance (Ainsworth & Bell, 1974; Bradshaw, 1969), Cattell performance (Beckwith, 1971), Gesell and Casati–Lezine performance (Beckwith *et al.*, 1976; Cohen & Beckwith, 1979), or a composite score based on infant performance across several tests (Klein *et al.*, 1977). Indeed, evidence is available indicating a negative relationship between parental vocal activities and object permanence level at 12 months of age as measured by the Einstein scales (Goldberg, 1977a).

Evidence indicating a non-significant relationship between verbal stimulation and development beyond 12 months of age is harder to find. Some evidence is available, however. Deschner (1973) does report a nonsignificant relationship between the conceptual level of maternal language and the competence level of 2-year-old children.

For follow-up, amount of maternal talk at 6 months is related to 36-month Binet only for children not in day-care; amount of maternal talk between 18–20 months is related to 36-month Binet for both day-care and non-day-care children (Ramey *et al.*, 1979). Follow-up data indicating no significant relationship between maternal vocalizations to the child at 10 months of age and 6-year PPVT IQ are also consistent with the above nonsignificant results (Tulkin & Covitz, 1975). Olson, Bates, Pettit, and Bayles (1981) report data indicating that continuity of verbal stimulation is critical if second year stimulation is to have a long-term impact upon later cognitive competency; without stability of verbal stimulation significant longitudinal results do not occur.

Particularly for verbal stimulation, the question of causality becomes paramount. Even if one ignored nonsignificant evidence, it would not be clear from most correlational studies whether parental verbalization leads to brighter children or whether brighter children pull for more verbalizations. Obviously, one approach that would allow causal inference is experimental studies. Unfortunately, experimental evidence, wherein infants are provided with extra verbal stimulation, is equally inconsistent. Again, the most positive effects are found for children above 2 years of age and suggest that having parents serve as verbal stimulation models to their children results in accelerated development across both general and language-based intelligence tests (Levenstein, 1970; Madden, Levenstein, & Levenstein, 1976).

For young infants, Katz (1971) reports that exposing premature infants to 30 extra minutes of verbal stimulation until the infants reach 36 weeks gestational age leads to significantly greater general maturation, as well as improvement on auditory and visual function as measured by the Rosenblith neonatal exam. Again, however, nonsignificant results also are found. Casler (1965b, 1975) reports that providing extra verbalization to institutionalized infants in the first year of life has little effect upon development as measured by the Gesell scale. Evidence is also available (Jason, Gesten, & Yock, 1976) indicating no advantage on Bayley performance for infants between 12 and 24 months of age for a language-based remediational program over other types of remediation. Similarly, Madden et al. (1976) report that a short-term experimental study using random assignment of subjects (their previously successful research had not utilized random assignment) indicates no effect on the developmental level of preschool children of having parents serve as verbal stimulation models.

Overall, if one looks at the number of studies indicating positive versus negative results, it seems clear that the relevance of verbal stimulation to development is nowhere near as consistent as reviewers have made it out to be. However, if one attempts to look at the characteristics of studies showing significant versus nonsignificant results, a number of interesting factors appear.

First, as we noted above, a majority of studies reporting positive results for verbal stimulation use infants 24 months of age or older. In contrast, a majority of studies yielding nonsignificant effects looked at the effects of verbal stimulation on infants below 12 months of age. From this it can be hypothesized that verbal stimulation may be age-specific, relating to cognitive intellectual development only after the first year of life.

Available evidence on the relationship between specific measures of verbal stimulation and development at different ages tends to support this hypothesis. Thus, Wachs et al. (1971) report no significant relationship between measures of maternal vocalization or naming and IPDS scores at 7 and 11 months, but do report a significant relationship between these parameters and sensorimotor development between 15 and 22 months of age. Along the same lines, Clarke-Stewart (1973) reports no significant relationship between parental verbal stimulation and Bayley performance at 10 to 12 months of age but does note a significant relationship between these parameters at 17 to 18 months of age.

As for long-term prediction, Farran et al. (1977) report that 6-month measurements of maternal verbal interaction do not predict Binet at 36 months; the same measures taken at 20 months of age do predict. Thus, on the basis of the present evidence it appears clear that verbal stimulation is relevant to cognitive intellectual development but primarily after 15 months of age.

An alternative possibility may be environmental specificity, such that only specific types of cognitive parameters are sensitive to verbal stimulation. Unfortunately, little direct evidence is available. As we noted earlier, studies looking at verbal patterns across social classes in the first year of life have suggested that amount of verbalization does not differentiate social class but that verbal contingencies may (Lewis & Wilson, 1972). However, as we mentioned earlier in this chapter, there appears to be no relationship between verbal contingencies and intellectual development in the first year of life. In the second year of life, Wachs (1979) reported that measures of maternal reading to the child primarily predicted the child's level of schemes (principally verbal schemes) but did not predict performance on other Piagetian abilities. Similarly, Tizard et al. (1972) report that the language environment of older children relates primarily to the child's language comprehension but is unrelated to the child's language expression. Tizard et al. (1972) also note that the amount of talk is unrelated to subsequent development, whereas specific aspects of the language environment such as giving information are significantly related. A training study recently reported by Ogston (1981) comparing the impact of language and gross-motor training also yields results consistent with a position of environmental specificity.

In addition to the possibility of environmental specificity, other evidence suggests that organismic variables may also lead to additional specificity. Sex of infant has been one individual dimension that has been hypothesized to be relevant to differential sensitivity to verbal stimulation (Parke, 1979). In general, the available evidence on this point has been inconsistent. Thus, Moss (1974) reports that amount of maternal vocalization significantly predicts female conditioning rate but not male conditioning rate at 3 months of age. Herman (1971) reports that degree of maternal vocal interaction significantly differentiates high-scoring from low-scoring male children on the Bayley; the prediction for females is essentially nonsignificant. The differential results across studies may suggest that specific abilities for specific children are influenced by verbal stimulation (environmental and organismic specificity).

Summary: Verbal Stimulation

In general, the available evidence suggests that the relationship of parental verbal stimulation to infant cognitive development is mediated by the age of the infant. Contrary to popular belief, verbal stimulation appears to bear little relationship to cognitive development prior to 12 months of age. A possible mechanism for this age specificity has been suggested by Uzgiris (1980). Working within a cogni-

tive framework, Uzgiris has suggested the need for certain cognitive prerequisites before the infant can utilize verbal stimulation.[2] Chief among these is the use of verbal interchanges to impose a shared structure on actions. This is a level of cognitive functioning that is typically not found until after 12 months.

In addition to age specificity, there also appears to be environmental and possibly organismic specificity in the relation of verbal stimulation to development. From this we may hypothesize that specific types of verbal interaction may only predict specific types of performance for specific children. This hypothesis is obviously highly speculative, but it is a researchable question and may offer an approach to explaining the inconsistencies noted for the area of verbal stimulation.

On the basis of available evidence, one could also speculate on a developmental progression relating specific aspects of the verbal environment to development. In the second year of life amount of verbal stimulation could be seen as critical in terms of giving a child a storehouse of syntactic and semantic information to draw upon. Similarly, one could hypothesize that after 2 years of age such factors as complexity of parental language, accuracy of communication, or parental use of language in problem-solving situations might be more relevant to development. At present, there appears to be no likely candidate for a verbal stimulation parameter relevant for intellectual development in the first year.

Parental Restrictions of Exploratory Behavior

As we noted in the physical environment chapter, the importance of exploration to cognitive intellectual development has been emphasized by a number of reviewers. For the social environment, the available evidence also suggests the relevance of parental restriction (parental prohibition, discouragement, or punishment for child's exploration) for subsequent cognitive development, particularly after 12 months of age. Negative correlations between parental restrictions of exploration and cognitive performance (or positive correlations between parental encouragement of exploration and cognitive performance) after 12 months of age have been found for infants' level of rated competence in the second and third years of life (Deschner, 1973; Wenar, 1976; White & Watts, 1973), infants' Gesell performance through 18 months of age (Williams & Scott, 1953), infants' level of object permanence at 12-14 months of age and Bayley performance at 17-18 months (Clarke-Stewart, 1973), infants' IQ performance at 24-30 months of age (Clarke-

---

[2]In a recently reported training study, Kahn (1981) has obtained results indicating that training severely retarded children in cognitive skills prior to training in language leads to higher levels of language than language training *per se.*

Stewart *et al.*, 1979), preschool children's IQ performance between 3 and 4 years of age (Kagan & Freeman, 1963; Elardo *et al.*, 1975), and language delay between 2½ and 6 years of age (Wulbert *et al.*, 1975).

As for long-term prediction, avoidance of restriction at 20 months of age has been found to be positively related to Binet performance at 4½ years (Bradley & Caldwell, 1976a), while parental restriction between 2 and 4 years of age has been found to be negatively related to IQ performance at 5½ and 9 years of age (Kagan & Freeman, 1963). Kagan and Freeman do note, however, that when maternal IQ is covaried out the relationship between restrictiveness and subsequent IQ becomes nonsignificant; this suggests that one reason for the relationship between parent and child IQ may be the association of certain rearing practices with parent IQ levels. For example, it may well be that lower IQ parents provide more restrictions on exploration than upper IQ parents. As a result, the child's IQ would also be depressed. This suggests the possible operation of neither genetic nor environmental effects directly, but rather the operation of type-one organism–environment correlation (Wachs & Mariotto, 1978) in the relation of restriction to development.

Nonsignificant evidence occurs primarily in the data by Elardo *et al.* (1977). Elardo indicates that avoidance of restrictiveness at 30 months shows little relationship to 36-month ITPA performance. This may reflect a lack of sensitivity of the ITPA to restriction effects. In addition, Ramey *et al.* (1979) report a positive relationship between 18–20 month absence of restriction and 36-month Binet, but only for children not in day-care.

Several studies also suggest the possibility of environmental specificity in the relationship of restriction of exploration to development. Clarke-Stewart (1973) reports, for example, that although there is a negative relationship between restrictiveness and IPDS object permanence between 12–14 months, there is a positive relationship between restrictiveness and the IPDS objects-in-space scale obtained at the same time. Other evidence suggests a possible age or age-by-environment specificity. Looking at data obtained over a 12-month period, Radin (1972a) reported that laboratory measures of paternal restrictiveness were negatively correlated with male children's 4-year Binet but were unrelated to PPVT IQ. When the children reached 5 years of age, the laboratory procedure was repeated. For the 5-year-olds, Radin (1973) reports a nonsignificant relationship between restrictiveness and Binet, but a negative and significant relationship between restrictiveness and PPVT IQ. The Kagan and Freeman results cited earlier also provide some evidence for specificity. Kagan and Freeman report that while early restrictiveness (between 2 and 4 years) is negatively related to subsequent development, later restrictiveness (after 4 years) is unrelated. This increasing specificity after age 4, as noted by Radin and Kagan and Freeman, may reflect the fact that home restrictiveness may be less critical as the child gains mobility to go outside the home.

For infants at or below 12 months of age, the relationship between cognitive development and parental restrictiveness—encouragement of exploration—appears to be generally nonsignificant. Measures of parental restrictiveness or encouragement prior to 12 months of age are generally found to be unrelated to infant performance on the Gesell (Cohen & Beckwith, 1979), Cattell (Beckwith, 1971), Bayley (Clarke-Stewart, 1973; Cohen & Beckwith, 1979; Elardo et al., 1975; Fields et al., 1978; Plomin and DeFries, 1980; Stevenson & Lamb, 1979), Griffiths (Blank, 1964), Einstein scales (Goldberg, 1977a), IPDS (Stevenson & Lamb, 1979), and Casati-Lezine (Cohen & Beckwith, 1979), or to changes in cognitive level between 6 and 36 months of age (Bradley & Caldwell, 1976b).

Longitudinally, the available evidence is inconsistent. It indicates nonsignificant relationships between 6-month avoidance of restriction and 36-month Binet (Bradley & Caldwell, 1980), 54-month Binet (Bradley & Caldwell, 1976a), or 36-month ITPA score (Elardo et al., 1977). Measures of restriction at 12 months are found to be unrelated to cognitive competence at 30 and 36 months (Siegel, 1979). This finding may reflect the operation of organismic specificity in that Bradley and Caldwell (1980) report 12-month restrictiveness predicting 36-month Binet for girls but not for boys. In contrast, in an earlier study, Elardo et al. (1975) report a significant relationship between 6- and 12-month avoidance of restriction and 36-month Binet. Ramey et al. (1979) report a significant relationship between 6-month absence of restriction and 36-month Binet, but only for infants enrolled in day-care programs. Tulkin and Covitz (1975) report a significant correlation between a measure of 10-month restriction and 6-year PPVT for middle-class but not for lower-class children. Interestingly, the correlation between 10-month restrictiveness and 6-year ITPA is nonsignificant in the Tulkin and Covitz study. The fact that 12-month restrictiveness predicts 30-month language comprehension and expression (Siegel, 1979) may only further emphasize the insensitivity of the ITPA to restriction effects as noted earlier.

Differences between longitudinal studies may, in part, reflect differences in predictor variables. The Ramey, Siegel, Bradley, and later Elardo studies all utilized the Caldwell HOME restrictiveness subscale. In the earlier Elardo study the Caldwell scale was also used. The correlations between this scale and subsequent development, while significant, are not highly impressive (i.e., $r = .24$). It may well be that only through the use of more powerful predictor variables, such as the direct observational data obtained by Tulkin, can one hope to find significant longitudinal relationships between early restrictiveness and later development. The question of why there may be significant (but weak) relationships between early restriction and later development but not between early restrictiveness and early development is an interesting one. These delayed effects may be a function of the fact that restrictiveness may be a stable phenomenon. Thus, mothers who are restrictive with their 10-month-olds may also be restrictive in the second and third years of life when restriction begins to relate to development. Recent data by Ramey *et al.* (1979) reporting no significant changes in the HOME restrictiveness subscale between 6 and 18 months tend to support this hypothesis. The implications of delayed effects of early experience for our understanding of the nature of early environmental action is a topic that will be discussed at greater length in Chapter 9.

Summary: Restrictiveness

Overall, in spite of some inconsistencies, the evidence generally suggests that parental restriction of exploration between 12 and 48 months of age is negatively related to cognitive development; encouragement of exploration during this time period is positively related to cognitive development. The lack of relationship between parental restrictiveness and development prior to 12 months of age may not mean that early restrictiveness is irrelevant to development. Rather, it may reflect the nature of the child prior to 12 months of age.

As we noted in our chapter on the physical environment, physical restrictions such as the use of barriers or playpens are negatively related to development prior to 12 months of age. A number of reviewers (White, 1975; Farran & Ramey, 1980; Burchinal & Farran, 1980; Hunt, 1976), have argued that parental restrictions do not become relevant to development until the infant has at least a moderate degree of mobility and can begin to get into physical danger or cause disruptions of household routines. For the infant younger than 12 months of age, mobility is essentially limited, and as a result the infant's exploratory excursions can be effectively restrained by barriers such as gates or stairs or by the use of playpens. It is only after 12 months of age (when most infants are walking) that the infant has enough mobility to begin to circumvent physical barriers. Thus, at this time there may well be an increase in parental restrictions and hence the onset of the relevance of these restrictions to development.

A direct test of this hypothesis would predict a radical increase in parental restrictiveness (as opposed to the use of barriers or other physical restrictions) once the child becomes mobile. Unfortunately, such data are not available to provide a test of this hypothesis. However, when the senior author visited the homes of poverty families in Bogotá, Colombia, it was learned (Mora, 1979) that the Colombian infant has the free run of the house as long as it does not disrupt the mother's routine. Once the infant begins to disrupt the mother's routine both physical barriers and parental punishment are utilized to keep the child in one corner of the house so the mother can go about her daily tasks. This evidence, although only descriptive, is supportive of our hypothesis that social restrictions *per se* do not come into play until the child has a moderate degree of mobility. Thus, there should be no relation between social restriction of exploration and development until the child begins to display mobility or until physical restrictions no longer suffice.

DEGREE OF SPECIFIC PARENTAL TEACHING

In all previous studies relating parental behavior to cognitive intellectual development, the parental behavior has been relatively nonspecific in the sense that the parents were not trying to stimulate a particular skill. Rather, the parents have been interacting with their children in ways that, although facilitative or detrimental to development, were not designed to be teaching experiences in the classical sense. In contrast, Engelmann (1970) has suggested that cognitive intellectual development can be more quickly facilitated by the teaching of specific skills to children than by general cognitive stimulation. Unfortunately, with the exception of this training study by Engelmann, a review of the literature reveals no systematic comparisons between general and specific cognitive skill training. Engelmann's report indicates significantly greater gains for preschool children receiving specific skill training than for control children enrolled in nonspecific nursery school programs. However, there are a number of problems with the Engelmann study. For one thing, there is the question of the degree to which Engelmann's subjects were directly taught the material the children were later tested on; unfortunately, there is no generalization test in the Engelmann study. In addition, although Engelmann's specific training group showed significant gains, there were notable individual differences within this group. Overall changes in the group ranged from a loss of 5 points to a gain of 42 points. Clearly, specific training, while relevant to development, is susceptible to a variety of other influences. For example, as Herman (1971) notes, the gains children make in specific training programs may, in part, be a function of the attitude of the parent toward these programs.

In addition to the above problems, Engelmann's approach, based on a training study, suffers from the question of ecological validity; that is, one must ask the degree to which parents normally utilize specific training in the home. Further, if specific training is used in the home, one must ask the degree to which this training in the home relates to development. Happily there is some literature available on at least the second question.

Across studies, definitions of specific teaching have varied tremendously, but most seem to center around either the concept of independence training or the concept of parental acceleration-pressure for specific skills. In general, parental independence training or use of accelerational techniques is found to be positively correlated to developmental level (L. J. Yarrow, 1963) and Griffiths IQ performance in the first year of life (Blank, 1964; Roberts & Rowley, 1972), positively correlated with measures of the competence level of the child in the second (White & Watts, 1973; Wenar, 1976) and third years of life (White & Watts, 1973), and positively related to PPVT (Radin, 1973) and Binet IQ through ages 4 and 5 (Radin, 1973; Hanson, 1975).

The only inconsistent evidence appears in three studies. Beckwith *et al.* (1976) report no significant relationship between 8-month parental use of intellectual stimulation and infant performance in either the Casati–Lezine or Gesell. In a follow-up, Cohen and Beckwith (1979) report no relationship between the 8-month measure and 24-month performance on a variety of psychometric and sensorimotor assessments. Williams and Scott (1953) report that, for infants from 4 to 18 months, those infants left to develop at their own rate showed significantly faster gains in development than children whose development was pushed by their parents. The Williams and Scott finding may reflect the effects of too much parental pressure, perhaps leading to negativistic behavior by the child on the specific skills trained for.

Longitudinally, several studies also suggest the relevance of early specific teaching to later developmental levels (Werner, 1969; McCall, Appelbaum, & Hogarty, 1973). However, Kagan and Freeman (1963) report that measures of parental acceleration taken between 2 and 7 years of age are generally unrelated to IQ performance through age 9. Inconsistencies found for both short-term and longitudinal effects of training may reflect limited generalizability associated with training studies (Wohlwill, 1973b). Alternatively, differences between training studies may reflect differences in predictor variables.

The problem of inconsistencies is further complicated by some evidence suggesting that at least some of the significant parental training relationships may be a function of child effects rather than parental effects. Using a cross-lag design, Clarke-Stewart (1977) reports that there is a significant effect of direct teaching from the mother upon the child's subsequent development. However, for paternal teaching the causal direction is from child's level to subsequent paternal behavior. This suggests that whereas maternal teaching may have an effect upon the child's subsequent development, for fathers the degree of paternal teaching is a function of the child's level of achievement rather than the contrary.

Summary: Parental Teaching

Overall, it appears clear that there is a positive relationship between direct teaching of skills and development. Contrary to Engelmann, however, we cannot recommend this approach unequivocally at this point. Inconsistencies in the data and the question of causality make direct teaching a subject more suitable for future research than for immediate application.

Parental Teaching Style

In contrast to Engelmann (1970), who suggests that direct teaching of material is a major contribution to cognitive development, a number of theorists (White & Watts, 1973; Carey, 1974) have suggested that it is not so much what is taught that is critical but rather the means by which the parent presents material to the child (i.e., the teaching style of the parent). Available data do suggest that when such variables as maternal intelligence, maternal social class, and maternal teaching styles are related to children's level of cognitive development the major share of variance in children's cognitive level is attributable to the teaching style of the parent (Hess & Shipman, 1967). This section focuses on available evidence relating differences in parental (or program) teaching style to differences in children's cognitive intellectual development.

Use of Rewards versus Punishments

Gray and Klaus (1968) have suggested that disadvantaged children receive fewer rewards and more punishments for cognitive activities than do middle-class children. These authors suggest that it is this difference in the ratio of rewards to punishments that is relevant to the class differences often found in cognitive performance. The available evidence, though sparse, tends not to support this conceptualization. A number of studies have measured such parameters as the number or relevance of rewards and punishments used by parents while attempting to teach their child a task. Thus, Filler and Bricker (1976) report that for preschool-age mentally retarded children the use of parental rewards while the child was being taught match-to-sample tasks was unrelated to the child's subsequent performance in either a similar or a dissimilar task. These nonsignificant results could be attributed either to the special population or to the special task utilized. However, in an earlier study, Hess and Shipman (1967) used both general and specific cognitive performance tasks and normal children. These authors report that the correlation between performance and the ratio of positive to negative parental reinforcements, though significant, is quite low ($r = .19$). Along the same lines, Jacobson et al. (1971) report that the use of reinforcement by teachers in a training situation, while related to gains in Binet performance, was less effective than other teaching styles such as the use of modeling.

One could argue that the artificial nature of training studies limits the relevance of the above data. However, naturalistically derived correlational studies are no less inconsistent. Levenstein (1970) notes that after training, mothers utilized significantly more reinforcements in their interactions with their children than nontrained mothers. Levenstein suggests that these maternal differences relate to offspring cognitive levels. However, other differences in maternal style resulting from training make this conclusion highly speculative.

Williams and Scott (1953) do report that parental punishment with infants from 4 to 18 months leads to significantly lower Gesell scores than those obtained by nonpunished infants, while McCall *et al.* (1973) report significant relationships between IQ patterns between 3 and 13 years and a number of parental parameters, including degree of punishment. However, as we noted previously, the McCall paper measures experience over a 10-year period and hence the effects cannot readily be attributed to early experience *per se.* Ainsworth and Bell (1974) report a nonsignificant correlation between frequency of punishment and 8-month Griffiths, but a significant correlation ($-.34$) between frequency of punishment and 11-month Griffiths. In contrast, Blank (1964) reports that use of parental punishment bears no relationship to Griffiths performance by either 20- or 28-week-old or 40- to 46-week-old infants. Differences between these studies in both age of subjects and criterion variables make it difficult to establish reasons for these differences.

Summary: Rewards versus Punishment. In general, contrary to Gray and Klaus (1968), the use of rewards and punishments as a means of teaching children cognitive skills has, at best, a weak and inconsistent relationship to subsequent cognitive-intellectual performance.

Praise versus Criticism

A parental style related to the use of rewards and punishment is the use of praise or criticism in cognitive teaching situations. Typically, punishment and reward involve material as well as verbal feedback, while praise and criticism primarily involve verbal feedback. However, in terms of their impact on the child, one would expect similar effects. In general, the evidence indicates the same degree of inconsistency for praise and criticism as for reward and punishment.

In terms of positive results, Seegmiller and King (1975) report significant correlations between maternal praise obtained while the child was being tested and Bayley performance at 14, 18, and 22 months of age. Hess, Shipman, Brophy, and Bear (1971) report that parental use of praise is significantly related to preschool children's performance on a variety of cognitive tasks including sorting and copying. For criticism, Beckwith *et al.* (1976) report that observationally based measures of maternal criticism at 3 months are significantly and positively related to Gesell performance at 9 months. However, Beckwith *et al.* also report that criticism at 1 and 8 months is unrelated to either Gesell or Casati–Lezine performance at 9 months. Follow-up to 2 years reveals no relationship of early criticism to a variety of psychometric and sensorimotor measures (Cohen & Beckwith, 1979).

McCall *et al.* (1973) report that degree of criticism is related to patterns of IQ change over time; however, comparison of variance accounted for suggests that criticism is relatively unimportant when compared to other parental factors. Kagan and Freeman (1963) report a positive correlation between degree of maternal criticism between 2 and 4 years of age and the female child's IQ at 3½, 5½, and 9 years of age. Correlations of criticism after 4 years with development are notably less significant. For males, the correlations, though negative, are nonsignificant. Kagan and Freeman suggest that the sex effect is a function of greater mother–daughter identification. Even if one can accept this explanation, the results by Kagan and Freeman only add to the available inconsistency, since most other studies do not report the existence of sex effects.

Summary: Praise and Criticism.   Overall, the data for praise and criticism suggest, at best, a weak and inconsistent relationship of this variable to development.

Use of Feedback

The use of punishment or praise as a manner of teaching may reflect a more general dimension, namely the use of feedback following the child's responses regardless of the content of the feedback. As with the previous dimensions, the available evidence on the relationship to development of feedback as a teaching style is highly inconsistent. Several studies utilizing preschool children from 2 through 5 years of age report significant and positive correlations between parental use of feedback and children's level of competence (Deschner, 1973), match-to-sample performance (Filler & Bricker, 1976), and sorting task performance (Hess *et al.*, 1971). In contrast, Hess and Shipman (1967) report significant and negative correlations between parental use of physical feedback and both IQ and placement task performance. However, the definition of feedback utilized by Hess and Shipman seems to refer more to parents telling children what to do than to parents responding to the child's actions. Thus, its relevance to other definitions is somewhat questionable.

In contrast to correlational research, the available experimental evidence, though sparse, is generally negative. Working with preschool children between 3½ and 4½, Jacobson *et al.* (1971) report that children trained on discrimination problems under a feedback condition do show significant gains on Binet performance but that these gains are no greater than those of children trained with other cognitive teaching styles. Filler (1976), using retarded children, reports that training mothers of these children to give feedback to their children during a teaching situation does not lead to significant gains in task performance.

Summary: Feedback.   The available evidence, though sparse, does not suggest that feedback is a powerful determinant of early cognitive-intellectual development.

Use of Structure

A number of reviewers (Gray & Klaus, 1968; Bronfenbrenner, 1974) have suggested the importance of parental structuring of the environment for the child during learning situations as a means of promoting cognitive growth. Unfortunately, little direct evidence is available on structuring *per se*. What evidence is available is primarily cross-cultural (Goldberg, 1972) and thus of questionable utility in terms of specifying exactly what role structuring plays in the developmental process.

Other evidence has looked at specific types of structuring procedures as these relate to cognitive intellectual development. One example in this literature is evidence on the role of the use of specific cues during the learning processes. Available studies suggest that providing specific cues to children either directly (Deschner, 1973), through instructions (Filler & Bricker, 1976; Hess *et al.*, 1971), or by parental use of modeling (Hess & Shipman, 1965; Jacobson *et al.*, 1971) are positively and significantly correlated with pre-school children's development on both specific and general cognitive tasks. What evidence is available from training studies also tends to support the above conclusion (Filler, 1976). However, use of hierarchial structuring[3] (Jason, Gesten, & Yock, 1976) does not appear to offer any special advantage for the development of children in the second year of life. Similarly, the use of explanation appears to be unrelated to either language comprehension or production of 2- to 5-year-olds (Tizard *et al.*, 1972).

In addition to these inconsistencies, certain cautions must be noted on the use of structuring. First, as Filler and Bricker (1976) indicate, the use of specific cues in ways that minimize the child's own problem-solving activities (i.e., through pointing to correct stimuli or directly guiding child's responses) does not promote development. Secondly, Sigel and Olmstead (1970) report that the use of specific cues tends not to generalize to other tasks and tends to wash out over time unless further training is provided to maintain the gains.

Besides specific cues, a number of other dimensions of structuring have also been documented. Carey (1974) has suggested that parental teaching can be facilitated through breaking material down into meaningful subunits which the child can more easily assimilate. Carey postulates that class differences in development may be less a function of maternal language differences than differences in the degree to which mothers break down the material for their children. Fowler (1964) has presented some data suggesting the relevance of breaking down material into small steps for subsequent cognitive development. Unfortunately, the Fowler study is poorly designed, lacking appropriate controls, Further, the data reported by Fowler indicate

---

[3]Training children initially on simple tasks and then moving on to training with progressively complex tasks.

tremendous individual differences in the degree to which children benefit from this approach to teaching.

Summary: Structuring. Overall, the above data suggest the relevance of providing specific cues for learning specific problems. However, this relationship appears to be short-lived, restricted to specific situations, and restricted to certain types of structuring. Further, there appears to be a fine line between providing specific cues and actually directing the child; at least the later strategy appears to be unrelated to cognitive intellectual development.

Miscellaneous Parental Variables

In addition to the parental dimensions noted above, a few reports have investigated other types of parent-child interactions as they relate to cognitive intellectual development. However, due to the paucity of studies on these alternate variables, few conclusions can be drawn. Several studies (Clarke-Stewart, 1973; Radin, 1973; White & Watts, 1973) have looked at the amount of parental caretaking activities (meeting the child's physical needs) as this relates to cognitive intellectual development; discrepancies between studies both in results and methodology make the contribution of this variable difficult to assess. There is some evidence (Blank, 1964; Roberts & Rowley, 1972) indicating a positive relationship between ratings of maternal competence and the infant's level of cognitive performance on the Griffiths scale. However, it is unclear from these data whether competent mothers produce brighter infants or whether brighter infants make their mothers look more competent to an outside observer. Ratings of severity of parental punishment have tended to relate negatively to both level (Kagan & Freeman, 1963) and pattern (McCall *et al.*, 1973) of intellectual development; detailed analysis of these results, however, suggests that severity may be related to other parental attitudinal and demographic variables. Thus, the extent of its unique contribution remains unclear. In the matter of teaching styles, Hess and Shipman (1967) have suggested the relevance of the type of parental control strategy utilized. This result appears in only one study and, because of inconsistencies noted earlier, replication seems essential.

MULTIVARIATE APPROACHES

Several studies, in addition to univariate analysis, have also attempted to utilize multivariate techniques as a form of data analysis. A variety of techniques have been employed. Condensing of environmental variables into factor scores and the use of multiple regression with these scores as predictors has been perhaps the most popular approach. Common to all attempts is the underlying rationale that a pattern of significant univariate relationships may, in part, be due to several underlying factors common to all the significant predictors. With a number of significant univariate correlations, multivariate analysis also allows one to specify what combination of factors or experiential dimensions are most relevant to development.

Some interesting findings have emerged from these attempts. This is particularly true when multiple regression techniques are used to determine which environmental variables predict the major share of variance in specific early cognitive–intellectual tasks. Thus, kinesthetic and inanimate stimulation seem most relevant for predicting early Bayley performance (L. J. Yarrow *et al.*, 1975); sensitivity in floor freedom accounts for most variance in predicting early Griffiths performance (Ainsworth & Bell, 1974); mothers who do not show the child what the relevant task skills are or who use nonspecific directions have children who do poorly in specific learning situations such as an Etch-a-Sketch task (Hess & Shipman, 1967).

Two potentially interesting uses of multivariate techniques have been recently noted in the literature. One approach has been to use multivariate techniques as a means of determining whether the pattern of environment–development relationships is similar for different ages (Farran *et al.*, 1977; Farran & Ramey, 1980) or sex groups (Kierscht & Vietze, 1977) or infants with different temperamental patterns (Wachs & Gandour, 1981). Differential environment–development patterns often can more easily be seen through the use of multivariate techniques than through comparison of a series of univariate correlations. A second interesting approach is the use of cluster analysis procedures to look at developmental changes across time and to relate these change patterns to different aspects of the environment (McCall *et al.*, 1973). One hopes that more use will be made of these approaches. It has also been argued (Clarke-Stewart *et al.*, 1979) that more replicable findings occur when multidimensional rather than unidimensional variables are used as predictors.

However, all too often multivariate approaches produce only vague generalities that are of little use either to the theoretician or to the practitioner. Thus, we find statements such as that optimal maternal care predicts infant competence (Clarke-Stewart, 1973) or that involved mothers have accelerated infants (Stern, Caldwell, Hersher, Lipton, & Richmond, 1969). Too often, this type of summary statement conceals information that is better revealed by use of univariate analysis.

An additional problem in the use of multivariate approaches in the area of early experience must be noted. A number of authors have utilized highly sophisticated multivariate analytic techniques on extremely small samples (i.e., Clarke-Stewart: $n = 36$; Stern *et al.*: $n = 30$). The difficulties in interpreting and generalizing multivariate results obtained on small samples have been discussed elsewhere (McCall, 1970) and will not be repeated here. Let it suffice to say that problems in replicating factor loadings obtained with small sample mutlivariate studies suggest the need for tremendous caution in interpretation of results. This is particularly true when factor analysis is used as a data-reduction technique and multiple regressions are then run using the factors obtained. The lack of replicability in early experience data so clearly documented by Clarke-Stewart *et al.* (1979) may well be more a function of the use of multivariate statistics with small samples than of the other factors discussed in her paper.

Multivariate techniques may be legitimate when there is a question as to whether an overall univariate correlation matrix is significant or as to what emphasis should be given to individual correlations within a matrix. However, even in this case univariate techniques such as the "cutting score" strategy (Wachs, 1979) may be more satisfactory for small samples. Too often it appears that researchers utilize multivariate statistics because it seems to be the proper thing to do rather than asking which statistical approach will be most valid given the constraints of the data base and the goals of the study.

The problem of small-sample multivariate analysis is not unique to the early experience area. However, it does appear to be a more critical problem here, given the fact that adequate measures of the infant's early environment often require detailed observation which in turn leads by necessity to a small sample size. Multivariate analysis may be a useful adjunct to univariate approaches but, particularly with small samples, it does not appear to be able to stand on its own. This is particularly true in studies which collapse across time periods or across sample subpopulations, thus minimizing the possibility of finding specific environment–development relationships. As we have seen (Farran *et al.*, 1977; Kierscht & Vietze, 1977; Wachs & Gandour, 1981), very often subsamples differ within themselves in terms of patterns of environment–development relationships. Obviously these differences would be lost if heterogeneous populations were collapsed in a multivariate analysis. Our recommendation would be to give equal weight to both univariate and multivariate approaches rather than exclusive reliance upon any one approach for data interpretation.

THE SOCIAL ENVIRONMENT: CONCLUSIONS

For the social environment, three experiential variables appear to show consistent relationships to development. However, the interpretation of each of these relationships is somewhat clouded. Thus, variety of stimulation is found to be positively related to development, but this conclusion is based on only a small number of studies. Parental sensitivity is also found to be positively related to cognitive-intellectual development, but widely varying definitions of sensitivity make it difficult to state exactly what we mean by this parameter. The use of direct teaching by parents is also positively related to development, but these effects appear to have limited generalizability.

Of the remaining environmental variables surveyed, the various parental teaching styles (with the exception of structure and providing specific cues) appear to bear little relationship to cognitive-intellectual development.

For the great majority of social environmental variables, their relationship to cognitive-intellectual development appears to be strongly mediated by the age of the infant (*age specificity*). Thus, physical contact stimulation appears to relate to cognitive intellectual development primarily between birth and 6 months of age. Parental orientation to the infant, responsivity (except for distress, which is related earlier), verbal stimulation, and restrictiveness do not appear to be relevant to cognitive-intellectual development until at least 12 months of age. Amount of involvement does not appear to show a consistent relationship to development until at least 24 months of age. Further, for certain of these parameters (verbal stimulation, responsivity) there appears to be a developmental progression in the kinds of stimulation the infant is sensitive to at different ages. Although for some environmental parameters the rationale for the existence of age specificity appears clear (physical contact, restrictiveness), for others (i.e., orientation) we are faced with a phenomenon without a clear-cut explanation.

In addition to age specificity, the evidence on the relationship between the early social environment and cognitive-intellectual development also indicates the possibility of environmental and organismic specificity, delayed environmental effects, and effects that fade with the passage of time. The existence of organismic specificity may be particularly critical in interpreting the results of multivariate approaches to relating environment to development. If the relationship of environment to development is mediated by specific, individual, organismic factors, then these relationships may be lost when multivariate tests are run requiring large-sample, heterogeneous groups. One could split a total group into several subsamples and utilize multivariate approaches, but this practice runs into the problem of the use of multivariate statistics with small sample sizes, as we noted earlier in this chapter.

CHAPTER 5

Early Experience and
Cognitive-Intellectual Development

The Emotional-Attitudinal Environment

A third component of the environment encountered by the young infant resides in the affect and attitudes of those around him. The study of the relationships between parental affect–attitudes and development has had a long history. This is particularly so in the area of personality development, with many of the classic longitudinal studies of development (i.e., Fels, Berkeley) falling within this model. Happily, many of these studies were also extended to the cognitive as well as to the personality domain.

As noted in Chapter 2, more recent approaches have turned away from the study of affect and attitudes. Methodological considerations are highly relevant to this loss of interest. Many of these criticisms seem to focus on measurement procedures. Like physical and social environmental studies, affect/attitudinal studies are often based on observational procedures. Unlike these other studies, however, affect/attitudinal data are often based on global summaries or global categorizations of the observations. Problems with global categorizations have been noted earlier, in Chapter 2. Given the limitations of global categorizations, one may question whether evidence on parental affect–attitudes should be considered at all. However, some theorists have made a case for continued study of attitudinal variables in spite of methodological problems (Parke, 1979). Instances have been reported in the literature in which parental attitude predicted development while observed behavioral interactions did not (Radin, 1976). Given these factors, plus the wealth of data available in this area, it would seem foolish not to consider this body of literature even though methodological constraints may limit the utility of the available results.

In reviewing the area of parental affect–attitude, one unique problem appears that should be noted. Unlike physical and social environmental studies, in which construct labels more or less clearly operationalize a specific parameter, for affective and attitudinal studies labels too often obscure rather than illustrate. In attitudinal studies, often the same label may describe totally different parameters, or different terms may subsume the same construct. As a result, in organizing this chapter, we have chosen not to rely on the label. Rather, we have attempted to organize constructs together in broad areas that appear to share some degree of general congruence, even if different terms or labels are utilized.

Specifically, we will be interested in five areas. The first three areas resemble the three major axes of Becker's (1964) hypothetical model. These are amount of parental involvement (Becker's emotional involvement–calm detachment factor), positive and negative attitudes toward the child (Becker's warmth–hostility factor), and use of parental controls (Becker's permissive–restrictive factor). In addition, we will also look at two other areas not covered by Becker. These are parental concerns for achievement and parental style. Although there may be some overlap between even these broad classifications, we feel that our organizational categories cover the field and have at least some degree of independence.

Amount of Parental Involvement

In terms of the amount of parental involvement, one popular approach has been to look at ratings of the degree of emotional involvement (high–low, strong–weak) between parent and child. A number of studies report a positive relationship between amount of emotional involvement and cognitive intellectual development. Thus, L. J. Yarrow (1963) reports a correlation of +.55 between ratings of degree of emotional involvement and 6-month infant IQ. Also for the first year of life, Stern et al. (1969) report that accelerated infant cognitive development loads on the same factor as close mother–infant emotional involvement.

Longitudinally, Werner (1969) has reported data indicating the relevance of early emotional involvement to IQ at 10 years. However, since this data is based on long-term retrospective reports, the validity of this relationship must be questioned. Honzik (1967a) reports that measures of mother–son closeness taken at 21 months are positively and generally significantly related to male IQ measured between 21 months and 18 years of age. The correlation between 21-month closeness and IQ measured at 30 years was nonsignificant. For fathers and sons the correlations tend to be significant and positive between 21 months and 4 years of age but not thereafter except at age 30, when the correlation is significant but negative. In sharp contrast to the male data, correlations for females tend to be generally nonsignificant.

In a second study, Honzik (1967b) reports evidence suggesting a good deal of specificity in the relationship between parental closeness and cognitive performance. Using 18-year WISC scores as the criterion, Honzik (1967b) reports that 21-month parental closeness predicts verbal but not performance abilities. In addition, parental closeness significantly predicts digit span and information for both sexes but predicts vocabulary, comprehension, and similarities only for males. The sex differences reported in the Honzik data are congruent with the data reported by L. J. Yarrow *et al.* (1973), who reported a significant prediction of 10-year WISC IQ performance from 6-month ratings of environmental closeness for males but not for females.

The above data suggest the relevance of degree of parental emotional involvement for both early and long-term cognitive development. This is true particularly for males and particularly for the mother–son dyad. Unfortunately, data inconsistent with these conclusions are available. Bayley and Schaefer (1964) report a number of significant correlations between ratings of maternal emotional involvement and female cognitive development over the first three years of life. Indeed, Bayley and Schaefer suggest that degree of mother–daughter emotional involvement may be the major factor for early female cognitive–intellectual development. In sharp contrast to the Honzik and L. J. Yarrow data, the Bayley and Schaefer correlations between degree of emotional involvement and male IQ from birth through 18 years are nonsignificant.

In terms of the critical relevance of mothers, Clarke-Stewart (1977) reports paternal rather than maternal emotional involvement with the child as being most predictive of early cognitive intellectual development. Using cross-lag correlations, Clarke-Stewart suggests that this relationship may be more a result of the child's level of development than the amount of paternal involvement. If replicable, Clarke-Stewart's cross-lag data would cast considerable doubt on the short-term findings of both L. J. Yarrow (1963) and Stern *et al.* (1969) since, from their concurrent relationships, it is difficult to determine whether the correlation is due to parent or child effects.

The Clarke-Stewart cross-lag results would be less easy to reconcile with the data from longitudinal studies unless one assumes an essentially stable amount of parent–child emotional involvement across time. With a stable amount of parent–child emotional involvement, the relationship between amount of early and later involvement could mediate the relationship between early involvement and later development. Indeed, evidence from England (Kent & Davis, 1957) indicates that older children from homes labeled as unconcerned (low involvement) do show low levels of intellectual functioning. Unfortunately, since Honzik (1967a, 1967b) L. J. Yarrow *et al.* (1973) each utilized only one measurement point, it is impossible to ascertain the autocorrelations in these studies. For Bayley and Schaefer (1964), the autocorrelations are not reported.

Summary: Emotional Involvement

Overall, the conflicting sex differences between studies make it difficult to interpret clearly the relationship between emotional involvement and development. There does appear to be at least some type of relationship, although its exact nature is still cloudy. Given both the age and subscale effects noted in the longitudinal studies, it may well be that there is a high degree of specificity in the relationship between emotional involvement and subsequent development. Unfortunately, given existing variations in the definition of emotional involvement, it is impossible to go beyond a general suggestion of the possibility of specificity.

DIRECTION OF EMOTIONAL INVOLVEMENT

Parental Emotional Warmth

Parental warmth is most often measured either in terms of discrete parental behaviors (i.e., smiling), which are thought to be indicative of quality of emotional involvement, or on the basis of global ratings.

In general, studies looking at specific indexes like smiling have tended to show either nonsignificant (Lusk & Lewis, 1972; Riksen-Walraven, 1978) or inconsistent (Clarke-Stewart, 1973; L. J. Yarrow *et al.*, 1975) relationships. For studies utilizing global ratings, the results tend to be somewhat more consistent. Studies using global ratings of parental warmth or degree of positive parental affect indicate a significant relationship between this parameter and 6-month IQ (L. J. Yarrow, 1963), 12-month Griffiths performance (Stern *et al.*, 1969), Bayley performance in the second (Clarke-Stewart, 1977; Seegmiller & King, 1975) and third (Herman, 1971) years of life, Minnesota preschool performance (Clarke-Stewart, 1977) and competence ratings (Deschner, 1973) in the third year of life, mental test performance and task independence between 3 and 4 years of age (Parker, 1972; Lawson & Ingleby, 1974), Binet and PPVT performance at 4 years, and gains in Binet performance from 4 to 5 years (Radin, 1971). In at least two studies (Clarke-Stewart, 1973; Seegmiller & King, 1975) results suggest at least some evidence for age specificity within the second year of life.

Longitudinally, degree of early parental warmth has been positively related to gains in intelligence between 12 months and 5 years (Champney, cited in Baldwin, Kalhorn, & Breese, 1945) and to IQ level from 21 months through 30 years (Honzik, 1967a, 1967b).

The Honzik data are particularly interesting in suggesting an age-by-sex specificity effect. For females, Honzik (1967a) reports significant correlations between both mothers' and fathers' positive feelings and daughters' IQ between 4 and 10 years of age; for males, significant correlations appear between 21 and 30 months and again between 8 and 10 years and primarily involve the mother–son relationship. Other studies also suggest the possibility of specificity, but the results between studies are highly inconsistent. Thus, Bayley and Schaefer (1964) report a significant relationship between maternal expression of affection and early female development between 10 and 30 months; the relationship for males is nonsignificant. In contrast, L. J. Yarrow et al. (1973) report significant correlations between 6-month ratings of maternal positive emotional expression and 10-year WISC for males but not for females.

Although the above studies do indicate at least some degree of association between degree of parental warmth and subsequent intellectual development, nonsignificant results must also be noted. These results are found across a number of studies. L. J. Yarrow et al. (1975) report few significant relationships at 6 months of age between a variety of general and specific cognitive measures and the degree of parental positive emotional expressiveness. Nonsignificant relationships are also reported between measures of parental warmth and Griffiths performance at 20 to 28 and 40 to 46 weeks (Blank, 1964), development of competence between 12 and 20 months (Wenar, 1976), and sorting and design-copying performance at 4 years of age (Hess & Shipman, 1965). Longitudinally, degree of early maternal affection has been found to be unrelated to IQ at 3½, 5½, and 9 years (Kagan & Freeman, 1963) or to changes in IQ between 3 and 12 years of age (Sontag, Baker, & Nelson, 1958). (Indeed, Sontag et al. suggest that mothers of ascending IQ children tend to be less affectionate than mothers of descending IQ children.)

In interpreting these divergent findings, a number of points should be noted. First, for a number of studies with negative results, parent affect measures were averaged across a time span of several years (Kagan & Freeman, 1963; Sontag et al., 1958). If one can accept the validity of the Honzik data, which suggest age specificity, this may mean that averaging over a time span of several years mixes significant with nonsignificant time periods leading to overall nonsignificance. Interestingly, the majority of significant studies measure affect over a time period of, at most, 12 months.

Secondly, in several of the nonsignificant studies, global ratings of parental affect were utilized (Wenar, 1976; Hess & Shipman, 1965). These ratings included measures of parental warmth but they also included other variables as well. It is unclear from the reports the exact degree to which parental warmth determined affect ratings. Available evidence does suggest that only certain dimensions of parental warmth may be related to cognitive development. Thus, Honzik (1967a) reports a significant relationship between ratings of parental friendliness (cluster 7) and development, but nonsignificant relationships for expression of affection (clusters 3 and 6) and cognitive development. Bayley and Schaefer (1964) report significant findings for positive expression of affect but nonsignificant relationships for positive evaluation of the child.

Summary: Emotional Warmth.   Overall, if one is willing to accept the possibility of age specificity (and possibly sex and environmental specificity as well), the overall pattern of evidence does suggest a positive and significant relationship between the dimension of parental emotional warmth and the child's subsequent cognitive-intellectual functioning. Less clear are the causal relationships between these parameters. One would like to think that parental warmth promotes cognitive development. However, Lawson and Ingleby (1974) have raised the possibility that bright children simply elicit more parental warmth than dull children. Unless one is willing to postulate a stable emotional climate, the longitudinal data of Honzik (1967a, 1967b) and L. J. Yarrow *et al.* (1973) are difficult to reconcile with Lawson and Ingleby's formulation.

Alternatively, Radin (1971) notes that if one covaries out the child's level of academic motivation, the relationship between the child's IQ and parental warmth becomes nonsignificant. Radin suggests that parental warmth may motivate the child to achieve in the presence of an adult, hence the relationship between warmth and performance. If correct, this hypothesis would suggest that only those components of parental warmth which relate to development of an achievement drive by the child would be relevant for subsequent cognitive functioning. This approach may be an avenue to further exploration of the notion of environmental specificity in terms of distinguishing between those components of parental warmth which are relevant to development and those which are not.

Parental Hostility

The overwhelming majority of studies on direction of affect have concentrated primarily on warmth. Surprisingly, there have been few other studies investigating the alternative, parental hostility. Within available studies the evidence is generally inconsistent. Seegmiller and King (1975) report no significant relationship between parental hostility and development between 14 and 22 months. In contrast, Wenar (1976) reports that negative affect tends to lower infant self-sufficiency between 12 and 20 months. Bayley and Schaefer (1964) report that the maternal attitude of perceiving the child as a burden is negatively related to male performance but not to female performance. Totally confounding matters, Ramey *et al.* (1979) report that parental hostility measures at 6 months are negatively related to 36-month Binet for non-day-care infants but not for infants in day-care; when hostility is measured between 18 and 20 months and related to 36-month Binet, the negative relationship appears for day-care infants but not for non-day-care infants.

One other parameter that appears to reflect hostility should also be noted. Several studies, based on the Fels population, have reported relationships between amount of parental criticism and cognitive performance. Kagan and Freeman (1963) report that degree of maternal criticism between 2 and 4 years of age is positively related to female IQ from 3½ through 9 years of age. The data for males is nonsignificant. Sex and age differences also are reported by Kagan and Moss (1962) who indicate that degree of maternal hostility (defined as criticism) from 0 to 3 years of age negatively relates to male achievement between 6 and 10 years, though not earlier. Degree of maternal criticism between 3 and 6 years of age negatively relates to female achievement during the same time period. Kagan and Moss suggest that sex differences may be due to the greater impact of the mother as a role model upon female development; however, this interpretation does not account for the sex-by-age specificity nor the radically different direction of effects for achievement (Kagan & Moss) and intelligence (Kagan & Freeman). A cautionary note on the role of criticism is cited by McCall *et al.* (1973). McCall notes that while degree of criticism does predict patterns of IQ change, when used in a multiple regression equation criticism *per se* does not show a high degree of predictive power.

Summary: Hostility. Comparing the data for hostility and criticism indicates highly inconsistent and conflicting findings both between and within each area. Given the general lack of research in this area, it is difficult to specify why these inconsistencies are occurring. Given reports of an increasing prevalence of child abuse and neglect, it appears clear that the relevance of parental hostility parameters to cognitive development deserves more study than it has heretofore received.

Parental Acceptance–Rejection of the Child

Although the accepting–rejecting dimension would seem to be almost identical to the hostility–warmth dimension, this is not necessarily so. It is possible for parents not to like a child but at the same time to accept the child ("an ill-favored thing, sir, but mine own": *As You Like It*, Act V, Scene iv). Thus, we will look at the relationship of acceptance–rejection to development as a separate subcategory.

In general, the evidence for the role of parental acceptance–rejection in cognitive intellectual development is equivocal at best. The most clear-cut evidence for the role of acceptance–rejection comes in the first year of life with several studies (Ainsworth & Bell, 1974; L. J. Yarrow, 1963) reporting positive and significant correlations between degree of acceptance and infant IQ performance. Unfortunately, inconsistent evidence also occurs in the first year. Ainsworth and Bell (1974) note that when a number of environmental variables are combined in a multiple regression equation, acceptance–rejection shows little overall predictive power compared to other variables. Supporting this, Farran *et al.* (1977) report no significant relationship between 6-month measures of acceptance–rejection and children's cognitive performance.

After the first year of life, relationships become even more inconsistent. The most consistent evidence is presented by Bayley and Schaefer (1964), who report that male preschool-age IQ is negatively related to degree of maternal rejection, while male school-age IQ is positively related to degree of maternal acceptance; for females, early acceptance is positively related only to early cognitive development. However, this conclusion is not based upon a direct measurement of acceptance–rejection but rather upon the assumption that the data from several scales taken together constitute a unitary dimension of acceptance rejection.

In contrast, Clarke-Stewart (1973) reports no relationship between rejection and Bayley or Piaget scale performance between 10 and 17 months of age. Farran *et al.* (1977) report a relationship between rejection and development at 36 months only for children who have previously been enrolled in a day-care center. Baldwin *et al.* (1945) report no relationship between rejection and IQ change over a three-year period and an effect for acceptance only when acceptance is combined with other parental dimensions such as democracy. Kagan and Freeman (1963) report no relationship between degree of early parental acceptance and male IQ between 3½ and 9 years of age; a relationship for females is found, but only at age 3½. In contrast, L. J. Yarrow *et al.* (1973), looking at the long-term predictive power of 6-months acceptance–rejection, indicate that this dimension predicts 10-year WISC scores for males but not for females.

Summary: Acceptance–Rejection. Overall, it appears clear that acceptance–rejection has, at best, a weak and inconsistent relationship to cognitive-intellectual development. This is not to say that acceptance–rejection is not relevant to other aspects of development but only that its relationship to cognitive-intellectual development seems highly tenuous.

PARENTAL CONTROL STRATEGIES

The studies to be reviewed in this section have, as a common core, an interest in parental control strategies. These can be defined as the degree to which the parent attempts to control the behavior of the child, the types of controls utilized, the way in which the parent presents controls to the child, and parental reactions to children's transgressions. Analogues of this section would be the control–autonomy factor of Schaefer (1959) or the restrictiveness–permissiveness dimension noted by Becker (1964).

Severity of Controls

Several studies have looked at the severity of parental controls as expressed by such categories as strictness, severity, or use of punishment. In general, results are fairly inconsistent, suggesting either a weak effect for this predictor or a high degree of specificity, particularly in terms of dimension and sex.

For sex specificity, Bayley and Schaefer report both punishment and strictness to be positively related to level of male IQ only between 4 and 6 months of age. In contrast, for females strictness is unrelated to development and punishment is negatively related to development between 13 and 54 months. Kagan and Freeman (1963) report negative relationships for both sexes, with degree of parental severity between 2 and 4 years predicting male IQ at 5½ years and female IQ at 3½ and 5½ years. In general, the above data suggest that severity may be more relevant for female development than for male development.

For environmental specificity, McCall et al. (1973) report that longitudinal decreases in IQ are related to either very low or very high levels of penalty–severity. However, use of severe penalties also produces a cognitive decline in middle childhood which does not occur in homes where there is little severity. However, since McCall et al. collapsed across experiential measures between 3 and 10 years, it is unclear whether these differential effects are due to early or later experiences.

Degree of Restrictiveness

An associated dimension is the degree of restrictiveness imposed by the parents, regardless of the severity of penalities used. In general, for restrictiveness the available information is congruent in terms of suggesting a negative relationship between early restrictiveness and subsequent development. Overall, the period between 12 and 48 months appears to be most sensitive in terms of the effects of restrictiveness. Prior to 12 months of age, evidence indicates no significant effect of restrictiveness upon development (Blank, 1964). Restrictiveness between 12 and 20 months of age was found to be negatively related to children's competence (Wenar, 1976), whereas restrictiveness between 2 and 4 years of age was found to be negatively related to IQ performance between 3½ and 9 years of age (Kagan & Freeman, 1963). For the upper limits of restrictiveness, Kagan and Freeman report that restrictiveness between 4 and 7 years of age is unrelated to later IQ. This upper boundary limit is less clear in that Kagan and Moss (1962) report that restrictiveness between 3 and 6 years of age, while unrelated to male achievement, is negatively related to female achievement between 3 and 10 years of age. In contrast, Radin (1976) reports that paternal restriction is negatively related to cognitive development in male preschool children but is unrelated to female performance. This may not be a case of organismic specificity, however, since apparently fathers behave in different ways to male and female preschool children. Given these sex differences and overlapping upper age boundaries, it is difficult to know whether there is a true discrepancy between studies or whether the Kagan and Moss findings for females are due primarily to parental restrictiveness between 3 and 4 years of age.

Evidence indicating no relationship between restrictiveness and subsequent development is reported primarily by McCall et al. (1973). However, as we noted earlier, McCall collected experiential data across a 10-year span. It may well be that these nonsignificant results are due to collapsing across restrictiveness measures taken during potentially sensitive periods (3–4 years) and nonsensitive periods (4–13 years).

Some evidence also suggests the possibility of an age-by-environment specificity for restrictiveness. Radin (1972a, 1973) reports that restrictiveness at 4 years of age is negatively related to male children's Binet performance but not to their PPVT performance; in contrast, restrictiveness at 5 years of age is negatively related to PPVT performance but is unrelated to Binet performance. This may suggest that the effects of restrictiveness are more closely related to specific abilities than to general abilities as the child develops. This hypothesis could account for the negative findings of McCall and Kagan and Freeman after 4 years of age, since these authors utilized general IQ measures rather than measures of specific abilities.

Several studies have looked at the dimension of parental coercion. As described, coercion appears to share a good deal of conceptual similarity with restriction. The evidence indicates that early parental coercion, from 24 to 48 months, is negatively related to children's competence in the second year of life (Deschner, 1973) and to children's IQ performance through 5½ years (Kagan & Freeman, 1963).

Summary: Restrictiveness. *Overall, both parental restriction and coercion show a consistent and negative relationship to development between 12 and 48 months.* Radin (1972a, 1972b, 1973) has suggested that one reason for the negative relationship between parental restriction and cognitive development is the possibility that restrictive parents may inhibit their children's exploratory behavior. This explanation would account for the lack of relationship prior to 12 months of age since children's explorations are limited by mobility prior to 12 months. This hypothesis might also indicate the reasons for limited findings after 48 months; as the child gets older and has greater freedom to move out of the home, children's explorations are increasingly out of the control of the parent. The evidence previously cited on physical and social restrictions of exploration would tend to support this hypothesis. Definitive support for this hypothesis would come in a study showing a significant relationship between restrictive parental attitudes and degree of limitations of children's exploration. Unfortunately, such a study has not yet been reported.

Parental Indulgence–Autonomy

The control dimension opposite that of restrictiveness would, of course, be indulgence. Little evidence is available on this parameter, though Wenar (1976) does report a lack of relationship between a laissez-faire attitude on the part of parents and children's competence between 12 and 20 months of age. What evidence is available more often encompasses parent attitudes of allowing the child autonomy.

In general, the evidence on autonomy is highly inconsistent. Deschner (1973) reports that maternal autonomy facilitates competence behavior in 2-year-old children. In contrast, Bayley and Schaefer (1964) report no relationship between autonomy and male development but a negative relationship between degree of autonomy and female development in the first year of life. Differences between the studies in definition of predictor variable and type of criterion variable used make it difficult to establish any consistency. However, in contrast to the data on restrictiveness, these data indicate little support for postulating a relationship between early parental indulgence–autonomy and later development. This is not to say that indulgence or autonomy later in life may not be relevant. However, in terms of early experience, parental indulgence–autonomy appears to bear little significant relationship to development.

Parental Concerns with Achievement

Parental achievement concerns may focus either on a concern for specific developmental achievements or for more general concerns such as the development of independence. Both approaches will be reviewed here.

Protectiveness

Protectiveness is most often defined as the degree to which the mother rewards dependency and prevents independent behavior by the child (Kagan & Moss, 1962). In general, the data relating early protectiveness to subsequent cognitive intellectual development tend to be either nonsignificant or inconsistent.

Based on the Fels population, available evidence reports no relationship between degree of early parental protectiveness and IQ level from 3½ to 9 years (Kagan & Freeman, 1963) or pattern of IQ change from 3 to 13 years (Sontag et al., 1958; McCall et al., 1973). Kagan and Moss (1962) do report a relationship between protection and general and intellectual achievement, but their results are inconsistent in regard to both sex and age. Specifically, Kagan and Moss note that the degree of maternal protection from 0 to 3 years of age is positively related to male achievement from 6 to 10 years of age but is negatively related to female achievement from 0 to 3 years of age. Blank (1964) does report that the degree of parental protection is related to Griffiths performance at 20 to 28 and 40 to 46 weeks, but her definition of protection (mother protects child from daily hazards) is different from the Fels definition (perhaps less restrictive) and may be more appropriate to development in the first year of life.

Overall, the results relating protectiveness to cognitive development are not highly impressive.

Fostering of Independence

A natural follow-up to parental protection would be studies relating the degree of parental concerns about independence to development. For this line of evidence, two dimensions (fostering of independence and fostering of dependence) seem particularly relevant. Congruent with earlier data noted for protection, early parental fostering of independence is either inconsistently or nonsignificantly related to development (though there is some evidence that fostering of independence for school-age children may be relevant—Hanson, 1975). Blank (1964) does report that the degree of independence training by the mother is positively and significantly related to infant Griffiths performance between 20 to 28 and 40 to 46 weeks. However, Hanson (1975) reports no significant relationship between early parental emphasis on independence and children's intellectual performance at 3 and 5½ years of age. Jordan, Radin, and Epstein (1975) do report a significant relationship between degree of parental expectancies for independence and development, but these occur only for middle-class boys and lower-class girls. Overall then, there does not appear to be a highly consistent relationship between parental fostering of independence and subsequent development.

Congruent with these results are data relating cognitive performance in children to the amount of parental babying (emphasizing dependency). In general, available studies report either nonsignificant relationships between parental babying and development (Kagan & Freeman, 1963; McCall *et al.*, 1973) or relationships that are significant but only at scattered points in time (Bayley & Schaefer, 1964).

Parental Acceleration

Another source of data reflecting parental concerns with achievement are those investigating parental desires for acceleration. An acceleratory emphasis is most often defined in terms of the parents' concern for the child's developmental level or high parental expectancies for development (Kagan & Moss, 1962). As with other attitudinal variables, inconsistent results appear to be the norm.

In general, for parental acceleratory concerns, when significant relationships occur they are found for males rather than for females (Honzik, 1967a; Kagan & Moss, 1962; Moss & Kagan, 1958). However even for males inconsistencies occur in terms of the age at which the relationship between acceleratory concerns and development become manifest. Honzik and Moss and Kagan report a positive relationship between acceleratory concerns and development prior to 3 years of age. In contrast, Kagan and Moss report no significant relationships between acceleratory concerns and development until after 3 years of age.

These differences may reflect criterion variable differences between studies. In the Kagan and Moss study the criterion variable was the child's level of intellectual (academic) achievement. In contrast, in the Moss and Kagan and Honzik studies the criterion variable was intelligence test performance. Acceleratory concerns over achievement may become relevant only when the child is put in a situation in which his achievement level is compared to that of other children (i.e., preschool or school age). In contrast, acceleratory concerns for younger children may well relate only to those items commonly tapped by developmental scales (i.e., alertness, fine motor coordination, verbal skills). Supporting this explanation is the finding by Shipman (1977) that maternal level of aspiration is positively related to infant's level of early intellectual alertness.

Besides inconsistencies among studies with positive results, nonsignificant results are also found. Using the Fels population, Kagan and Freeman (1963) report generally nonsignificant relationships between parental acceleratory concerns and IQ performance from 3½ to 9 years of age. Similar results using the construct of parental achievement demands are also noted by Bayley and Schaefer (1964).

Data relating parental acceleratory concerns to patterns of IQ change are equally inconsistent. Sontag *et al.* (1958) report positive but nonsignificant relationships between degree of parental acceleratory concern and children's patterns of intellectual development. In contrast, McCall *et al.* (1973) do report highly significant relationships between these parameters. However, McCall utilizes a definition of acceleratory concern that stresses skill training rather than concern *per se* and may thus reflect parental behaviors rather than parental attitudes.

Summary: Achievement Concerns

The above pattern of results indicates that, even when limited to males, the evidence for a relationship between parental acceleratory concerns and development is quite tenuous. This conclusion can be generalized to all of the areas relating parental achievement concerns to development.

PARENTAL STYLES

The above areas have been dealing essentially with parental emotions, expectations, and concerns about children. There is an additional body of literature that deals with parental personality and characteristics and parental attitudes about the nature of the family. This literature has been organized under the present heading.

Parental Equalitarianism

For many parents the form of discipline (restrictive–indulgent) is less critical than the need to treat children as adults and consult with the children on family matters. These attitudes are categorized by such terms as *democratic, equalitarian,* or *high in justification of discipline.* For the variable of democratic homes, Baldwin *et al.* (1945) report that the greatest gains in intelligence over a three-year period were made by children from homes that were democratic in orientation (democratic–accepting or democratic–indulging). However, caution must be taken in generalizing from these findings since Farran (Farran *et al.*, 1977) and Ramey (Ramey *et al.*, 1979) note that the relationship of democratic attitudes in the home to development is mediated by extraneous factors such as whether the child has been in a day-care program and the age of the child. Differences between studies may reflect differences in either predictors, age of subjects, or the fact that Baldwin *et al.* looked at IQ change while Farran and Ramey looked at IQ level. Alternatively, the fact that the Farran and Ramey data were reported 30 years after that of Baldwin may indicate the possibility of generational effects (Wohlwill, 1973a) changing the meaning of democratic attitudes over time.

For equalitarianism Bayley and Schaefer (1964) report that, for males, equalitarianism in the first year of life is negatively related to development while equalitarianism after 4 years of age is positively related to development. For females, equalitarianism is positively related to development primarily between the first and third years of life. The rationale for these age and sex differences is unclear. At least for age, it could be hypothesized that mothers who treat a young infant as an equal member of the family may be unrealistic about children's capacities and this (insensitive?) attitude may in some way inhibit development. In contrast, mothers who treat older children as equal may be fostering independence.

Data on justification of discipline to the child indicates strong positive correlations between justification of discipline after 4 years of age and both male and female intellectual development through 9 years of age (Kagan & Freeman, 1963). Kagan and Freeman suggest that this relationship exists because the mother who justifies her discipline to the child may be stimulating the child's language and showing faith in the child's ability to comprehend. This interpretation is supported by the fact that early justification between 2 and 4 years of age is also related to female IQ at 3½ and 5½ years of age (Kagan & Freeman, 1963). Since females tend to be accelerated in language development, they may be better able to comprehend early justification than males. Why justification of discipline should show a more consistent relationship to development than democracy and equalitarianism is unclear except for the possibility that justification of discipline is an attitudinal parameter that may be more easily translated into parent behavior than the latter two parameters.

Parental Nurturance

A dimension related to parental equalitarianism is that of parental nurturance. Nurturance is most often defined as the parents' listening to the needs of the child, consulting the child, and responding to the child as an active human being (Radin, 1972a) Most of the available work on nurturance has been done by Radin and her colleagues, who report that the degree of paternal nurturance is positively and significantly related to the performance of 4-year-old males on the Binet, PPVT (Jordan *et al.*, 1975; Radin, 1972a) and Piagetian problem-solving behavior (Jordan *et al.*, 1975). Nurturance has also been positively related to the performance of 5-year-old boys on both the Binet and PPVT (Radin, 1973).

Interestingly, however, in spite of the seeming consistency of these results, a number of curious exceptions have been noted. Thus, in the work of Radin and her colleagues, the relationship between paternal nurturance and development appears primarily for middle-class males. Using a similar population, Baumrind (1971) reports no significant relationships between nurturance and development. The fact that the Baumrind procedure involved both parents while Radin's approach involved only fathers may suggest the impact of family structure on the nurturance–development relationship (Radin, 1976). Further, different aspects of the nurturance scale appear to predict cognitive development differentially. Thus, paternal nurturance rated during an interview is positively related to intellectual competence; paternal nurturance rated during a problem-solving task is negatively related to IQ performance (Radin, 1976).

Sex differences may be attributed to the fact that only paternal nurturance was considered. Class variables are not so easy to account for. Whether these reflect the operation of a particular kind of specificity or whether there are other intervening variables that are suppressing a relationship between nurturance and development for lower-class boys is not clear at present. The possibility that differential aspects of nurturance are differentially predictive is interesting, but unfortunately little follow-up work on this hypothesis has been done.

Radin suggests that nurturance is relevant to development primarily through indicating to the child that interaction with the environment (i.e., exploration) is rewarding. Unfortunately, there has been no direct test of this hypothesis through looking at exploratory patterns of children from nurturant versus nonnurturant homes. One could speculate that greater interference with exploration in lower-class homes might relate to the fact that the nurturance development relationship occurs only for middle-class boys.

Parental Anxiety and Conflict

In addition to the above studies, several other papers have reported data on other parental style factors that may relate, although indirectly, to the child's cognitive-intellectual development. One of these variables is the degree of parental anxiety. Bayley and Schaefer (1964) report generally nonsignificant relationships between degree of maternal anxiety and cognitive performance for both males and females. In contrast, the majority of other available results do suggest at least some relationship between anxiety and development. However, the direction of relationship varies among studies. A number of studies (Davids, Holden, & Gray, 1963; Stern *et al.*, 1969) report a negative relationship between degree of maternal anxiety and child's level of cognitive performance. In contrast, several other studies (Honzik, 1967a, 1967b; Blank, 1964) report positive relationships.

This discrepancy between studies may reflect differences in causality. In those studies reporting negative relationships, maternal anxieties seem to be primarily a reflection of the child's slow rate of development. In contrast, for those studies reflecting positive relationships, anxiety appears to reflect a general concern for the child's well-being which is independent of the child's level of achievement. It may well be that mothers who are more concerned about their children's well-being interact more with their children and hence promote development. This interpretation receives some support from the data by Bleckman and Nakamura (1971) which indicate that the relationship of parental anxiety to performance may be mediated by the rewards and punishment systems parents use with their children. If correct, this would suggest that a fruitful area of study might be the relation of parental anxiety to specific parent–child interactions.

One other area that has received some study has been the degree of parental conflict. Unfortunately, all the available evidence comes from one population, namely the Berkeley study (Honzik, 1967a, 1967b) and thus has limited generalizability. At least for this population, the available evidence indicates a high degree of environmental and organismic specificity. Honzik's data indicate that a lack of parental conflict is related to accelerated female cognitive performance but is unrelated to male performance. Further, this relationship appears to be primarily for verbal rather than for nonverbal abilities. Whether this finding can be replicated outside of the Berkeley population is, as yet, an unanswered question.

Summarizing across the major parental style variables, one sees that the evidence indicates few main effect relationships between parental style and cognitive-intellectual development. The consistency which does exist in relationships appears to be restricted by such parameters as the criterion variable studied or the child's age or sex.

Other Stylistic Variables

Much of the other literature on parental styles is scattered among various parameters. As a result, it is difficult to do more than note some of the available highlights. In general, available evidence indicates that children's cognitive intellectual development is unrelated to parental emphasis of female sexual development, parental task orientation models (Hanson, 1975), parental autonomy or locus of control (Herman, 1971), parental affection and home adjustment (Sontag *et al.*, 1958), parental irritability or marital adjustment

(Honzik, 1967a), or parental accommodating attitudes toward the child (Clarke-Stewart *et al.*, 1979).

Evidence is available indicating that the degree of maternal abstract cognitive style may be related to children's creativity; paternal abstract cognitive style apparently is unrelated (Bishop & Chace, 1971). Evidence is also available (Honzik, 1967b) indicating that high verbal males have fathers who are often poorly adjusted socially; fathers of high-performance males lack self-confidence and have a strong sense of privacy. For high performance females, mothers tend to be irritable while for high verbal females, mothers tend to be worrisome (Honzik, 1967b).

Early language is also positively related to the degree of parental accommodation to the child (Clarke-Stewart *et al.*, 1979). For males, maternal rejection of homemaking, negative emotional states, and mood swings tend to be negatively related to cognitive development, while maternal narcissism is positively related; for females, negative emotional states and narcissism are relevant, but these relationships occur less consistently (Bayley & Schaefer, 1964).

Although, as we noted above, marital adjustment *per se* is unrelated to development, a close friendly relationship between parents appears to be particularly relevant to female developmental level; this is particularly true for the development of verbal abilities (Honzik, 1967b). The data by Sontag *et al.* (1958), although nonsignificant, also tends to be in the same general direction. Honzik (1967a, 1967b) also reports that early paternal energy tends to be negatively related to female development from 2 through 9 years of age. In contrast, early maternal energy is positively related to male development from 8 through 18 years of age. Honzik (1967b) suggests that maternal energy level may be particularly relevant to male verbal abilities and female performance abilities. Early maternal worrisomeness, which seems to tap many of the same dimensions as energy, is also found to be particularly related to male development from 2½ through 30 years of age.

Summary of Parental Attitude Studies

Overall, it appears that with some notable exceptions (emotional warmth, controls) the relationship between parental attitude parameters and development is highly inconsistent. This is particularly so when one compares findings in this chapter with findings from the previous chapters on the role of the physical and social environments. As we noted earlier in this volume, inconsistencies involving parental attitudinal parameters may be due to discrepancies in definitions between studies, the superordinate nature of parental attitude constructs, the problem of translating parental attitudes into actual behavior, and the fact that the child's perception of the attitude may be more critical than the attitude *per se*. Whatever the cause, the above review suggests that the study of the relationship of early parental attitudes *per se* to cognitive-intellectual development has not been as fruitful as we would wish. New directions, including systematic studies on children's perceptions of parental attitudes and studies on how attitudes translate into behavior, may be necessary for further progress.

CHAPTER 6

The Earliest Social Experiences and Their Effect on Social Development

Historically, great importance has been attributed to the relationship of the child with his first caregiver, usually the mother. Psychoanalysts have seen the quality of the child's relationship to his mother as the prototype of all his later relationships. Ethologists such as Bowlby (1964) have suggested that prolonged separation of the child from his mother (or mother substitute) during the first five years of life "stands foremost among the causes of delinquent character development and persistent misbehavior."

In this chapter, we will review studies that owe much of their impetus to this concern about the quality of the mother–child relationship and its role as a determinant of social development in young children. However, in many of these studies, especially the early ones, the effect of the maternal relationship to the child, or the absence of it, is confounded with variations in sensory stimulation, the trauma of separations of the child from his caregiver, institutionalization, family discord or disharmony, and other stresses on the child. We will attempt to separate these effects to the extent possible, but it must be admitted that many of these studies do not allow such separation of effects.

After reviewing these studies, we will turn our attention to recent studies which have focused on the "responsivity" of the caregiver as a factor affecting many social behaviors developing in the first year of life (including the mother–child relationship itself) and some later social behaviors, such as orientation toward peers.

Unfortunately, we will not be able to trace the effects of these early experiences on later social development with the same degree of specificity that was possible for cognitive development. This is especially true for the studies dealing with maternal deprivation and associated early stresses which we will review first. For the studies focusing on maternal responsivity, we will attempt to trace its effect on the development of what can be thought of

121

as a set of social competencies. These include the development of the smile, person permanence, competence in getting the adult's attention, the discrimination of the caregiver from others, attachment, exploration, and social orientation toward peers and adults.

Yarrow *et al.* (1971) have pointed out that the conviction of the importance of early experience for later development derives largely from data on extremely traumatic and depriving experiences (see also L. J. Yarrow, 1964, 1968). For example, many of the early studies of children reared in institutions (Freud & Burlingham, 1944; Goldfarb, 1945; Spitz, 1946; Spitz & Wolf, 1946) demonstrated profound and longlasting effects on children's intellectual and social development. In one series of follow-up studies of older children who had spent the first three years of their lives in an institution (Goldfarb, 1943, 1944, 1945), the following deficits were found in adolescence: serious learning impairments, disturbances in impulse control, both oversubmissiveness and uncontrolled aggressive impulses, a lack of anxiety or guilt following aggressive or antisocial behavior, impaired ability to form close interpersonal relationships, low frustration tolerance, lack of goal directedness, and a high percentage of delinquent behavior patterns. Studies of children outside institutions who have experienced extreme trauma and deprivation have similarly found long-lasting effects. For example, Bowlby (1944), in a retrospective study, related delinquency and what he called "affectionless characters" personality development to early separation from the natural mother or a mother substitute.

In addition to the long-term effects described above (Goldfarb, 1945), immediate effects of a diminished impulse to reach out toward people, limited and stereotyped emotional responses, failure to establish a personal attachment, and failure in the development of normal social discrimination (as evidenced by infants responding indiscriminately to caregivers and strangers) were also found. Two predominant social patterns were exhibited by these children: either they were socially indifferent and failed to form meaningful social attachments with their caregivers and later, with peers; or they were characterized by what Spitz called "affect hunger," characterized by an insatiable desire to obtain social attention and affection.

In a longitudinal study of children who had considerably fewer traumatic separations and depriving experiences as infants, Yarrow *et al.* (1971) looked at the cognitive and personality development at 10 years of age of children who were in adoptive homes. Most of the children had been placed in adoptive homes by 6 months of age, either being placed directly in upper-middle-class homes 7 to 10 days after birth or being cared for in foster homes until placement in adoptive homes. As far as social development was concerned, early maternal communication, individualization, positive emotional expression, and appropriateness of stimulation were found to be related to 10-year-old boys' "social effectiveness"—a measure of the degree to which the child could relate with ease and contribute to a social situation. No significant relationships were found for girls.

In addition, Yarrow compared three groups of children: (1) children who went directly from the hospital into their permanent adoptive homes (control group), (2) children who were separated from foster mothers before 6 months of age, and (3) children who were separated from their foster mothers after 6 months of age. While no significant effects of early separation from a mother-figure were found for the intellectual functioning of the children at 10 years, late-separated children were significantly lower at 10 years of age than either the control group or the children separated before 6 months on the variable "social discrimination." This variable reportedly reflects the "capacity to establish different levels of relationships with people." There was also a significant negative relationship between age of separation and discrimination in relationship ($r = -.43$) for the total group. Boys and girls did not differ on this variable. However, "social effectiveness" was negatively related to age of separation for boys but not for girls.

Since many of the relationships between infant experiences and 10-year-old characteristics were not significant in this study, and because even the significant correlations were not of great magnitude, Yarrow points out that one cannot conclude from this study that the early environment is decisive for later development. However, the affective relationship with the mother in infancy and maternal stimulation are variables that Yarrow believes must be considered in predicting later behavior.

More recently, Tizard and Hodges (1978) have followed up 51 (of an original sample of 65) children who had been hospitalized before the age of 4 months and continuously institutionalized until at least age 2. Between 2 and 4 years of age, 24 were adopted, 15 were restored to their natural parents, and 26 remained in institutional care; after 4 years of age, 7 more were adopted, 7 more were restored to their natural parents, and 4 were placed in foster homes. This particular institution had a generous staff–child ratio and toys and books were plentiful, but the care of the children had passed through many hands. An average of 24 nurses had worked with the children for at least a week in the first 2 years of life; by 4½ years the figure had increased to 50, and by 8 years it was estimated that at least 80 staff had worked with the children. The authors argue that institutions like this still fail to provide the warm, intimate and continuous one-to-one relationship with a mother substitute that Bowlby (1944) and others have stated is necessary for healthy development.

Compared with a London working- and middle-class control group, the exinstitutional children were more often described by their natural or adoptive mothers as restless, fidgety, quarrelsome, not liked by other children, irritable, more frequently suckers of their thumbs, disobedient, untruthful, resentful or aggressive when corrected, seeking attention from strange adults and from teachers. Interestingly, the adoptive parents, who were older and better educated than the natural parents, were more definite about wanting to keep their children, more often played and engaged in other activities with their children, and were more likely to put them to bed. The children restored to their natural parents, who often reported feeling ambivalent about wanting them, were the most attention-seeking group, more often had negative relationships with their siblings, and were the least affectionate. Also, the later the child was restored to the parents, the less likely was a mutual attachment formed. However, both of the exinstitutional groups were described as over-friendly to strangers, attention-seeking, and as having more problems at school.

L. J. Yarrow (1964) has reported on three major studies that have investigated the effects of short-term hospitalization (Faust, Jackson, Cermak, Burtt, & Winkley, 1952; Prugh, Staub, Sands, Kirschbaum, & Lenihan, 1953; Schaffer and Callender, 1959). All three of these found that the kinds and severity of reactions to hospitalization varied significantly with the age of the child. For example, Schaffer and Callender, studying 25 infants hospitalized less than two weeks, found a variety of disturbances associated with separation in infants over 7 months of age but none with younger infants. These disturbances included marked anxiety toward strangers, desperate clinging to their mothers, and vigorous crying on their departure. Prugh *et al.*, studying 200 children between 2 and 12 years of age, found the reactions of the youngest children to be primarily expressions of anxiety over separation from parents. Children 4 to 6 years old showed similar but less extreme evidence of disturbance. And in the older children, 6 to 10 years of age, there was less anxiety which could be directly attributed to separation.

Yarrow suggests that the developmental period during which children are likely to be most susceptible to damage by hospitalization extends roughly from 7 months to 7 years, with the most vulnerable period being 7 months to 3 years. However, he noted that the hospitalization experience need not be extremely traumatic if the child is given adequate preparation and if hospital procedures minimize separation anxiety and trauma regarding bodily injury. He also pointed out that separation from parents is but one among many factors influencing the child's adaptation to the hospital experience.

Rutter (1971, 1979) has provided evidence that it is not parent–child separation *per se* that is responsible for these effects of hospitalization. He has been particularly interested in the relationship between parent–child separations and antisocial or delinquent behavior. With the help of questionnaire and interview techniques, he classified the marriages of parents of boys who had either no separation from parents, separation from one parent at a time, or separation from both parents as either good, fair, or poor marriages. In each type of separation circumstance, the proportion of antisocial boys was higher when there was a very poor marriage than when there was a good or fair marriage. Thus, the largest differences in antisocial behavior in boys were associated with the marriage rating and not with separation experiences. In another comparison, he showed that boys from homes broken by divorce, when presumably marital discord and disharmony preceded the divorce, were more likely to be delinquent than boys from homes broken by the death of a parent or boys from unbroken homes. Thus, it was the discord that led to delinquency and not the breakup of the family as such (see also L. J. Yarrow & Klein, 1980).

Clearly, the effects of institutionalization early in life on subsequent behavior cannot be accounted for by one monolithic cause such as a lack of stimulation or maternal deprivation or separation. The effects of these experiences on the social development of the child depend on the age at time of separation (L. J. Yarrow, 1964; Tizard & Hodges, 1978), the quality of the relationship with the mother prior to the separation (L. J. Yarrow, 1964), the type of parental care obtained subsequent to the separation (Tizard & Hodges, 1978), the duration of separation experiences (Spitz & Wolf, 1946), the amount of marital discord or harmony in the parents' relationship (Rutter, 1971, 1979), individual differences including sex differences (Rutter, 1971, 1979; Tizard & Hodges, 1978; Yarrow et al., 1971), and, possibly, temperament differences (Rutter, 1971). Thus, the notion of "maternal deprivation" as the cause of the effects reviewed in these studies is obviously an oversimplification.

Many recent investigators (for example, Casler, 1961, 1967) also have rejected Bowlby's (1944) notion that the lack of maternal influence was totally responsible for these effects, but on different grounds. Casler believes that it is a lack of perceptual and sensory stimulation that is responsible for both the learning impairments and the atypical social functioning of institutionalized children. Impressive evidence has been gathered to support this latter hypothesis and this, in combination with the fact that many of the studies reviewed here have been severely criticized on methodological grounds, has led many investigators to reject maternal deprivation or separation as an adequate explanation of these effects. In a recent review of the early experience literature, Hunt (1979) stated that

> the importance attributed to continuous one-to-one relationship between infant and mother... proved to be exaggerated. Much of the retardation of the first year turned out to be reversible as Skeels and Dye had discovered in 1939 and as others have confirmed.... Moreover, from the findings of a follow-up study of 60 children admitted to a tubercular hospital for extended periods before they reached age 4, Bowlby and his collaborators were forced to conclude that the importance he had attributed to an infant of having a continuous one-to-one relationship with a mother figure had been exaggerated in his WHO report (Bowlby, Ainsworth, Boston, and Rosenbluth, 1956).

However, it must be said that it is impossible to tell from these early studies whether it was the reductions in sensory and perceptual stimulation

alone or the alterations in the social environment, or both, that were responsible for the institutionalization effects. While maternal influences *per se*
probably cannot account for the devastating effects of extreme deprivations,
there is increasing evidence that some form of social stimulation is necessary
for normal social development to occur.

PARENT–CHILD INTERACTION: THE IMPORTANCE OF A RESPONSIVE SOCIAL ENVIRONMENT

In less extreme environments in Western culture, parents are obviously
significant sources of stimulation as well as important determiners and
mediators of environmental effects. This is especially true with respect to the
first two years of life, when parents typically are the main objects of the
infant's social attachment and interaction.

One of the most important early experiences for infants, and one believed to have far-reaching effects on their later behavior, is the experiencing
of mutuality and reciprocity in interaction with their primary caregiver. For
example, in the context of mother–infant interaction, Ainsworth and Bell
(1974) have suggested that competence implies a competent mother–infant
pair—"an infant who is competent in his pre-adapted function . . . and a
mother who is competent in the reciprocal role to which the infant's behavior
is pre-adapted" (p. 98). According to this view, an infant is socially competent to the extent that he can elicit the attention and cooperative care of
others. In addition, "maternal responsiveness" to the infant's signals and
sensitivity to his needs are seen as very important for normal social development.

Goldberg (1977b) has drawn upon and extended this model of mother–
infant interaction proposed by Ainsworth and Bell. She has argued very
effectively that the infant is preadapted to "be selectively attentive to the
kinds of stimulation provided by people and that the infant is equipped with
a repertoire of behaviors which effectively capture adult attention and facilitate effective adult-infant interactions. This in turn facilitates development"
(p. 163). The model which she proposes focuses upon conditions that contribute to feelings of efficacy generated in caregivers and infants by their
interactions, namely the extent to which each member of the dyad provides
the other with *contingency experience*.

Other investigators have also emphasized the importance of these early
contingency experiences for the development of social competence. For
example, Watson (1967) has argued that infants are programmed to search for
contingencies from birth. He has (Watson, 1972) elaborated on what he has
termed an "ethologisociocognitive" hypothesis, to which he mercifully gave
the shorter name "The Game." He noted that during the 13th week infants
smile approximately twice as much to an upright (0°) face as they do to a face

with a 90° orientation (see Watson, 1966). While a hypothesis of innate responding to a 0° face could explain this finding, Watson (1972) suggests an experiential hypothesis—namely, that a special experience called "The Game" is associated with the 0° face. The Game hypothesis is that the 0° face becomes a

> special marker of the situation in which the infant first becomes aware of a clear contingency between his behavior and a stimulus occurrence in the environment. With the experience of "The Game" the infant emits vigorous smiling and cooing, and these in turn are very likely received by the caretaker as inspiration for new games both with other responses and with the smile and coo themselves. (p. 1,090)

What is unique about the Game hypothesis is that no special significance is given to the fact that the infant is interacting with another person. Rather, the perception of a relationship of contingency between a specific stimulus and a specific response is what is important. Presumably, mechanical contingencies provided by the infant's nonsocial environment would be as effective in eliciting smiling and cooing in the infant as the human face, if they were correctly arranged. To quote an often cited statement by Watson (1972, p. 338): " 'The Game' is not important to the infant because people play it but rather, people become important to the infant because they play 'The Game.' "

One does not have to take such an extreme position to recognize that contingency-seeking is an important characteristic of infant behavior or that adults tend to adapt their behavior to the infant's contingency-seeking in gamelike activities. It probably would be very difficult, if not impossible, to construct artificial instruments that could provide contingencies mechanically in such a way that the frequency, intensity, and timing of environmental responses could be as flexible and appropriate as those of the typical caregiver. Still, Watson has called attention to the importance of contingency experiences by his extreme stand.

The hypothesis of the importance of early contingency experiences suggests another explanation for the effects of the extremely depriving institutional environments referred to above: It may have been the lack of an opportunity for the infant to establish the perception of contingencies in those environments that (at least partially) accounts for the devastating effects that resulted (cf. Provence & Lipton, 1962). The institutional environments studied by the early investigators were undoubtedly very nonresponsive to the infants' emerging social skills such as smiling, crying, and vocalizing. Infants were fed, and their physical needs met, on a schedule rather than in response to their needs. Since caretaking events were mostly noncontingent on their own behavior, these infants may have developed a kind of "learned helplessness" (Watson & Ramey, 1969, 1972; Maier, Seligman, & Solomon, 1970) that resulted in the apathy that was observed in the institutionalized children.

Returning to Ainsworth and Bell's (1974) concept of maternal responsiveness, we see that there is a strong relationship between their argument
and those of Watson and Goldberg with respect to the importance of a
contingent environment for the infant's development. Ainsworth, Bell, and
Stayton (1974), drawing both on their own empirical work and Bowlby's
(1958, 1969) formulations, view adults generally as biased to respond to the
species-characteristic signals of an infant in ways that are also species-
characteristic. Reciprocally, infants are genetically biased toward interaction
with adults from the beginning:

> Their sensory equipment is responsive to stimuli most likely to stem from people,
> and many of their behavioral systems are most readily activated (or terminated) by
> such stimuli. A child is preadapted to a social world, and in this sense is social
> from the beginning. (Ainsworth *et al.*, 1974, p. 99)

In their view, a mother responsive to infant signals is an important feature of
the infant's environment and, in an evolutionary sense of adaptiveness, ful-
fills a significant function that forwards survival of not only the individual
but the species.

Responsivity and Social Competence

These infant signals to which a sensitive parent responds are the first
specific index of social competence in the infant, at least according to
Ainsworth and Bell's (1974) definition of social competence: the extent to
which the infant can elicit the attention and cooperative care of others. It is
argued that the degree to which the infant is successful in eliciting attention
and care from his social environment has longlasting effects on his social
development. This is largely an assumption shared by a significant number
of investigators and supported by evidence of at least short-term effects of
differential environmental responsiveness.

Before discussing these short-term effects, we must ask what the signals
that make up this rudimentary "social competence" in the infant are.
Goldberg (1977b) has provided illustrative examples of some of the more
salient and more systematically studied infant behaviors. These include feeding behavior, crying, smiling, and vocalization and are part of the behavioral
repertoire with which the infant comes into the world and which bias him for
social interaction.

For example, during feeding the cessation of sucking behavior in the
infant has been observed to elicit various behaviors from the adult, including
"jiggles" and looking, talking, and touching (Dunn & Richards, 1974). These
investigators have proposed a reciprocal interaction model of the mother–
infant relationship that recognizes the mutuality involved in this context.
Terms such as *communication, conversation, dialogue,* and *waltz* have been used
to describe this relationship (Brazelton, Tronick, Adamson, Als, & Wise,
1975; Schaffer, 1977; Stern, 1974b).

Infant crying is another powerful stimulus for eliciting adult behaviors, behaviors usually designed to terminate crying behavior. For example, Moss and Robson (1968) found that 77% of 2,000 episodes in which infant crying occurred resulted in maternal intervention of some sort. Ambrose (1963) has suggested that crying behavior initially serves the function of maintaining proximity with the caregiver and later smiling takes over this function. Goldberg (1977b) also suggests that early parent–infant interactions are controlled by parents seeking to terminate crying, while in later interactions parents increasingly seek to elicit and maintain smiling.

These are only a few of the "preadapted" patterns of behavior of infants that elicit the attention and cooperation of adult caregivers and lead to mutuality and reciprocity in producing contingency experiences both for the infant and the adult. To emphasize the importance of contingency experiences for producing feelings of efficacy for adult caregivers as well as for infants, Goldberg (1977b) proposed that the infant's readability, predictability, and responsiveness were crucial in her reciprocal interaction model.

In their model of mother–infant interaction, Ainsworth *et al.* (1974) have also viewed the behavioral repertoire with which the normal infant comes into the world as setting him up for social interaction. The caregiver's role has four components: (1) awareness of the infant signals, (2) accurate interpretation of signals, (3) appropriate response to signals, and (4) promptness in responding to signals.

What are the effects of maternal responsiveness or, more generally, caregiver responsiveness on the infant's development? We will review these effects during the first year and then turn to the later effects.

THE EFFECTS OF THE SOCIAL ENVIRONMENT DURING THE FIRST YEAR

Development of Attachment

Maternal responsiveness has been found to be related to secure attachments primarily by Ainsworth and her colleagues. In her work, the quality of the infant's attachment to the caregiver has been assessed typically by using the Ainsworth strange situation paradigm (Ainsworth & Wittig, 1969). This is an eight-step cumulative stress situation involving two separations and reunions, two exposures to interaction with a stranger, and two periods of being left alone. Behavior during the reunion episodes is weighed particularly heavily in classifying infants into one of three main groups: securely attached (Group B), avoidant (Group A), and ambivalent or "anxiously attached" (Group C) infants. About 75% of all infants fall into Group B. Classification into Group A, B, or C is determined by ratings by judges on four variables: (1) *proximity seeking*—seeking to be near the caregiver in terms of physical distance; (2) *contact maintenance*—clinging, not wanting to be separated from the caregiver; (3) *contact resistance*—angry resistance when the mother attempts contact with the infant; and (4) *proximity and interaction avoidance*—easy separation from and continued avoidance of caregiver. Inter-rater reliability for these behaviors and the threefold classification have been reported to be high (Ainsworth & Wittig, 1969; Sroufe & Waters, 1977).

Securely attached infants (Group B) typically engage in behaviors of types 1 and 2, that is, proximity seeking and contact maintenance. These infants occasionally sought to be near their mother and touch her when she was present, but did not cling and whine and were explorative and manipula-tive in dealing with toys in the unfamiliar situation when their mothers were with them. They comfortably left their mother to explore their surroundings in the mother's presence and sought proximity and contact with her during reunion episodes following separation from her. Minor separations in familiar situations such as home resulted in only minimal disturbance, and they typically greeted their mother's return with enthusiasm. Avoidant (Group A) infants also left their mother easily but, unlike Group B infants, did not go back to her when a stranger was introduced into the situation. They were not upset when the mother left and tended to avoid her when she came back. In play situations, they also spent less time with each toy than did Group B infants. In general their behavior was predominantly type 4, that is, prox-imity and interaction avoidance. The ambivalent or anxiously attached in-fants (Group C) seldom left their mothers and became terrifically upset when a stranger came in. They had high scores on behaviors 2 and 3, contact maintenance and contact resistance, during the reunion episodes, being in their mother's arms but clinging and kicking; they often indicated intense distress and cried whether the mother was present or absent.

The Ainsworth strange situation procedure for assessing ataachment generally has been found to be a reliable classification technique (Ainsworth & Wittig, 1969; Matas *et al.*, 1978; Sroufe & Waters, 1977) appropriate for use with infants less than two years of age. Within the 12–18 months age period, this procedure has been found to be developmentally robust in that stable individual differences in the quality of the infant–mother attachment relationship over a six-month period have been found (Waters, 1978). How-ever, most of these findings have been based on data with middle-class families with presumed environmental stability. A recent study with an urban poor population (Vaughn, Egeland, Sroufe, & Waters, 1979), reported somewhat less stable individual differences in the attachment relationship. Specifically, 38% of the attachment relationships of this sample changed over a six-month period (12–18 months) compared with 4% in a stable middle-class sample (Waters, 1978). The changes in classification were found to be related to stressful events—for example, loss of a job—and a generally less stable environment.

These different attachment patterns may be considered the effects of earlier mother–infant interactions, and Ainsworth and her colleagues clearly believe that they are. Generally, mothers of securely attached (Group B) infants have been found to be highly sensitive and responsive to their infant's needs, whatever their particular childcare practices. They had earlier permitted their infants to play an active role in determining such things as the pacing, onset, and termination of feeding. On the other hand, mothers of avoidant (Group A) infants typically have been found to be generally unavailable to the infant in the home. Mothers of the anxiously attached, ambivalent (Group C) infants have been described as inconsistent, vacillating between smothering their children with attention and avoiding them. They were also rated as being insensitive in their interactions with their infants during earlier feeding situations.

The degree of mutuality or synchrony in caregiver–infant dyads also has been found to be important in determining the development of secure infant attachments to parents. For example, Blehar, Lieberman, and Ainsworth (1977) found adult–infant face-to-face play patterns at 6–15 weeks to be positively related to the quality of attachment at 12 months. Generally, infants termed securely attached at 1 year had been described as more responsive in earlier playful encounters with their mothers; their mothers, in turn, were more likely to have responded in a sensitive and contingent manner to the infant's behavior and to have encouraged social interaction. Interestingly, the infants labeled securely attached at 1 year had been more positively responsive to their mothers than to an unfamiliar figure in face-to-face interactions at 6–15 weeks; infants labeled anxiously attached, on the other hand, had responded equally to familiar and unfamiliar adults at 6–15 weeks.

Clarke-Stewart (1973) has provided evidence to support this expectation of a generally positive relationship between maternal responsivity and young children's social development. In a comprehensive investigation, she made repeated observations of 36 mothers and their firstborn children during the nine-month period from 9 to 18 months old. Seven visits were made to observe naturally occurring infant behavior and mother–infant interactions. Six additional visits were made to conduct standardized probes. The home observations included ratings of attachment to mother, reaction to stranger, exploration and play, and measures of contingencies between sequential maternal and child behaviors. The mother's responsiveness to specific infant behaviors (crying, making a vocal demand, calling, getting hurt and crying, etc.) were recorded as well as the infant's responses to specific maternal behaviors (giving, offering, showing an object, ordering, etc.). The mother's behavior was classified as effective and appropriate if, for example, the infant smiled and went to his mother when an object was offered or carried out the mother's order. Thus, maternal effectiveness scores were calculated by classifying each of the maternal behaviors, summing them, and converting them to proportions by dividing them by the total recorded frequencies of these maternal behaviors. The standardized probes included maternal interviews and questionnaires, Bayley Scales of Infant Development, a social-play (laboratory) probe, the four developmental series from the Uzgiris–Hunt Scales, and a language assessment.

The infant and maternal measures were reduced to a manageable set of data by a principal components factor analysis. The strongest relationship found by regression analysis of maternal and infant factors was between a factor labeled "optimal maternal care" and two child factors: the maternal factor was positively related to a child factor labelled "children's competence" and a negatively related to a child factor labelled "fretfulness." The maternal variable most highly related to the factor of children's competence was verbal stimulation. Another finding concerned the relationship between maternal and infant emotional expression: the mother's expression of positive emotion was closely related to the child's positive involvement with his mother and his expression of happiness. Warm physical contact or "cuddling" by the mother was positively related to the child's attachment to her as evidenced by the fact that he tended to stay close to her and to hold her often, was distressed when she left the room, and exhibited marked anxiety when a stranger approached or touched him. Maternal effectiveness was negatively related to infant irritability (by definition and empirically).

Corroboration for Ainsworth's finding of a strong relationship between maternal responsivity and infant attachment also was found. Mothers who were highest on each of three maternal variables—stimulation, contingent responding, and expressing affection—had the most securely attached children. Children of mothers with the lowest scores on these variables displayed maladaptive social behaviors in the laboratory situation. Optimal secure attachment occurred in homes in which the child was not constantly exposed to a great number of people and where the mother was socially responsive and affectionate, but not excessively physical in her contact.

Clarke-Stewart also tried to separate the degree to which the mother's impact on the child's development was due solely to sensory stimulation, as suggested by Casler (1961, 1967), and the degree to which it was responsive, that is, contingent upon the age, state, mood, desire, or need of the infant and the mother's responding immediately and appropriately to the signals which indicated these needs and feelings—in other words, whether the mother's behavior was more than just indiscriminately stimulating. The child's positive involvement with his mother and his language scores were associated more highly with maternal stimulation than responsiveness; but the infant's expression of positive emotion and his Bayley mental test score were more closely related to maternal responsiveness than to stimulation.

A cross-lag correlational analysis indicated that in the area of social interaction the reciprocal nature of mother–child influence was clearly demonstrated. In this area, the child's effect on the mother's activities was clear. The more the child looked, smiled, or vocalized to his mother, the more affectionate and attached to the child she became and the more responsive she was to distress and demands. In turn, the mother's responsiveness to the

child's social signals enhanced the child's later intellectual and social performance.

A recent study of the effects of routine daily separations occasioned by
out-of-home care on the formation and maintenance of infant–mother attachment relationships (Vaughn, Gove, and Egeland, 1980) suggests that
early separations (prior to 12 months) of this sort are associated with
anxious-avoidant attachments. In this study, three groups were constituted
on the basis of the time in the infant's life when out-of-home care began: (1)
before 12 months, (2) between 12 and 18 months, and (3) home care controls.
The mothers of these infants were economically disadvantaged and had returned either to work or to school. The Ainsworth strange situation test was
administered at both 12 and 18 months and the infants were classified as
secure, anxious-avoidant, or anxious-resistant. The major finding was that
physical inaccessibility of the mother due to out-of-home care was associated
with anxious-avoidant attachments. At 12 months, 47% of the infants whose
mothers had returned to work or school were so classified, whereas the other
two groups did not differ significantly in the proportions of infants assigned
to the three attachment classifications. At 18 months, 41% of the infants of
early working mothers were classified as anxious-avoidant and the proportion
so designated in infants whose out-of-home care began after 12 months did
not change. Conclusions regarding these results must be guarded, however,
since mothers who worked in this sample were also reported to have higher
levels of life stress than mothers who stayed home with their infants. In
addition, this sample of mothers and infants was atypical in that there was a
much lower percentage of secure attachment relationships (ranging from
23.5% to 39%) than Ainsworth and other investigators typically find. Still,
the results are suggestive, within this population, of an association between
physical inaccessibility of the mother and anxious-avoidant attachments.

The naturalistic and correlational approach used in the above studies
makes causal inferences problematic. Even though the above authors stress
the bidirectional nature of mother–infant attachment, they appear to favor,
or at least give greater emphasis to, the view that maternal responsiveness
"causes" or "affects" the infant–mother attachment. For example, several
investigators doing this kind of research have suggested that maternal behavior which interferes with (Ainsworth, Bell, & Stayton, 1971; Beckwith,
1972) or restricts (Clarke-Stewart, 1973) ongoing infant activity is positively
related to anxious infant–mother attachment and to the infant's ignoring the
mother's social overtures, and that it is negatively related to eye contact with
the mother, object-sharing with her, and positive affect (Clarke-Stewart,
1973).

In a rare laboratory experiment in this area, Gray, Tracy, and Lindberg
(1979) attempted to examine this hypothesis. They examined the short-term
effects of maternal interference on social behavior toward mother and exploratory play of 40 1-year-old children (20 boys and 20 girls). Mothers in the
experimental group frequently interfered with the exploratory play of their

infants during the first (but not the second) half of the observation session. Interference consisted of repeatedly picking up their infants and temporarily restraining them from playing with attractive toys. This was uniformly aversive to the infants. Mothers in the control group permitted their babies to play without interference throughout the session. A postinterference (or control) free-play period immediately followed. Interestingly, no significant differences between children in the two groups were found in the free-play period in social initiatives directed to the mother (looking, smiling, vocalizing, showing toy, and touching), in responsiveness to mother's social bids, or in exploratory play. Although the authors concluded that these findings do not rule out a causal role for interference when conjoined with other deficiencies of maternal care (for example, lack of maternal warmth or maternal responsiveness), they do suggest that maternal interference *per se* may have no measurable short-term effects on subsequent infant attachment or exploratory play behavior.

Clearly, this experiment does not address the questions of the long-term effects of interference or the ways in which maternal interference may interact with the infant's history with the mother in natural settings. Yet, it does illustrate the need to be very cautious in drawing conclusions from the bulk of the studies on attachment which are naturalistic and essentially correlational. What is needed now are more experimental studies, with long-term follow-up, to put the hypotheses and findings raised by this literature to more rigorous test.

Development of Person Permanence

Another effect of maternal responsivity has been noted by Bell (1970), who found person and object permanence to develop earlier in infants with harmonious mother–infant relationship. She found an interesting horizontal decalage in this group in that the acquisition of person permanence occurred prior to object permanence. She also suggested that harmonious mother–infant relationships appear to act as a buffer for the effects of impoverished environment such as those associated with low socioeconomic status (SES). Low SES infants of disharmonious mother–infant relationship were slower to obtain either object or person permanence than were middle SES infants of disharmonious relationships. This was not true for low SES infants of harmonious mother–infant relationships.

Development of Communicative Competence

A third variable that can be considered an indication of early social competence, communicative ability, also has been found to be related to maternal responsiveness. For example, Bell and Ainsworth (1972) focused on the infant's cry as a communicative signal and assessed maternal responsiveness to it during each quarter of the first year. They then related maternal responsiveness in each quarter to the frequency and duration of crying episodes of infants in subsequent quarters. They found a positive correlation, in the third and fourth quarters, between the frequency of infant crying and the frequency of *non*responding on the part of the mothers. In general, maternal ignoring in one quarter was positively correlated with greater infant crying in the subsequent quarter. The authors concluded that an unresponsive mother is likely to increase the frequency of her infant's crying episodes across the first year of life. They suggest that the lack of a response to the infant's cry on the part of the mother interferes with the development of more mature signalling behaviors. At the end of one year, infants of responsive mothers possessed a wider range and more differentiated modes of noncrying communication. These findings are at variance with the typical advice given to mothers by behavior modifiers and others who recommend ignoring infant crying as a means of reducing (extinguishing) its frequency.

Stevenson and Lamb (1979) have provided some evidence that indirectly supports Bell and Ainsworth's (1972) hypothesis that the caregiver's responsivity facilitates the development of mature communication signals and, thereby, the infant's skill in eliciting others' cooperation. They found that the infant's reciprocal interaction with an experimenter during a home visit when the infant was one year old was positively correlated with emotional and verbal responsivity of the mother as assessed by the Caldwell HOME stimulation inventory. In other words, the mother's responsiveness toward her child not only was important for maintaining the mother-child interaction but facilitated the development of infant communicative competence and sociability with other people as well.

The Social Smile

Another early index of social competence that has been investigated is the social smile. It has been widely acknowledged as very important in sustaining parents through the early months and as instrumental in facilitating interaction and responsiveness in the caregiver. The developmental course of the social smile, in turn, is apparently greatly influenced by the responsiveness of the caregiver.

Observers of the smile in infants (cf. Ambrose, 1963; Wolff, 1963) have reported that the first social smiles typically appear at 4–5 weeks of age. From 5 to 14 weeks of age, a wide variety of stimuli evoke a smile in the infant, including mother's face, nonhuman objects, and strangers. For the normal infant, many of the stimuli that evoke smiling are mediated through vision. This has led some investigators (e.g., Rheingold, 1961) to suggest that it is visual contact, and not physical contact, that is the basis of human sociability.

But what about blind infants? How is smiling stimulated for them? Evidence bearing on these questions suggest that it is not so much a matter of which receptor modality is important but the variations in the manner in which mothers interact with their infants that matters. Fraiberg (1975) has observed that for the blind infant, familiar voices are the prime elicitors of smiles. Like the sighted infant, blind infants smile selectively by 4–5 weeks, but to the caregiver's voice rather than the caregiver's face. She noted that whereas sighted infants smile regularly to a human face, no stimulus except gross tactile stimulation (tickling) regularly elicited smiling in blind infants; and, although sighted infants showed preferential smiling to their mother from 2½ to 6 months, blind infants continued to smile selectively but irregularly to their mother's voice.

Most important for our discussion, unless smiling in blind infants was reinforced through touching, cooing, or tickling, the quantity of smiling quickly diminished. Further, if the blind child ceased to smile because of lack of response, it was very difficult to retrieve it.

Discrimination of the Primary Caregiver from Others

One more indication of the importance of responsiveness in the caregiver for the early social development of the infant is seen in the relationship between mother–infant attachments and the age at which infants begin to discriminate their primary caregiver from other adults. Schaffer and Emerson (1964a), in their well-known study of 60 Scottish infants, found that infants developed indiscriminate attachments to strangers, close acquaintances or parents during the first six months of life. However, intense attachments to specific persons appeared by 7 months of age as indicated by the fact that protest behavior occurred only when separation from specific persons occurred.

However, the beginning of this discrimination and attachment to the primary caregiver undoubtedly occurs much earlier. For example, we know that infants prefer faces to other visual stimuli from an early age (Fantz, 1961); and Haith, Bergman, and Moore (1977), using a technique that allowed them to determine which parts of the face were being scanned, found that 3- to 5-week-old infants focused mainly on contours and edges of faces while older infants, 7 to 11 weeks old, looked more at the eyes. Haith et al. interpreted the increased face-looking, and especially eye contact, as important for the formation of attachment to a specific figure: it "carries special social meaning for the infant's caretakers and plays an important role in the development of the social bond" (p. 8). Further evidence that infants begin to discriminate their parents from strangers very early comes from Carpenter's (1974) demonstration that 2-week-old infants look longer at their mother's face when presented with either the mother's or a stranger's face through a porthole in their cribs. And Yogman, Dixon, Tronick, Als, and Brazelton (1977) report that by 2 months infants can discriminate not only their parents from strangers but their mothers from fathers as well.

This discrimination also may be inferred from the commonly reported "fear of strangers" syndrome in infants. This anxiety reaction to unfamiliar adults has typically been found to peak somewhere between 7 to 9 months. Spitz (1950) was so impressed with the regularity of the time at which this fear first appeared in infants that he called it "eight-month anxiety." Cross-cultural studies suggest that even when childrearing practices differ greatly, such as those in Uganda (Ainsworth, 1963) and on Hopi Indian reservations (Dennis, 1940), infants show the fear of stranger reaction at approximately the same time as do Western infants. This evidence, in addition to Freedman's (1965) finding of a greater concordance of age of onset of stranger anxiety between identical than between fraternal twins, led Freedman to conclude that the onset of fear of strangers is influenced by genetic factors.

However, experience apparently plays some role in the age of onset of fear of strangers. Schaffer (1966) found fear of strangers to manifest itself earlier in families with a small number of children and also when the number of strangers seen by the child was small. In addition, infants exposed to multiple mothering (Fox, 1977; Kagan, Kearsley, & Zelazo, 1977; Maccoby & Feldman, 1972) have been found to exhibit considerably less fear of strangers. It appears that infants who spend a great deal of time with one primary caregiver, such as Ugandan infants (Ainsworth, 1967), are most likely to develop the fear of stranger syndrome, with more intensity and at an earlier age than others. Morgan and Ricciuti (1969) have suggested that fear of strangers may be more marked after specific maternal attachments have been formed, as is likely to occur with prolonged interaction with a responsive caregiver (Bell & Ainsworth, 1972).

Although the notion of stranger anxiety as a typical reaction to unfamiliar adults has been criticized by Rheingold and Eckerman (1973) and Ross (1975) on the basis that greeting and smiling are the frequent reactions of some infants to strangers, there is little doubt that many infants do exhibit fear of unfamiliar adults. However, the age of onset, frequency of occurrence, and the intensity of the reaction may vary depending on the context (Sroufe, Waters, & Matas, 1974), the proximity of the infant to the mother (Morgan & Ricciuti, 1969), distance of the stranger from the infant (Lewis & Brooks-Gunn, 1972), relative familiarity of the stranger (Ross, 1975), or other factors.

In terms of the infant's ability to discriminate the caregiver from others, we can conclude (1) that discriminating the caregiver from unfamiliar adults is a developmental milestone; (2) that fear of strangers must necessarily be based on such a discrimination; and (3) that the intensity, frequency, and age of onset of fear of strangers is influenced by the nature of the mother–infant bond, and indirectly, the maternal responsivity which promotes such bonds.

Development of Obedience

Finally, the origins of "socialization," as exemplified by infant obedience, have also been traced to the responsiveness of the caregiver (Stayton, Hogan, & Ainsworth, 1971). Consistent with their original hypothesis,

Stayton *et al.* found that mothers who were accepting, cooperative, and sensitive to signals had infants who tended to obey their verbal commands (such as "No! No!" and "Come here!") and prohibitions. This was in contrast to mothers who were described as rejecting, interfering, and insensitive, who had infants who did not comply as readily. These authors challenge the predominant assumptions of both social learning and psychoanalytic theory regarding the socialization process: (1) that a fundamental antagonism exists between a child's natural behavioral tendencies and cultural constraints; (2) that a child acquires a set of specific roles, attitudes, and responses that typically conform with social pressures; and (3) that socialization is a result of specific intervention tactics designed to foster social learning or identification. In a manner reminiscent of Rousseau, they propose instead that:

> A disposition for obedience and indeed a disposition to become socialized tends to develop in children reared in a social environment similar to that in which the species was adapted. This disposition does not require as a condition for its acquisition a rigorous and specialized training regimen. (p. 1059)

Although there is very little research bearing on the origins of infant obedience which would allow one empirically to test these authors' notion of a "disposition for obedience," their finding of a relationship between maternal behaviors which promote mother–infant harmony and an infant's compliance to commands appears to be consistent with their position.

The Effects of the Early Social Environment on Later Social Development

Although social development has been less extensively studied in the second than in the first year of life, there are some recently reported observations of mother–child interactions from 12 to 24 months of age which suggest that the effectiveness of this interacting dyad typically increases during this time (Bronson, 1974). There is also some evidence suggesting a relationship between maternal responsivity and secure attachment during the first year of life and social competence during the second and third years of life.

Bronson's (1974) observations can be viewed as extending those of Bell and Ainsworth (1972) with respect to the continued development of the infant's communicative skills and success in eliciting cooperation from the caregiver. She characterized the toddler's attempts to elicit the attention of the mother's behavior directed toward her child as "interactive bids." Generally, she found that children's interactive bids between 1 and 2 years of age became clearer and more markedly differentiated as the children got older. Increased linguistic competence was evident in changes with age such as the employment of fewer "visual check," "reach to," and "give" bids and a higher frequency of "vocal verbal check," "request for information," and "request for help" bids. An increase in maternal responsivity over the second year was observed in that the frequency of the mother's responses to the child's bids increased over the course of the year. This could reflect the child's developing skill in gaining the mother's attention and in communicating needs. Interestingly, the child's ability to elicit positive affective responses ("transmit positive affect" bids) from the mother substantially increased over the second year.

In summarizing her observations, Bronson noted that when you look at the toddler you see a developing, changing organism; but when you look at mothers you see relatively unchanging modes of behavior. An interesting paradox, or contradiction, is that when you look at the *mother–toddler interaction*, you see an increasingly effective dyadic unit. She suggests a "gears model" explanation of those observations, such that successful "meshing of gears," or adjusting of mother and child to one another's style, requires a change not so much in kind of maternal behavior, but in selectivity. That is, the mother more readily recognizes the toddler's moods, emotions, and needs and responds more appropriately to them. The child, in turn, uses feedback from the mother to alter his own behavior and gradually becomes more "socialized."

The investigation of this relationship between mother–child interaction and other behaviors is just beginning. Sroufe and his colleagues (Matas, Arend, & Sroufe, 1978; Sroufe, 1978; Sroufe & Waters, 1977; Waters, 1978) have reported strong relationships between secure attachment in infancy and social and cognitive competence at 2 years. To give a specific example of this kind of research, Matas *et al.* studied infants classified at 18 months as to the quality of their attachment relationship based on the Ainsworth strange-situation behavior paradigm. At 23 months, the same infants were given a measure of cognitive competence (Bayley Mental Developmental Scales) and at 24 months the children's play behavior and problem-solving behavior were assessed. Matas *et al.* found that children classified as securely attached in infancy subsequently engaged in more imaginative, symbolic play than did both avoidant and ambivalent infants, even though the groups did not differ in DQ. In tool-using tasks they were significantly more enthusiastic, affectively positive, and persistent. They also exhibited less nontask behavior, ignoring of mother, and noncompliance on these tasks. However, the securely attached group did show more oppositional (though less angry) behavior in the clean-up period. Matas *et al.* interpret the difference between noncompliance behavior in the clean-up and problem-solving situations for the securely attached group in terms of the adaptiveness of the behavior. That is, they suggest that when cooperation has a clear adaptive advantage, as in the tool-using situation, the securely attached children become readily involved in the task and enthusiastic about it. Sroufe (1978), as well as Matas *et al.*, has further interpreted these results as indicating a fundamental continuity between earlier and later adaptive functioning.

Another interesting question is whether early mother–child relationships have any effect on children's later interactions with same-age peers. To what extent does social competence in the infant, demonstrated in interactions with an adult caregiver, generalize to interpersonal competence with peers? Easterbrooks and Lamb (1979) found a significant relationship between quality of infant–mother attachment and infant peer competence at 18 months of age. They divided securely attached infants into two groups, those infants who explore more and rely less on proximal modes of interaction with their mothers and those for whom proximity and contact-seeking were heightened. Basically, what they found was that the former group engaged in more frequent and more sophisticated interaction with peers. More specifically, they played more with an unfamiliar peer in a 30-minute free play situation, they engaged in more positive peer interaction, spent more time playing with the same materials, and vocalized and imitated their peers more often. Main (cited briefly in Mussen & Eisenberg-Berg, 1977) found a relationship between secure attachments in infants at 12 months and their orientation toward peers, but she examined their peer orientations nine months later. She found that infants securely attached at 12 months were more likely than other infants to demonstrate a friendly interest in peers and to participate in social interactions with them when 21 months old.

Lieberman (1977) also has examined directly the relationship between secure attachments in infancy and social competence of the preschool child in peer interaction. The attachment relationship was assessed by: (1) the child's attachment and exploratory behaviors in the Ainsworth strange-situation, (2) the child's initiative, cooperation, and anxiety expressed during a structured mother–child play session, and (3) interview information gathered from the mother concerning the stability of the caretaking environment and the child's response to maternal separation. Social competence with an unfamiliar peer of the same sex was assessed in a free-play situation. The "unfamiliar peers" were chosen on the basis of having received high scores on a social competency scale. Three areas of peer competence were considered: (1) social maturity assessed in terms of the child's verbal and behavioral initiation of interaction, responsivity to another's overtures, and a number of interactive exchanges; (2) expression of positive and negative affect; and (3) withdrawal from interaction.

One of the most interesting findings from this study was that security of attachment was positively correlated with the competence behaviors grouped as reciprocal interactions (e.g., sharing, giving, showing) and negatively correlated with negative behaviors directed toward the peer (e.g., physical aggression, verbal aggression, and leaving the room). Lieberman suggested that security of attachment is related primarily to nonverbal indexes of social competence with a peer and that experience with peers was positively related to the development of competence in verbal interaction (as indicated by verbal responsiveness and number of exchange chains). The most important implication of this study, however, is that the quality of the mother–child relationship significantly affects (four months) later peer relations.

However provocative these results are, they should be interpreted with caution. It is not possible to determine from this study the causal influences on the interrelationships between attachment, peer experience, and peer competence because the data are correlational. In addition, the correlation between peer experience and attachment was highly significant, and therefore the independent influences of these two variables cannot be separated completely (even though the author used partial correlations). Apparently, children who have developed a secure attachment with a caregiver are given more opportunities to interact with peers.

Further caution is recommended because of the findings of a recent study by Bakeman and Brown (1980). These authors reported finding little relationship between early mother–infant interaction and either social or cognitive ability at age 3. Mothers and infants were seen in 30-minute sessions centered around feedings just before hospital discharge, four times in the first 12 months after the infants left the hospital, twice during the baby's second year, and once late in the baby's third or early in the fourth year. Mother–infant interaction was assessed three times in the first three months of the infant's life. In addition to measures of mother and infant responsiveness, four "behavior dialogic" categories that characterized a broad class of communicative behaviors were applied to the interaction. These were thought to summarize the interaction especially well and included: (1) the percentage of time the infant alone was active; (2) the percentage of time the mother alone was active; (3) the percentage of time mother and infant were active concurrently; and (4) a "measure of how variable or unpatterned the interaction was as a whole"—in information theory terms, how uncertain or unpredictable the events in the sequence were. In addition, ratings of the caregiving environment based on the HOME inventory (Elardo *et al.*, 1975) were obtained. At 3 years of age, when these children were at a day camp for three weeks, measures of social and cognitive ability were obtained. Two aspects of social ability were assessed: social competence (derived from staff ratings) and social participation (derived from videotapes). In general, early mother–infant interactions did not predict social ability at age 3. The only early variable that did predict social ability at age 3 was infant emotional and verbal responsiveness during a home visit at 20 months. This may well have been an infant temperament variable rather than an interaction variable. This finding is consistent with a recent finding by Clarke-Stewart, Umeh, Snow, and Pedersen (1980) of the predictability of children's "sociability" (smiling, vocalizing, and playing) at 2½ years from their sociability at 1 year. Thus, these data provide little support for the notion that how a mother interacts with her baby during the first few months has any particular consequences for later social development.

The Negatively Responsive Environment

Finally, there are children whose signals and needs are responded to but in a negative way. Some of the studies reviewed in the first part of this chapter may have been of this sort. One group of children who very definitely have experienced negative responses to their needs are abused children. In a very interesting recent study, George and Main (1979) conducted what is probably the first controlled investigation of the social interactions of physically abused infants between 1 and 3 years of age. They compared 10 physically abused children with 10 controls (matched on sex, age, race, marital status of parents, mother's education and occupation, father's education and occupation, and the adults with whom the child was living at the time of study.) Trained observers made four half-hour observations of each child over a period of three months at a protective day-care center (raters, however, were not blind regarding the identity of the abused and control children). The abused children differed significantly from the controls in their approach behavior to adult caregivers when the adults made a friendly overture toward them. Interestingly, six of the abused, but only two of the controls, responded by approaching to the rear of the adult or by turning about and backstepping. The abused children also avoided other children almost four times as often and avoided adult caregivers about three times as often as the controls did. All 10 of the abused children but none of the control children responded to friendly overtures from other children with approach–avoidance behavior. Approach–avoidance behaviors involved combinations of locomotor approach with gaze aversion and visual orientation with moving away (crawling toward the child with head averted; creeping away while looking at the child). Seven of the abused, but only one of the controls, engaged in approach–avoidance behavior with adult caregivers. Finally, the abused infants physically assaulted other infants over twice as often as the controls did, and abused infants were found to aggress against caregivers over four times as often as the controls did.

We are just beginning to understand the causes and effects of child abuse. One of the most interesting questions for further research is why abuse in childhood often has the long-term effect of leading to abusive parenting in the next generation.

CONCLUSIONS

The origins of social competence appear to be found in the quality of the relationship between caregiver(s) and infant. In this context, the single most important early experience for infants may well be a contingently responsive social environment. This is probably true whether one defines social competence in broad terms to refer to "feelings of efficacy" or in terms of specific developmental achievements. This may be the single most important early experience that is missing for hospitalized or orphanage children.

A responsive caregiver, sensitive to the signals the infant gives regarding some need, provides the kind of environment in which the infant will most likely achieve the first milestone in the development of social competence, namely, the ability to elicit the attention and care of the caregiver (Ainsworth & Bell, 1974). Although the infant may be innately predisposed to emit the signals involved (crying, smiling, vocalizing, etc.), the maintenance of these behaviors and their appropriate employment probably depend on what happens after they are emitted. To use Goldberg's (1977b) terms, the infant's readability, predictability, and responsiveness may depend in large measure on the extent to which his signals are met in a responsive manner.

The "fit" between the behaviors of the infant and those of his caregiver may be the crucial variable here. Although it may be difficult to measure such meshing of behaviors in the caregiver–infant dyad, several notable attempts have already been made with apparent success in both the first year (Brazelton, Koslowski, & Main, 1974) and second year of life (Bronson, 1974).

This review has indicated that such a fit is related to several early developments that might be considered further indexes of social competence: secure attachments, compliances, early development of person permanence, increasingly mature communicative signals, maintenance and appropriate use of social smiling, and ability to discriminate the caregiver from others. In addition to this kind of fit in caregiver–infant interactions, however, variations in the manner in which the caregiver interacts with the infant may be important for maintaining specific social behaviors such as the smile.

By inference, caregiver responsiveness may also be related to the 2-year-old's social maturity in interacting with peers, since responsiveness is related to attachments and secure attachments were found to be positively related to reciprocal interactions with peers. Tentatively, Lieberman (1977) has suggested that this relationship is strongest for nonverbal reciprocal interactions such as sharing, giving, and showing.

The absence of longitudinal follow-up studies makes it impossible to know the long-term effects of the relative presence or absence of an early socially responsive environment. We can only infer from the follow-up studies of hospitalized and other children separated from their parents, who very likely were exposed to a nonresponsive social environment, that many of the later social behavior aberrations of these children may have been at least partially due to a nonresponsive environment. The degree to which a continued socially responsive environment, beyond infancy, is needed to maintain early positive effects of responsiveness—analogous to the reinstatement process—is also not known. Peer interactions undoubtedly become increasingly important in social development as the child grows older. Although some continuity may exist between the development of social competence in the context of parent–infant interactions and that in the context of peer–peer interaction (Easterbrooks & Lamb, 1979; Lieberman, 1977; Main, 1973), the degree of continuity and the particular forms it takes are largely unknown. The reversibility of the effects of a nonresponsive or inappropriately responsive environment which may result in delay or distorted social development is also not known. Perhaps children's peers, just like the monkey "peer therapists" (Suomi, Harlow, & McKinney, 1972), can be important in overcoming the effects of unfortunate or broken parent–child relationships (cf. Furman, Rahe, & Hartup, 1979). The research bearing on these issues has barely scratched the surface and leaves many questions unanswered, but it is provocative and suggests potentially fruitful directions for continued research in these areas.

CHAPTER 7

The Socialization of Young Children

Thus far, in talking about early experience effects on social development, we have focused primarily on the young child's immediate, proximal environment and its effects on the child, or on the effects of specific dyadic relationships. In this chapter we will turn our attention to the cultural context in which the young child is reared. More specifically, we will turn our attention to the context provided by the childrearing practices employed by parents, the context provided by the child's peer group, and that provided by the larger cultural environment. Both parents and peers will be considered in terms of their roles as socializing agents.

PARENTAL DETERMINANTS OF SOCIAL DEVELOPMENT

Classic Studies

In a monumental effort to describe parental behavior, Becker (1964) factor-analyzed his own data and data from studies using the Fels Parent Behavior Rating Schedule, studies by Schaefer (1961), and the work of Sears, Maccoby, and Levin (1957). The results indicated that parental behavior could be described within a three-factor model. The three dimensions along which parent behavior may be described, according to the analysis, are (1) restrictiveness vs. permissiveness, (2) warmth vs. hostility, and (3) anxious-emotional involvement vs. calm-detachment. The first two factors were dominant and correspond to Schaefer's (1959) earlier work, in which he described a hypothetical circumplex model for maternal behavior. Schaefer's two dimensions in his model were (1) autonomy vs. control and (2) love vs. hostility.

Summarizing a vast literature, Becker believed parent behavior (usually the mother's) could be classified in one of the four quadrants produced by the two-dimensional model shown in Table 1. In this table, he also attempted to show how the parent behavior was related to children's behavior. This table,

Table 1.   Interactions in the Consequence of Warmth–Hostility and Strictness–Permissiveness

	Restrictiveness	Permissiveness
Warmth	Submissive, dependent, polite, neat, obedient (Levy)	Active, socially outgoing, creative, successfully aggressive (Baldwin)
	Minimal aggression (Sears)	Minimal rule enforcement, boys (Maccoby)
	Maximum rule enforcement, boys (Maccoby)	Facilitates adult role-taking (Levin)
	Dependent, not friendly, not creative (Watson)	Minimal self-aggression, boys (Sears)
		Independent, friendly, creative low projective hostility (Watson)
Hostility	Inconsiderate, quarreling with peers (Radke)	Delinquency (Gluecks, Bandura, and Walters)
	Compliant to adults (Meyers)	Noncompliance (Meyers)
	Socially withdrawn (Baldwin)	Maximal aggression (Sears)
	Low in adult role-taking (Levin)	
	Maximal self-aggression, boys (Sears)	

of course, oversimplifies the actual complexities involved in relating parent behavior to child behavior, since factors such as age, sex of child, sex of parent, social class, method of assessment, and place of assessment are known to affect the interpretation of these results (cf. Becker, 1964). Nevertheless, it serves to illustrate the dominant approach that has been taken to investigate parental effects on children's behavior. Typically, some behaviors or attitudes that characterize the parent are correlated with some behaviors or attitudes in the offspring and, when the correlations reach some conventional level of statistical significance, a causal, unidirectional inference is made, that is, that the parent behavior caused the child's behavior. Many of the correlations summarized in this table are of the magnitude of .2 to .4 but reach statistical significance because of the large numbers of subjects used. Becker and many other investigators have recognized the weaknesses in this methodological approach but have been hard-pressed to come up with a more acceptable alternative.

In the well-known Birth to Maturity project, Kagan and Moss (1962) brought back 71 subject who had participated in the Fels Longitudinal Study for further study when they were 20 to 29-year-old adults. Although the primary aim of their study was to look for stability and change in certain characteristics (e.g., dependence and independence) of people over time, they were able to look also at maternal practices early in a child's life and use these as predictors of adult behavior. Four types of maternal practices were evaluated which were defined and rated on a 7-point scale. The maternal ratings were repeated separately for the first three developmental periods, 0 to 3, 3 to 6, and 6 to 10 years of age. For our purposes, the first two of these periods are of particular significance.

The four maternal variables they studied were:

1. Maternal protection—the degree to which the mother rewarded dependent overtures and prevented independent development. Major sources of data included (a) unsolicited and unnecessary nurturance of the child, (b) consistent reward of the child's requests for help and assistance, (c) encouraging the child to become dependent on her, (d) overconcerned when the child was ill or in danger.
2. Maternal restrictiveness—the mother's attempt to force the child, through punishment or threat, to adhere to her standards; the degree to which she punished deviations from her standards. Major sources of data included punishment for any deviation from maternal standards and "channeling the child into activities the mother valued, without regard for his abilities or interests."
3. Maternal hostility—maternal criticism of the child and hostile statements expressed directly to the child or to other adults. Major sources of data included (a) criticism of the child's behavior and derogation of his skills and personality, (b) statements of preference for another sib, and (c) active rejection or neglect.
4. Maternal acceleration—the degree to which the mother showed excessive concern for her child's cognitive and motor development. Major sources of data included (a) concern over the age when the child walked, talked, rolled over, (b) showing off the child's skills and abilities, (c) maternal dissatisfaction with the child's cognitive development, and (d) maternal encouragement of the child to master various skills.

On the basis of ratings of selected aspects of the child's behavior at each of the developmental periods, some significant relationship were found between these maternal variables measured in the first 6 years of the child's life and his later behavior. For example, maternal protection of sons during the first 3 years (period I) predicted passive and dependent behavior in the boy for the first 10 years of life. Protection of daughters during period I, on the other hand, was highly associated with adult withdrawal behavior in the women. There was also a positive relation between protection during period II (3–6 years) and passivity in girls during period III (6–10 years).

Maternal restrictiveness during all three periods was associated with childhood passivity and dependence in girls. However, early restrictiveness of girls was not related to adult dependent behavior. Boys whose mothers were restrictive during period I were minimally dependent (on friends or love object) as adults. However, restrictiveness during period II did have a slight positive association with dependence (on a love object) in adulthood for boys.

Hostility toward girls during period I by the mother predicted independence with love objects and a reluctance to withdraw from stress during the adult years. However, hostility toward girls during periods II and III showed no relationship with these adult behaviors. Maternal hostility toward sons was not associated with later passivity or dependency in boys.

Maternal acceleration showed no striking relationship with dependency for boys. For girls, acceleration during period III predicted an independent approach to problems in childhood and high dependency conflict during early adulthood.

Kagan and Moss pointed out that protectiveness was a better predictor of passivity for boys while restrictiveness was a better predictor for girls. Overall, the four maternal variables were not highly predictive of adult dependency, especially for men. They were, interestingly, poorer predictors of adult passive or dependent behavior than the child's own behavior during age 6–10 or 10–18.

One "sleeper effect" found in this study was that protection and hostility toward girls during period I were the best correlates of adult withdrawal (positive for protection and negative for hostility). The same maternal variables at periods II and III did not predict adult withdrawal as well. Also, maternal protection of sons during period I was slightly better predictor of passivity in boys 6–10 than protection for periods II and III.

Other findings of interest related to these maternal variables are these: maternal restrictiveness during periods II and III were the best predictors of aggressive behavior in adult men and women; acceleration of girls was consistently related to aggressive behavior toward the mother during preadolescence; and maternal hostility was the best correlate of aggression to peers during childhood.

With respect to adoption of sex-roles, maternal protection of sons was the major predictor of nonmasculine sex-role interests in boys as adults; protection of girls predicted the adoption of feminine interests during childhood and adulthood; and the adoption of masculine activities in adult women was highly associated with maternal hostility during period I. Thus, maternal protectiveness apparently "feminized" both boys and girls whereas maternal hostility "masculinized" girls. Maternal protectiveness during period I was also associated with uneasiness in social situations for both males and females and with fear of physical harm in boys aged 3–10. For girls, maternal restriction predicted fear of harm for this age span rather than protection.

Perhaps a reminder that correlation does not imply causation would be appropriate here. The bidirectional nature of parent–child interaction makes cause–effect statements between these maternal treatments and child behaviors dangerous. In addition, the large number of correlations obtained in this investigation makes it very likely that some of these significant correlations were spurious.

Recent Studies

Such parent–child interaction studies have been the major source of our information about the socialization of the child in spite of the fact that they are fraught with methodological problems. Lytton (1971) has observed that the central objection is that distortion of data attaches to all methods of collecting information about parent–child interactions. Therefore, the "experimenter's dilemma consists in deciding, given his basic aims and opportunities for research, which kind of distortion he is willing to tolerate, at the same time doing his best to minimize it" (Lytton, 1971, p. 678). It is difficult to discern a way around these distortions.

For example, the method of naturalistic observation in the home (Baumrind, 1967; Moss, 1965) is immediate and provides firsthand information, but it is limited because the presence of the observer may change the relationship that normally occurs between parents and child (Patterson & Reid, 1969). Similarly, observation of parent–child interaction in an experimental playroom situation permits isolating and manipulating the conditions under which interaction occurs; but, because of both the presence of an observer and the problem of generalizing from laboratory to the home setting (cf. Baumrind, 1968; O'Rourke, 1963), this method of observation is limited as well. Parental interviews are relatively easy and inexpensive but suffer from the fact that parents are extremely ego-involved in describing their interactions with their children (cf. Yarrow, 1963). Consequently, responses to attitude questionnaires may be distorted for the same reasons that parental interviews are distorted. Questionnaires have generally been found to be of low utility for making valid predictions about parent–child interactions (cf. Becker, 1964).

Lytton concluded that combining home and/or laboratory observation with a detailed interview or questionnaire may be the most fruitful approach to take in studying parent–child interactions. This appears to be the most reasonable conclusion to make given the available research. Firsthand observation, preferably in the home, should supplement secondhand data such as that obtained through questionnaires or interviews

> The inclusion of observation would very likely serve to ensure greater accuracy in parents' reports and, thereby, increase the validity of the interview. In this way, two complementary methods could counterbalance each other and thus greatly enhance their combined effectiveness. (Lytton, 1971, p. 79)

Several investigators have attempted to use approaches consistent with Lytton's suggestion. For example, Baumrind (1967, 1971) included parent behavior ratings based on observation by trained raters in the home combined with a parent attitude questionnaire in her longitudinal study of parental authority patterns and their effects on children's behavior. Hoffman (1963) combined home observation with a detailed interview in some of his studies. By confining the questions to events during the preceding 24 hours, Hoffman and others (cf. Douglas, Lawson, & Cooper, 1968) were apparently successful in increasing the reliability of the interview. We shall look at the work of these investigators more closely.

By using a combination of home observation and parent questionnaires,

Baumrind (1967) identified three patterns of parent behavior associated with children's behavior. Parents of preschool children previously identified as self-reliant, self-controlled, explorative, and content were themselves controlling and demanding—but also warm, rational, and receptive to the child's communication. This pattern of parents' behavior Baumrind labeled *authoritative*. Parents of children who were discontent, withdrawn, and distrustful were described as detached and controlling, and somewhat less warm than other parents. These parents were called *authoritarian*. Parents of the least self-reliant, explorative, and self-controlled children were themselves described as noncontrolling, nondemanding, and relatively warm. Baumrind labeled these parents *permissive*.

A second study of preschool children (Baumrind & Black, 1967) confirmed the first in showing that authoritative parental control was related most to responsible conformity to group standards without loss of individual autonomy or self-assertiveness. In a subsequent study, Baumrind (1971) defined membership in one of the three patterns of parent behavior on the basis of scores from measures of parent behavior and attitudes rather than by observations made on the children's behaviors. In this latter study she treated child behavior clusters as dependent upon antecedent parent behavior. In addition, the parent–child relationships were examined for boys and girls separately.

Baumrind was able to differentiate further among patterns of parental authority in this study and to measure their effects on the behavior of preschool schildren. She isolated eight specific patterns of parent behavior and combined them into four general patterns: authoritarian, authoritative, permissive, and nonconforming.

In a follow-up paper, Baumrind (1977) noted an unexpected similarity of the effects of authoritarian and permissive childrearing—namely that both boys and girls reared under these parenting patterns were low on measures of social responsibility and social and personal agency. Social and personal agency refer to internal dispositions that lead children to perceive themselves (rather than forces outside themselves) as largely responsible for their own successes and failures. This is a notion very similar to Rotter's (1966) concept of internal locus of control. Preschool children of authoritative parents, on the other hand, received high schores on measures of social responsibility and personal agency.

Further, these follow-up data from Baumrind's Family Socialization Project indicated sex-differentiated effects of the same parental practices. Personal agency in preschool girls was associated with a childrearing pattern of firm control and somewhat stressful, even abrasive interactions with both parents, but especially with their fathers. Encouragement of independence and individuality had positive effects for girls only if it was *not* associated with lax control or passive acceptance. The results for boys were quite different, the boys with the highest personal agency measure coming from home environments characterized by nondirectiveness, parental warmth, and the active encouragement of independence.

Baumrind (1977, p. 10) believes that for girls competency is actively elicited as part of the pattern of parental directiveness, whereas for boys competency need only be permitted to occur. She argues that these sex differences are due to "three distinct sources of developmental influence: 1) biological predispositions; 2) parental socialization practices; and 3) interaction with teachers, peers and other out-of-family socialization agents" (1977, p. 10–11). That is, biology and society conspire to emphasize passivity in girls, but girls apparently learn and practice personal agency primarily in interaction with abrasive, challenging parents. This argument is reminiscent of the finding in the Kagan and Moss (1962) Birth to Maturity study that maternal hostility "masculinized" girls, that is, hostility was associated with independence and reluctance to withdraw from stress during adult years. Given boys' presumed biological predilection towards aggression and the social support they receive for displays of antagonistic behavior, Baumrind reasons that "boys, unlike girls, appear to benefit from a noncontrolling upbringing which permits their 'natural' assertiveness to be displayed and rewarded" (p. 11).

Baumrind developed models of parent and preschool child behavior inductively on the basis of cluster analysis of items from her various rating scales. With a more theory-based approach, Hoffman (1963, 1970) has attempted to relate parental behaviors to an important aspect of the socialization of the preschool and older child, moral development. Hoffman (1963) consistently has found that parental *power assertion*, defined as including physical punishment, deprivation of material objects or privileges, the direct application of force, or the threat of any of these, leads children to develop a moral orientation based on the fear of external detection and reprisal. On the other hand, nonpower-assertive discipline, called psychological, indirect, or love-oriented discipline, typically leads to a moral orientation characterized by independence of external sanctions and high guilt.

Various explanations have been offered for the effects of power assertion, including (1) the role of the parent as model (Allinsmith & Greening, 1955) during the disciplinary encounter, that is, the parent overtly expresses anger with the power assertion orientation rather than controlling it; (2) the relative brevity of punishment, with accompanying quick relief of the child's anxiety or guilt is more common to power assertive kinds of parenting techniques; (3) the importance of the timing of the punishment according to Hill (1960), in that the physical punishment is likely to terminate at the time of the deviant act with the power assertive parent, whereas love-withdrawal more often terminates when the child performs a corrective act; and (4) the information communicated by different types of discipline (Aronfreed, 1961), for example, power assertion is associated with less information being communicated to the child regarding which acts will lead to reward or punishment.

Most of these explanations, except the last one, stem from the psycho-analytic and learning-based theories of behavior which emphasize anxiety over the loss of love as the primary motivational basis for moral development. But Hoffman (Hoffman, 1963; Hoffman & Saltzstein, 1967) has suggested and provided some evidence to show that the effectiveness of nonpower-assertive techniques might lie in their "empathy-arousing" capacity rather than their love-withdrawing properties. Hoffman and Saltzstein (1967) made a distinction, therefore, between two kinds of nonpower-assertive parenting techniques: *induction* and *love withdrawal.*

Induction refers to techniques in which the parent points out the painful consequences of the child's act for either the parent or others. This includes, generally, a reference to the covert feelings or thoughts, for example, the hurt or disappointment, of other individuals. Love withdrawal refers to the parent's openly withdrawing love by ignoring the child, turning his back on the child, refusing to speak to him, explicitly stating that he dislikes the child, or isolating him. Hoffman and Saltzstein (1960, 1967) have hypothesized that induction, and not love withdrawal, relates most strongly to various measures of moral development. In their view, induction capitalizes on the child's capacity for empathy, and "it is this capacity which provides a powerful emotional and cognitive support for development of moral controls." Indeed, their research has indicated that moral maturity is associated with infrequent use of power assertion and with frequent use of induction. It is, furthermore, infrequently associated with love withdrawal.

In support of Hoffman and Saltzstein's (1967) position, Dlugokinski and Firestone (1974) have recently found with older children (grades 5 and 8) that children who perceived their parents as "inductive" reported greater importance of "other-centered" values and more mature understanding of the meaning of kindness and were rated by their peers as kind and considerate. Power assertiveness, on the other hand, had little value in predicting other-centeredness.

However, the effects of more sophisticated child-rearing techniques, such as inductive techniques, depend upon child attributes. Hoffman & Saltzstein (1967), for example, found no consistent differential effects of various child-rearing techniques on lower-class children. And Borgman (1972) found inductive techniques related to the child's level of moral development only in children with mental ages (MAs) greater than 6 years. With MAs less than 6 years the relationship was reversed. That is, maternal directedness was negatively related to levels of moral development with MAs greater than 6 and positively related with MAs less than 6.

Another current approach to studying parent–child relationships is based on Bernstein's (1970) sociolinguistic theory, which posits that family control systems are reflected by the way parents use language. Starting from this position, Bearison and Cassel (1975) conducted one of the few studies that bears directly on the question of whether parental factors are related to social-cognitive development. They looked specifically at parents' "appeal strategies," of types of reasoning, in some parent–child conflict situations. Their results suggested that some parents appeal to *position-status* factors, whereas other parents appeal to *person* factors involving the feelings, needs, and intentions of particular people in particular situations. The authors found person-oriented appeals by parents were significantly related to role-taking skills in children aged 6 to 7.

The literature also suggests that child-rearing techniques have an impact on very young children's orientation toward others and moral development. This has been demonstrated recently with children 1½–2½ years old by Zahn-Waxler, Radke-Yarrow, and King (1979). These investigators assumed that the core of moral behavior is the child's sense of concern and responsibility for the welfare of others and that altruism and reparation share this core. They investigated the relationship between the ways mothers handle children's transgressions against persons and children's reparation for transgressions and altruism as bystanders to distress in others. They trained mothers to record their children's reaction and their own behaviors in everyday encounters with expressions of distress in other children, such as sorrow, discomfort, and pain. Distress was also simulated by mothers and investigators who went into the homes to observe. Ratings were made during the home visits of the mother's empathetic caregiving and affectively delivered explanations regarding the distresses their children had caused to others. Empathetic caregiving by mothers was positively associated with children's reparation and altruism. Affectively delivered explanations ("You made Doug cry. It's not nice to bite." "You must *never* poke anyone's eyes." "When you hurt me, I don't want to be near you.") also were associated with children's reparations for transgressions and with children's altruism when they were bystanders to another's distress. The authors hypothesized that what is being taught by mothers is a basic orientation toward others.

Another recent study suggests that this basic orientation may facilitate the development of empathy in 4- to 6-year-old girls. Barnett, King, Howard, and Dino (1980) found that girls (but not boys) this age whose mothers were empathic also tended to be empathic. This was particularly true when the mother was markedly more empathic than the father (the sex-stereotyped pattern). The authors suggested that with this parental pattern, empathy may have been identified as distinctly gender appropriate for females, thereby enhancing its internalization in young girls.

A relationship between maternal child-rearing practices and preschoolers' social problem-solving strategies also has been found (Jones, Rickel, & Smith, 1980). In this study mothers were classified according to two dimensions similar to Becker's (1964) restrictiveness and nurturance. Restrictiveness suggested a concern with the child's adherence to a set of adult-imposed rules and expectations. Maternal nurturance referred to warmth, involvement, and recognition of the child's desires and emotional needs. These maternal variables were then related correlationally to children's responses and social problem-solving strategies as derived from a modified version of the Preschool Interpersonal Problem Solving Test (Spivack & Shure, 1974). Maternal restrictiveness was found to be positively related to children's use of an "evasion" strategy—for example, in order to resolve mother–child problems more frequently resorting to escape, denial, or total resignation (e.g., "I'd run away and hide"). Restrictiveness was negatively related to "personal appeal" and "negotiation" strategies in resolving mother–child and child–child problems. Personal appeals involved attempts to mollify the mother's anger with affective appeals or with verbal compensations. Negotiation strategies included obtaining a toy by reciprocal recognition of each child's rights and wishes.

Maternal nurturance was negatively related to reliance on authority. Mothers who considered themselves high providers of nurturance had children who were less likely to turn to an authority figure to resolve a dilemma with a peer. In addition, more highly educated mothers had children who could use a delay of gratification strategy, that is, children who suggested waiting for a desired toy as the appropriate problem-solving strategy.

It is evident in these studies, particularly those by Hoffman, Baumrind, and Bearison and Cassel, that the parental choice of disciplinary strategy is viewed as the antecedent rather than the consequence of the child's behavior. Hoffman (1975) has argued strongly that parents have greater power to intervene in the child's behavior and to elicit compliance. He argues that parents have consistent ways of reacting to their children's behaviors, making it possible to study the effects of their socialization practices on children's subsequent behavior.

However, Bell (1968) and others have pointed out that children differ on congenital characteristics such as temperament and person orientation. Because of these individual differences, they respond differently to the same disciplinary technique. Parents in turn tend to use the childrearing technique that works best with their child. Grusec and Kuczynski (1980) recently reported some evidence that supports the latter position. Mothers of children 4–5 and 7–8 years old described the discipline they would use with their children in situations involving 12 different misdemeanors. Mothers were not consistent in their reported discipline techniques across situations, but, rather, situations tended to elicit the same discipline techniques from different mothers. Mothers were more flexible than the conceptualizations of the child-rearing process described above would lead us to expect. Rather than use a particular technique (e.g., induction) indiscriminately, they tended to vary their discipline technique according to the situation. In addition, mothers frequently said they would use multiple techniques in dealing with a misdemeanor—for example, power assertion in combination with reasoning. Clearly, caution is required in applying existing conceptualizations of parent–child influence.

THE FATHER'S IMPACT ON SOCIALIZATION

Most of the research reviewed in the previous chapter and this one thus far, with the exception of Baumrind's work, has focused on mothers and neglected fathers as the source of influence on the child. However, many behavioral scientists acknowledge that the father plays a critical role in such aspects of the socialization process as sex-role development, moral development, and personality development. In spite of this recognition, relatively few investigators have directly studied the father's impact on these variables. It is interesting to note that the effect of father *absence* has been used as one of the primary techniques to study father effects. Relatively few studies have been designed to get at the unique parental qualities associated with the father's presence. This is, of course, not true with respect to the study of mother effects. The neglect of the father as parent may also be seen in the fact that there has been considerable interest of late in the effects of working mothers on their children but few, if any, studies of the effects of working (or nonworking) fathers. These asymmetries in research on mother and father effects on preschool children probably reflect the temporary cultural forces and theoretical biases that currently exist.

However, a number of recent investigations indicate that fathers and mothers provide different types of social stimulation to infants. For example, Lamb (1976a) drew upon Bretherton and Ainsworth's (1974) distinction between attachment and affiliative behavioral systems to investigate this question. Certain behaviors, such as wanting to be held by an adult or wanting to be comforted when distressed, appear to be directed almost exclusively to attachment figures; other behaviors, such as those involved in the context of social play, are directed to both attachment figures and other friendly adults. The infants were observed in their homes at 7 and 8 months. Both parents were found to be "preferred" over the visitor, especially on measures of physical contact such as seeking to be picked up, fussing to, reaching to, and touching. Over all measures of interaction, fathers were "preferred" to mothers but this was accounted for largely by more affiliative interactions with fathers. No preference was demonstrated on measures related to close physical contact and distress. Lamb concluded that infants appear to relate to their mothers mainly as attachment figures or sources of security. They relate to their fathers to some extent as attachment figures but mainly as the focus of more frequent distal affiliative behaviors such as play. Clarke-Stewart (1978) also found that at 18 months, if children were given a choice of play partners, they chose their fathers more often than their mothers.

With respect to infant play behaviors, mothers and fathers differ qualitatively. Generally, mothers tend to stimulate their babies more verbally from the first months (Yogman, Dixon, Tronick, Als, & Brazelton, 1977) and play more conventional games at 8 months such as peek-a-boo (Lamb, 1977;

Clarke-Stewart, 1978). Fathers typically engage in more unusual and physically arousing games.

Interestingly, there appear to be some sex differences in the effects that paternal stimulation, or its absence, may have. Pedersen, Rubenstein, and Yarrow (1979) have reported positive relationships between male infant social responsiveness and paternal stimulation, but female infants in their sample appeared unaffected by the father's presence or absence. Their sample included 55 black infants (age 5–6 months) living in the inner city in lower socioeconomic circumstances; 27 infants were being reared by their mothers in single-parent families. In addition to a simple classification of the infants as father absent or present, a more refined (5-point rating) scale, based on the mother's report, provided a measure of the amount of interaction the father had with the infant—from no contact to daily interaction involving play and caregiving activities. Father-present male infants were significantly higher on a cluster of eight Bayley items measuring social responsiveness: behaviors such as vocalizing to a social stimulus, making anticipatory adjustment to being lifted, and enjoying frolic play. Male infants who had experienced greater amounts of interaction with their fathers appeared more responsive to social instigations in the testing situation. These findings supported and extended an earlier study by Pedersen and Robson (1969), who had found that the level of stimulation in paternal play was positively related to the male infants' attachment to their fathers. Attachment was assessed in this study by the age of onset and intensity of greeting behavior directed at the father.

Many of the studies concerned with the father as a socializing agent have focused on his role in the sex-role typing of children, particularly of boys. Both learning theorists and psychoanalytically oriented theorists have emphasized modeling and identification as important processes in this sex-typing. However, in reviewing the literature relevant to this hypothesis, Maccoby and Jacklin (1974) and Lamb (1976b) have concluded that modeling *per se* probably plays a minor role in sex-typing. In fact, the evidence is even somewhat contradictory to this hypothesis. For example, there is more evidence that paternal masculinity is related to femininity in daughters (Heilbrun, 1965; Johnson, 1963; Sears, Rau, & Alpert, 1965) than evidence that masculine fathers have masculine sons (cf. Lamb, 1976b, p. 13). Presumably such a relationship would be fundamental to the modeling hypothesis.

When the quality of the father–child relationship is considered, however, the modeling hypothesis does gain some support. Several studies using children of a variety of ages have shown that fathers who are warm and nurturant and participate extensively in child-rearing do have masculine sons (Bandura & Walters, 1959; Biller, 1969; Distler, 1964; Moulten, Burnstein, Liberty, & Altucher, 1966; Mussen & Distler, 1959, 1960; Mussen & Rutherford, 1963; Sears et al., 1957). Bandura and Walters found that even paternal punitiveness enhanced masculinity when the father was nurturant.

There is some evidence also that fathers play a direct role in shaping sex-typed behavior in boys. Hetherington (1967), working with nursery school children, found that highly masculine boys perceive their fathers, but not their mothers, as more nurturant and rewarding than do less masculine boys. Also, fathers of highly masculine boys have been found to have fathers who are decisive and dominant in setting limits and dispensing both rewards and punishments (Biller, 1968; Hetherington, 1965; Moulten et al., 1966; Mussen & Distler, 1959).

The effects of father absence on sex-typing are most apparent if separation occurred prior to age 5. Older boys who were separated from their father prior to age 5 are found to be less aggressive and more dependent, to have more feminine self-concepts, and to use more verbal aggression and less physical aggression (a feminine pattern) than boys separated after 5 years (Hetherington & Parke, 1979). Using observations of male directors of boys in a recreation center, Hetherington (1966) found additional differences between sons whose fathers left prior to, rather than after, 5 years. If the father left before the son was 5 years old, the son scored as less masculine on the IT Scale for children (a measure of sex-role preference). He also was rated as more dependent on peers, less assertive, and engaging in fewer rough physical contact sports. Results with older boys were less consistent.

Lamb (1976b) has suggested that there may be an even earlier critical period during which the father–child relationship is most important. He cites three sources of evidence for this assertion: (1) there is evidence that many fathers interact extensively with their infants (Clarke-Stewart, 1978), that the type of interaction differs from that between mothers and infants (Lamb, 1977), and that infants do not show consistent preferences for either parent (Kotelchuck, 1976); (2) the severity of the effects of father absence is negatively correlated with the age of the child at separation; and (3) Money, Hampson, and Hampson (1957) have shown that sex-role assignment should be made before 18 months of age, suggesting that the child is aware of the sex-appropriate expectations early in life. Since fathers are typically more concerned than mothers about sex-role adoption, Lamb argues that the father's role may be crucial from the first years of life.

Boys raised without fathers are reported to be either less masculine in their sex-role preferences and behavior (Biller, 1969, 1974; Biller & Bahm, 1974; Hetherington, 1966; Lynn & Sawrey, 1959; Santrock, 1970) or else they are described as exhibiting "compensatory masculinity" (Bartlett & Horrocks, 1958; Lynn & Sawrey, 1959; Pettigrew, 1964; Tiller, 1958, 1961). Delinquents have often been reported to have the combination of flamboyant, swaggering toughness and sexuality accompanied by dependency that is usually referred to by the term "compensatory masculinity."

In girls, father absence is associated with difficulties in interacting with males. It is interesting that studies of adolescent girls suggest that early paternal absence may have a delayed effect on their sex-typing. For example,

Hetherington (1972) found that girls with fathers absent showed patterns of heterosexual behavior different from those of girls from intact nuclear families. The form of this disruption, however, differed for daughters of widows and divorcées and also for those whose fathers were lost early (before age 5) and those lost later. When separation had occurred because of the father's death, the adolescent girls exhibited excessive sexual anxiety, shyness, and discomfort around males. When separation was a result of divorce, the adolescent girls were described as sexually precocious and as showing inappropriately assertive behavior with male peers and adults. Generally, these differences were exaggerated when the separation occurred early (before 5 years). Early as opposed to late separation was associated with greater attention-seeking from both male and female adults, greater subject-initiated physical contact with male adults and female peers, and more time spent in male activities and less in feminine ones. One interaction effect occurred reflecting the fact that girls from divorced early families exhibited more prosocial aggression than girls from divorced late or widowed early families. Further, a follow-up study of these girls (reported in Hetherington & Parke, 1979, p. 589) indicated that the effects of father absence on daughters' relationships with men are long-lasting:

> Not only did daughters of divorcees marry younger, but more of them were pregnant at the time of marriage and several are already separated or divorced. No differences in frequency of marital sexual intercourse were reported for the three groups, but orgasmic satisfaction was less in girls from single-parent families.

The presence of an alternative masculine model such as an older brother may inhibit the effects of the father's absence on boys and girls to some degree (Birm, 1958; Rosenberg & Sutton-Smith, 1964; Santrock, 1970; Sutton-Smith & Rosenberg, 1965; Wohlford, Santrock, Berger, & Liberman, 1971). Lamb (1976b) suggests that this kind of finding illustrates that the effects of father absence cannot be determined without considering important ecological variables such as age of separation, reason for the separation, the family composition and structure, socioeconomic status, and the mother's reaction to the separation. Because of failure to take such factors into account, Lamb believes that we can conclude little more than that an affectionate father–child relationship appears to facilitate the sex-role development of boys and girls. We are unable at this time to be more specific.

The evidence bearing on the father's role on children's moral development is equally inconclusive. In support of the hypothesis that the father plays a role in moral development, it has been found that delinquent sons are likely to come from homes where the father is either antisocial, unempathetic, and hostile (Bandura & Walters, 1959; Glueck & Glueck, 1950, 1959; McCord, McCord, & Howard, 1961, 1963; Schaefer, 1965) or absent (Bandura & Walters, 1959; Burton & Whiting, 1961; Glueck & Glueck, 1950, 1956; Gregory, 1965; Rohrer & Edmondson, 1960; Siegman, 1966; Stephens, 1961).

On the other hand, Holstein (1969), with older children, found little father–child similarity in moral judgments but a significant mother–child similarity on Kohlberg's Moral Judgment Scale. And Hoffman (1970), in a review of moral development, concluded that relationships between the child's morality and maternal behavior were more common than relationships between paternal behavior and the child's morality.

Finally, there is fairly good agreement that father presence does facilitate general psychological adjustment in both boys and girls (Barclay, Stilwell, & Barclay, 1972; Baumrind & Black, 1967; Hetherington, 1972; and Palmer, 1960). Consistent with this hypothesis, Hoffman (1961) found that boys from mother-dominated homes have difficulty being accepted by peers. On the other hand, paternal warmth is correlated with a boy's feeling of self-esteem (Coopersmith, 1967; Medinus, 1965; Rosenberg, 1965; Sears, 1970) and his personality adjustment (Mussen, 1961).

In concluding this section, it should be emphasized that most of the studies dealing with the effect of the father on children's socialization have been correlational and have relied heavily on questionnaire procedures to gather information. Investigators have provided little evidence that the questionnaires used have any reliability or validity. And even if these problems were cleared up, we would still be unable to infer cause–effect relationships between father and child variables because of the correlational approach taken. Clearly, more longitudinal studies that include direct observation of father–child interaction are required if we are ever to get more useful data. In addition, many of these research efforts have been flawed methodologically. Characteristics of the parents, such as socioeconomic status, age, sex, reasons for being absent (in parent absence studies); characteristics of the children, such as race, sex, age at onset of parental absence, duration of absence; and problems in design, representative sampling, and generalizability of results are especially troublesome in this area of research.

Peer Effects on Social Development

Although parents may have their greatest influence on young children in the areas of sex-role preferences, attitudes toward social responsibility and moral development, and educational aspirations, peers may be more influential in situations involving friendship choices, prosocial behavior, challenges to authority, aggressiveness, and personal or group identity (Brittain, 1963; Whiting & Whiting, 1975). In settings in which peer interaction can occur, such as nursery schools and neighborhood playgrounds, children have the opportunity to practice and develop these kinds of behaviors.

Description of Peer Interaction Development

Social play with peers of the same age has generally been reported to exceed solitary play in the presence of peers at about 2 years of age (Bronson,

1975; Mueller & Lucas, 1975). Prior to this age, initial meetings between peers are characterized as object-centered contacts (Mueller & Lucas, 1975). Curiosity in an object tends to be aroused by the action on that object performed by the initiating child. When the same infants are repeatedly exposed to one another, however, proximity, sharing, and offering behaviors have been found to increase even prior to 2 years of age. In contrast to the interaction with unfamiliar peers, infant "friends," that is, those repeatedly exposed to one another, engaged each other more proximally, imitated each other more often, and displayed more positive affect toward each other (Doyle, Connolly, & Rivest, 1980; Lewis, Young, Brooks, & Michaelson, 1975). However, Bronson's (1975) observations of infants throughout their second year of life suggest strong individual differences in peer interactions in that those children in her study who were most likely to interact with their peers at 1 year were also more likely to do so at 2 years. By 2 years of age, however, social play was fairly frequent among peers. Actual regulation of one another's behavior through actively seeking and receiving contingent responses from each other probably occurs typically after 2 years.

Descriptively, then, it appears that around 1 year of age, children interact predominantly with their mothers and toys and only distally with peers. By the end of the second year, social play has begun and children interact proximally with peers. Reinforcement and modeling are important determinants of peer interaction in that preschoolers respond to the attention, approval, and acceptance of peers, especially peers of the same sex (Charlesworth & Hartup, 1967). There is a strong, positive relationship between giving and receiving reinforcement and also between giving reinforcement and popularity (Hartup, 1964; Titkin & Hartup, 1965). These observations primarily result from the investigations of researchers with a social learning orientation. In the next chapter, when we consider the interrelationships between social and cognitive development, we will look at the contributions made by researchers with a cognitive-developmental orientation.

The Effect of Early Peer Interaction on Social Development

Probably the most dramatic evidence that early peer interaction is significant for social development is the series of observations on six 3-year-old German-Jewish children by Anna Freud and Sophie Dann (1951). Willard Hartup (1977) has succinctly summarized these observations:

> Earlier that summer, these children—three boys and three girls—had been found living by themselves in a "motherless" ward in a concentration camp in Moravia. Various scraps of information revealed the following: Each of the children had been in a concentration camp since before its first birthday. The mothers of each had been killed within a short period of the confinement, and the children had mostly been passed from camp to camp until they ended up at Theresienstadt. Their care, in terms of food and facilities, was impoverished but not extreme. Socially, however, the children had essentially reared themselves. Adults had not

cared for them other than minimally. Thus, one may regard these 3 year-olds as peer-reared.

After being discovered, the children were removed to a relocation center in a nearby castle and fed lavishly for several weeks until they were flown by bomber to a children's facility established by Miss Freud in England. The significance of this "natural" experiment is recorded in the following three excerpts from the report. First, the children's behavior toward adults was bizarre. ". . . they showed no pleasure in the arrangements which had been made for them and behaved in a wild, restless, and noisy manner. . . . They destroyed all the toys and damaged . . . the furniture. . . . Toward the staff they behaved either with cold indifference or with active hostility. . . . At times they ignored the adults completely." Second, the children showed a high degree of mutual attachment: ". . . positive feelings were centered exclusively in their own group . . . They cared greatly for each other and not at all for anybody or anything else. They had no other wish than to be together and became upset when they were separated. When separated, a child would constantly ask for the other children, while the group would fret for the missing member." Last, the most important observation from this study: "They were neither deficient, delinquent, nor psychotic. They had found an alternative placement for their [attachments] and, on the strength of this, had mastered some of their anxieties, and developed social attitudes. That they were able to acquire a new language in the midst of their upheavals, bears witness to a basically un-harmed contact with their environment." In spite of the horrendous deprivations experienced by these children, peer-rearing had kept their social repertoires intact and preserved a large measure of what may be called "social competence." (pp. 1–2)

It is also very significant that low acceptance by peers in childhood has been found to be one of the best predictors of later behavior problems. These include later behavior disorders and psychiatric difficulty (Cowen, Pedersen, Babigan, Izzo, & Trost, 1973); juvenile delinquency (Roff, Sells, & Golden, 1972); and dropping out of school (Ullman, 1957). In the Cowen et al. study, a diversified test battery including school records, IQ, grade point average, achievement test performance, absenteeism, teacher ratings, self-report data, and peer ratings were gathered on relatively young children (8 to 9 years old). The best predictor of emotional problems 11 years later was peer ratings. Children who were less liked by their peers were more likely to have mental health problems later. These children received more frequent nomination for negative roles and they were nominated for fewer positive roles. Although these children were not observed as preschoolers, these data suggest that children identify troubled peers early and that the identified ones are in some way aware of these perceptions.

Another source of evidence regarding peer effects on later social development is the cross-cultural comparison research. Peers play an influential role in affecting each others' behavior in many cultures, but the way in which this manifests itself varies considerably from one society to another. For example, Swiss (Boehm, 1957) and Russian (Bronfenbrenner, 1967) children have been found to be more resistant to peer influences which conflict with adult societal values than American children. The peer group in Russia is used to assist adult authorities in enforcing the dominant social values of the society from the earliest years (Bronfenbrenner, 1970). The main focus of concern is the collective rather than the individual, that is, the goals and aims of the collective are the standard against which the individual's behavior is evaluated; and the group is held responsible for the actions of its individual members. The primary method of social control is public recognition and criticism, and peer monitors are chosen to evaluate and criticize behaviors deviant from the group goals. Bronfenbrenner believes that the peer collective surpasses the family as the principal agent of socialization at an early age in Russia. However, it functions in a way that helps to maintain the adult system. In the United States, on the other hand, there are often conflicts between the peer group pressure and adult norms. It is not clear from these studies, however, precisely which experiences are important to effect these differential outcomes of direction of peer influence.

Similarly, it has been suggested that the child-rearing processes in China, the Israeli kibbutzim, and the Soviet Union have resulted in children who compete in groups rather than as individuals (Smart & Smart, 1977). Shapiro and Madsen (1974) have shown that kibbutz children behave more cooperatively than city children when presented with Madsen's "cooperation board," a game-like task designed to elicit either cooperative or competitive behavior. In this task, reward conditions can be changed so that rewards are contingent either on group success or on individual performance.

Under conditions in which cooperation among children to reach a desired end was possible but rewards were contingent on individual performance, striking differences were found between Mexican village children and three urban United States groups (Shapiro & Madsen, 1974). In the three United States groups there was no instance of group cooperation. In the Mexican village group, on the other hand, there was no competitive behavior. Anglo-American and Afro-American groups were especially aggressive and competitive. Urban Mexican-Americans were also competitive, but less vigorously so. Kagan and Madsen (1972), in a related study, found that Mexican children made few or no attempts to take toys from peers, whereas Anglo-Americans took satisfaction in preventing a peer from getting a reward even if they themselves received nothing. They suggest that cooperation in Mexican children results, in part, from an extreme avoidance of personal conflict.

One might speculate on the exact manner in which the cultural values of individualism versus collectivism are mediated through both adults and peers. Certainly, the experiences of public recognition and criticism from peer monitors for behaviors deviant from group goals must be important. Extreme avoidance of situations fostering competition and emphasis on cooperation by providing settings in which it is possible and rewarded may be other factors in these cultures. Games children play are typically competitive in America and may be less so in these other cultures.

In addition to cross-cultural comparisons such as these, comparisons of subgroups within a dominant culture have also been made. The early experiences associated with these subgroups are then related to the stable differences between persons which are presumably a consequence of being reared under one condition or another. Perhaps the most often cited studies of this nature are the studies of the Israeli kibbutzim.

The kibbutz is a collective which exists as one life-style within a larger society rather than as the dominant cultural pattern. Each kibbutz is free to establish its own pattern, but kibbutz child care generally covers the first four years of life. A stable caregiver, the *metapelet*, has the primary responsibility for the care of a small group of children. According to Newman and Newman (1978):

> The primary goals of the child care environment include sensory stimulation, motor activity, emotional security, and independence. There is an appreciation of individual differences in tempo, skill, and preference. Freedom of movement inside the house and in the yard are encouraged. A variety of toys are provided at each age level to stimulate motor skills and fantasy play. The introduction of the peer group takes place gradually. Children begin eating together in twos and threes at age one. By age two, the children sit together regularly for meals. Other group activities include taking a walk together, listening to a story, and celebrating the Sabbath and other holidays. (p. 406)

What is the effect of this greater emphasis on peer interaction and group activities from a very early age on social development? Although Newman and Newman caution against assuming that all kibbutzim provide the same socialization milieu, most studies of collective child-rearing have compared kibbutz-reared to home-reared children.

Since kibbutz-reared children spend less time with their parents, the questions of how these children view their parents and how attached they are to them arise. With respect to the latter question, there is mainly controversy and little evidence. Spiro (1954) has argued that kibbutz-reared children have a strong attachment to both parents and peers. He viewed the quality of parent–child interactions as very special times not diluted by the many chores and adult activities that characterize most parents. Bettelheim (1969), on the other hand, has argued that the infant's early attachments in the kibbutz are diffuse and that the kibbutz infant has a less intense bond with the mother.

A study by Maccoby and Feldman (1972) comparing American and kibbutz-reared mother–infant pairs indicates little, if any, effect of these different forms of child-rearing for attachment behaviors—at least, at 2½ years of age. A youngster from either cultural group as equally likely to talk, smile, and show things to the mother and to a female stranger entering the room and also about equally distressed at the mother's departure.

With respect to the question of how parents are viewed by children reared in a kibbutz, Devereaux, Shouval, Bronfenbrenner, Rodgers, Kav-Venaki, Kiely, and Karson (1974) provide some data. Children queried at 11 or 12 years of age described their metapelet as the agent of punishment, disapproval, and discipline, whereas they saw their parents as warm, supportive, and encouraging. Compared to urban family-reared children, they perceived their parents as equally supportive but considerably less critical. Interestingly, the peer group was also viewed by the kibbutz-reared children as serving a controlling or disciplinarian function. Physical punishment, social isolation, and emotional withdrawal were all attributed to peers. Of course, since these children were not questioned until 11 or 12 years, their views of their earlier experiences were confounded and probably distorted to some extent by their later experiences.

Other differences between kibbutz- and family-reared children at later ages include higher self-esteem and more social interest in kibbutz-reared children (Long, Henderson, & Platt, 1973) and earlier development of internal locus of control (attribution of one's own success or failure to personal efforts) in home-reared children (Lifshitz, 1973). At age 9 the home-reared children were much more "internalized," but by age 14 there were no differences between groups. Lifshitz also discovered differences in locus of control scores among three kibbutz groups, particularly at ages 9 and 10. The highest internality scores were made by children who were given the most freedom to organize their affairs and had been reinforced for autonomous behavior, taking responsibility, and making decisions.

Conclusions

It is obvious that the socialization process, whether mediated through parents or peers, has significant effects on the development of individuals. Although current research methods reflected in the literature, do not allow for clear statements of cause–effect relationships, there are certain recurrent consistencies. None of these consistent relationships permit strong conclusions about long-term effects of early socialization experiences, although some are certainly suggestive.

With respect to parental effects, Baumrind's (1971) identification of the "authoritative" parent, as distinct from the authoritarian or permissive parent, has been more than a conceptual contribution (although it certainly is that). Her data consistently support her expectation that authoritative parenting is associated with an orientation toward greater social responsibility, independence, and a sense of personal agency in preschool children. Whether this relationship continues to hold up as the children get older must be documented before long-term effects can be assumed. The application of newer statistical techniques, such as path analysis, to data such as that collected from Baumrind's Family Socialization Project may allow some causal inferences to be made if these children are followed longitudinally. Such analyses would indeed be very informative.

Baumrind also has made it clear that the differential aspects of various forms of parenting on boys and girls must be taken into account in statements regarding the effects of parenting on children. Perhaps her most provocative and important finding in this regard is that personal agency in girls was associated with a child-rearing pattern characterized by firm control and somewhat abrasive, challenging interactions with parents (especially fathers). This finding must be replicated because it has obvious practical implications for parenting.

One of the results of the Birth to Maturity study (Kagan & Moss, 1962) may be analogous to Baumrind's finding, even though the focus was on maternal determinants of child behavior. Maternal hostility in the first three years of life was associated with adult independence and reluctance to withdraw from stress in girls. Maternal protectiveness of girls was negatively correlated with these adult behaviors.

The effects of these maternal variables were, however, highly dependent on the sex of the child. Maternal hostility and protectiveness were not highly associated with adult independence and withdrawal in boys. But maternal protectiveness was the best predictor of dependence and passivity in boys. For girls, maternal restrictiveness was a better predictor of passivity.

Hoffman's (1963) concept of inductive child-rearing and Bearison and Cassel's (1975) concept of person-oriented childrearing share with Baumrind's notion of authoritative parenting the common features of individualized give-and-take, explaining and listening, and emphasis on the child's and others' feelings, thoughts, and behavior. One would expect this emphasis on covert psychological events, particularly in others, to facilitate the development of role-taking ability in children. Dlugokinski and Firestone's (1974) finding that induction is related to "other-centeredness" appears to support this expectation. Hoffman's suggestion that inductive childrearing has empathy-eliciting properties also is consistent with this notion and certainly has face validity. More evidence is needed, however, before these speculations can be definitely accepted.

With respect to father effects, there is considerable evidence that the father plays an important role in the sex-typing of both boys and girls and in the intellectual and academic achievement of boys. Father presence is associated with good psychological adjustment, self-esteem, and peer acceptance in boys. Father absence, on the other hand, is associated with less masculinity and with increased verbal but decreased mathematic achievement on tests and in school for boys particularly if father absence began prior to age 5. There is less evidence that the father significantly affects moral development.

The father effects on girls detailed by Hetherington (1972) are interesting because they suggest long-term effects of early father absence. That is, father absence in the early years, especially prior to 5 years of age, is related to adolescent girls' sexual and social behavior. Further, Hetherington's finding that the reason for the father's absence was related to different outcomes in adolescence is particularly provocative. These findings deserve further substantiation.

With respect to early peer effects on later development, the findings of Cowen *et al.* (1973) that low acceptance by peers is one of the best predictors of behavior disorders at maturity is important. Also impressive are the effects of the "peer collective" (Bronfenbrenner, 1970) on the social development of children in cultures such as those in Russia, China, and Israel. The peer collective apparently operates as an effective socializing agent leading to more cooperative and less competitive behavior between individuals. Peers in these cultures apparently reinforce and enforce adult norms, and competition between groups is more likely for them than individualistic competition. Just the opposite appears to be true for children reared in the highly individualistic American culture.

The specific processes involved in peer interaction that produce these results need further elucidation. For example, giving and receiving reinforcement, particularly from 4 years of age on (Charlesworth & Hartup, 1967), may be one important factor, as may modeling (Hartup & Coates, 1967). These factors have been found to play important roles in establishing peer acceptance and popularity. However, the development of role-taking ability (Piaget & Inhelder, 1969) may also facilitate positive peer interaction, although at this time it is unclear whether role-taking ability is a determinant or a consequence (or both) of peer interaction.

Further investigations with variables such as these should enable greater articulation of the specific processes responsible for early experience effects. Experimental studies are possible and should become more frequent in the study of these processes. However, naturalistic longitudinal studies also are required for studying many aspects of the effects of parents and peers as socializing agents. There is certainly enough correlational evidence to indicate that efforts in these directions would have a high probability of being fruitful even though they might be expensive in terms of time and resources. One hopes that more attention will be directed toward the long-term effects of the home environment in future research.

The Relationship between Social and Cognitive Development

The young child's interpersonal environment obviously has powerful effects on both his cognitive and social development. To consider these effects separately, as we have attempted to do thus far, is instructive but in many ways artificial. It is becoming more and more obvious that social and cognitive competencies develop from shared organizational processes and are inextricably bound up with each other. Thus, any specific kind of social interaction is inevitably partially dependent on cognitive processes; cognitions, in turn, are influenced and modified by interpersonal interactions.

In this chapter we will explore some of the interrelationships between these two threads of development and, where possible, attempt to interweave them into a more complete tapestry of what the infant and young child are like. We will not do this in any exhaustive way, but rather try to give some representative samples of areas of study in which this kind of integration is further developed. We will also attempt to look at the common role that early experience plays in both social and cognitive development and how it forms a kind of inevitable bridge between the two.

SOCIAL-COGNITIVE RELATIONSHIPS IN INFANCY: THE MOTIVATIONAL LINK

In thinking about the role that early experience plays in both social and cognitive development, it is helpful first of all to recognize the complete interdependence of cognition and motivation in infancy. Piaget (1952), for example, has emphasized the goal-directedness of intelligent behavior and did not draw the neat boundaries typical of the academic psychologist between thinking and motivation. Although his theory is thought of as a "cognitive theory," his notions of cognitive development have provided the basis for some modern conceptualizations of intrinsic motivation. One such conceptualization has been provided by Hunt (1961), who was influenced by Piaget and others in defining intrinsic motivation as "motivation inherent in information processing and action." From this point of view, activity is a goal in itself and intrinsic motivation is inherent in all forms of organism-environment interaction and, especially, in the organism's use of his senses.

In order to understand how early experiences influence behavior from this cognitive-motivational view, one other aspect must be emphasized. Hunt (1965) assumed that behavior is most strongly activated when there is a moderate discrepancy between the individual's "standards" and the ongoing input. As Ulvund (1980) has put it, "these standards . . . may take the form of adaptation levels, of expectations . . . and these expectations are *derived from previous experience*" (p. 24, italics ours). Thus, the epigenesis of standards becomes an important aspect of motivational development.

For our purposes, it is important to recognize two features of this argument. First, some existing level of cognitive organization is a precondition for the operation of this motivational principle, that is, some standard against which incoming information can be matched; and second, the existing level of cognitive organization or, in Piaget's terms, the cognitive structure itself results, at least in part, from early experiences. That is, the discrepancy hypothesis implies that the individual's reaction to a new stimulus is a function of the degree of discrepancy between new informational input and the individual's earlier experience—what Hunt (1965) has labeled the "problem of the match."

In infancy, cognition and motivation are two closely intertwined processes that probably cannot be identified as two separate processes in operation. As L. J. Yarrow and Pedersen (1976) have noted, "the need to reconcile discrepancies, to master the environment, and to repeat activities that produce interesting results all involve more than cognition. They require the coordination of intellect with motivation."

The amalgamation of the infant's cognitive and affective processes is evident in his interaction with both the physical and social environments. These encounters influence both social and cognitive development, and these two lines of development are themselves interrelated. For example, perceptual discrimination and some form of rudimentary memory must be involved in the infant's ability to recognize his mother and discriminate her from other people; some central imagery process must be present for the development of "person permanence," and the infant's association of his own actions with their effects on other people is a learning process dependent on experience.

The nature and quality of the infant's early experiences, therefore, simultaneously affect both his cognitive and social development. In the infancy period we can scarcely separate what is cognitive from what is social. A responsive social environment has facilitative effects on both social and cognitive development, and advances in cognitive development permit more complex levels of social interaction. Early experiences establish the standards against which new input, whether social or nonsocial in nature, is compared and, from the above analysis, determine the degree of interest the infant has in these events.

In order to illustrate the complex way in which cognitive and motivational factors are interrelated with each other and also with social development, let us consider the development of the social smile. One explanation that has been offered for why different events cause smiling at different ages in infants presumes that they develop schemata, or memory images, of objects they encounter in their environments (Kagan, 1967). From this point of view, the infant is seen as an information-processing organism who makes sense of incoming information by forming mental representations of external events. After a sufficient amount of experience with an object or event (for example, with the mother's face), the infant retains or builds up a schema of it. This schema is described as an inexact duplicate of the represented phenomenon, like a caricature highlighting the most distinctive elements of it. In the case of the mother's face, the most distinctive elements are probably the eyes and, perhaps, the oval shape. During the period when the schema for the face is not yet firmly established, probably in the first 4–6 months of life (Kagan, Henker, Hen-Tov, Levine, & Lewis, 1966), repeated presentations of a face (or facelike) stimulus gradually come to elicit a smile. According to this explanation, the infant apparently begins to assimilate the stimulus to his schema of the face, or, in other words, shows perceptual recognition of it. After the schema has been firmly established, discrepant stimuli, that is, stimuli which are similar yet different in some salient way (such as a "scrambled face") elicit more attention and smiling. It is generally thought that moderate discrepancies from established schemata attract the greatest attention (McCall & Kagan, 1967).

Another application of this kind of cognitive processing theory is seen in interpretations of the classical "fear of strangers" and "separation anxiety" syndromes in infants which are often explained in terms of discrepancies from an already established schema. Let us look at these phenomena more closely. The general developmental sequence in the course of attachment/development is from smiling at a strange face at 4 months, to displaying anxiety to a strange face by 6–8 months, to protest of separation from a familiar person (including their face) at about 12 months. Schaffer and Emerson (1964a) conducted a well-known study of attachment emergence that illustrates this typical sequence. The amount of protest behavior emitted by children in specific separation situations, such as being left in a crib, was reported by mothers in monthly interviews. In addition, monthly observations were made of the infants' fear responses to the approach of a stranger. It was not until about 7 months of age that very intense, specific attachments occurred. Prior to this time, infants were relatively undiscriminating in their attachments to people, that is, they cried with (and smiled at) contact and attention from strangers and parents alike. However, at 7 months, the children protested only when separation from certain people, usually the mother, occurred. And it was about this time that fear reactions to strangers also occurred. Other investigators have reported similar findings, although there is considerable variation among babies in the age at which specific attachments peaked. For example, Kotelchuck (1972) found that separation protest peaked between 12 to 18 months in American babies, while Ainsworth (1967) found that Ugandan babies developed specific attachments slightly earlier, and fear of strangers later, than the American or Scottish samples. However, the same general developmental sequence is typically found.

From a cognitive view point, the infant must have already developed object permanence, or, more accurately, person permanence, through the establishment of a schema representing the primary caregiver in order for separation protest and fear of strangers to occur. That is, the person must still exist for the infant even when out of sight; and some memory respresentation must be available for recognition of the caregiver or stranger to occur. Ainsworth (1973) and Schaffer (1958) have stated clearly that attachment itself, in the sense of an enduring tie of the infant to the mother, requires a certain level of cognitive competence. That is, the infant must appreciate that objects outside the perceptual range still exist in order for the special relationship with the mother to span the times when she is away. (See Corter, Zucker, & Galligan, 1980, for a recent laboratory experiment that supports this hypothesis.)

However, it is important to recognize that the schema that develops is not for the mother as an individual so much as for the mother in particular contexts. For example, Littenberg, Tulkin, and Kagan (1977) found that infants protest less when the mother leaves them at home than when she leaves them in a strange laboratory, and more in the house when the mother departs through a seldom used door than when she leaves through a door she often uses.

Evidence of another sort confirming the close relationship between cognitive and social developmental processes in infants comes from a study by L. J. Yarrow and Pedersen (1976). These investigators used the items of the Bayley infant scales to distinguish a number of aspects of infant development that formed a series of item clusters. These clusters of items were grouped together on a conceptual basis rather than on the basis of a factor or cluster analysis. Then they examined the statistical interrelationships among these clusters (for those items applicable to 6-month-old infants). One cluster, labeled "social responsiveness," was composed of eight items measuring the infant's early responses to people. The infant's smiling, vocalizing, making anticipatory adjustments to being picked up, approaching and smiling at his mirror image, and engaging in simple play were the kinds of behaviors tapped by these items. Yarrow and Pedersen viewed these as the infant's first positive approaches to others. They compared this cluster of behaviors to

Piaget's secondary circular reactions in that they were goal-directed and involved obtaining feedback. But for this "social responsiveness" cluster, the feedback is from people rather than objects.

There was a high correlation between the social responsiveness cluster and the Bayley Mental Development Index ($r = 0.71$) which Yarrow and Pedersen interpreted as reflecting the common psychological properties in both measures, a reaching out and responding to people and objects. The social responsiveness cluster was generally more independent of other clusters than were the motor or cognitive-motivational clusters.

Another cluster, labeled "vocalization and language" was significantly related to social responsiveness. This cluster was composed of six items dealing with rudimentary aspects of language: responding to his own name or nickname, making appropriate responses or adjustments to words, vocalizing simple syllables, and vocalizing expressive aspects of language such as attitudes and jargon. This vocalization and language cluster had very low relationships with all other clusters except social responsiveness ($r = 0.61$), which Yarrow and Pedersen interpreted as reflecting the common social character of these two measures. This cluster was also correlated ($r = 0.48$) with the Bayley Mental Development Index.

Thus, it is clear that cognitive factors play an important role in social exchange processes from infancy. It is equally clear that the people in the infant's environment, particularly the primary caregiver, stimulate cognitive growth through direct and indirect interaction with the infant. Although cognitive, motivational, and social processes remain intertwined to some extent in the individual's adaptive functioning throughout life, they are probably never so inseparable as in the first two years of life. With the increasing differentiation that comes with development, each of these areas of functioning becomes increasingly identifiable as an entity worthy of study in its own right, although never totally divorced from its relationships with other aspects of the organism's functioning.

SOCIAL-COGNITIVE RELATIONSHIPS DURING THE PRESCHOOL YEARS

As the child grows older, it is likely that the development of interpersonal competence depends even more heavily than before on cognitive factors. Lee (1975) has pointed out that social encounters inevitably involve such processes as "decision making, problem solving, information processing, and role taking" and that cognitive and social processes are inextricably bound up together in some manner (p. 208). Lee has suggested that we view the developmental course of interpersonal competence in terms of structures similar to Piaget's cognitive structures. Thus, social competence could be defined as "the attainment of a set of logically consistent structures and operations through which a person can view and act on the world" (Lee, 1975, p. 221).

From this point of view, research in this area should be concerned with how children acquire *knowledge* about interpersonal relations and the ability to make accurate *predictions* and *inferences* about the thoughts, feelings, and behavior of others (and to interact accordingly). Lee suggests that this approach will eventually lead to study of the development of *strategies* of interaction, particularly those which permit the maintenance of reciprocity or mutual exchange, and of how children acquire the ability to *conserve* the social situation and social partner, that is, to perceive "the invariant features of social partners and social settings, despite their transformation in space and time" (Lee, 1975, p. 211).

For the most part, however, this area of research is underdeveloped. In addition, apart from the area of "perspective-taking" development (discussed below), initial efforts at examining these social-cognitive relationships have been somewhat discouraging. For example, Emmerich, Cocking, and Sigel (1979) found little evidence for reciprocity between the cognitive and social domains in preschool children. They examined short-term longitudinal relationships between test measures of cognitive processes—syntax production, word meanings (Peabody Picture Vocabulary Test), nonverbal and verbal operativity in problem solving—and ratings of classroom behaviors observed during free play. Social measures were derived from a three-dimensional model defined by (a) extroversion versus introversion, (b) love versus hostility, and (c) a variable described as "task orientation" (autonomous achievement, cognitive activity, fine manipulative activity, artistic activity, gross motor activity, sociodramatic activity, and fantasy activity—see Emmerich, 1977). The results did not demonstrate strong relationships between social and cognitive variables. Certain cognitive processes facilitated social adaptation, but social adaptation apparently did not feed back to modify these cognitive processes. The authors concluded that cognitive and social functioning are linked by partially overlapping processes rather than by strong mutual interactions.

This view is similar to Lee's (1975) view that social and cognitive functioning depend on shared organizational properties (structures) that are primarily cognitive in nature. The body of literature that gets most directly at these social-cognitive relationships in preschool children is that dealing with the development of perspective-taking skills. This area of research provides one of the richest sources for studying the acquisition of social knowledge and the testing of strategies in interpersonal exchanges.

After a brief review of the development of perspective-taking skills in preschool children, we will look at parental and peer effects on the development of perspective-taking skills. Since we have reviewed already (in Chapter 7) the parental effects on role-taking ability in preschool children, we will only briefly summarize these effects in this context. We will devote more space to peer effects on social-cognitive development.

Finally, we will examine the relationship between perspective-taking skills and social behavior, particularly prosocial behavior; and the interactive effects of perspective-taking skills and personality variables as they relate to social behavior in the preschool child.

The Development of Perspective-Taking Skills

Piaget has demonstrated that with increasing age (from 4 to 11 years) children show an increasing ability to visualize literally alternative spatial position, for example, to predict the appearance of three papier-mâché mountains from various vantage points (Piaget & Inhelder, 1956). This developing capacity for perceptual shifting or decentering has been methodologically replicated with tighter experimental controls (Cowan, 1967; Lovell, 1959; Sullivan & Hunt, 1967). In addition, conceptual perspective-taking skills assessed through game and story tasks (DeVries, 1970; Feffer, 1959; Selman, 1971; Selman & Byrne, 1974) have been demonstrated to follow an age-related trend toward increasing perspective-taking ability. Most of these earlier studies have indicated that the preschool child is mainly egocentric with little or no perspective-taking ability. The implication of this research for the social development of preschoolers is that their inferences about others' thoughts, feelings, and intentions are likely to be distorted and inaccurate.

However, there is increasing evidence that the preschool child is not so profoundly egocentric as Piaget's early findings may have suggested. Studies by Flavell (1974)—and also the study by Masangkay, McCluskey, McIntyre, Sims-Knight, Vaughn, and Flavell (1974) with children between 2 and 5 years of age—indicate that the preschooler has at least a primitive understanding that others can have a visual perspective other than his own but he is limited to identifying *what* another person sees that he himself does not see and cannot tell you *how* it appears to the other. For example, Masangkay *et al.* showed a card with different pictures on each side to their subjects. Then they placed the card vertically between subject and experimenter. Next, these questions were asked: "What do *you* see?" and "What do *I* see?" Two- and three-year-olds typically failed the second question—they could apparently represent objects but not another's perspective. However, many 3- to 5-year-olds demonstrated the ability to answer the second question correctly, indicating that they had the capacity to represent *what* another person sees when they themselves do not see the object. According to Flavell (1974), however, they are not yet able to represent *how* objects appear to the other person, as is demanded in the three-mountain task.

Several recent studies go even further in that they challenge Flavell's conclusion that 4- and 5-year-olds are unable to represent *how* objects appear to a person who has a different vantage point. Borke (1975) has argued that the task typically presented to children for communicating their perceptual role-taking skills has frequently been beyond the cognitive response capabilities of most children below 9 years of age. She cites a number of investigators (Fishbein, Lewis, & Keiffer, 1972; Hoy, 1975; Huttenlocher &

Presson, 1973) who have studied the effects of altering both the task and the mode of responding on children's ability to reproduce another's perspective. All of these studies indicate that success in demonstrating perceptual role-taking by preschool and elementary school children varies with both the dimensions of the task and the type of response required. In two of these studies (Fishbein *et al.*, 1972; Huttenlocher & Presson, 1973) as well as in Borke's own study, the researchers had subjects rotate a three-dimensional scene on a turntable device (like a "lazy Susan") to reproduce the other's point of view. This procedure was apparently easier for the preschoolers than either (a) indicating another's perspective by pointing to a picture representing it or (b) reconstructing the other's viewpoint with replicas of the display objects. Significantly fewer errors by children of all ages were reported when they were simply required to rotate the scene to reproduce the other's view. Fishbein *et al.* reported that 3- to 5-year-olds correctly predicted the other's perspective 90% of the time when they used the rotation task. Similarly, Borke found that 3- and 4-year-olds correctly reproduced the other's perspective 79% to 90% of the time with various displays differing in complexity. However, on Piaget and Inhelder's mountain scene, 3-year-olds gave only 42% correct responses and 4-year-olds gave 67% correct responses. Clearly, the nature of the task and the mode of response required of children are important considerations in spatial decentering tasks.

Interrelationship among Perspective-Taking Abilities

Piaget (1970) has suggested that cognitive and social empathy skills are highly interrelated. As Shantz (1975) has noted, Piaget suggested this interrelation by his use of the term *egocentrism* to apply to a number of cognitive problems in which the child lacked the ability to differentiate his own perspective or needs from those of another. However, at no time did Piaget test for the generality of egocentrism by measuring the same group of children on a battery of tasks measuring egocentrism (Shantz, 1975).

To test for the generality of egocentrism or, conversely, perspective-taking skills among preschool children, Van Lieshout, Leckie, and Smits-Van Sonsbeek (1973) administered nine perspective-taking tasks to 142 3- to 5-year-old children. The tasks measured the following: (a) recognition of role attributes, (b) recognition of role behavior of family member, (c) choosing a gift, (d) recognition of needs, (e) empathy (Borke, 1971), (f) visual perspective (Flavell, 1968), (g) three-dimensional visual perspective, and (h) left–right identification. Except for the left–right identification task, all correlations between the tasks were significant. The magnitudes of the correlations were not high ($r = .48$ to $.12$). This study suggests a low to moderate relationship among various role-taking skills in preschool children. Factor analysis, on the other hand, revealed that one major factor accounted for a third of the variance between the correlated measures. The authors interpreted this latter finding to indicate that perspective-taking is either a single or a series of parallel constructs.

Rubin and Maioni (1973), testing older children on a series of perspective-taking tasks, were able to identify a single factor which accounted for 57% of the variance among role-taking tests. However, test intercorrelations were moderate (.31 to .36), even after mental age and chronological age were statistically controlled.

In a more recent study on the congruency of perspective-taking abilities, Hudson (1978) controlled for three sources of variance which she felt were primarily responsible for the low correlations among measures. Specifically, she selected three tasks to assess children's abilities to infer another's intentions, thoughts, and feelings. The tasks were designed to control for variance due to inconsistencies in (a) the type of inference, (b) the type of response, and (c) the task format. The resulting measures examined children's abilities to make inferences about another's psychological properties. All tasks required verbal responses to structured interview questions and were adapted from videotaped presentations to approximate the full range of cues typically available to children to make social inferences.

The correlation between thought and feelings tasks was .25, but neither task was significantly correlated with intentions. Within-task correlations among items were also low to moderate. However, when the researchers divided the scores on each task, grouped the children into four categories (high, moderately high, moderately low, and low), and assessed the consistency with which each child scored at the same level on all tasks, more children than expected by chance alone obtained consistent and moderately consistent scoring patterns.

Although Hudson controlled for these measurement problems, the failure of her research to find significant intercorrelations among role-taking tasks may reflect an additional measurement problem—the use of a restricted range of scores. In existing measures, a child is given one score, either a perspective-taking or nonperspective-taking score for each test item. The scores then are summed across all items to form the child's overall perspective-taking index. Unless a sufficient number of test items are used, little variation in total test scores exists. Comrey (1973) suggested that measures must have at least a 12-point variance in scores before reliable correlations may be assessed. Few measures meet this criterion. Thus, the failure to obtain consistent results among studies may be due, in part, to the restricted range of scores in present measures.

The Effects of Parents and Peers on Social-Cognitive Development

Parental Effects.   In Chapter 7, several parent–child interaction styles were found to be related to the development of perspective-taking skills in children. Hoffman and Saltzstein's (1967) identification of the "empathy-arousing" capacities of nonpower-assertive parenting techniques, particularly the parental use of induction, is one such style. The explaining of consequences of the child's acts on others, the references to the covert feelings and thoughts of others, and the guilt induction associated with this style of parenting appear to be associated with greater role-taking ability in children, greater importance of "other-centered" values, and a more mature understanding of the meaning of kindness (Dlugokinski & Firestone, 1974). In addition, parental use of "person-oriented" as opposed to "position-oriented" appeals has been found to be related to role-taking skills in children (Bearison & Cassel, 1975), as has just the simple opportunity for social-verbal interaction (Hollos & Cowan, 1973). Thus, the early experiences associated with these kinds of parent–child interaction syles and opportunities for social-verbal interaction are the most likely precursors of the development of adequate perspective-taking abilities in young children.

Peer Effects. Piaget suggested that one of the most important factors leading to the development of role-taking in the child is the interaction of the child with the peer. It is the process of

> social exchange . . . [between peers] that gives rise to the process of gradual structuration or socialization which leads from a state of relative lack of coordination or differentiation between the child's own point of view and that of others to a state of coordination of points of view and cooperation in action and communication. (Piaget & Inhelder, 1969, p. 120)

From this viewpoint, the development of role-taking skills comes primarily through social interactions with peers, especially through conflicts and arguments. During these interactions the child receives information that is dissonant with his views, thus creating a conflict in which he may be required to take another's point of view.

Unlike the child–adult interactions in which the type of play and structure of the social interaction are controlled primarily by the adult, the peer environment requires that the child actively construct his interactions with others around play. The type of play, then, both encourages and demands the development of peer interactions which in turn lead to the development of role-taking skills. The facts that social play is contingent on interactions and activities between children, that it creates a long-sustained contact which invites mutual discovery of interpersonal contingencies, and that it allows for conflict over differing points of view all suggest that social play stimulates the development of role-taking. Thus, the type of play and exposure to peers are both important factors influencing the development of role-taking skills.

The development of role-taking skills, in turn, may have an important effect upon the child's behavioral interaction with peers. For example, Feshbach and Feshbach (1969) found that role-taking was an inhibitor of overt aggression in older boys. In general, these findings suggest that for older boys the ability to take the role of another is related to a reduction in aggression. However, the Feshbachs' findings for preschool boys and girls are somewhat confusing and not supportive of the expected relationship between role-taking and social behavior stemming from Piaget's theory.

Levine and Hoffman (1975), in an investigation of the relationship between conceptual role-taking and cooperative acts in 4-year-olds, found no relationship. This finding, coupled with Feshbach and Feshbach's (1969) findings, suggests that preschool children's performance on role-taking tasks is not very predictive of their behavior in interaction with their peers. The results are not clearcut, however.

Deutsch (1974) investigated the relationship between communicative egocentrism and two measures of popularity in 60 female preschoolers. Popularity was measured by a picture sociometric test and observational measures of the occurrence of interactions in the classroom. Communicative egocentrism was measured by a modified version of the Glucksberg, Krauss, and Weisberg (1966) task. Specifically, each child was asked to describe six nonsense figures, one at a time, to a female experimenter who sat directly behind the child. The mean number of distinctive features used by the child to describe each item was added to a score representing the child's responses to the listener's inquiry for additional information. Communicative egocentrism was significantly related to the amount of social interactions of female preschoolers but not to the sociometric measure of popularity.

Thus, Deutsch's findings suggest a relationship between preschoolers, social interactions and role-taking but not between sociometric popularity and role-taking. However, it should be noted that her measures of popularity were incomplete. In asking children to list the names of the two children they preferred to play with she failed to control for the possible effect that some of the most popular children may also be those who are rejected as friends by others. By not considering rejection scores, she failed to differentiate those children who are liked by the majority of children from those who are equally liked and disliked by their peers. Furthermore, in taking the frequency of interactions as a popularity measure, she failed to differentiate positive from negative interactions. It seems quite plausible that the type of interactions that children engage in will influence role-taking skills. However, this information is not available from this study, so nothing definitive can be said about the relationship between popularity and communicative role-taking. Many studies of popularity suffer from the same methodological problems.

Rubin and Maioni (1975) examined the relationship between type of play, popularity, spatial role-taking, and conceptual role-taking skills. The four categories of play as defined by Piaget (1962) were functional, constructive, dramatic, and games with rules. Sixteen preschool children ages 3.7 to 4.7 years were administered Borke's (1971) conceptual role-taking task and then a modified version of the Piaget and Inhelder (1956) three mountain experiment. Sociometric popularity consisted of an interview with the children in which they were asked to name their three best friends. Ratings on play were made during observations of the children in free play activities. Results of the study are not complete because the small number of subjects

(n = 16) prevented the authors from using any multivariate analyses. However, correlational findings indicated that the frequency of dramatic play was positively related to spatial role-taking and popularity. Spatial role-taking was also related to popularity in a positive direction. Functional play was found to be negatively related to spatial role-taking, conceptual role-taking, and popularity.

The authors suggest that peer interactions during which children take the roles of others provide situations in which they learn to understand reciprocal relationships. However, in view of the fact that a sociometric measure was used which did not control for rejection choices, and no measures of the frequency of interactions or type of behavior used in interactions were made, this interpretation of findings was at best suggestive.

An incidental finding reported in the study was that the most common forms of play observed were functional, constructive, and dramatic. Few children engaged in games with rules. Since functional play was found to be negatively related to all experimental measures, it may be that this type of play provides no role-taking opportunities for the children. Dramatic play, on the other hand, does seem to provide opportunities for role-taking. One finding of interest was that the majority of children were observed in constructive play. However, this type of play did not relate to any of the role-taking or popularity indexes. It may be that constructive play serves as a transition activity from the development of nonrole-taking to role-taking. However more research is needed to clarify the relationship between type of play and the development of role-taking abilities. When adequate measures of peer relations are used and type of play can be examined under experimental conditions, the relationship between popularity, play, and role-taking will be better clarified.

The Relationship between Perspective-Taking Skills and Prosocial Behavior

Although Piaget (1965) suggested a direct relationship between perspective-taking and cooperation, few studies have investigated this relationship. Johnson (1975) found cooperation as measured by a choice-cards task (Kagan & Madsen, 1972) to be related to affective perspective-taking scores in 44 working-class fifth-grade students. Levine and Hoffman (1975) examined the relationship between empathy and cooperation in 4-year-old children. These 60 children were rated as cooperative or noncooperative on two measures, teacher ratings and performance on the Kagan and Madsen (1971) cooperative gameboard. Empathy was assessed using Feshbach and Roe's (1968) affective perspective-taking task. No differences between cooperative and noncooperative children were found with respect to empathy. Additionally, the two measures of cooperation were found to be unrelated.

In the Johnson (1975) and the Levine and Hoffman (1975) studies, cooperation was measured by a cooperative-competitive game. On these tasks children may either cooperate (by taking turns) or compete (by not taking turns). When they cooperate, they are rewarded. Competition leads to no individual rewards.

However, when cooperation is measured by the above procedures, the intent underlying a child's response is not necessarily prosocial. The child cooperates to receive a reward and not for the mutual benefit of self and partner. As the prosocial intent underlying the child's behavior is essential in defining a cooperative response, it is important that cooperation be assessed as a voluntary act based on the desire to work with another for the mutual benefit of each.

The relationship between perspective-taking ability and indexes of generosity and helping was assessed in 7-year-olds by Rubin and Schneider (1973). The correlations between communicative egocentrism and generosity and helping were $-.31$ and $-.44$, respectively. With mental age statistically controlled, the generosity correlations for helping remained significantly related to egocentrism ($r = -.64$).

M. R. Yarrow and Waxler (1975) and Waxler, Yarrow, and Smith, (1977) investigated the development and relationship of perspective-taking skills to prosocial behavior among children aged 3-7 years. Prosocial behaviors were defined as acts of helping, sharing, and comforting in response to the needs of another. They were assessed in six experimental situations. In two situations, helping was assessed by the child's response to an adult's spilling materials during play activities. Limited amounts of supplies which might be shared were presented to the children in two different play situations to measure sharing behaviors. Finally, comforting was measured by presenting each child with two situations where he witnessed someone expressing pain.

Using a battery of perspective-taking tasks, M. R. Yarrow and Waxler (1975) found that abilities on spatial and conceptual tasks increased with age. The most substantial age difference occurred between 4½ and 5 years. Prosocial behaviors, however, showed neither systematic changes nor significant correlation with perspective-taking abilities.

Developmental differences among a variety of prosocial behaviors have been estimated from children's descriptions of kind acts. Youniss (1975) asked 50 children in kindergarten and first, fourth, and seventh grades to define kindness and to create a story in which one child did something kind for a peer.

Giving or sharing material items and playing with a peer characterized most of the actions described by kindergarten and first-grade children. Fewer responses in these categories were given by older children. Categories of teaching and helping another in distress were used exclusively by older children. Differences in the ability to describe the state of the peer recipient were also noted. The younger children failed to describe the recipient state; the older children almost always did. The common feature of the older children's responses was that they depicted the recipient of a kind act in either a condition of need or a state of distress. The younger children considered as kind only those acts that produced states of well-being. For younger children, kind acts apparently did not alter conditions of need or states of distress.

Although very little research attention has been given to the joint relationship of perspective-taking ability and personality variables to prosocial behavior, several characteristics of prosocial children have been identified. Children who tend to behave prosocially have been found to be more gregarious, outgoing, independent, and assertive than their peers (Hartup & Keller, 1960; Murphy, 1937; Rutherford & Mussen, 1968; Staub, 1971). Throughout the preschool years, these children have been described by their teachers as bright, reasonable, generous, considerate, adept at planning, reflective, attentive, creative, dependable, responsible, calm, and relaxed (Block & Block, 1973 as reported in Mussen & Eisenberg-Berg, 1977).

The results from the one study that investigated the relationship between perspective-taking ability and personality characteristics provide evidence of the interactive role which these variables play as predictors of prosocial behavior. Barrett and Yarrow (1977) hypothesized that assertiveness would predict prosocial behaviors for children high in perspective-taking ability. For children low in perspective-taking ability, assertiveness would account for little variance in prosocial behavior. Their results were in line with their predictions. Assertiveness among high perspective-takers was highly correlated with observations of prosocial behaviors ($r = .52$). No significant relationship were found for low perspective-takers. To clarify the interaction further, the relationship between perspective-taking ability and prosociality was assessed for different levels of assertiveness. Although few significant findings were reported, there was a trend for inferential ability to be positively related to prosocial behaviors for highly assertive children and negatively related to prosocial behaviors for highly assertive children and negatively related for nonassertive children. Thus, the data clearly support the authors' contention that perspective-taking ability plays an indirect mediating role rather than a direct main effect with respect to prosocial behaviors. However, they do not rule out the alternate hypothesis that personality variables such as assertiveness act as mediators between perspective-taking ability and prosocial behaviors.

CONCLUSIONS

From a cognitive-developmental point of view, early experiences in infancy are crucial in establishing the infant's first perceptual and conceptual schemata, or ways of representing his environment. These schemata are the standards against which ongoing input, social or nonsocial, is compared. The degree of discrepancy between any new input and the established standards appears to serve the function of arousing the infant's attention in people and events in his immediate environment. It is virtually impossible in early infancy to separate cognitive, motivational, and social processes because of the degree of intertwining (or lack of differentiation) among them. With increasing development and the concomitant increase in differentiation of these processes, they become more identifiable and investigatable as separate entities, although undoubtedly all are involved to some extent in any adaptive act the individual makes.

Viewing the young child, even the infant, as an information processor has been helpful in trying to make some sense of the earliest developments. These include the developmental course of the smile, the development of person permanence, and various aspects of the development of the infant's attachment to the caregiver—including stranger anxiety and separation protest. This cognitive approach has given a central role to the infant's *experiences* in determining these key social-cognitive developments, but biological constraints have not been totally ignored.

Much more information is needed at the infancy level. For example, we are just beginning to be able to specify with any precision the degree to which specific cognitive structures have been established or, for that matter, the level of general cognitive development that has been achieved at any point in time. Until we do, advice to present the child with information (objects, social encounters) just beyond his present level of development is not very useful. This is, of course, the "problem of the match" discussed in an earlier chapter. From a scientific point of view it is a very difficult concept to test. Although the model proposed appears to be consistent with the evidence accumulated thus far, alternative models may prove equally viable.

The social-cognitive literature for preschool-aged children is also problematic. It is doubtful that perspective-taking, the key development in social interactions from a cognitive-developmental point of view, is a unitary construct. Relationships between performances on the various role-taking tasks are often weak. This weakness is even more evident when variance due to IQ or mental age is removed. Even when specific kinds of perspective-taking (emotional, conceptual, perceptual) are examined, the studies often produce conflicting results. Some of these contradictions can be resolved by a careful examination of specific task requirements. Incredible variation in the stimulus materials presented, the degree of reliance on verbal modes of presentation and response, and the type of response formats used (pointing, physically reconstructing, verbally explaining) exist. This makes comparison across tasks difficult, if not impossible.

Nevertheless, a steady increase in perspective-taking ability (or abilities) does appear to be taking place during the preschool years. The most important early experiences related to the development of perspective-taking skills in young children appear to be those associated with parent–child and child–child interactions during the preschool years. Likely parent effects identified in this review include nonpower-assertive parenting techniques such as induction, which includes explaining the consequences of the child's acts on others and reference to others' covert feelings, thoughts, and emotional states; person-orientation, which appears in the parent's language; and opportunities provided by the parent for social-verbal interaction. Peer effects for preschoolers include simple exposure to peers, amount of social interaction with peers, and some types of play—particularly dramatic play—and actual experiences in role-playing.

Paradoxically, the social-cognitive research is neither very "social" nor systematically "cognitive." It is not very social because the child's view of others, or their perspectives, is treated in much the same manner as the child's view of physical objects. Interactive processes, dialogue, degree of prior relationship with another, and the general give-and-take of what we usually think of as social interactions are rarely investigated in these studies. Thus, our knowledge of how children develop socially is quite limited by this approach. At the same time, our knowledge of how cognitive development proceeds is not advanced very much either. Apart from the fact that it is easier to study children's cognitive processes as they interact with physical rather than social objects, most of the social-cognitive research has not been designed to elucidate strategies of interaction, decision-making processes, or other aspects of problem-solving in a social context. Rather, they seem designed to determine whether children of a certain age are egocentric. Thus, children are classified in one of two categories on the basis of tasks that differ from one investigator to another with little attempt to specify the specific cognitive processes being tapped. Virtually no attempts have been made to examine, let alone improve, the psychometric properties of these tasks designed to measure role-taking. Thus, their reliability and validity are questionable. Some (M. R. Yarrow & Waxler, 1975) have suggested that we use batteries of these tasks, rather than a single measure, in assessing perspective-taking abilities. Although this may be a move in the right direction, it will help very little if no attempt to establish reliability and validity is made.

The relationship between perspective-taking skills and prosocial behavior deserves further study. Studies with children in the fourth and fifth grades have typically found significant relationships, although studies with preschool children have been contradictory. Apparently, individual differences in personality characteristics such as aggressiveness (Friedrich & Stein, 1973) and assertiveness (Barrett & Yarrow, 1977), which have been found to be related to prosocial behavior, have an interactive effect with perspective-taking. That is, children who are both assertive and skilled in perspective-taking do engage in prosocial behavior more than others. The suggestion by Barrett and Yarrow (1977) that perspective-taking plays an indirect mediating role with respect to prosocial behaviors appears well taken, although it needs confirmation through further studies.

All in all, the complex relationships between the development of social behavior and cognitive processes will be difficult to disentangle and organize in any comprehensible manner. To the extent that social and cognitive processes derive from shared organizational processes, however, models depicting these relationships should eventually emerge. We are just beginning to understand exactly which early experiences have a significant impact on later social-cognitive organization.

CHAPTER 9

The Nature of Early Environmental Action

In previous chapters we have reviewed available evidence on the nature of relationships between specific early experience parameters and subsequent cognitive and social development. For some early experience parameters, clear-cut relationships with development have been shown; for others, few relationships have occurred, and for the remainder unsystematic or weak relationships have been revealed. One question that emerges is what this body of data tells us about the nature of early environmental action *per se*, over and above the specific relationships reported.

Three specific areas are of concern to us here. The first is the pattern of early environmental action, the second the direction, and the third the duration. Discussion of these areas is of more than academic interest since our concept of environmental action often determines, to a great degree, the types of intervention strategies we use with at-risk infants and preschoolers.

The Pattern of Early Environmental Action

In analyzing the relationship of early experience to development, we perceive that previous theory has been formulated along the lines of global, all-encompassing constructs. Specifically, early experience effects were typically construed in such terms as "stimulus deprivation" or "match." The underlying assumpion of these theories appears to be that experience is essentially a unidimensional phenomenon that equally affects all individuals across all phases of development. Thus, a depriving environment (most often defined as low social class) is one that will uniformly depress intellectual or social parameters for all children unfortunate enough to reside in such an environment; similarly, an enriching environment (often defined as a nursery school experience) will have uniformly facilitative effects on the social and

185

cognitive development of all children fortunate enough to encounter such a developmental Shangri-la.

There are a number of historical reasons why such a view of early experience emerges. The critical influences of psychoanalytic theory and Gestalt psychology for the development of a global model of environmental action have been delineated by Hunt (1977). In addition, the early concordat between individual (correlational) and general (experimental) psychology had clearly come unglued by the 1920s (Cronbach, 1967). Thereafter, the experimental approach to psychology clearly became the dominant approach. Within the mainstream approach individual differences were regarded, at best, as annoyances and "cast into that outer darkness known as error variance." (Cronbach, 1967). In this atmosphere, early experience was naturally regarded as a unidimensional phenomenon, with individual differences in reactivity being considered error variance.

The effects of this historical dominance of experimental methodology upon early experience research can be most clearly seen in the designs of studies in this area in the 1930–1950 period (Hunt, 1961). Following a nursery school model, global experiences were applied to a heterogeneous sample of children. If statistical significance was reached, the procedure was considered a success regardless of how many children in the experimental sample failed to show change; if an acceptable level of statistical significance was not reached, the procedure was considered a failure, again regardless of how many children in the enriched group showed notable changes. This global approach to early experience research only reified the concept of a global pattern of environmental action.

This hypothesis of global environmental action was further confirmed by the strongly held belief that intelligence, the major criterion variable in so many studies, was essentially a unidimensional, quantitatively changing trait (Hunt, 1961). With the dual concepts of a unidimensional environment and global intelligence, differential effects of early experience were considered impossible since the predictor and criterion variables were essentially unidimensional.

These views of early environmental action as a global, unidimensional phenomenon have recently been challenged by a number of sources. Theoretically, Wohlwill (1973a) has pointed out that the term *experience* may involve the influence of both antecedent stimulus conditions and the acquisition and practice of specific responses. The relevance of these different types of experience to development may change as the child develops. Empirically, Bloom (1964), L. J. Yarrow *et al.* (1975), Wachs (1979), and Hunt (1977, 1979) have suggested that early environmental action may be highly specific in nature. These authors have suggested that specific components of experience predict specific aspects of development. Wachs (1979, in press) has taken the specificity notion one step further by hypothesizing that specific components of experience may be relevant only for specific individuals. Such a rethinking of early environmental action is in line with current notions on the nature of intelligence (McCall *et al.*, 1972) which indicate that intelligence is a multidimensional, qualitatively changing phenomenon, that is, that the nature of intelligence changes as the child develops.

A theory invoking a concept of global environmental action would predict the following hypotheses: (1) little evidence for age changes in the types of environmental parameters relevant to development; (2) different aspects of development predicted equally by any aspect of the environment; (3) little variation in level of developmental change for children reared in essentially the same environmental conditions; and (4) no evidence for a systematic relationship between specific individual differences and differential reactivity to the same environmental parameters. In contrast, a specificity hypothesis would predict exactly the reverse of each of the above points. Each of these predictions will be reviewed in turn.

Age Changes in Environmental Action

A hypothesis of age specificity would predict differential predictor–criterion relationships as a function of the age of the individual. Generality of environmental action would predict that different aspects of the environment show approximately the same relationship to development at all ages. In general, a review of the available evidence as presented in Chapters 3 through 7 suggests that age specificity is the more correct formulation.

First, recent evidence suggests that the first six months of life are a period of time when environmental influences exert much less of an effect on cognitive (Bradley & Caldwell, 1980, 1981; Burchinal & Farran, 1980; Farran & Ramey, 1980), motivational (Rubenstein, Pedersen, & Yarrow, 1977), and social (Bakeman & Brown, 1980) development than influences occurring after six months of age.[1] This could suggest that age specificity is simply a form of the critical period hypothesis were it not for other evidence indicating systematic changes in the nature of environment–development relationships as the child develops.

Specifically, for cognitive intellectual development, available evidence suggests that age specificity occurs particularly for four aspects of the early environment: (a) degree of physical contact, wherein significant relationships occur primarily before 6 months of age (Farran *et al.*, 1977; Goldberg, 1972, 1977a); (b) verbal stimulation, wherein few relationships are found prior to 12 months of age (Wachs *et al.*, 1971; Clarke-Stewart, 1973); (c) parental restrictiveness, which is found to be related to development primarily between 2

---

[1]M. R. Yarrow (1981) has recently obtained data on the development of infants of clinically depressed mothers. Her results suggest no impact of maternal psychopathology on infant development until after the first year of life.

and 4 years of age (Kagan & Freeman, 1963; Borgman, 1972); (d) a predominance of object variety over person variety as the prime predictor in the first year of life, whereas the reverse holds true after 12 months. (Clarke-Stewart, 1973; Elardo *et al.*, 1975; L. J. Yarrow *et al.*, 1975).

In addition to these "marker" dimensions, our previous review has also shown age specificity for a number of other variables. For physical environmental parameters, availability of stimulus material appears to relate to development only during the first year of life (Gottfried & Gottfried, 1981; Riksen-Walraven, 1974); organization of the child's home environment relates to development only after 12 months of age (Elardo *et al.*, 1975). For social environmental parameters, maternal orientation to the child relates to development only through 12 months of age (Clarke-Stewart, 1973); verbal contingencies appear to relate to development starting somewhere between 12 and 30 months; amount of parental involvement with the child does not appear to be relevant for development until at least 12 months of age (Elardo *et al.*, 1975). Parental equalitarianism is negatively related to development in the first year of life and positively related to development after 4 years of age (Bayley & Schaefer, 1964).

For social development, although available data is much more sparse, what relationships do exist also support a concept of age specificity. Thus, parental inductiveness, "person-orientation," and use of reasoning are positively related to moral development but only in children with mental ages greater than 6 (Borgman, 1972). Analogous findings are also shown for role-taking ability. Similarly, father absence when the separation occurred prior to 5 years of age was found to be related in males to later increased physical aggressiveness, verbal aggressiveness, and dependency, and to less masculine self-concepts (Hetherington, 1966; Hetherington & Parke, 1979). The same pattern of findings does not occur with separation after 5 years of age.

Looking over the available literature, one perceives that only physical responsivity of the environment, number of sibs, and specified parental training appear to show any age generality. For these dimensions, evidence on physical responsivity has been limited to the first three years of life. Training effects, although relevant to development across a wide age span, appear to have limited generalizability over time. Thus, the overall pattern of evidence clearly suggests age-specific relationships between the majority of environmental parameters and subsequent cognitive and social development.

Environmental Specificity

A hypothesis of environmental specificity would predict that different aspects of the environment would relate to different aspects of development. A hypothesis of environmental generality would predict that all aspects of the environment would have essentially similar effects upon development (either raising or depressing development) and that for different criterion variables any aspect of the environment would be salient. A review of the evidence presented in Chapters 3 through 7 clearly supports the former hypothesis, particularly for cognitive-intellectual development.

For the physical environment, the strongest evidence for environmental specificity is seen with the parameter of floor freedom. In the first year of life, floor freedom has been found to predict Gesell performance but is unrelated to Casati–Lezine performance (Beckwith et al., 1976). In the second year of life, floor freedom has been found to predict certain aspects of Piagetian sensorimotor development (object permanence, foresight, schemata, gestural imitation) but not others (means, objects in space, verbal imitation) (Wachs, 1979). Also within the physical environmental sphere, regularity of the home environment has been found to predict object permanence (Wachs, 1979) but to be unrelated to language development (Elardo et al., 1977). Ambient subway noise affects psychomotor development but not memory performance (Hambrick-Dixon, 1980). Finally, complexity of the physical environment predicts cognitive-motivational and exploratory parameters but not language or general cognitive functioning (L. J. Yarrow et al., 1975).

For the social environment, maternal involvement predicts recognition memory but not Bayley performance (Gottfried & Gottfried, 1981); maternal orientation has been found to be positively related to object permanence and Bayley performance but negatively related to performance on early spatial abilities (Clarke-Stewart, 1973); parental restrictions are positively related to early spatial abilities, negatively related to early object permanence (Clarke-Stewart, 1973), and unrelated to language development (Elardo et al., 1977). Language development itself is predicted by informational content of adult vocalizations but not by amount of adult vocalizations. Language comprehension appears to be more related to language environment (Tizard et al., 1972) and to maternal invovement (Siegel, 1979) than is language expressiveness, which is uniquely predicted by maternal involvement (Siegel, 1979). The amount of parental reading to infant also predicts early language but is unrelated to other early cognitive parameters (Wachs, 1979). Experimental intervention studies clearly indicate that groups of children who receive different types of environmental input show different patterns of cognitive development (Hunt, 1977; Ogston, 1981; Riksen-Walraven, 1978).

In terms of the interpersonal environment, early parental closeness is found to predict subsequent verbal abilities but is unrelated to performance abilities (Honzik, 1967a, 1967b); similarly, early parental conflict relates to subsequent verbal abilities but is unrelated to nonverbal performance (Honzik, 1967a, 1967b). Active maternal involvement with the child is found to predict the development of person permanence prior to the development of object permanence (Chazan, 1981).

Interestingly, evidence supporting a concept of environmental specificity also exists at the infrahuman level. Singh (1969) has reported differences in patterns of exploration and social behavior by Rhesus monkeys living in either urban or rural settings. Looking at environmental demands in each setting, Singh concludes that it is the different experiences encountered by rural and urban rhesus monkeys that leads to the behavioral differences.

Evidence also exists indicating that different developmental parameters are predicted by different aspects of the environment at different ages (age-environmental specificity). Results suggesting the existence of such a phenomenon are most clearly seen in the data by Wachs (1979) relating physical environmental parameters to Piagetian development at different ages. Wachs notes, as an example of age-environmental specificity, that development of object permanence prior to 18 months of age is primarily related to environmental predictability, whereas development after 18 months of age is a function of exploratory opportunities and a lack of strangers in the home; in contrast, for the development of foresight, the early development of this ability is predicted by a responsive physical environment, whereas the development of foresight after 18 months is a function of exploratory opportunities, the presence of a stimulus shelter, and a lack of overcrowding. For older children, Radin (1972a, 1973) notes that paternal restriction at 4 years of age facilitates general intelligence but is unrelated to language competence; in contrast, at 5 years of age the reverse is true. Similar age-by-environmental specificity involving language and cognitive functioning and variety of stimulation in the home have been reported by Siegel (1979). A look at the overall pattern of evidence demonstrates that only physical responsivity of the environment (up to 3 years) and number of sibs appear to be immune to environmental specificity. Thus, the available evidence clearly supports the hypothesis of environmental specificity over that of environmental generality.

Organismic Specificity

A hypothesis of organismic specificity can be considered at a number of levels. At a molar level, this hypothesis would predict differential responses by different children encountering an essentially similar environment. At a more molecular level, the hypothesis would predict that specific, individual differences would be systematically associated with differences in reactivity to environmental parameters.

Looking at molar predictions, one can ask whether essentially similar environments, if applied to a heterogeneous group of children, lead to essentially similar results. Evidence on this point is most clearly seen in studies of preschool or early intervention where, within a given program, all children receive an essentially similar curricular experience. In general, the available evidence supports organismic specificity rather than generality. Following intervention, IQ range differences of 30–50 points are the rule rather than the exception. Within specific programs, some children have gained as much as

40 points while others have lost as much as 28 points. These tremendous individual differences occur whether one is talking about Head Start, general preschool programs (Horowitz & Paden, 1975; Williams, 1977), or highly structured and regimented instructional programs (Engelmann, 1970; Fowler, 1964).

In one of the most dramatic demonstrations of this point Stevenson, Parker, Wilkinson, Bonnevaux, and Gonzalez (1978) reported on the effects of early social experience on development in Peru. In spite of the fact that a rigid curriculum and overcrowded classrooms made differential treatment of the children all but impossible, individual differences in reactivity to schooling were the rule rather than the exception.

A similar phenomenon also exists at the infrahuman level. In a review of infrahuman data, Globus (1975) reports that even when littermates are compared, identical environmental manipulations may produce quite different physiological effects in individual animals. This tremendous range of differences suggests that individual differences may be more critical in understanding the results of cognitive intervention than the type of remediational technique utilized.

Given this tremendous range of individual differences within highly similar environments, one can ask whether there are specific individual difference parameters associated with differences in reactivity. Some evidence has been reported indicating social class (Moore, 1968; Tulkin & Covitz, 1975) and racial differences (Bradley & Caldwell, 1980; Clarke-Stewart, 1973) in environmental reactivity. The above findings, while further strengthening the case for organismic specificity, are less than satisfactory since they make an assumption that individuals within a group are essentially homogenous (i.e., all lower-class children are similar). More relevant would be evidence looking at the relationship between specific individual difference parameters and reactivity to subsequent environmental stimulation. The hypothesis that specific classes of individuals may respond differentially to similar environmental stimulation has received much theoretical speculation (Caspari, 1968; Clarke, 1978; Korner, 1971) but, unfortunately, little research.

The overwhelming majority of studies in this area have dealt primarily with differential responses by male and female infants to environmental stimulation. For the social environment, L. J. Yarrow et al. (1973) report that males are more sensitive than females to early match, specific training, closeness, positive emotional expression, and rejection. Bradley and Caldwell (1980) report an association between male cognitive development and the organization and degree of encouragement for development in the home; for females, the salient environmental predictors are level of punishment and maternal responsivity.

Most of the available evidence, however, has dealt with interpersonal environmental variables. As we noted earlier in Chapter 5, the pattern of available evidence suggests that parental criticism and conflict predict female development rather than male development, whereas parental acceleration and nurturance relate to male rather than female development. In the area of social development, personal agency and a sense of responsibility have been found to be associated with firm parental control and abrasive parent–child interactions for girls, but with encouragement of independence, warmth, and nondirectiveness for boys (Baumrind, 1971).

Rather than straight organismic specificity, most evidence suggest an interaction between organismic and environmental specificity such that different aspects of the environment predict different aspects of development for males and females. Thus, Honzik (1967b) reports that high verbal males have fathers described as poorly adjusted socially, whereas high-performance males have fathers described as lacking self-confidence and having a strong sense of privacy; high verbal females have mothers characterized as worrisome, whereas high-performance females have mothers described as energetic. Close, friendly parental relationships predict female verbal abilities but are unrelated to male verbal abilities (Honzik, 1967b). Parental vocalizations have been found to predict female conditioning performance (Moss, 1974) and male Bayley performance (Herman, 1971) but not male conditioning or female Bayley performance.

Evidence also exists in the work of Honzik (1967b) for an age-by-environment by organism interaction. Specifically, Honzik reports that early paternal energy is negatively related to female development from 2 to 9 years of age, but early maternal energy is positively related to male development from 8 to 18 years of age.

Apart from sex differences, only a few studies have looked at the role of other individual difference variables in mediating environmental effects. Greenburg (1965) has reported preliminary evidence suggesting that nursery-reared infants are more sensitive to incoming stimulation, assimilate less, and have more labile heart responses than home-reared infants. Data from the Head Start project suggest that different teaching techniques may be necessary for children with different IQ levels (Horowitz & Paden, 1975). Using hospitalized infants, Schaffer (1966a) has reported data indicating that inactive infants may be more sensitive to environmental deprivation than active infants. Similarly, Wachs and Peters-Martin (1981) have obtained data indicating that placid infants living in inadequate home environments show lower levels of sensorimotor development than nonplacid infants. Schaffer and Emerson (1964a), using retrospective data, report that contact comfort is relevant to the social development only of babies considered as "cuddlers"; for "noncuddlers" maternal contact was unrelated to social development. Siegel (1981) has presented evidence suggesting that preterm infants may be more sensitive to environmental stimulation than full-term infants.

One problem is common to all of the above findings. Specifically, it is unclear whether the results are due to genuine differential reactivity of individuals to similar environmental stimulation or whether the differences are due to different environments provided to male/female, active/inactive infants. In only a few studies has this potential confounding of individual with environment been eliminated. Pedersen, Rubenstein, and Yarrow (1979) report a greater impact of father absence on male than on female infants. These differences occur in spite of a lack of differences in maternal behavior toward male or female infants. Wachs (1978, 1979) reports that male infants, in spite of having essentially identical physical environments, were significantly more sensitive to the detrimental effects of noise–confusion existing in the home than were female infants; female infants were significantly more sensitive to the facilitative effects of long-term stimulus variety in the home than were male infants. Wachs and Gandour (1981) have recently obtained data indicating that temperamentally "easy" 6-month-old infants appear to be significantly more sensitive to social interactions than temperamentally "difficult" 6-month-olds. In contrast, difficult infants appear to be significantly more sensitive to the negative aspects of the physical environment such as noise–confusion. These differences occur in spite of a lack of differences in either the physical or social environment for the two groups of infants.

With respect to social development, Gunnar (1980) reports that control of fearful stimuli significantly reduced fear responses only for boys; predicting the onset of the stimuli increased fear responses only for girls.

Although evidence is limited, what evidence is available does suggest that individuals do react differently to similar environments and that specific types of parameters, such as sex and temperament, are mediating differential responsivity. Suggestions for other types of organismic parameters that may be relevant to differential responding have been discussed in a chapter by Wachs (1977).

Specificity—A Phenomenon in Search of a Rationale

On the basis of the available evidence, it appears clear that although certain environmental parameters may be general in nature, for the vast majority of environmental factors specificity of early environmental action appears to be the more correct formulation. This pattern of evidence has led Wachs (1979) to suggest a model of environmental action dubbed the bifactor environmental action model (BEAM). The BEAM model suggests that there are two types of environmental parameters: a small subset which are general in nature and a larger subset which are highly specific. Although the existence of general environmental parameters fits many of our preconceptions about early experience, the possibility of specificity of environmental action causes many developmentalists concern. If nothing else, specificity would seem to violate our treasured concept of parsimony. Certainly, from the standpoint of parsimony, it would seem more reasonable to have only a few critical environmental parameters accounting for almost all development.

Yet, the available evidence suggests that most environmental parameters will be highly specific in their action. What appears to be lacking is a theoretical framework within which the existence of specificity of environmental action can be encompassed.

Given the three types of specificity on which we have previously reported (age, environmental, organismic), one sees clearly that, with one exception, no single framework will fit all types of specificity. The one exception is, of course, the possibility that specificity is some kind of statistical artifact. Factors that have been suggested as contributing to artifact include small sample size (Lusk & Lewis, 1972), inadequate statistical analysis (Kamin, 1978), a lack of variation within measures (Lusk & Lewis, 1972; Tizard et al., 1972), attrition of some particular subgroup of individuals from the sample (Shipman, 1977), differential variability or differential mean levels of critical variables between groups (Clarke-Stewart, 1973; Kamin, 1978), lowered reliability or stability for certain critical measures (Tizard et al., 1972; L. J. Yarrow et al., 1975), or random variation across studies (Clarke-Stewart et al., 1979).

However, even if one grants the existence of artifact, it is difficult to attribute all the specificity results to artifact. Age and organismic specificity may be sensitive to many of the above artifactual problems; however, there are studies showing both age specificity (Clarke-Stewart, 1973; Bradley & Caldwell, 1976a) and organismic specificity (Wachs, 1979; Wachs & Gandour, 1981; Pedersen et al., 1979), in which artifactual factors have been minimized. Further, artifact could not easily explain environmental specificity when, at a given age, a certain subset of environmental variables predicts one criterion while a second subset predicts another. Thus, although artifact may be relevant for certain studies, it is difficult to attribute all evidence for specificity to artifact. Rather, one must look elsewhere for a theoretical framework. A number of suggestions for possible causes for specificity are given below.

Age Specificity

Historically, the idea of critical periods has been most often used as a framework for age specificity. Critical periods refer to time periods when, for maturational or physiological reasons, the organism is particularly sensitive to environmental stimulation. Stimulation occurring before or after the critical period will have little effect upon development. As we noted earlier, the buffering of the human infant in the first six months of life against the normal range of experiences encountered may be one example of a critical period phenomenon. However, as we have also noted, the concept of age specificity encompasses more than just buffering. Unfortunately, for explanatory purposes, most critical period theories have been based primarily on infrahuman populations (Thompson & Grusec, 1970). Few critical period approaches have been aimed specifically at the human levels (Hunt, 1979), and those that have been are primarily concerned with social-interpersonal behaviors. In general, the scientific usefulness of these approaches has been shown to be extremely limited (Caldwell, 1962; Hunt, 1979).

A variant of the critical period hypothesis, which may have some explanatory power at the human level, is based on attempts to relate variations in level of central nervous development to the types of stimulation that the infant or preschooler can most efficiently process. In terms of general sensitivity to stimulation, Epstein (1974a, 1974b) has suggested that spurts of myelinization or biochemical changes in the central nervous system coincide with periods when the organism is most sensitive to environmental stimulation. Such an explanation would not, however, account for different patterns of stimulation predicting development at different age periods.

For the latter type of finding, Korner (1973) has suggested that the prepotence of certain types of stimulation may reflect the states of the infant's central nervous system. Specifically, she points to the early prepotence of vestibular stimulation in the developmental process as being due to the fact that the young infant's vestibular system is fully myelinated at birth (Korner, 1972). A similar suggestion has been made by L. J. Yarrow (L. J. Yarrow et al., 1975). Evidence relating different levels of central nervous system development to the processing of different types of stimulation clearly would offer a framework for age and age-by-environmental specificity. However, with the exception of certain infrahuman studies (i.e., Floeter & Greenough, 1979), we are not aware of any direct evidence showing parallels between central nervous system changes and changes in the types of environmental parameters relevant to development. This lack of hard data may well reflect the fact that the concept of specificity is a fairly new one in the area of early experience. As we have noted, previous approaches to an understanding of early environmental action have utilized a general model of early experience. Perhaps with a greater understanding of the specificity of early environmental action, a fruitful collaboration can occur between early experience researchers and neurobiologists as a means of determining existing parallels between central nervous system development and the types of experience the organism is sensitive to at various ages. Until such evidence is presented, conclusions must remain at only a speculative level.

A motivational approach to age specificity has been suggested by Bronfenbrenner (1968, 1974). Bronfenbrenner suggests that early stimulation will be most effective when it is tied in with a strong bond between parent and child. The stronger the parent–child bond, the more sensitive the child is to specific aspects of parental behavior. This approach would suggest that certain critical periods, particularly during the first three years of life, would exist for sensitivity to interpersonal environment variables. However, the available evidence, as reviewed in Chapter 5, does not suggest that the interpersonal environment is more prepotent in the early years than in later years.

No data indicate that the early social environment may be more critical than the early physical environment. Further, Bronfenbrenner's hypothesis would not explain age-by-environmental specificity wherein one aspect of parental involvement is prepotent in one age but not at earlier or later ages.

A third alternative to critical periods lies in the interface between the specific experience and the organism's developmental stage or level of behavioral functioning. At the infrahuman level, Thompson (1972) has postulated a developmental differentiation theory wherin the type of early experience to which the organism responds is mediated by the organism's stage of development. For Thompson, habituation is most critical in mediating experiential effects early in development; for development after early infancy, classical emotional conditioning becomes the critical mediator, whereas instrumental conditioning factors are most critical in mediating later development. Thus, experiences involving a classical conditioning component would be salient for development primarily during only one time period.

General analogues to Thompson's theory have been noted at the human level. The role of the infant's cognitive level in mediating its reaction to verbal stimulation (Uzgiris, 1980) has been noted earlier. Similar arguments have also been noted in the field of language development (Greenbaum & Landau, 1977). Behaviorally, a number of authors have taken a transactional position in suggesting that the development of mobility by the young infant is a critical point in development which may lead to radical shifts in the nature of parent–child interaction (Bakeman & Brown, 1980; Burchinal & Farran, 1980; Farran & Ramey, 1980). These hypothesized shifts in parent-child interactions lead to the changes in environment–development relationships which we have labeled as age specificity. Along the same lines, Bradley and Caldwell (1976a) have reported that parental organization of environment is less related to development after 36 months. These authors suggest that older children are better able to organize the environment for themselves and rely less on parental organization, which thus decreases in salience. Similarly, the greater independence of the older child may mediate the decrease in importance of severity of punishment as the child grows older. Although plausible for some environmental dimensions (organization, restrictiveness) these hypotheses would not explain physical environment age specificity; nor would they explain age specificity for those social environmental parameters not dependent upon mobility or organization (i.e., vocal interaction). The evidence reviewed in Chapter 7 with respect to the development of perspective-taking in children also provides an example of the interface between stage of (cognitive) development and various environmental factors— person-orientation (Bearison & Cassel, 1975) and inductiveness (Dlugokinski & Firestone, 1974) in parents; and amount of verbal-social interaction (Hollos & Cowan, 1973). This is especially relevant to Thompson's postulate if one adopts Flavell's biologically flavored view that perspective-taking development is a species-specific "cognitive-developmental universal" because

(a) it is not present at birth, (b) it must therefore be the product of a development process in any organism that displays it, (c) it has probably developed to some nontrivial level in all biologically intact human adults around the world, and (d) it may not develop to any significant degree in any species but our own (Flavell, 1974, p. 70).

Like the hypothesis of differential central nervous sytem development mediating age specificity, a functional approach to age specificity is quite plausible on the surface. Unfortunately, like the earlier hypothesis, little direct evidence has been obtained at the human level in terms of the specific developmental or behavioral parameters characterizing functioning during specific age periods. Thus, the value of a functional approach to age specificity must also remain at a speculative level.

Finally, it may well be that neither the biological nor functional approaches to age specificity will be relevant. Although the constancy of the environment has been stressed by reviewers (Wohlwill, 1980), some evidence is available (Lawson & Ingleby, 1974; Barnard, 1979; Cohen & Beckwith, 1979) indicating differences in patterns of parent–child interaction as children get older. If this evidence proves to be replicable, age specificity may turn out to be due to different environments rather than to differential reactions.

Environmental Specificity

The only existing explanation for environmental specificity is that given by Wachs in regard to cognitive-intellectual development (Wachs, 1979; Wachs, Francis, & McQuiston, 1979).[2] Wachs hypothesizes that environmental specificity is primarily a function of the multidimensional nature of both early environment and early intelligence.

If either early intelligence or early environment were unidimensional, one would not expect specificity, since we would be dealing with global, undifferentiated phenomena. However, if *both* early intelligence and early environment are regarded as multidimensional in nature, then specificity is the logical outcome of this situation, since we are dealing with predictor–criterion components. Available evidence clearly indicates that early intelligence, whether measured in a psychometric (McCall, Hogarty, & Hurlburt, 1972; McCall, Eichorn, & Hogarty, 1977) or a Piagetian framework (Uzgiris, 1973; Wachs & Hubert, 1981), is multidimensional. Similarly, evidence is available to support the multidimensional nature of both the physical (Wachs *et al.*, 1979) and social environment (Roff, 1949; Stern *et al.*, 1969). Within this framework, age-by-environmental specificity could be seen as due to qualita-

---

[2]Though Greenough and Juraska (1979) have recently presented infrahuman evidence indicating that specific regions of the central nervous system are modified by stimulation in specific modalities; these data seem to offer the possibility of a psychobiological explanation for environmental specificity.

tive changes in either the predictor (Barnard, 1979) or criterion components (McCall *et al.*, 1972, 1977; Wachs & Hubert, 1981).

Although the multidimensional hypothesis of environmental specificity is logical and appears to fit available evidence, further research must be generated to determine how useful this hypothesis is in predicting specific patterns of development.

Organismic Specificity

As we noted earlier, most of the available evidence on organismic specificity deals with sex differences. Historically, between-sex genetic differences have been postulated as one likely cause for differential reaction of the sexes to environmental variables. The phenomenon of gene–environment interaction (different genotypes reacting differently to environmental factors) is well known, and specificity may be one example of this phenomenon.

The strongest proponents for genetically based sex differences are Bayley and Schaefer (1964). Looking at the different environment-development patterns for males and females in their sample, these authors suggest that the determinant of cognitive development for males is primarily environmental while that for cognitive development in females is primarily genetic in nature. Other more recent results, however, suggest that females may be equally or more sensitive to the environment than males (Werner, 1969; Bradley *et al.*, 1977). Further, a reanalysis of the Bayley and Schaefer data by Kamin (1978) indicates clearcut sample differences between the sexes in variability plus a lack of statistical tests indicating whether the differences between male and female environment–development correlations were actually statistically significant. Overall, a hypothesis of genetic differences between males and females as a cause for specificity clearly does not appear to be upheld by available evidence.

A related hypothesis suggests that differential reactivity may be a function of behavioral or stimulus processing differences between the sexes which, in turn, may be biologically based. Thus, Hutt (1972), citing evidence that males orient more toward visual patterns while females orient more toward auditory sequences, has suggested that verbal experience may be more critical for female cognitive development. Along the same lines, Kagan (1969) has also suggested verbal factors as particularly critical for female development and has noted that this differential sensitivity may be genetically based. Wachs (1979), noting evidence indicating greater sensitivity of males to environmental stress than females, has suggested that females may be more genetically buffered than males against environmental stress and thus may be less reactive to the presence of noise–confusion in the home environment. It should be noted, however, that all of the above authors also agree that environmental differences between males and females may be as important as biological differences. Thus, the greater vocalization given to female infants could well account for the greater salience of vocalization for female development.

For differential reactivity as a function of temperament, Wachs and Gandour (1981) have suggested the relevance of Field's (in press) arousal model for their data. Working with high-risk infants, Field has hypothesized that certain classes of high-risk infants have a higher threshold for orienting responses and a lower threshold for defensive reactions (i.e., a narrower arousal range). The lower threshold of difficult infants to noise-confusion, combined with their higher threshold to social interactions, clearly appears to parallel the high-risk infant data. However, direct evidence documenting biologically based arousal differences in either high-risk or difficult infants has not yet appeared. Clearly, until someone identifies the specific biological or genetic parameters that underlie differences in reactivity to specific environmental parameters, the role of these factors in producing specificity must remain at a hypothetical level.

More researchable as a cause is the question of differential treatment. It may well be that the different treatment received by male and female infants produces specificity either directly or indirectly through mediated factors associated with differential treatment (Bronfenbrenner, 1968). Evidence is available indicating that greater amounts of physical stimulation (holding) are given to male infants (Korner, 1974; Lewis, 1972), whereas female infants receive a greater degree of verbal stimulation (Cherry & Lewis, 1976; Korner, 1974; Lewis, 1972). These differences in treatment may lead to what appears to be differential reactivity to environmental stimulation. However, negative evidence against a differential treatment hypothesis also exists. Many sex differences in reactivity occur well after the period when differential treatment of the sexes is most clearly seen (Lewis, 1972). Further, evidence is available indicating that when differential treatment of the sexes is shown not to exist, differential reactivity of males and females to environmental stimulation continues to appear (Pedersen, Rubenstein, & Yarrow, 1979; Wachs, 1978, 1979). Further, in many cases, clear-cut differential treatment does not produce expected differences in behavior (Cherry & Lewis, 1976). Thus, differential treatment may explain certain aspects of organismic specificity but clearly is not the whole story.

Using a modification of the differential treatment hypothesis, Korner (1974) has adopted a transactional position. For Korner, differential treatment is based on initial differences in infant characteristics. These initial individual differences may be either biologically based (Korner, 1974) or a result of differential rearing (Moss, 1974). In either case these initial individual differences are magnified through the differential treatment they evoke. Differences in specific male and female behaviors have been noted as early as the neonatal period (Korner, 1974; Osofsky & Danzger, 1974). Further, evidence is available suggesting that statistically controlling for initial infant behaviors eliminates much (though not all) of the variance associated with subsequent differential treatment (Moss, 1974). However, few studies are available which point to specific patterns of relationships between particular infant characteristics and subsequent parental behaviors. Further, what evidence is available from the study of infant temperament is clearly contradictory to Korner's transactional position. Her approach would predict that initial differences in temperament should be related to differences in parental treatment and thus lead to different developmental patterns for infants with different temperaments. However, evidence indicates that easy versus difficult temperamental patterns are unrelated to patterns of parent–infant interaction at 6 months (Bates, Olson, Pettit, & Bayles, 1980; Wachs & Gandour, 1981) or 13 months (Bates, Pettit, & Bayles, 1981). Further, in spite of the lack of interaction differences, differential reactivity still occurs for easy versus difficult infants (Wachs & Gandour, 1981).

It appears clear from the available evidence that differential reactivity to environmental stimulation does exist. Given the complexity of the human organism, such specificity is not surprising. What is not clear is the rationale for this specificity. Three positions have been discussed: differential biological heritage, differential treatment, and a transactional model based on initial individual differences. At present, none seems completely satisfactory as an explanatory device.

Summary of Specificity

On the basis of available evidence, it appears obvious that a global, undifferentiated model of early environmental action is inadequate. Although global environmental parameters do exist (i.e., physical and social responsivity), they reflect only a small subset of environmental parameters. The majority of environmental parameters will be specific to particular abilities, particular ages, or particular classes of individuals. It appears clear that any model of early environmental action must include information on both the general and specific nature of the environment. Why specificity occurs is not yet clear, although a number of hypotheses exist and may be useful in explaining this phenomenon. Perhaps, as an understanding of the specific nature of early experience evolves, research on these various hypotheses will allow us to choose between competing alternatives. Perhaps we may then begin to understand specificity both as a theoretical as well as an empirical phenomenon.

THE DIRECTION OF EARLY ENVIRONMENTAL ACTION

Even through the late 1960s it was commonly assumed that environmental action was essentially unidirectional. Specifically, the environment of the child was thought to affect the child's development directly but the impact of the child on the environment was rarely, if ever, considered. Historically, this emphasis on a unidirectional pattern of environmental action can be traced to psychoanalytic theory with its insistence that early events clearly structured later development and its emphasis on the role of the parents in causing deviant development in children. In addition, the adoption by the behavioral sciences of a mechanistic model, often based on the study of lower organisms, reified the notion of a unidirectional concept of environmental action.

The construct of a unidirectional pattern of environmental action has been challenged in recent years in reviews in a number of areas including socialization (Bell, 1968), parent–child interaction (Lewis & Lee-Painter, 1974), and the development of high-risk children (Sameroff & Chandler, 1975). These reviews clearly indicate the inadequacy of a unidirectional model of environmental action. It appears clear that one must look to the continuous interplay of environmental characteristics and child characteristics if one is truly to understand the role of the environment in the developmental process. Specifically, recent reviews have emphasized the importance of two-way or transactional models. These models postulate that while environment affects the organism, differences in the organism reflect back on and change the subsequent environment. Thus, development consists of a continuous transaction between an organism and its environment.

It appears clear that the general transactional hypothesis is valid. What has been lacking until recently is evidence for what specific child parameters cause changes in the physical, social, or interpersonal environment (Belsky, 1981). Also lacking is evidence on how changes in the environment, caused by individual characteristics, are subsequently translated into changes in the organism's cognitive or social development.

The Transactional Model and Cognitive Development

Many of the studies relating infant characteristics to environment have been based on concurrent correlations between infant development and environmental parameters. As such, these studies do not offer definitive proof of the effect of the infant's behavior upon subsequent parental behavior nor do they deal with the question of how parental behavior changes relate to later infant development. However, the studies are interesting in at least suggesting the types of infant parameters that might be critical in promoting environmental change. In addition, a number of longitudinal studies have recently appeared relating infant characteristics to subsequent parent behavior (although not to subsequent changes in the infant's development). Concurrent and longitudinal studies relating infant characteristics to patterns of parent interactions have been reviewed in two recent chapters by Osofsky and Connors (1979) and Parke (1979). These reviews suggest clearly that there is a good deal of inconsistency in the literature. Rather than repeat information already available in these chapters, we will focus on one infant characteristic not covered in detail in these chapters, as an indication of the status of the field.

Many studies have dealt with the relationship of the infant's level of competence to concurrent parental behavior. Roberts and Rowley (1972) have suggested that competent infants obtain more contact and more skills training from their parents. Similar results indicating greater amounts of interaction and approval for more competent infants have been noted in a variety of studies (Beckwith *et al.*, 1976; Lawson & Ingelby, 1974; White & Watts, 1973; Zeskind & Ramey, 1978). In sharp contrast, other studies (Beckwith & Cohen, 1978; Stern *et al.*, 1969) have reported data indicating that slower infants may receive more responsiveness and physical contact from their mothers, perhaps as a result of maternal anxiety about the infant's development. Differences between studies on a variety of parameters (age of subjects, reasons for delay) make it difficult to rationalize these discrepant results. The overall pattern of correlational studies does suggest that infant competence may in some way be related to the degree of parental interaction even if the direction of this relationship is inconsistent.

Other evidence on the role of infant competence in structuring the environment comes from intervention and longitudinal studies. Evidence is available indicating that early intervention, besides directly affecting infant performance, may also lead to changes in subsequent parental behavior. For premature infants, both Solkoff *et al.* (1969) and Siqueland (1973) have reported greater maternal stimulation following premature infants' participation in early intervention programs. For preschool children, Falender and Heber (1975) have reported more use of verbal and physical feedback by mothers whose young children were in an early intervention program than for mothers of controls. The rationale behind these results is that the early intervention increases the child's competence level; this increase in competence in some way cues greater parental stimulation.

More directly, a number of longitudinal studies have looked specifically at the relationship of infant competence to subsequent parental behavior. For the physical environment, Wachs has reanalyzed his 1979 data. This reanalysis indicates that more competent infants (defined by level of object permanence) received more floor freedom and had a greater number of visitors in the home than less competent infants. These data suggest that parents of brighter infants allow more exploratory freedom and are less prone to protect their child from people than parents of less bright infants.

For the social environment, using a cross-lag design, Bradley *et al.* (1979) report that bright infants elicit higher levels of maternal involvement and receive more age-appropriate play materials from 6 to 12 months of age than duller infants. Past 12 months of age, the results indicate a "steady state" phenomenon such that brighter children continue to receive more age-appropriate materials and involvement, which further advances their capacities. Cross-lag analysis of the relationship between infant intelligence and maternal responsivity did not reveal any clear causal pattern (Bradley *et al.*, 1979). Also using the Caldwell scale, Barnard (1979) has looked at direction of environmental action for high-risk infants between 12 and 24 months of age. In contrast to the "steady state" pattern reported by Bradley *et al.*, the data by Barnard indicate no effect of 12-month infant competence on any subsequent maternal behavior (although maternal responsivity, organization of the environment, and involvement with the child at 12 months are all predictive of 24-month Bayley performance). Similar nonsignificant results using different measures and ages have been reported by Clarke-Stewart (1973). The data from these three studies could be used to suggest that transactional effects involving competence occur primarily in the first year of life, with unidirectional environmental effects becoming more prominent after that time. However, the physical environment results of Wachs noted above occurred after 12 months of age. Further, data by Kagan and Freeman (1963) have indicated a positive relationship between the child's intellectual level at 42 months and subsequent maternal justification of discipline through 7 years of age. Again, differences between studies on subject populations and measures makes it difficult to reconcile inconsistencies.

Two recent studies by Clarke-Stewart (1973, 1977) suggest that inconsistencies in studies on transactional effects may, in part, be due to methodological parameters. In an initial study (Clarke-Stewart, 1973), cross-lag correlations were computed between various maternal variables and Bayley scores between 11 and 17 months of age. Results indicated that components of optimal maternal stimulation (looking, positive emotions, responsiveness, playing) predicted subsequent Bayley performance, whereas initial competence levels did not predict subsequent maternal behaviors. However, in a more recent study, Clarke-Stewart (1977) suggests that a transactional pattern becomes apparent only when one looks at the entire family structure. Specifically, looking at child and parent interaction from 12 through 30 months, Clarke-Stewart (1977) reports a pattern of interactions indicating that maternal variables affect the child's cognitive levels; the child's subsequent cognitive level in turn affects subsequent paternal interaction patterns. These paternal interaction patterns in turn feed back into subsequent maternal interactions with the child.

This pattern clearly supports a transactional model in indicating both child and environmental effects. However, these data suggest that the transactional pattern becomes manifest only when the entire family is considered over a longitudinal time span. In the overwhelming majority of previous studies only mother–child interactions were considered and only over a 2-point time span. Clarke-Stewart's data suggest that transactional patterns are less likely to be revealed with the type of paradigm used in most early experience studies.

Overall, as we have noted earlier, there appears to be little doubt about the existence of a transactional process, with a child's being affected by and affecting his subsequent environment. However, inconsistencies in the literature make it difficult to state clearly what are the specific child characteristics that lead to subsequent environmental change. Even more critical is the almost total lack of evidence on how these environmental changes relate to future development of the child. The state of available evidence on transactional patterns resembles the state of early experience research 10 years ago. At that time it was known that early experience was related to development, but the hows and whys of the relationship were unclear. At present, we know that transactional patterns exist; the hows and whys of these patterns and their contribution to development currently remain unclear. More longitudinal studies clearly are called for. The use of path models (Wachs & Mariotto, 1978) as a means of distinguishing transactional from unidirectional effects may be particularly useful here.

THE DURATION OF EARLY ENVIRONMENTAL ACTION

The Transitional Nature of Early Experience

Available reviews of evidence clearly indicate that the effects of a *single* or *isolated* experience (such as a year of preschool intervention) fade with the passage of time (Bronfenbrenner, 1974; Clarke & Clarke, 1976; Fowler, 1969; Kagan *et al.*, 1978; Weisbender, 1969; Winick, Meyer, & Harris, 1975).[3] Some behavioral exceptions have been found in the literature (Darlington *et al.*, 1980; Friedman *et al.*, 1968), and early experiences that affect the development of the central nervous system may be an exception to this pattern. In general, however, most reviewers agree that early experience effects will fade unless steps are taken to maintain these early effects.

Theoretically, Bloom (1964) has pointed to the characteristics of later environmental input needed for maintaining early changes. Specifically, Bloom hypothesizes that the later environment must be consistent with and mutually reinforcing of the characteristics of the early environment in order for long-term stability to occur. Evidence, both with infrahuman (Wachs, 1973b) and human populations (Sigel & Olmstead, 1970), suggests the importance of either "reinstatements" of the initial experience or further training based on gains obtained from the initial experience. Later reinstatement experiences may be built in either through specially designed training programs (Sigel & Olmstead, 1970) or by keeping the child in a relatively constant and enriched environment over an extended period of time (Bradley &

---

[3]In an elegant demonstration of this point, Olson *et al.* (1981) used a path model approach to show that early differences in rearing had long-term cognitive consequences only to the degree that they were associated with later environmental inputs to the child.

Caldwell, 1981; Ramey, Campbell, & Nicholson, 1973). Most reviewers, however, have stressed setting up naturally occurring reinstatements in the child's natural environment.

Typically, some type of transactional process is envisioned wherein the parent–child dyad becomes the mechanism which stabilizes the initial gains provided by enriched early experiences. This may occur naturally, through enriching experiences promoting gains in the child. These gains are sensed by the parent, who is then inspired to do the extra work necessary to maintain the gains (Siqueland, 1973; Shipman, 1977). A naturally occurring reinstatement is a chancy proposition, however, in that it assumes that the parent will be able to perceive changes and that the parent will be inspired by this perception to provide further enrichment for the child. As Ainsworth and Bell (1974) have clearly indicated, parents differ in their level of sensitivity to their child's behavioral patterns; as Bayley and Schaefer (1964) have noted, parents also differ in the degree to which they are willing to accept the responsibilities of parenthood. Environmental stresses may interfere with parental attempts to provide continuity, as seen in the dramatically lower continuity scores over a 5-year period for lower class homes (Beckwith, 1981). As a result, current theorizing suggests that it may be more economical to involve the parent directly in working with the child rather than assuming that the parent will automatically continue to work with the child.

Efforts to involve the parent directly may be purely empirical (Levinstein, 1970), or they may be based on specific theories (Bronfenbrenner, 1974). In either case, the goal is to get the parent directly involved with the child as a means of providing a natural source of "reinstatement." In general, the available evidence suggests that more lasting effects of early experience will occur with home-based programs where the parent is directly involved than with center-based programs where the parent is not directly involved (Bronfenbrenner, 1974). However, the evidence also indicates tremendous inconsistencies, with washout effects occurring even with home-based intervention programs (Madden et al., 1976; Williams, 1977). This may be due, in part, to purely ecological causes; in severely disadvantaged families survival needs may take precedence over child care needs (Bronfenbrenner, 1974). Failures may also be due to individual differences in parents. Not all parents are highly involved with their infants and some parents may interact with their infants only as long as there is outside encouragement. When encouragement ceases, the parents' interests may also fade. Unfortunately, little research is available to tell us what types of parents may be trusted to continue stimulation when direct program intervention ceases or what are the characteristics of parents who will stop intervention as soon as direct involvement is terminated. Undoubtedly many of the parental variables, such as sensitivity, which have been shown to be relevant to development, will also be relevant here. All of this has implications for intervention and will be considered in the final chapter.

Delayed Effects of Early Experience

One interesting exception to the general rule that most early experiences, taken in isolation, will fade over time is evidence for delayed or "sleeper" effects. Delayed or sleeper effects refer to a situation wherein early experiences are not found to relate to concurrent development but are found to relate to subsequent development perhaps years and years later. The distinction between the two terms lies in the relationship of later experience to development. For delayed effects, one typically finds a pattern wherein early experiences do not predict concurrent development, but both early and later experiences do predict later development. In contrast, for sleeper effects, only the early experience predicts later development; later experiences are found to be unrelated to development.

Delayed effects are quite common in the literature. The most clear-cut cognitive example is that in the study by Elardo, Bradley, and Caldwell (1975), who showed that specific measurements of the home environment at 6 and 12 months did not predict development at these ages but did predict development at 36 months. Examples are also found in the work of Radin (1973), Honzik (1967a), and Bayley and Schaefer (1964).

For social development, an apparent delayed effect is that of the early absence of the father on females' later (adolescent) relationships with males. Generally, these girls tended to have difficulties in interacting with boys, but the form of this difficulty varied for daughters of widows and divorcées. The former exhibited excessive shyness, sexual anxiety, and discomfort around males, whereas the latter were described as assertive with males and sexually precocious, marrying and becoming pregnant earlier than other girls.

The most obvious explanation for delayed effects is given by Hanson (1975), who suggests that delayed effects may reflect the cumulative effects of weak but consistent experiences. A similar formulation has been developed by Bradley and Caldwell (1981). Specifically, an early experience parameter may be too weak to have a direct initial effect upon development. With continued exposure to the experience over time and with a stable environment, one eventually finds a relationship between the early experience and later development (an artifact due to the stability of the experience over time) as well as a relationship between the later experience and later development.

Sleeper effects are rarer, but some examples do exist in the literature. Kagan and Moss (1962) note that critical maternal attitudes from 0 to 3 years of age predict female adult achievement whereas later maternal criticism does not. In the Bayley and Schaefer (1964) data on males, maternal ignoring, irritability, and perceiving the child as a burden are all sleepers for later mental test performance; for females, maternal intrusiveness shows the same pattern.

In contrast to delayed effects, sleeper effects are much more difficult to explain. Kagan and Moss suggest that early maternal practices may provide a more sensitive index of the mother's attitude toward the child and thus have long-term predictive value. This does not explain why the effects appear only later in life if the early practices are that sensitive. L. J. Yarrow *et al.* (1975) suggest that transactional patterns may lead to a sleeper effect, but they are relatively nonspecific as to how this occurs. It seems clear that sleeper effects exist. It also seems clear that they are unexplainable by current theory.

SUMMARY

From the above pattern of evidence a number of statements can be made about the nature of early environmental action.

1. Although some early experience parameters may be global in nature, the vast majority are highly specific: related to development only at certain time periods, related only to certain aspects of development, or related to development only for certain classes of individuals.
2. Early experience can affect the level of the child's development; however, the child's level of development can then, subsequently, affect the environment in which the child is living. This leads to a bidirectional ("transactional") causal chain. The specifics of this process are still relatively unclear.
3. With certain exceptions, the vast majority of early experiences, *taken in isolation,* will not have lasting effects unless later experiences occur which stabilize the effects of the initial experiences. These later stabilizing experiences may occur naturally, as a result of the transactions set up by the initial early experiences, or they may be built in to intervention strategies.
4. Not all early experiences have immediate effects. Delayed effects of early experience can occur when weak but stable experiences exist. Genuine long-term, sleeper effects can also occur, but the nature of the mechanism underlying these is much less clear.

The above four points represent the state of the art in our knowledge of early environmental action. It appears clear that current global experiential theories, based on such concepts as match (Hunt, 1961), dependency drives (Bronfenbrenner, 1974), or stimulus deprivation (Das, 1973) are clearly inadequate in terms of reflecting the above pattern of evidence. This suggests that it may be time, at least temporarily, to move away from global theories into a lower level of inquiry, or mini-theorizing. As we have noted earlier, the infrahuman mini-theories noted by Thompson (1972) may be a useful model to follow in the human area. These theories may be less glamorous than global theories, but they may have more explanatory power, given the nature of early environmental action.

Our ultimate aim, of course, would be to develop an all-encompassing "unified field" theory of early environmental action. However, it appears clear that the current generation of global theories is simply inadequate in the light of the available data. Mini-theories may be useful in terms of posing specific questions (what is the nature of sleeper effects; what are the biological factors underlying age specificity) which may be answered and which may ultimately contribute to development of a more comprehensive theory. The integration of current knowledge about the physiological and behavioral development of the young child (Appleton, Clifton, & Goldberg, 1975) into mini-theories would be a useful approach in expanding the scope of these theories.

In addition to theoretical considerations, the above points have definite implications for applied uses of early experiences. These implications will be considered in the final chapter.

CHAPTER 10

Early Experience and Development

Implications and Applications

Up to the present point, the major thrust of the book has been to review available evidence on the relationship of early experience to both cognitive and social development. In addition to its implications for theory, as we noted earlier, this evidence also has potential practical applications for child-rearing and early intervention. It will be the aim of this final chapter to specify some of the implications of basic research in early experience for applied work with children.

COGNITIVE DEVELOPMENT

In discussing the implications of early experience for human cognitive development, the area that immediately comes to mind is that of early intervention. The historical factors underlying the promotion of early intervention as a tool for facilitating human cognitive development have been noted by Bronfenbrenner (1974). These include infrahuman data on the beneficial effects of early experience stemming from the theorizing of Hebb (1949), and the integration by Hunt (1961) of both basic human and infrahuman data and his relating of these data to the field of early education.

From this background a number of assumptions have been made regarding the importance of early cognitive intervention. These assumptions would undoubtedly include the following: (1) intelligence develops very early, perhaps as much as 50% being developed in the first four years of life; (2) intellectual development is primarily due to experiential factors; (3) certain infants, particularly those who are economically disadvantaged, are being reared in evnrionmental circumstances which are detrimental to optimal cognitive-intellectual development; (4) unless proper experiences are provided, these infants will fall further and further behind intellectually and

209

eventually will be classified as mildly retarded; (5) the earlier remedial experiences are provided, the greater the individual's chance for subsequently normal cognitive development.

Although one could now question the validity of many of these assumptions, the fact remains that during the mid-1960s these assumptions were not questioned. As a result, early intervention as a tool to remediate potential cognitive deficits became fashionable, supported not only by government grants (e.g., Head Start) but also by private foundations (e.g., Sesame Street). At least in the 1960s it seemed clear that early intervention was the means by which we would wipe out all nonorganically based retardation (perhaps 85–90% of all retardation).

It is now clear that many of the goals for early intervention set in the 1960s were quite unrealistic. In part, this is because certain of the assumptions underlying early intervention were clearly invalid, or, at best, limited in their scope. The early intervention approaches, particularly those started in the 1960s, were not based on sound scientific grounds. Specifically, a global model of environmental action was used based on infrahuman data which suggested that disadvantaged children were the human analogues of rats living in laboratory cages; this model postulated that providing massive amounts of stimulation would overcome natural environmental deficits. Few, if any, attempts were made systematically to review available evidence on the role of early experience in development and to construct an "empirical curriculum" based on this review. Almost no one considered the possibility that specific interventions might have to be tailored for specific children. Rather, it was assumed that intervention was good for everyone (the earlier the better). Thus, selection of curriculum was based on intuitive grounds (downward extensions of nursery school techniques, "expert" opinions) in terms of what variables were selected and when they were introduced (Riksen-Walraven, 1978). The result was that heterogeneous groups of infants and toddlers were brought into the "booming, buzzing confusion" of various massive intervention programs.

The consequences of this unbridled enthusiasm for early intervention only now are being recognized. It is now clear that not all children benefit significantly from early intervention; some, in fact, may even show further losses as a result of intervention (Williams, 1977). It is also clear that gains resulting from early intervention are modest indeed and may perhaps serve only to attenuate the declines in cognitive functioning that occur in populations at risk for either biomedical or environmental factors (Belsky & Steinberg, 1978). Some have concluded that this pattern of results represents a failure of early intervention as a remediational technique. We would agree that, as currently practiced, early intervention has clearly failed to meet the goals which were set out for it in the early 1960s. However, one must distinguish between the failure of a model and a failure of the means by which the model was effected.

We strongly maintain that the failure is in the means rather than the model. By blindly rushing into early intervention without understanding the nature of early environmental influences, by assuming a global and linear model of early environmental action, and by assuming that intervention would benefit everyone equally, proponents of early intervention set themselves up for failure from the start. We further maintain that early intervention might meet the goals originally designed for it if these interventions were soundly grounded in basic research on the role of the environment in cognitive development.

It will be the focus of the present section to bring together existing evidence on early experience as the basis for developing an empirically validated curriculum for intervention and to discuss the implications of our understanding of early environmental action for early intervention programs.

The Empirically Validated Curriculum Defined

Up to the present we have talked about an empirical curriculum without actually attempting to define what is meant by this term. The empirical component refers not to the fact that a total curriculum may produce gains in some children. Rather it refers to a curriculum in which are integrated empirically valid components of experience; that is, those experiential components which empirical research has shown to be positively related to specific aspects of cognitive intellectual development for specific children at specific ages. Sets of empirically validated experiences are organized into a coherent and logically organized body of interventions (the curriculum) to be provided to specific children at specific times for specific purposes.

We maintain that such an empirical curriculum would have a maximum probability of enhancing specific aspects of cognitive development at specific ages for specific classes of children. Obviously such a curriculum is limited to current knowledge of the relationship of specific experiences to development. However, adoption of an empirical curriculum strategy would demand, as new hypotheses emerge on potentially relevant experiences, that these hypotheses would be tested by basic research *before they are inserted into the curriculum*. Only if validated could new experiences be integrated into the ongoing empirical curriculum.

As of now, an empirical curriculum, as we have defined it above, does not exist to our knowledge in the early intervention field. Current intervention curriculum may contain some empirically validated aspects but these are there by chance rather than by design. Most intervention curricula are still relatively nonspecific and are based on opinion rather than on actual basic research data (Riksen-Walraven, 1978).

It is also worth noting that most current curricula follow an "inoculation model," on the assumption that the gains obtained will continue through the child's development. It is our contention that unless there is follow-through on the original empirical curriculum we will continue to find our evaluations indicating wide variability of results and washout over time of whatever gains were made.

We therefore challenge early childhood specialists interested in early intervention to utilize the information contained in this volume as a means of designing an empirical curriculum for specific populations of infants and young children. The authors of this book are not educators or curricular specialists and do not presume to have the skills to organize empirically validated experiential components into curricular format. Rather, we see our job as presenting the types of experiences which have been empirically validated and noting the limits of the environmental components in such a way that early educators can take this information and use it to design an empirical curriculum. To aid in this process, we would first like to present those components of the environment which we feel deserve representation in such an empirical curriculum. Because of the evidence for environmental specificity, these components are organized in terms of the cognitive operations they are most likely to affect.

The Components of an Empirical Curriculum

Psychometric Intelligence. Operationally, psychometric intelligence most often refers to general intellectual and problem solving skills as tapped by measures such as the Bayley or Binet scales. These are the tests most often used to evaluate infants' progress in intervention programs and therefore would be of interest to most intervention specialists. Obviously, specific abilities underlie these general skills, but we have not yet, with certain exceptions (e.g., the work of L. J. Yarrow *et al.*, 1975), begun in any systematic fashion to relate specific components of the environment to the development of specific psychometric abilities. Therefore, the present section will be devoted to the role of environmental factors in promoting general psychometric intelligence defined either by test scores or global measures of competence.

Environmental factors which have been shown to be related to the development of psychometric intelligence between birth and 5 years of age (see Chapters 3–5 for specific references) are shown in Table 2. For the first 6 months of age two environmental components appear particularly salient. These are the availability of stimulus material to the child when the child wants to view this material and a high level of physical contact between the child and the caretaker. If one looks at these components in terms of mechanisms, it appears to be clear that physical contact increases the child's attentional capacities (Korner, 1971), whereas the presence of available stimulus material appears to be critical in giving the child something to pay attention to.

After 6 months of age, physical contact seems less and less relevant for development. Rather, amount of interaction with one or two emotionally warm, sensitive caretaking adults who provide the child with a variety of experiences becomes salient to development. Care must be taken not to expose the infant to too many people. Rather, the caretakers must do a variety of activities with the child, particularly after 6 months of age. This suggests the necessity of using home- rather than center-based intervention for the very young infant.

In addition, when the child is about 6 months of age, we can begin to teach specific skills. Care must be taken not to force skills on the child, particularly for less cognitively adept children. As the child becomes mobile after 6 months of age it also becomes more and more important to allow as much exploratory (floor) freedom as possible within the limits of safety. Available stimulus material in the first year should not be just visual but rather should be within easy reach (i.e., things to handle as well as things to look at). Particularly relevant for general cognitive development is the presence of objects with a good deal of variety (a multivariate component—color plus shape plus size) and objects that are in some way responsive (auditory-visual changes) to the child's interactions.

Except for environmental variety, which appears to have a high degree of sex specificity, there is little evidence to suggest that the above stimulus factors would not be relevant for most children through the first year of life (but one must bear in mind that little evidence on organismic specificity in the first year of life is available). Components of experience which current evidence indicates are not particularly relevant to *psychometric intelligence* during the first year include verbal stimulation or responsivity to verbal signals. This may fly in the face of much intervention literature, but available evidence clearly indicates little relevance of these parameters to psychometric development until at least 12 months of age. In addition, as long as the child has adequate exploratory freedom, the degree of parental coercion or restriction appears to be irrelevant to development prior to 12 months of age.

Starting at 12 months of age, a number of early experiences which were relevant in the first year can be carried on through the second year of life. These include the presence of multidimensional toys, particularly of the responsive variety, provision of adequate exploratory freedom for the child, provision of different types (variety) of parent–child interactions (though not physical contact *per se*), specific skill teaching, and provision of sensitivity and emotional warmth. In addition to these earlier factors, a number of other environmental variables become salient during the second year of life and must thus also find their way into our empirical curriculum. For most children, three aspects of environmental stimulation become more and more salient during the second year of life. These are appropriate adult responsivity to the child's nonverbal social signals and needs, increased verbal stimulation (reading, talking), and the active promotion of other forms of exploration (for example, handling of objects) besides allowing the child locomotor (floor freedom) exploration. Along with providing a variety of alternate forms of

Table 2.   Validated Environmental Components Related to the Development of
General Psychometric Intelligence

Add to curriculum	Maintain in curriculum	Drop from curriculum
0–6 months		
Assuring availability of visual material		
Providing physical contact		
6–12 months		
Promoting primary caretaker–infant interaction	Assuring availability of visual material	Providing physical contact
Providing a variety of activities		
Promoting specific skills teaching		
Providing floor freedom		
Placing objects within reach of child		
Assuring object variety for child		
Providing responsive objects		
12–24 months		
Promoting responsivity to infant's social signals	Assuring object variety for child	
Providing verbal stimulation	Providing responsive objects	
Promoting exploration	Providing floor freedom	
Avoidance of restriction/coercion of child	Providing a variety of activities	
Providing long-term object variety (δ)	Promoting primary caretaker–infant interaction	
Providing an environment with temporal/spatial regularity (δ)	Promoting specific skills teaching	
Avoidance of environmental noise–confusion (δ)		
Avoidance of environmental overcrowding (δ)		
24–36 months		
Caretaker responsivity to infant's verbal signals	Providing responsive objects	Assuring object variety for child
	Promoting responsivity to infant's social signals	Avoidance of environmental noise–confusion (δ)
	Promoting exploration	
	Providing floor freedom	
	Promoting primary caretaker–infant interaction	
	Providing verbal stimulation	
	Promoting specific skills teaching	

Table 2. (Continued)

Add to curriculum	Maintain in curriculum	Drop from curriculum
	Avoidance of restriction/coercion of child	
	Providing long-term object variety ($\male$)	
	Providing an environment with temporal/spatial regularity ($\male$)	
	Avoidance of environmental overcrowding ($\male$)	
36–48 months		
Allowing infant to interact with a variety of persons	Promoting responsivity to infant's social signals	Providing responsive objects
	Promoting primary caretaker–infant interaction	Providing floor freedom
	Providing verbal stimulation	Providing long-term parent variety
	Promoting responsivity to infant's verbal signals	
	Promoting exploration	
	Promoting specific skills teaching	
	Avoidance of restriction/coercion of child	
	Providing an environment with temporal/spatial regularity ($\male$)	
	Avoidance of environmental overcrowding ($\male$)	
48–60 months		
Avoidance of environmental noise–confusion ($\male$)	Allowing infant to interact with a variety of persons	Avoidance of restriction/coercion of child
Providing adult nurturance to child ($\male$)	Promoting primary caretaker–infant interaction	
	Promoting responsivity to infant's social signals	
	Promoting responsivity to infant's verbal signals	
	Providing verbal stimulation	
	Promoting exploration	
	Promoting specific skills teaching	
	Providing an environment with temporal/spatial regularity ($\male$)	
	Avoidance of environmental overcrowding ($\male$)	

exploration we would also strongly emphasize avoiding restriction or coercion of the infant during the second year.

In addition, four other components become salient during the second year but only for males or only for females. For females, available evidence suggests the importance, during the second year of life, of providing long-term stimulus variety, that is, allowing the child to be exposed to different types of toys and objects over time rather than continually leaving the child with familiar ones. For males, long-term variety appears to be significantly less relevant for development. In contrast, for males, available evidence indicates the importance of providing a temporally and spatially regular environment during the second year of life, that is, a home where everything has a place and a time. Again, the evidence indicates the irrelevance of this component for the female's development during 12 and 24 months of age.

In addition to variety and regularity, two other environmental factors are relevant for psychometric development during the second year of life, particularly for males. These components are not those which should be built into a program but rather ones which should be avoided in a curriculum or in a home situation. We refer specifically to the presence of noise–confusion and overcrowding. What appears critical here is a survey of infant's natural home environment at the start of the second year of life to determine whether either noise–confusion (number and intensity of stimulus sources) or overcrowding (high number of sibs or low rooms-to-people ratio) exists in the child's home environment.

Particulary for male children, where these conditions exist it may be a mistake either to provide intervention experiences in the home situation or to bring the child into the typical noisy, crowded day-care center. Rather, for children during the second year of life who live in these conditions, it may be important to set up a small room in the intervention center away from the noise, confusion, and other children, where the child can be alone with an adult, one or two other children, and several toys. Alternatively, if home-based intervention is used, one could attempt to set up a separate room in the home which would serve these functions during intervention periods. The goal of this "stimulus shelter" would be to avoid treating the child in environmental conditions which are not conducive to cognitive growth and to which male infants are particularly sensitive. Obviously, such a strategy may require more investment of personnel time and building requirements than direct intervention without considering the child's natural ecology. However, if one is truly serious about providing optimal interventions for individual children, such steps may have to be taken, particularly in the second year of life. Indeed, we would go so far as to suggest that a home survey be taken routinely, if only to get an idea of the relevant ecological components present or lacking in the natural environment.

Starting in the third year of life, certain components become less and less salient for development, while several new components begin to emerge.

Specifically, for two classes of environmental stimulation little evidence is available on their relevance to development between 24 and 36 months of age. These are presenting multidimensional toys to the child and the presence of noise and confusion in the home. This is not to say that these factors may not be relevant for development but only that their role in the third year of life has not been systematically investigated. Therefore, until appropriate evidence is gathered, their role in an empirical curriculum is unclear.

The majority of factors found relevant in the second year of life continue to remain salient during the third year of life as well. Thus, providing a physically and socially responsive environment to the child, providing various forms of exploratory freedom, providing adequate amounts of warm adult interaction, giving the child adequate amounts of verbal stimulation, providing training in specific skills, and avoiding restrictiveness and coercion are all relevant to development in the third year of life. In addition, for girls, providing long-term variety of objects is still salient, and for males, promoting temporal and spatial regularity and avoiding overcrowding also continue to be relevant.

In addition to these factors, one new environmental factor that should be added in the third year of life is appropriate adult responsivity to the child's verbal signals. In previous years, nonverbal social signals were responded to as were the child's needs; the literature now suggests the importance of responding to verbal signals after 24 months of age.

Between 36 and 48 months of age, many of the previously noted environmental factors continue to remain salient. However, the presence of a number of factors in the empirical curriculum becomes less clear, again primarily due to a lack of evidence rather than to negative evidence. These factors include promoting physically responsive objects, providing floor freedom and, for girls, providing long-term variety of objects.

Still relevant for development are providing adequate amounts of responsivity to social signals, adult warmth, verbal stimulation, promoting the child's exploratory freedom, teaching specific skills, and avoiding restriction and coercion. Again, for males, providing a regular temporal and spatial environment and avoiding overcrowding also appear to be salient.

Available evidence indicates that one new environmental factor becomes increasingly salient for development after 36 months of age. This factor involves exposing the child to a variety of different people with whom to interact. The increasing importance of person variety parallels the shift to a more social-interactional loading of intellectual factors as discussed in earlier chapters. The relevance of person variety after 36 months suggests that this may be the important time to shift the child from home- to center-based intervention, where the child will encounter more people.

A number of interesting shifts occur in the period from 48 to 60 months. Again, providing experience with a variety of people, providing available, warm, socially responsive, and verbally stimulating adults, promoting exploration, and teaching specific skills are salient. For males, promoting temporal and spatial regularity and avoiding overcrowding also continue to be relevant. Also, for males, available evidence indicates that it again becomes important to avoid noise–confusion in the child's environment. Thus, the importance of home or preschool visits again becomes particularly critical during this time. Scrutinizing the ecology of the day-care center may be particularly critical, since many lower-class children may now be eligible for Head Start programs. If the centers are overcrowded and noisy in nature, enrollment of the child may be detrimental rather than beneficial. In addition, particularly for middle-class males, the providing of a nurturant figure also gains salience as a relevant environmental factor after 48 months. The relevance of avoiding adult restriction and coercion becomes less and less salient after 48 months, suggesting that emphasis on minimizing these factors be shifted to other more critical areas of the environment.

Sensorimotor (Piagetian) Intelligence. Uzgiris (1976) has differentiated between sensorimotor and psychometric approaches to intelligence on the grounds that the former measures the level of organization of actions and the latter assesses the degree of competence or the dimensions related to individual differences. Operationally, tests of sensorimotor development often are designed to identify specific dimensions of early cognitive functioning, while psychometrically based instruments often yield a single composite score such as a DQ. Significant but moderate correlations are found between sensorimotor and psychometric assessment instruments. As a result, one would expect to find some, but not complete, overlap between environmental factors predicting sensorimotor intelligence and those predicting psychometric intelligence. Further, one would expect to find a higher degree of specificity for environmental factors predicting sensorimotor intelligence than for factors predicting general psychometric intelligence. In general, the available evidence to be described below bears out these hypotheses.

In developing an empirical curriculum for acceleration of sensorimotor abilities, we cannot, therefore, simply adopt a curriculum intended for the development of general psychometric intelligence and expect optimal results. Rather, a curriculum must be tailored not only for sensorimotor intelligence but also for the specific components of sensorimotor intelligence which have been identified. Obviously, many of the same factors influencing psychometric abiliies will also influence sensorimotor intelligence, but the pattern and direction of these relationships may be notably different.

Specifically, a number of factors found to influence psychometric intelligence have been shown to be completely irrelevant to the development of sensorimotor intelligence. Thus, the teaching of specific skills, which was found to be quite salient for psychometric intelligence between birth and 5 years of age, shows little or no relationship to the development of sensorimotor intelligence. Similarly, parental warmth, which is positively related to infant psychometric intelligence from the first years of life, shows little consistent relationship to sensorimotor intelligence. Indeed, some evidence indicates a negative relationship between measures of warmth and the sensorimotor ability on the object relations in space scale during the second year of life (Clarke-Stewart, 1973). Floor freedom, which is a major predictor of psychometric intelligence in the first year of life, is irrelevant to sensorimotor intelligence during this time period. Even within the sensorimotor domain components of the environment that specifically predict one aspect of sensorimotor intelligence do not specifically predict other aspects of sensorimotor intelligence. Environmental factors which available evidence (see Chapters 3–5) implicate as relevant to sensorimotor development are shown in Table 3. In general, unless otherwise specified, the time periods for environmental items will reflect those noted for psychometric intelligence.

The overwhelming majority of evidence relating environmental factors to sensorimotor intelligence deals with the development of object permanence. Specifically, object permanence levels are facilitated by providing physical contact stimulation and a variety of different interactions between parent and child in the first year of life (particularly for temperamentally "easy" infants). Providing multidimensional toys, adequate amounts of social stimulation, responsive toys, and contingencies following the child's behavior are also relevant both in the first and second years of life.

Giving the child adequate amounts of floor freedom and providing alternative forms of exploration become salient in the second year of life. Also in the second year of life, for males, providing adequate temporal spatial regularity and avoiding overcrowding and noise–confusion are critical. After 15 months, the verbal interaction between caretaker and child becomes quite salient in the development of object permanence. Care must be taken, however, to de-emphasize verbal stimulation prior to 15 months, for some evidence is available (Goldberg, 1977a) indicating negative relationship between parental vocalizations and object permanence level prior to 15 months of age. Little or no evidence is available for environmental factors predicting object permanence after the second year of life. Indeed, with the exception of retarded children, it is expected that most infants will have achieved the top levels of object permanence after the second year of life.

Available evidence, though highly limited, is available for other sensorimotor components. (For a more detailed description of these components see Uzgiris & Hunt, 1975.) For the development of foresight after 12 months, an organized home environment, the provision of age-appropriate, responsive play materials, promoting exploratory freedom, and providing vocalizations directed at the infant are all relevant. Available evidence also suggests the relevance of long-term variety for females after 12 months of age. Avoiding overcrowding, avoiding noise–confusion, and providing exploration opportunities are relevant to the development of male foresight after 11 months of age.

For schemes, in the first year of life, high levels of activity and noise–confusion in the home are negatively related to development. Between 12 and 24 months of age, long-term variety, a lack of overcrowding, and temporal-

Table 3.   *Validated Environmental Components Relevant to the Development of*
Sensorimotor Intelligence

Sensorimotor ability	Environmental components	Age period (months) during which environmental component should be in curriculum
Object permanence	Providing physical contact	0–12
	Providing a variety of activities	0–12
	Assuring object variety for child	0–24
	Promoting primary caretaker–infant interaction	0–24
	Providing responsive objects	0–24
	Promoting responsivity to infant's social signals	0–24
	Providing floor freedom	12–24
	Promoting exploration	12–24
	Providing verbal stimulation	15–24
	Providing an environment with temporal/ spatial regularity	♂ 12–24
	Avoidance of overcrowding	♂ 12–24
	Avoidance of environmental noise– confusion	♂ 12–24
Foresight	Providing a temporally and spatially organized environment	12–24
	Providing age-appropriate play materials for child	12–24
	Promoting exploration	15–24
	Providing responsive objects	15–24
	Providing verbal stimulation	15–24
	Providing long-term object variety	♂ 12–24
	Avoidance of environmental overcrowding	♂ 11–24
	Avoidance of environmental noise–confusion	♂ 11–24
	Providing floor freedom	♂ 11–24
Schemes	Avoid exposing infant to too many people in home	0–12
	Providing responsive objects	15–24
	Providing verbal stimulation	15–24
	Avoidance of environmental noise– confusion	0–12; ♂ 12–24
	Providing long-term object variety	♂ 12–24
	Avoidance of environmental overcrowding	♂ 12–24
	Providing an environment with temporal and spatial regularity	♂ 12–24

Table 3. (Continued)

Sensorimotor ability	Environmental components	Age period (months) during which environmental component should be in curriculum
Causality	Promoting exploration	♂ 12–24
	Assuring availability of visual material	♂ 12–24
	Providing responsive objects	♂ 12–24
	Avoidance of environmental noise–confusion	♂ 12–24
Spatial relations	Providing physical contact	0–12
	Avoidance of environmental noise–confusion	0–12; ♂ 12–24
	Avoidance of environmental overcrowding	♂ 12–24
	Providing responsive objects	♂ 12–24
Verbal imitation	Avoidance of environmental noise–confusion	♂ 15–24
	Providing verbal stimulation	♂ 15–24
Gestural imitation	Avoidance of environmental noise–confusion	♂ 0–24
	Providing floor freedom	♂ 12–24
	Providing responsive objects	♂ 12–24

spatial regularity are all positively related for males, while noise–confusion is negatively related. In addition, providing physically responsive toys and vocalizations directed to the child after 15 months of age are also positively related the the development of schemes.

For the development of an understanding of causality, with the exception of data suggesting the sensitivity of difficult infants to ambient noise–confusion at 6 months, all available evidence occurs between 12 and 24 months of age. These data suggest the relevance, for males, of providing exploratory freedom, availability of visual stimulation, a responsive physical environment, and a lack of noise–confusion in the home. In contrast, for females, the development of causality is positively related to the presence of noise–confusion in the home and negatively related to the availability of visual stimulation.

For the development of early spatial relationships, in the first year of life we find positive relationships between the degree of physical contact and negative relationships with noise–confusion in the home. In the second year of life, a lack of overcrowding and noise–confusion for males plus a physically responsive environment become more relevant to an understanding of object relations in space.

For verbal imitation, again the need to avoid noise–confusion stress with difficult infants is noted in the literature. Most salient for males in the second year of life is an avoidance of noise–confusion and vocal stimulation directed toward the child after 15 months of age. For gestural imitation, most relevant is a lack of noise–confusion for males in the first and second year of life plus floor freedom, and a physically responsive environment for males after 12 months of age.

The above evidence clearly shows that although some environmental factors (noise–confusion, a physically responsive environment) relate to most components of sensorimotor intelligence, there is a high degree of age-by-environment-by-organismic specificity in available relationships. This must be taken into account if one is attempting either home- or center-based intervention directed at sensorimotor intelligence.

Language. In the present section language development is defined primarily in the terms a psychologist would use (naming, word recognition, use of language to solve problems) rather than in the terms a linguist would use (mean length of utterance, correct grammatical usage, nouns or verbs used per utterance). The study of the relationship of specific environmental factors to these latter linguistic parameters is a relatively recent innovation which has not been dealt with in this volume. For the reader interested in this topic, a number of excellent references have appeared recently (e.g., Nelson, 1973; Furrow, Nelson, & Benedict, 1979; Moerk, 1980).

If one is interested in developing an empirical curriculum to accelerate language development, it becomes quickly apparent that a number of environmental components which are relevant to the development of psychometric or sensorimotor intelligence are unrelated to the development of language. These include dimensions of the physical environment such as the presence of multidimensional toys, varied stimulus material, a responsive physical environment, a lack of overcrowding, temporal and spatial irregularity, and floor freedom. Measures of the social environment such as physical contact stimulation, and most available measures of the interpersonal environment (i.e., parental warmth, coercion) are also unrelated to the development of language. In terms of environmental factors available for inclusion in an empirical language curriculum, what evidence is available is summarized in Table 4 (see Chapters 3–5 for specific references).

The summary presented in Table 4 reflects the fact that little if any evidence supports the salience of specific environmental factors in the first year of life. One can, of course, get an increase in phoneme production through reinforcement in the first year, but the relevance of this intervention to language development is unclear. Bruner (1975) has speculated that early mother–child interaction patterns are a precursor to acquisition of language concepts and rules. However, his analysis is purely on a descriptive level; nowhere do we see an attempt to relate differences in interaction patterns to differences in later language development.

Table 4.   *Validated Environmental Components Related to the Development of Language*

Environmental component	Age period (months) during which environmental component should be in curriculum
Providing an environment with temporal and spatial regularity	12–24
Providing age-appropriate play materials to child	12–24
Promoting primary caretaker–infant interaction	12–24, 36+
Avoidance of environmental noise–confusion	12+ ($\male$)
Providing verbal stimulation	12–36
Caretaker responsivity to child's verbal signals	24–36
Availability of adults as problem-solving resource for child	36+
Accuracy of child–caretaker, referential communication	36+

In the second year of life, the most relevant environmental factors appear to be an organized environment, the presence of age-appropriate play materials, verbal stimulation directed toward the infant, a variety of social interactions, a lack of restrictiveness, and, for males, an avoidance of noise–confusion. In the third year of life, beside verbal stimulation directed toward the infant, responsivity to infant verbal signals and "matching" the infant's speech level become increasingly salient. After 36 months, accuracy of referential communication between the child and caretaker, the amount of adult interaction, and the availability of adults as problem-solving resources become important. From the above pattern of evidence, unlike psychometric and sensorimotor abilities, it appears clear that only a small and specific subset of environmental influences are relevant for the development of language.

Other Developmental Parameters

In addition to intelligence and language, a little evidence is available on the relationship of specific components of the environment to other aspects of cognitive development. A summary of these data are shown in Table 5 (for references see Chapters 3–5).

For the development of habituation, maternal involvement at 9–12 months, maternal availability at 12–24 months, and responsivity to the infant's social signals after 12 months have proven to be relevant. For goal-directed exploratory behaviors in the first year of life, complexity of stimulus material provided, maternal involvement, responsive toys and parents, and

Table 5. Validated Environmental Components Relevant to the Development of Nonintellectual Cognitive Components

Cognitive component	Environmental component	Age period (months) during which environmental component should be in curriculum
Habituation	Promoting active maternal involvement with infant	9–12
	Promoting maternal availability to infant	12–24
	Promoting responsivity to infant's social signals	9–24
Exploration	Providing infant with objects of increasing complexity	0–12
	Providing responsive objects	0–12
	Providing an environment with temporal/spatial regularity	0–12
	Promoting active maternal involvement with child	0–24
	Promote parental responsivity to infant	9–12
	Assuring object variety for child	12–24
	Providing floor freedom	12–24
	Avoid interference with child's actions	12–24
Task persistence	Promoting primary caretaker–infant interactions	0–24
Attention/information-processing	Providing physical contact	0–6
	Avoidance of environmental noise–confusion	48+
	Provide specific cues for infant in training situations	48+

environmental regularity are all critical. After 12 months, maternal involvement, variety of stimulation, and a lack of environmental restriction or interference are also relevant. The evidence suggests, however, a high degree of environmental specificity for exploratory behavior (McQuiston & Wachs, 1979).

Maternal involvement also predicts the development of recognition memory between 12 and 24 months. Perceptual discrimination and task persistence are related to the variety of adult interactions in the first and second years of life. For preschool children, psychomotor performance, information processing, and attention are negatively related to noise–confusion after 4 years of age, while provision of specific cues is relevant to performance of specific tasks. One hopes that more evidence can be gathered on the above, nonintellectual cognitive parameters to provide more than just the skeleton of an empirical curriculum for development in these areas.

Summary of Current Knowledge of the Empirical Curriculum

It appears clear from the above pattern that enough environmental components have been validated to write at least a tentative empirical curriculum for psychometric intelligence covering the first five years of life. Writing this curriculum would essentially involve translating validated environmental components into a set of center- or home-based curricular experiences for infants and children.

Validation of such a curriculum could be done on a yearly basis by comparing gains in psychometric intelligence for a group of infants or children receiving the empirical curriculum with those in standard, nonempirical intervention programs. Undoubtedly, the standard curriculum would contain some empirically validated elements, but it would also contain elements that might prove to be either irrelevant or detrimental to cognitive growth. Our prediction would be that for a given year there would be significantly greater gains and less variability of gains under an empirically validated curriculum than under a standard, nonvalidated curriculum (i.e., the empirical curriculum would be valid for more children, hence lower variability than the standard curriculum).

As for writing an empirical curriculum for other aspects of cognitive development, our knowledge is inadequate at present. The most promising area outside of psychometric intelligence appears to be that of language, wherein a small but well-validated set of environmental components can be found. The majority of these occur after 12 months of age. Certain environmental components may be relevant to language development prior to 12 months of age, but at this point they have not been discovered.

For the specific components found under sensorimotor intelligence (or indeed for individual components of psychometric intelligence), the outlook is clearly not promising. Only a limited number of studies exist in this area.

Almost all deal with the age period between 12 and 24 months, and much of the available evidence deals with the physical rather than the social environment. Further, most evidence here is centered around a single sensorimotor ability, namely that of object permanence. Clearly, a great deal more evidence must be generated before we can hope to write an empirical curriculum for specific components of either sensorimotor or psychometric intelligence. A similar statement can be made with regard to nonintellective aspects of cognitive development such as habituation, exploration, or information processing skills. Given this state of affairs, we recommend that most early intervention efforts concentrate on the development of either language or general psychometric intelligence.

Two further points must be made in regard to the development of an empirically validated curriculum. First, it must again be emphasized that an empirically validated curriculum is not carved in stone. Rather, as further basic research reveals new experiences which are relevant to development, these should be introduced into the curriculum. Unless this is done, in ten years any empirically validated curriculum will undoubtedly be dated and thus not worthy of the name. Second, given the current state of knowledge, any attempts to write an empirical curriculum at this time will undoubtedly contain gaps which must be filled, either by overgeneralizing experiences to areas where there is little support or extending the experiences downward or upward past their optimal point. This may be necessary to provide a curriculum, but one hopes that in validating the curriculum care will be taken to distinguish between those time points at which an empirically validated curriculum is used and those time points at which an empirically validated curriculum is generalized before or past its optimal point.

The Nature of Environmental Action and the Intervention Process

Up to the present we have been talking primarily about available knowledge of the role of specific experiences and development and the implications of this knowledge for writing a curriculum. However, writing a curriculum involves more than just simply translating experiences into a set of interventions. Rather, to have intervention programs with any chance of success one must take cognizance not only of empirical findings *per se* but also the implications of these findings for early intervention. As we have noted earlier, available evidence suggests a high specificity of early environmental action, suggests that early experiences may fade with the passage of time, and implicates the child's role in promotion of his own experiences and development. The importance of each of these factors for early intervention must be seriously considered, and we will do so in the following section.

Specificity and the Intervention Process.   The concept of specificity indicates the need for highly specific curricula for different individuals at different ages and for different outcomes. At present this concept must be seen more as a caution than as something to be integrated into intervention *per se*. In good part this is due to the relative newness of the concept and the paucity of empirical evidence on specific organism–environment–development relationships. At least to some extent, environmental specificity has been dealt with in the previous section in terms of delineation of environmental factors that predict specific aspects of development. As we have shown, although there is clearly some overlap, certain environmental factors are highly unique to certain areas of functioning. For those interested in intervention, the implications of environmental specificity are that one should define the processes one hopes to facilitate prior to intervention and attempt to provide curricular experiences that are most specific for development of the selected target behaviors.

Similarly, age specificity implies that experiences chosen for the curriculum should be appropriate for the age of the particular child in question. Also implicit in the concept of age specificity is a critical period notion, namely, that there may be some age period when the infant may be well buffered against environmental stimulation. Evidence on this latter point is mixed. Some studies have presented evidence indicating minimal relationships between environment and either cognitive (White, Kaban, Shapiro, & Attanucci, 1977; Rubenstein *et al.*, 1977; Farran & Ramey, 1980; Burchinal & Farran, 1980) or social development (Bakeman & Brown, 1980) in the first six months of life. Other studies have reported significant correlations between environment and development during this time period. (L. J. Yarrow *et al.*, 1975; Beckwith *et al.*, 1976; Cohen & Beckwith, 1979).

Factors that have been implicated in leading to differences between studies include differential sensitivity of developmental instruments (Sloven-Ela & Kohen-Raz, 1978) and differences in population (Wachs, in press; many of the studies showing significant relationships prior to 6 months utilized infants who were either biomedically, temperamentally, or environmentally at risk). The relevance for intervention of the possibility of age-mediated buffering against very early environmental stimulation hangs on the question of when intervention should begin. Obviously, if the infant is very well buffered against most forms of environmental stimulation during the first six months, then the implication is that intervention should not take place until the insensitive period has passed.

At present, the question of when to begin intervention is still an open one. About all that can be said with any confidence is that environmental effects become much more dramatic after 6 months of age. At least for biologically nonimpaired infants or infants who are at risk only for environmental reasons (i.e., disadvantaged), intervention in the first six months of life may be justified only when one considers the possibility of delayed effects upon development. Weak but consistent environmental influences starting in the first year of life could have significant long-term effects upon development which are not evident immediately but are nonetheless real (Elardo *et al.*, 1975).

Justification of very early intervention is easier with infants who are biologically high risk or at risk (developmentally disabled). Available evidence indicates significant cognitive gains associated with environmental intervention with biologically vulnerable babies in the first year of life (Powell, 1974; Scarr-Salapatek & Williams, 1973). Given these facts and the available evidence indicating that environmental factors come to overshadow biological deficits over time (Sameroff & Chandler, 1975; Jordan, 1978), it is our conclusion that intervention should be started as early as possible for infants who are at risk either for biological or developmental deficits.

The implications of organismic specificity for intervention, although shadowy in outline, may be more critical than either of the other specificity factors. One specific implication of the concept of organismic specificity is the notion of an idiographic rather than a nomothetic treatment strategy. Specifically, at its most extreme point, the organismic specificity hypothesis would suggest that intervention must be tailored specifically for the individual child, it is not sufficient simply to place the child in a group and hope that enough positive stimulus elements for that child are present in that group situation.

Such an idiographic approach is more feasible when one is dealing with home-based intervention because the parent can be trained to respond to the individual child (when one can assume that the home environment is not part of the child's problem; if it is, the organismic specificity hypothesis would suggest that intervention should be outside of the home environment). If center-based intervention is used, we can only suggest careful, ongoing monitoring of the targeted cognitive growth paths of children in the intervention program. Rather than assuming that all children will be benefiting from the intervention, it is critical to assess whether specific, individual children are benefiting in the desired ways. If a specific child in an intervention program shows little ongoing progress, it may be time to look carefully at that child to determine what aspects of the intervention program may be irrelevant or even detrimental to the specific child's cognitive growth.

Even within a home-based intervention program one is faced, of course, with the problem of what individual, idiographic aspects should go into curriculum formation. Unfortunately, available research is of little help here since, with the exception of research on sex and temperament differences, there is little evidence on what individual characteristics interface with the environment to produce optimal growth for the individual. In the absence of hard evidence, suggestions for empirical programs for individual children must of necessity be vague.

Certain caveats can be specified: (1) do not provide the same experience or set of training experiences for all parents to give to their children; (2) do not provide any experience to the child without first considering salient qualities of the child which may mediate the experience provided. Salient qualities which should be considered (see Chapter 9 for specific studies) include the child's sex, temperament, preintervention history, level of cognitive functioning, biomedical history, and current pattern of cognitive function. As we noted in our previous review, these have all been shown to mediate the effects of early experience upon development. Other relevant organismic parameters will undoubtedly emerge as research continues on this question in the future.

Of the above organismic factors, biomedical history must be considered as especially relevant, particularly when one attempts to intervene with identified developmentally disabled children. The overwhelming majority of studies relating experiential parameters to subsequent development involve disadvantaged but biologically normal populations. Only a few studies are available looking at parent–child interaction with developmentally disabled children as these relate to development (Beckwith *et al.*, 1976; Cohen & Beckwith, 1979; Piper & Ramsay, 1980). Thus, in generalizing information obtained with normal children to developmentally disabled children, one must make two assumptions. The first is that experiences relevant for the cognitive development of normal infants are also relevant for the development of developmentally disabled infants. At present, not enough evidence is available to assess the validity of this assumption. The second assumption is that these experiences will be salient at the same age for both populations (i.e., there will be no age-by-organismic specificity). Available evidence, though scant, suggests the lack of validity for this assumption. Studies of visual behavior indicate that experiences relevant for normal infants at a specific age may be inappropriate for infants with biological or neurological problems (Parmelee & Sigman, 1976). In addition, reviews of available evidence suggest that for premature or retarded infants measures of mental age or estimates of central nervous system immaturity may be more crucial in determining stimulus-processing ability than measures of chronological age (Wachs, 1977). These data could be used to suggest that mental age or developmental quotient, rather than chronological age, be used as the basis for deciding what experiences an infant receives. However, Scott (1978) has reviewed a number of statistical problems associated with the use of intelligence level as an independent or predictor variable. Scott cautions that these problems may severely limit the use of intelligence as a guide to programming specific interventions.

Clearly what is needed is research to determine whether the same environmental parameters predict development for normal and developmentally disabled children of the same age. In the absence of such research, our clinical judgment suggests that stimulation validated for younger, normal children may be more appropriate for developmentally disabled children than stimulation used for same-age normal children. It must be emphasized, however, that this conclusion is based on clinical judgment and has little empirical validation *per se.*

Implications of the Transactional Position and the Transient Nature of Early Experience to Early Intervention

In a perfect universe, theory would predict that the effects of early intervention would be automatically stabilized and maintained throughout the life span. Enhancing the infant's cognitive growth and making the infant more attentive to environmental stimulation should ensure that he will demand and receive more stimulation from his caretakers in the future. The infant's demanding and receiving more growth-producing stimulation from his parents would, in turn, lead to further accelerations of cognitive growth, setting up a positive spiral. As we have documented in Chapter 9, however, available evidence is quite inconsistent as to whether more competent infants, or infants who have graduated from intervention programs, actually do get more stimulation from the environment.

It is not only methodological factors which produce these inconsistencies. A number of existing parameters clearly limit the degree to which changing the infant's level of functioning leads to subsequent provision of growth-producing experiences. Three factors appear to be particularly relevant. First, as we have noted earlier, the ecological conditions of the child's environment may be such as to attenuate any subsequent growth-producing experiences provided by the parent. For example, Bronfenbrenner (1974) has reported data indicating that with three or more sibs in the home, attempts to stimulate the child have little value. Even if the home conditions are positive, parental survival needs may have more salience for the parents than child stimulation needs. As long as the parent and the child are in the intervention project, adequate stimulation is provided. However, once the project is discontinued, ecological-personal pressures on the parents may be so great as to minimize the parents' ability to contribute any further input to the infant's development (Bronfenbrenner, 1974; Rynders & Horrobin, 1975). And even when the home environment is supportive and survival needs are not critical, many parents are either unable or unwilling to put time and effort into facilitating or promoting their infant's development (Rynders & Horrobin, 1975). The increasing numbers of reports of battered or neglected children is a clear indication that, for many parents, children are a burden, or at best irrelevant to the parents' needs and goals.

Given these factors, it seems particularly naive to expect that facilitating the child's development will automatically cause maintenance of early gains. Thus, the debate as to whether home- or center-based intervention is more likely to cause the parents to continue subsequent work with the children seems irrelevant (Bronfenbrenner, 1974). Home-based intervention may be more likely to maintain gains if the environmental ecology is favorable, if survival needs are not critical, and if the parent has the motivation and skills to continue working with the child in the absence of external social pressures. However, if the ecology is unfavorable, if survival needs are critical, or the parent is not motivated or skilled, neither home- nor center-based intervention will produce much in the way of long-lasting parental contributions to the child's progress once the original intervention program has ceased. As Gray and Klaus (1970) have noted, early intervention simply cannot be considered a form of early inoculation which will forever protect the child from life's subsequent adversities. In the absence of ideal conditions promoting transactional effects, something else must occur to maintain the gains resulting from early intervention.

Given the above, what are the implications for early intervention programs? The major implication, of course, is that one simply does not start an early intervention program without considering the long-term consequences and the possible methods of maintaining early gains. Specifically, three questions should be asked for every child who is terminating an early intervention program.

1. Do the parents have the time and social support systems to continue some type of future intervention with the child?
2. Do the parents have the motivation and skills to continue to work with the child after the intervention has ceased?
3. Will the natural ecology of the child's home environment permit parental intervention to be effective?

Careful observation during intervention of the child's home environment and the level and pattern of parent–child interaction is critical for answering each of these questions. Repeated regular visits to the child's home should be made to assess the ecology of the home in terms of such factors as overcrowding, noise–confusion, or a lack of temporal and spatial regularity. Also critical to note would be whether both parents have to work to survive, the extent to which the child is left with a sitter, and the types of social stresses the parents may be undergoing. In a center-based program, records can be kept of the degree to which the parent observes sessions or at least attends parent–teacher meetings as an indication of motivation. In addition, either in the home or in the center, direct observation should be made of parent–infant interaction sequences, both in a free play situation and at various times during the intervention phase. These sequences should then be coded for variables such as parental sensitivity, parental responsiveness, and parental warmth as a further indication of the parents' interest and competence in interacting with the child.

On the basis of the above information, for a situation wherein the answer to the above three questions is yes, one could expect with a reasonable degree of confidence that intervention gains probably will be maintained without future major interventions. Even in this case it would be desirable to follow-up on each infant to confirm these hypothesized gains and to provide a rationale for further intervention if gains seem to be fading. For a situation in which parental survival needs seem to preclude child care needs, efforts should be made to provide social or economic support to the parent to allow the freedom to continue working with the child. In a situation wherein the natural ecology seems to be hostile for future growth, either working with the parents to restructure the environment or beginning center-based intervention as a follow-up may be critical. When the parent lacks only specific skills, these may be provided either by home-visitor demonstration or by parent classes. When the parent seems unable or unwilling to continue follow-up intervention, using some form of center-based follow-up intervention is probably critical. Obviously, in the latter case, except for the rough indexes noted above, we have few if any specific markers to determine whether parents are genuinely motivated to do follow-up work with their infants. In the absence of clear-cut marker variables, intervention personnel must be prepared to make a clinical guess based on whatever information they have as to whether the parents are likely to continue working with their children. Since follow-up cognitive analyses should be part of the program, a guess, if incorrect, will be detected within a reasonably short period of time and can be corrected by center-based follow-up.

Some may object that the above program puts heavy economic and personnel demands on early intervention programs. But unless the early gains are maintained, it makes little economic or human sense to involve children in an intense intervention program which will have few if any long-term consequences. Early intervention makes sense only if one can talk about long-term remediation. To guarantee long-term remediation, the pattern of evidence clearly indicates that when ideal conditions do not exist other measures must be taken.

SOCIAL COMPETENCE

There have been a number of efforts in the last decade to increase the social competence of infants, preschool children, and older children who are identified as lacking in social competence. Many of these efforts have been either atheoretical or adevelopmental in nature and therefore have lacked the impact and importance they might otherwise have had. Few of these interventions could be considered as fitting within our conception of an empirically based curriculum. Because of this, it is difficult to generalize their results beyond the specific populations and programs employed in the particular settings in which they were conducted.

There are, however, a number of concepts derived from the current research and theory we have reviewed that suggest meaningful practical applications. In addition, there are some relatively specific training techniques and programs which are solidly based on this literature. These will be reviewed here, starting with their practical implications for institutional and day-care centers, and then moving to the implications for preschool settings and finally to parent training in the home.

Implications for Institutional Environments

The essential implication of the literature reviewed in this book is that both the physical and social environments must be highly responsive to the infant's and young child's needs and behavior if positive social development is to occur. The physical responsive environment has already been discussed. In nonsocially responsive environments, such as institutions where the child is separated from his parents, the most obvious intervention would be to train the administrators and caregivers who will be working directly with children. This training should include both information about the need for a contingently responsive social environment and some of the "nuts and bolts" techniques for appropriate, sensitive interaction with infants and young children. For example, Clarke-Stewart (1973) found that the maternal variable that was most positively related to the development of competence in children was verbal stimulation; next were the expression of positive emotions and "cuddling." These findings reinforce the view that institutional caregivers must be aware of the importance of providing a stimulating, contingently responding, affectively expressive, and sensitive social environment for infants.

Also, apropos of institutionalized children, the work reported in an earlier chapter by Tizard and Hodges (1978) confirmed Bowlby's concept that infants need a warm, continuous, and intimate relationship with at least one caregiver. Excessive turnover of staff working directly with infants, therefore, may have negative effects on the infants' social development by either preventing a stable attachment relationship from being formed in the first place or by forcing a separation after a strong bond has been established. Interestingly, the effects of lack of caregiver stability appear to be much more critical for social than for cognitive development (Rutter, 1979). L. J. Yarrow (1964) has suggested that such separations can be devastating to children between 7 months and 7 years, but particularly in the last half of the first year.

Thus, in a preventative sense, maintenance of a stable personnel team may be of major importance in minimizing detrimental social effects associated with institutionalization. Continual reinstatement of the socially responsive environment by caregivers in orphanages and other institutions where parent substitutes are required may well be necessary for the earliest experiences to have a long-lasting effect. This suggests that the staff in such institutions should include persons whose primary responsibility is "mothering" a small group of children. Such staff need not be highly trained, as the Skeels and Dye study (Skeels, 1966) indicates. In that study retarded adolescent girls functioned as caregivers. However, training would ensure more informed caregiving. The idea of using older people as "foster grandparents" of children in institutions also has been suggested and tried by Saltz (1973). This experiment was interesting because both the children and the caregivers benefited from the interaction. The important thing is that some relatively *stable*, warm individual be made available for infants and young children in environments that typically are undermanned and, therefore, relatively nonresponsive.

Particularly when deviations from the normal child-rearing pattern occur, parents of institutionalized children also must be aware of the importance of providing a socially responsive environment for infants and young children. In addition to the factors mentioned above, the research literature suggests several other points important for parents whose children have been separated from them early in life (for hospitalization or other cause). First of all, the Tizard and Hodges (1978) and L. J. Yarrow (1964) studies indicate that the earlier a child is restored to his natural or adoptive parents, the better the adjustment of the child is likely to be. Further, the Tizard and Hodges study indicated that the quality of parent care subsequent to separation from the child was very important. The parental characteristics most strongly and positively related to the establishment of a good parent–child relationship following separation were: (1) that the parents said they wanted the child, (2) that the parents spend some time playing with the child, and (3) that the parents said they enjoyed putting the child to bed. All of these factors suggest a warm, affectively positive, stimulating environment with a give-and-take relationship between the parents and child. This is the kind of interaction that might characterize a socially responsive environment and certainly is consistent with Clarke-Stewart's (1973) description of a stimulating, responsive environment.

Implications for Day-Care Programs

Although studies of the effects of day-care centers primarily have emphasized cognitive development, some have examined selected aspects of day-care program effects on social development as well. Specifically, the attachment of the child to his mother and his orientation toward peers have been investigated in terms of the effects of day-care experiences on them.

With respect to the attachment behavior of children, Blehar (1974) reported an early study purporting to show that day-care may adversely affect the emotional attachment or bond between the child and mother. However, subsequent studies have been unable to replicate this finding. Belsky and Steinberg (1978), in a comprehensive review of day-care center effects, conclude that there is no evidence that day-care is disruptive of the child's emotional bond with his mother even when day-care is initiated in the first year of life. Perhaps the most damaging study to Blehar's conclusion was one done by Portnoy and Simmons (1978). These investigators attempted to replicate Blehar's findings by comparing the mother–child attachments of children reared entirely at home and those reared at home until 3 years and then enrolled in day-care. In order to test age of entry effects, they also included a group of children reared at home until age 1, placed in family day-care until age 3, and then transferred to a day-care center. They found no differences between the groups in their reactions to Ainsworth's strange situation test. They concluded that age of entry into day-care does not systematically affect children's attachments to their mother either. In reviewing these and other studies, Belsky and Steinberg (1978) concluded that, at least in high quality day-care, there is no indication that exposure to day-care decreases the child's preference for his mother in comparison with an alternative familiar caregiver.

However, generalizations like this about the degree to which day-care affects mother–child attachments may have little usefulness. Day-care centers are complex environments, and it may well be that some interfere with attachments and some do not. Specific features of day-care that may contribute to its quality need to be examined. For example, there is increasing concern in day-care centers, as in institutional settings, with caregiver stability and continuity. Honig (1976) has suggested that the random rotation of caregivers in day-care centers should be replaced by major caregiver systems in which each adult takes primary responsibility for specific children over time. Presumably, this would allow greater opportunity for caregiver bonding and decrease unpredictability and inconsistency of care. Similarly, Anderson (1980) concluded that the quality and stability of caregiving relationships and of care setting may well override the daily separation experience from the mother in determining a child's reactions in day-care centers. Rarely, however, have variables such as continuity and stability of caregivers in day-care centers been employed as independent variables or even strictly controlled in studies of day-care effects.

An exception to this is a recent study by Cummings (1980), in which the effects of caregiver stability, defined as how long a child and a caregiver had been together in a day-care center, were directly investigated. Cummings found in the day-care setting that children preferred stable over nonstable caregivers and became less distressed when their mothers left them if a stable caregiver was present at the center. After separation from the mother had occurred, positive affect by the child was more common when observations involved stable caregivers than when they involved nonstable caregivers. In addition, there were nonsignificant trends for infants to show greater proximity-seeking, less distress, and more stranger eye contact when stable caregivers were present than with nonstable caregivers.

Clearly, more studies of this sort are needed. As Cummings pointed out, the generalizability of day-care research will be limited until more is known about the assessment of the quality of care offered by day-care centers.

Practical implementation of such findings is possible. Caregiver schedules, for example, can be adjusted to provide greater stability and continuity, and this would seem desirable on the basis of these findings.

Implications for Preschool Settings

Relatively few programs designed for enhancing the social development of preschool children are based solidly on either research or developmental theory. Some of the current behavioral approaches to training social skills are of this sort, but these have generally been designed for children older than preschool age. In this section we will briefly review only those training techniques relevant for preschool children. Our main focus will be on two rather innovative approaches to enhancing preschoolers' social development which have their basis in the areas reviewed in this volume. One, Spivack and Shure's (1974) cognitive approach to interpersonal problem solving, is uniquely based on cognitive-developmental theory and capitalizes on the knowledge gained from the research reviewed in Chapter 8. The other is based on Harlow's (Harlow, 1971; Suomi, 1974; Suomi, Harlow, & McKinney, 1972) work with nonhuman primates but represents an apparently successful attempt to extend this work to preschool children. This work deals with the use of peers as therapists.

Behavioral Approaches to Social Skills Training. The last decade also has seen the proliferation of a number of different approaches to teaching specific social skills to children. Most of these attempts have been with socially isolated or withdrawn children. Programs based on these approaches implicitly make the optimistic assumption that low social competence in children is reversible.

The term *social skills* generally refers to the complex behavioral and cognitive factors associated with confident, responsive, and mutually beneficial social interactions. Combs and Slaby (1971) define a social skill as "the ability to interact with others in a given social context in specific ways which are societally acceptable or valued, and at the same time personally beneficial, mutually beneficial, or beneficial primarily to others" (p. 2). Social skills training can be seen as adult intervention to guide children in ways aimed at increasing the number of behavioral choices available to the children in their peer interactions.

The primary focus of social skills training programs, regardless of the theoretical orientation, has been the socially isolated or withdrawn child (O'Connor, 1969, 1972; Keller & Carlson, 1974). Unfortunately, the term *social isolate* has had different meanings to different investigators. For example, Gottman, Gonso, and Rasmussen (1975) have identified the social isolate as a child who has low levels of peer acceptance on sociometric measures. O'Connor (1969, 1972), on the other hand, identifies the social isolate as one who has low relative frequencies of peer interaction. However, Gottman

(1977) found no relationship between peer acceptance as measured by sociometric status and the relative frequency of peer interaction as measured by behavioral observation of Get Set (Head Start) children. He classified five orthogonal clusters of children which included sociometric stars, sociometric rejectees, children who had highly negative interactions with the teacher, children who interacted frequently with peers, and children who were frequently "tuned out" or off-task when alone. The children described as "tuned out" were lowest on peer acceptance and were high on a set of shy, anxious, and fearful behaviors. This group appears to fit the construct of the shy, socially anxious child who is neither accepted or rejected, but rather ignored by peers. These children have been characterized as "hovering" (McGrew, 1972; Gottman, 1977) and must be distinguished from sociometric rejectees in empirical investigations of socially isolated children.

Three major approaches to social skills training have been reported in the literature. These include training based on contingent reinforcement (shaping), training through observational learning (modeling), and training utilizing a combination of cognitive mediation, verbal counseling, and other techniques. The latter is a verbally oriented group approach which is probably inappropriate for preschool children.

A variety of studies have been reported which have utilized reinforcement training (Clement & Milne, 1967; Hart, Reynolds, Browley, & Harris, 1968). Successful results have occurred, but the manipulations have tended to foster prosocial skills in a specific "deficient" child rather than in all children. Further, the failure of these studies to produce long-lasting effects of shaping limits the effectiveness of this treatment procedure. Perhaps a gradual decrease or fading out of the reinforcement rather than an abrupt termination would alter this finding. However, the contingent reinforcement has tended to focus solely on discrete behaviors rather than on more complex social behaviors. Ethical considerations are also raised when peers are used as reinforcers of specific behavior (e.g., orientation and debriefing issues).

A variety of studies have also used modeling procedures to treat preschool children with social interaction problems (Cooke & Appoloni, 1976; Evers & Schwartz, 1973; Keller & Carlson, 1974; O'Connor, 1969, 1972). These investigations suggest that the frequency of peer interactions can be increased in socially isolated children through modeling and that the frequency of positive behaviors such as smiling, imitation, and verbalization can be increased as a result of individual social skills training. However, there are several limitations of the observational learning approach. First, this procedure primarily concerns increasing the child's tendency to approach other children without regard for the quality of the interaction. Second, from these findings it is not clear whether the increased frequency of approach has had any impact on the child's peer acceptance or whether the "target" children were perceived by their peers as being "problem" children since low behavioral interactions are not equated with social isolation (Gottman, 1977).

SUMMARY: SOCIAL SKILLS TRAINING.   Overall, studies using shaping or modeling procedures with preschool children provide some useful information as well as innovative approaches for training socially inept children. However, their findings lack generalizability because they are not systematically tied into either theory or previous empirical research. The operant conditioning studies are specific in technique, but the evidence does not indicate that these techniques produce long-lasting effects. In addition, they focus on discrete behaviors and ignore complex social behaviors and developmental factors associated with them. The modeling techniques may be more promising, but although the studies clearly demonstrate that increases in peer interaction can be obtained with social isolates, it has not been demonstrated that *peer acceptance* can be improved as a result of modeling techniques.

A Cognitive Approach to Social Skills Training.   The work of Spivack and Shure (1974) typifies a cognitive approach in a specific intervention program for solving interpersonal problems. This approach is based on the concept that if children can be helped to develop a cognitive problem-solving style and can be taught to generate their own solutions for resolving typical interpersonal problems that arise daily, then they will manifest an improvement in overt behavior. In order to achieve this level of overt functioning, young children must have specific language and cognitive skills which are prerequisite for solving problems, and they must be taught how to use those skills in solving representative interpersonal difficulties. This approach, then, focuses on problem-solving skills which indicate how a child views and handles personal needs or interpersonal situations rather than impersonal cognitive tasks, such as paper-and-pencil maze tests or puzzles (Simon & Newell, 1971). It is consistent with the cognitive-developmental point of view that provided the basis for much of the research reported in Chapter 8, that is, the social-cognitive literature.

Empirical support for the cognitive-based training program was derived from several studies which examined the relationship of specific problem-solving variables and the behavioral adjustment of 4- to 5-year-old children. A test (The Preschool Interpersonal Problem-Solving Tests) was created to measure the child's ability to name alternative solutions to two life-related situations (e.g., ways a child might obtain a toy from another child and ways a child might avert his mother's anger caused by his destruction of property). The primary behavioral indexes of adjustment were the child's rated impatience, his display of emotional control, and the amount of physical or verbal aggression shown in the classroom. Findings indicated that poorly adjusted children generated a narrower range of solutions to the problems presented (e.g., "Hit him," or "Grab it," rather than "Ask him," "Let's play together," or "I'll let him have my toy"), as well as more irrelevant solutions. Children from poverty areas gave solutions that were more aggressive. These findings suggest that children may behave differently because they conceive of different types of solutions and because they do not think of the variety of alternative solutions which could be used in the situation and which might help them avoid difficulties and frustrations if they were considered.

Shure, Spivack, and Jaeger (1971) implemented a 12-week training program with 20 Get Set (Head Start) classes in inner-city schools. In all, 113 children from 10 classes were trained and 106 children from 10 classes were controls. Pretraining teacher ratings were made to assess the child's level and type of classroom-behavioral adjustment. Children were classified as impulsive (impatient, nagging, grabby, easily upset with low frustration tolerance), inhibited (exhibiting abnormal control of feelings and behavior), or behaviorally adjusted (neither impulsive nor inhibited). Other behavioral measures were (1) the degree to which the child showed concern for others and offered help to other children in distress, (2) the extent of peer acceptance, (3) the degree to which the child demonstrated initiative, and (4) the degree to which the child was autonomous in his functioning. The teachers conducted the classroom training under the pretense of enhancing each child's problem-solving, language, and thinking skills; there was no mention of expectations regarding specific behavioral changes.

The results indicated that the training program (1) enhanced alternative, consequential, and cause-and-effect thinking, (2) decreased superfluous and irrelevant thinking, (3) enhanced problem-solving ability among the impulsive and inhibited groups, and (4) shifted the priority away from aggressive solutions. Inhibited children made the greatest positive change in adjustment and increased the frequency of demonstrating empathic interest in their peers and willingness to extend help. Consequently, overt behavioral adjustment was improved in addition to the enhancement of problem-solving skills. The six-month posttreatment follow-up indicated that more trained children remained adjusted than did the control group children.

This study goes beyond mere correlational evidence of a relationship between cognitive skills and behavioral adjustment. The children who improved the most in the trained cognitive skills also improved most in their overt behavioral adjustment. Further, they maintained their adjustment longer than the control children. Unlike the shaping and modeling approaches, there was some evidence of generalization of interpersonal problem-solving skills to situations outside the specific training program. This kind of generalization may be the most important advantage of the cognitive approach.

The cognitive mediation training approach has several other advantages over the previously presented social skills training approaches. For example, it encourages the child to generate independent and flexible problem-solving approaches and to evaluate them on the basis of their potential consequences. Further, it utilizes the child's point of view in judging the value and appropriateness of a social skill. Also, an entire classroom is involved in the training with beneficial results for all of the children, whereas the other training approaches are designed to work with a specific target or problem child away from the classroom. Teachers can become effective implementers of this approach. And the effects of this kind of training are potentially long lasting.

Peers as Therapists

An interesting twist on the role that peers play in the development of social competence has been to treat peer interaction as an independent variable rather than a dependent variable. Hartup and his colleagues at Minnesota have drawn upon the monkey "peer therapist" research of Suomi, Harlow, and McKinney (1972) and extended it to working with socially withdrawn, isolated children. Both Suomi, Harlow, and McKinney's work and Hartup's attempt to extend it are important because they suggest that "the social pathology induced by early isolation can be reversed through a carefully managed program of play with peers who are younger than the subject" (Hartup, 1977, p. 2). While Hartup appears to believe there may be "sensitive" periods for the development of social competence, he is somewhat skeptical that there are truly "critical" periods (in primate development) in which social interaction must occur in order for social behavior to emerge normally.

One direction Hartup and his colleagues (Lougee, Grueneich, & Hartup, 1977) have taken has been to look at the way in which children's interaction with agemates differs from their interaction with children who are not the same age. These authors point out that Barker and Wright (1955), in their book *Midwest and Its Children*, reported that 65% of the child–child encounters they observed involved individuals who differed in age by more than 12 months; and, excluding contacts between siblings, 52% of these encounters involved individuals who were one year older or younger than each other.

Their data suggest that normative data based on same-age interaction may not be generalized to mixed-age situations. Using children in the age range 3.4 to 5.4, they conducted observations of three kinds of dyads: (a) same-age younger dyads, whose members' ages ranged from 3.2 to 4.1 ($\bar{x} = 3.8$), but for each dyad the children did not differ by more than two months; (b) same-age older dyads, whose ages ranged from 4.5 to 5.3 ($\bar{x} = 4.10$) with less than a two-month spread between members of each dyad; and (c) mixed-age dyads, composed of children ranging in age from 3.4 to 5.4 and a difference in age within dyads of 16 months, ± 3 months. In this study, they found that the mixed-age pairs were intermediate between younger and older children observed in same-age pairs in the number of social contracts made. In the mixed-age condition, older children typically decelerated their rates of social activity whereas younger children elevated their levels of social behavior.

In the mixed-age pairs, even the very young children were able to make subtle adjustments in social behavior according to the demands and needs of other children. However, verbal communication was more appropriate among the younger members of the mixed-age dyads and less appropriate among the older members than among children in same-age situations. Accommodation to the developmental status of the comparison child was evident more in the appropriateness of the communication than in the amount of social interaction.

Furman, Rahe, and Hartup (in Hartup, 1977) also attempted to answer the question: Does play with younger children possess the same kind of therapeutic potential for socially withdrawn children that it seems to possess for socially debilitated rhesus monkeys? These investigators selected 24 4- and 5-year-old children identified as "noninteractive." One third of these children participated in 15 special play sessions over three weeks with one other child who was 16 months younger than the subject. Another third played with a child who was within 4 months of the subject's own age. A third group received no treatment.

Children exposed to younger peers were found to be significantly more sociable in these observations than were children in the control group. Although children exposed to same-age peers were also more sociable than the control children, they were not reliably so. Longer-term follow-ups of these children are being conducted. Hartup believes that "unique socialization potential resides in play with younger peers for children who are at risk in the development of social competence" (1977, p. 3).

The importance he places on peer interaction for normal social development is underscored in another quote from Hartup (1977):

> In point of fact it is difficult to conceive of normal human development in the absence of peer interaction. New evidence shows that, without an opportunity to encounter individuals who are co-equals, children do not learn effective communication skills, do not acquire the competencies needed to modulate their aggressive actions, have difficulties with sexual socialization, and are disadvantaged with respect to the formation (of) moral values. Peer relations are not luxuries in human development but necessities. . . . Poor peer relations in childhood are among the most powerful predictors of later social and emotional maladies. (p. 1)

Although much more research is clearly needed, these preliminary studies suggest that one empirical approach to the remediation of young children with social-interactional problems is play with younger peers.

Parent Training in the Home

So far as parent training is concerned, a wide variety of books on parenting currently exists. Few of these, however, are actually based on empirical evidence. This is not to say that they are not useful, but only that it would be preferable, from our point of view, to base suggestions for child-rearing on empirically verified information to as great an extent as possible.

The research literature on parenting styles indicates the kind of parental orientations most likely to produce children with (1) an orientation toward others, (2) a sense of personal agency, and (3) dependency and passivity. The Zahn-Waxler *et al.* (1979) study indicated that the mother's empathic caregiving coupled with affectively delivered explanations was positively associated with children's reparations and altruistic behavior. The description of an empathic caregiving mother by these authors sounds very much like the inductive parent who explains to the child the consequences of his acts on others—and particularly on others' covert feelings or thoughts. The research literature suggests that inductive (Hoffman & Saltzstein, 1967), person-oriented (Bearison & Cassel, 1975) parents are most likely to produce children who are other-oriented. The Zahn-Waxler *et al.* study adds that they may also be more altruistic. Perhaps parents could be readily trained to be inductive and person-oriented (see Chapter 7 for a fuller description of these styles). Since the literature suggests that lower socioeconomic status parents are least likely to use these parental styles, perhaps a special effort could be made through welfare, family service, or other agencies to train parents in how to respond to children's feelings and how to get them to lead their children to be aware of others perspectives, feelings, and thoughts (as an inductive parent might do).

The authoritative parental style, characterized by controlling and demanding parents who are also warm, rational, and receptive to their child's communication, appears to be most clearly related to a sense of personal agency in both boys and girls (Baumrind, 1971). However, for girls, personal agency was also associated with somewhat challenging, even abrasive interactions with parents, and particularly with fathers. For boys, warm, nonabrasive encouragement of independence in combination with the authoritative parental style appears to be most related to personal agency and a sense of social responsibility. Parents who view these attributes as important ones for their children could be instructed regarding these findings and trained to respond "authoritatively" to their children.

For parents who want to avoid "passivity" in their children, the Kagan and Moss (1962) findings indicate that maternal protectiveness was a strong predictor of passivity in boys whereas restrictiveness was the best predictor for girls. Thus, avoidance of overprotection of young boys and overrestriction of young girls may lead to less dependent and passive adults.

While all these suggestions must be presented quite tenuously and are indeed speculative, they are at least based on some empirical evidence. One hopes that these could be integrated into parent training programs and child-rearing books in a beginning effort to establish a research-based" curriculum" or procedure for encouraging the development of social competence in young children.

One example of an empirically based parent training program is seen in a recent study by Dickie and Gerber (1980). This study illustrates the effects that parent training can have on the social competence of infants. The authors were interested in looking at the mother–father–infant triad as well as father–infant interactions and mother–infant interaction. Competence was defined in accord with Goldberg's (1977b) definition, that is, in terms of the parent–infant dyad when both parent and child provide crucial contingency experiences for one another (see Chapter 6). For parents, competency involved anticipating infant needs, reading infant cues, and responding contingently, as well as initiating contacts with the infants. For infants, competency involved providing readable, predictable cues to parents, eliciting responses from the environment, and responding often and contingently to parents and the environment. An experimental group was involved in a training program which included lectures, discussion, and demonstrations, and emphasized child development, individual infant variation, knowledge of the infant's temperament and cues, provision of contingent experiences, and awareness of the infants' effect on the parents and the parents' effect on infants. The control group was offered the class at the completion of the study. Infants in the experimental group were more responsive and predictable. Trained parents anticipated infant needs, responded more appropriately to the infant's cues, and provided more frequent verbal and nonverbal contingent responses. The importance of studying the mother–father–infant triad was emphasized by the finding that as trained fathers increased their interactions with the infant, the trained mothers decreased their interaction. There was a shift toward more father–infant interaction when the mother was also present. Much more applied research of this type is needed.

EVALUATION OF EARLY INTERVENTION

In addition to intervention *per se*, an understanding of the nature of early environmental action also has implications for evaluation of the results of this intervention. In terms of general evaluation strategies, two points should be noted. As we mentioned earlier, for most evaluation programs the major criterion for gain is mean change in developmental quotient between two points in time (Williams, 1977). As we have noted repeatedly, obtaining a significant mean gain says nothing about the response of the individual infant to the intervention program. In addition to idiographic treatments, a more idiographically oriented evaluation strategy is needed.

At a minimum, what appears to be critical is reporting not only mean differences, but also variances and range of responses to intervention. In addition to a range score, it would be helpful if the number of children within designated range units could be presented as a means of determining whether mean gains were due to a few children showing major gains or whether the gains were more modest but were distributed across all children. A program in which only a few children show major gains clearly could not be regarded as a major success since, for the majority of children, the intervention would have been more or less ineffective (i.e., the majority of children gained less than one would expect based on test–retest effects alone). Only a program wherein at least a majority of children gain significantly more than would be expected by chance or test–retest effects alone could truly be considered as a successful intervention.

This use of an idiographic evaluation strategy would have the additional virtue of allowing us to differentiate between gainers and nongainers in terms of individual characteristics (temperament, parent–child interaction pattern, initial level of specific cognitive skills). With enough information it may be possible, before the intervention is begun, to identify a subgroup of children who will not respond well to traditional intervention programs. For these children alternate forms of intervention might be provided.

As far as number of evaluations, two factors we have noted previously argue against evaluating only once, at the termination of the program. First, repeated longitudinal evaluations are critical as a means of assessing whether a fading of intervention gains is occurring. If such a pattern is found, we can begin to build in reinstatements for individual children to minimize the loss of initial gains. In addition, available evidence also indicates delayed or sleeper effects. The existence of these phenomena suggests that certain environmental effects may not become manifest until years after the original experience has been terminated. To dismiss a program based on only a single evaluation may be an unduly conservative strategy in view of the possibility that the full extent of the program's impact on individual children may not be revealed until later in life. Recent evidence on the positive impact of early intervention upon later school performance (Darlington *et al.*, 1980) clearly supports the utilization of a longitudinal evaluation strategy.

Cognitive Assessment

In the past, most evaluations of intervention programs have utilized global instruments such as the Bayley or Binet which are given once, at the end of the program (Belsky & Steinberg, 1978).

In terms of assessment devices, the high level of environmental specificity we have documented clearly argues against the use of global tests that collapse homogeneous abilities into a single heterogeneous score. This is particularly so for programs attempting to accelerate the development of some specific, targeted ability. By using a global scale, which taps both target and nontarget functions, gains occurring for target abilities may not appear when the measurement of these abilities is combined with that of nontarget abilities, which do not show any gain (Wachs, 1973b). Rather, assessment should be based on performance, on specific ability measures, with a choice of measures being based on the specific abilities targeted for intervention.

Given the number of available psychometric and sensorimotor tests, finding appropriate measures should not be a major effort.

In testing for specific abilities, one must be careful, of course, not to teach to the test. Teaching to the test may promote better test scores on a specific ability; however, there will be little generalizability to alternate measures of the same ability (Robinson & Robinson, 1978). Ideally, the testing procedure (and indeed the criterion items making up the test) should be done blindly in regard to the interventions the child received. Further, whenever possible, a variety of test procedures centering on the target ability should be given as a means of determining the generalizability of the specific targeted behavior (i.e., are gains restricted only to one way of measuring the criterion variable?). This suggests the use of both norm-referenced (psychometric) and criterion-referenced (edumetric) measures as a means of maximizing evaluation of generalizability.

This is not to say that criterion testing should be restricted only to those specific abilities which have been targeted for intervention. It may well be that intervention targeted for a specific ability may influence the development of other nontargeted abilities to a lesser extent. Given our understanding of the interface of social and cognitive skills, as described in Chapter 8, having cognitive as well as noncognitive data may help us understand the implications of intervention upon the developmental process *per se* and may thus have much theoretical value. Given this possibility, a broad-based selection of evaluation instruments could be utilized. These instruments should be designed so that they can measure not simply global psychometric functions (although this could be one of the measures if people are interested) but also the development of specific abilities so that we may know the effective boundaries of our intervention program. Overall, what would be optimal in assessing the effects of early intervention is a multitrait, multimethod approach; here, specific abilities are measured by a variety of approaches to determine not only if the target ability is affected but also what other abilities are affected and what the generalizability of effects is across alternate measures of the same ability.

Some authors (e.g., Belsky & Steinberg, 1978) have criticized the intervention literature for undue reliance on global psychometric tests. Belsky and Steinberg have called for the adoption of more ecologically based competence measures. We agree with their point regarding the use of global psychometric measures but see little point in using global measures of competence in place of global psychometric measures. If ecologically based competence measures could be derived that would reflect specific aspects of competence (i.e., social competence in getting desired reactions from adults; cognitive competence in dealing with naturally occurring environmental obstacles), such measures would be extremely useful and would fit in with our multitrait, multimethod approach in terms of providing a useful supplement to specific psychometric measures. Indeed, the existence of such measures would provide a clear-cut test of generalizability of intervention effects and offer much more dramatic support for the effects of intervention.

Social Assessment

Unfortunately, measures of social development are even less well developed than those in the cognitive area. There is nothing comparable to an IQ test, for example, to measure social competence. Those standardized measures that do exist depend on either parental or teacher report rather than on direct behavioral observation (for example, the Vineland Social Maturity Scale).

A fairly large number of assessment devices have been developed to measure social perspective-taking. As we pointed out in Chapter 8, it is doubtful that these devices are measuring the same phenomenon. One of the problems with the perspective-taking measures is that each investigator has developed his own measure to suit the population and particular aspect of perspective-taking in which he was interested. Thus, measures of perspective-taking that have been used at different ages appear to be getting at very different phenomena (see Chapter 8), and even measures developed by different investigators for children of the same age vary considerably. Until something better comes along, researchers interested in social perspective-taking probably would be wise to use a battery of several of these perspective-taking measures.

There have been a number of direct behavioral observational techniques developed that may be useful in assessing children's social competence (Hartup, 1970; Gottman, 1977; Lieberman, 1977). However, these techniques are appropriate only for the particular age group and situations for which they were designed. The kinds of information these techniques provide is usually in terms of frequency of interaction, or whether the interaction was positive or negative. Since norms do not currently exist for the amount of positive or negative interactions children of a given age typically engage in, only the extremes, exceptionally high or low frequencies of interaction, are meaningful. Summary data reflecting children's relationships with their peers can be obtained from sociometric devices, but these only measure one aspect of social behavior, that is, popularity. Nevertheless, these behavioral and sociometric techniques do permit fairly reliable and valid data gathering. As such, they may be the most promising approaches developed thus far.

FUTURE DIRECTIONS

A review of the available evidence, contained in Chapters 3-7, has enabled us to discuss both the basic nature of early environmental action and implications of knowledge about early experience for early intervention. In concluding this volume we would like to devote some space to our thoughts on the future directions of the early experience field, both on a basic and on an applied level.

Future Directions: Basic Research

On a basic level, three areas of study clearly appear to warrant future intensive research efforts. First, there is the question of the interface between individual differences and reactivity to environmental stimulation. Both from basic and applied data it has become increasingly clear that the relationship of early experience to development will be mediated by the nature of the organism on which the experience impinges. Unfortunately, virtually nothing is known about the specific organismic characteristics which mediate differential reactivity to the early environment. One hopes that future research and theory will begin to delineate the specific organismic characteristics which are relevant to this process.

One initial approach to this problem would be to identify organismic characteristics (i.e., temperament, preference for specific stimulus dimensions, biomedical history) which maximally differentiate individual reactivity to early intervention. These initial data could form the basis for future prospective studies wherein specific predictions are made as to what clusters of children (clustered by organismic characteristic similarity) will react best to standard intervention experiences. The ultimate goal of this research would be to predict what specific organismic and environmental combinations maximize development of specific cognitive or social parameters.

Related to the first goal is the need for future research on the nature of the transactional process. As we have pointed out in earlier chapters, it has become increasingly obvious that the relationship between organism and environment is a two-way street; the child can affect its environment just as the environment can affect the child. However, it is also distressingly clear that we know little about the nature of the transactional process, in terms of what specific child characteristics are most likely to influence what specific environmental characteristics. What is required are longitudinal studies looking at the relationship between child and environmental characteristics over time. It may well be that certain child parameters are more salient for promoting environmental change than others; it may also be that certain aspects of the environment or family configurations are more sensitive to child influences than others. However, unless longitudinal research is initiated to look at changes in the child–environment relationship over time (perhaps using approaches such as path analysis as a conceptual model), we will not progress much beyond the general statement that development is transactional.

Up to now we have been dealing primarily with predictor variables (i.e., the environment). In the writing of this volume, it has become increasingly clear to the authors that there may well be an artificial separation of our criterion variables. Specifically, in most cases we have been forced to treat social and cognitive factors as different because almost all available research assumes them to be different and studies them accordingly. As we have pointed out in Chapter 8, it may well be that certain aspects of social and cognitive development have more in common than previously thought. The role of sociability in influencing an infant's test-taking performance, or the role of cognitive level in influencing a preschool child's understanding of other children's feelings, are just two instances wherein social and cognitive factors interface with each other.

As with organismic specificity and the transactional process, in discussing the interface of social and cognitive development, we are again faced with a general principle but little specific supporting data about the nature of the process. One approach to looking at the nature of this relationship may well lie in the study of early experience. Specifically, it could be hypothesized that social and cognitive factors which share common experiential determinants may do so because of commonalities in the nature of each parameter. Social and cognitive factors which are differentially determined by highly specific and unique environmental components may reflect distinctly different developmental processes. Thus, looking at the degree of overlap of environmental correlates with cognitive and social factors may serve as an initial approach to identifying those aspects of social and cognitive development which are likely to be interrelated. From these data we could then begin to develop testable hypotheses about the nature of the relationship between specific cognitive and social parameters. Such a research program would be important not only for an understanding of the developmental process but also for an increased understanding of the nature of early environmental action.

In addition to the above suggestions as to where the early experience field should be headed, it seems worthwhile to devote a few lines to directions which perhaps should be avoided. Clearly, the study of global experience parameters (social class, institutions) which are not broken down into their specific components appears to be an approach whose time has passed. Similarly, studies which avoid an understanding of process in favor of comparing two extreme dimensions (nature vs. nurture, early vs. later experience) also seem to offer little of substance. One hopes that as the field matures fewer of these studies will be in evidence.

Future Directions: Applied Research and Intervention

To continue the above discussion of where not to go in terms of applied directions, the use of global intervention strategies with heterogeneous groups of children who are tested once on global measures is an obvious pitfall to avoid. Ideally, future early interventions and applied research in the early experience field will concentrate on programming specific experiences for specific children directed toward specific aims. When heterogeneous groups of children must be seen, ideal programs will try to provide empirically based "best fit" programs of stimulation which maximize desired progress in specific areas for the majority of children enrolled in such programs.

In developing such specific and "best fit" programs in the future, it is critical to set up an atmosphere such that intervention specialists and basic researchers in the early experience area can work closely with one another. Too often in the past the potential contributions of basic research to early intervention have been ignored by applied workers; similarly, the specific needs and problems continually confronted by those in the applied areas have been dismissed by researchers interested in more basic problems. If we are to have any hope of progress in the application of early experience principles to basic human problems, such an artificial split between the basic and applied fields must be avoided.

Basic researchers must learn to view applied settings as potential field laboratories where specific hypotheses can be tested; the role of individual difference factors governing the child's reaction to intervention is one example of a problem that has both basic and applied components and which could easily be carried out in an applied setting. Similarly, clinicians working in early intervention must learn to view basic research as a potential source of answers to perennial problems encountered during the remediational process. Determining whether the same environmental dimensions are relevant for the development of handicapped babies as for normal babies is an example of a problem which is best studied within a basic research framework and yet has major implications for planning specific interventions. On the basis of our joint experience in both basic and applied settings, it is clear to us that basic researchers in the early experience area want to feel that their work has relevance for society; similarly, applied workers are eager for input into their remediation strategies. With time, training programs and joint meetings must allow for greater contact between these two groups. Such contact is critical for future progress in both basic and applied areas.

One final area of importance in the applied area is the need to begin to look at parameters which maximize or minimize the long-term impact of early intervention. It is clear that in most cases an "inoculation" of enriched early experience will wash out over time unless future conditions are developed to maintain the initial gains. Unfortunately, what must happen to maintain these early gains is not yet clearly understood. Whether the locus is in the nature of the follow-up process, the characteristics of the parent–child relationship, or the school system encountered after 5 years still remains an open question. What we do know is that intervening and simply assuming permanence of effects is a dated concept and a dangerous one as well for the well-being of the children involved. Again, this is the kind of problem which can best be dealt with through a close collaboration between basic and applied workers.

Overall, if one makes the assumption that the modern era of human early experience research began sometime during the 1950s, then it is clear that the discipline is still very much in its infancy. It is also clear that how we choose to study and to apply early experience in the future will govern whether the field grows up to be viable or whether its early promise will remain unfulfilled. Clinging to outmoded conceptions and practices is the sort of early experience that will guarantee stunted development, not only for children but also for areas of study. A willingness to respond to new information and a sensitivity to critical issues are the sorts of early experience that guarantee successful development not only for children but for disciplines as well. Those of us dedicated to the study of early experience at the human level hope to demonstrate the wisdom to provide the stimulation and nourishment that will ensure future growth and development both for our discipline and for future generations of children.

References

Acredolo, L. Laboratory vs. home: The effect of environment on the 9 week old infant's choice of spatial reference systems. *Developmental Psychology*, 1979, *11*, 666–667.

Aiello, J., Nicosia, G., & Thompson, D. Physiological, social and behavioral consequences of crowding on children and adolescents. *Child Development*, 1979, *10*, 195–202.

Ainsworth, M. D. S. The development of infant–mother interaction among the Ganda. In B. M. Foss (Ed.), *Determinants of infant behavior* (Vol. 2). New York: Wiley, 1963.

Ainsworth, M. D. S. *Infancy in Uganda: Infant care and the growth of love*. Baltimore: Johns Hopkins University Press, 1967.

Ainsworth, M. D. S. The development of infant–mother attachment. In B. Caldwell & H. Ricciuti (Eds.), *Review of child development research* (Vol. 3). Chicago: University of Chicago Press, 1973.

Ainsworth, M. D. S. Infant development and mother–infant interaction among Ganda and American families. In P. Leiderman, S. Tulkin, & A. Rosenfeld (Eds.), *Culture and infancy*. New York: Academic Press, 1977.

Ainsworth, M. D. S., & Bell, S. M. Mother–infant interaction and the development of competence. In K. J. Connolly & J. S. Bruner (Eds.), *The growth of competence*. New York: Academic Press, 1974.

Ainsworth, M. D. S., & Wittig, B. A. Attachment and exploratory behavior of one-year-olds in a strange situation. In B. M. Foss (Ed.), *Determinants of infant behavior IV*. London: Methuen, 1969.

Ainsworth, M. D. S., Bell, S. M., & Stayton, D. J. Infant–mother attachment and social development: Socialization as a product of reciprocal responsiveness to signals. In M. P. M. Richards (Ed.), *The integration of a child into a social world*. Cambridge: Cambridge University Press, 1974.

Allen, G. Intellectual potential and heredity. *Science*, 1961, *133*, 378–379.

Allinsmith, W., & Greening, T. C. Guilt over anger as predicted from parental discipline: A study of superego development. *American Psychologist*, 1955, *10*, 320.

Ambrose, A. *Stimulation in early infancy*. New York: Academic Press, 1969.

Ambrose, J. A. The concept of a critical period for the development of social responsiveness in early infancy. In B. M. Foss (Ed.), *Determinants of infant behavior II.* London: Methuen, 1963.

Anderson, C. Attachment in daily separations: Reconceptualizing daycare and maternal employment issues. *Child Development,* 1980, *51,* 242–245.

Antonovsky, H., & Feitelson, P. An observational study of intellectual stimulation in young children. *Early Child Development and Care,* 1973, *2,* 329–344.

Appleton, T., Clifton, R., & Goldberg, S. The development of behavioral competence in infancy. In F. Horowitz (Ed.), *Review of child development research IV.* Chicago: University of Chicago Press, 1975.

Aronfreed, J. The nature, variety and social patterning of moral responses to transgression. *Journal of Abnormal and Social Psychology,* 1961, *63,* 223–230.

Ausubel, D. How reversible are the cognitive and motivational effects of cultural deprivation? Implications for teaching the culturally deprived child. *Urban Education,* 1964, *1,* 16–38.

Bakeman, R., & Brown, J. Early interaction: Consequences for social and mental development at three years. *Child Development,* 1980, *51,* 437–447.

Baldwin, A., Kalhorn, J., & Breese, F. Patterns of parent behavior. *Psychological Monographs,* 1945, *58.*

Ball, B. Some relationships among infant preference for tactile stimulation, infant developmental level and maternal behavior. *Dissertation Abstracts,* 1969, *29,* 4838B.

Bandura, A., & Walters, R. H. *Adolescent aggression: A study of the influence of child-rearing practices and family interrelationships.* New York: Ronald, 1959.

Barclay, J. R., Stilwell, W. E., & Barclay, L. K. The influence of parental occupation on social interaction measures of elementary school children. *Journal of Vocational Behavior,* 1972, *2,* 433–446.

Barker, R. G., & Wright, H. F. *Midwest and its children.* New York: Harper & Row, 1955.

Barnard, K. *Child, parent and environmental correlates of child development: A longitudinal study.* Paper presented to the biennial meeting of the Society for Research in Child Development, San Francisco, March 1979.

Barnett, M. A., King, L. M., Howard, J. A., and Dino, G. A. Empathy in young children: Relation to parents' empathy, affection, and emphasis on the feelings of others. *Developmental Psychology,* 1980, *16,* 243–244.

Barrett, D. E., & Yarrow, M. R. Prosocial behavior, social inferential ability, and assertiveness in children. *Child Development,* 1977, *48,* 475–481.

Bartlett, C. J., & Horrocks, J. E. A study of the needs status of adolescents from broken homes. *Journal of Genetic Psychology,* 1958, *93,* 153–159.

Bates, J., Olson, S., Pettit, G., and Bayles, K. *Individuality in the mother–infant relationship at six months.* Paper presented to the International Conference on Infant Studies. New Haven, Conn., April 1980.

Bates, J., Pettit, G., & Bayles, K. *Antecedents of problem behaviors at age three years.* Paper presented to the Society for Research in Child Development, Boston, April 1981.

Baumrind, D. Child care practices anteceding three patterns of preschool behavior. *Genetic Psychology Monographs,* 1967, *75,* 43–88.

Baumrind, D. Authoritarian vs. authoritative parental control. *Adolescence*, 1968, *3*, 255-272.

Baumrind, D. Current patterns of parental authority. *Developmental Psychology Monographs*, 1971, *4*(1), Part 2.

Baumrind, D. *Socialization determinants of personal agency*. Paper presented at the biennial meeting of the Society for Research in Child Development, New Orleans, 1977.

Baumrind, D., & Black, A. E. Socialization practices associated with dimensions of competence in preschool boys and girls. *Child Development*, 1967, *38*, 291-327.

Bayley, N., & Schaefer, E. Correlations of maternal and child behaviors with the development of mental abilities: Data from the Berkeley Growth Study. *Monographs of the Society for Research in Child Development*, 1964, *29*.

Bearison, D. J., & Cassel, T. Z. Cognitive decentration and social codes: Communicative effectiveness in young children from differing family backgrounds. *Developmental Psychology*, 1975, *11*, 29-36.

Becker, W. C. Consequences of different kinds of parental disciplines. In M. L. Hoffman & L. W. Hoffman (Eds.), *Review of child development research* (Vol. 1). New York: Russell Sage Foundation, 1964.

Beckwith, L. Relationship between attributes of mothers and their infants' IQ scores. *Child Development*, 1971, *42*, 1083-1097.

Beckwith, L. *Preterm children's cognitive competence at five years and early caregiver-infant interactions*. Paper presented to the Society for Research in Child Development, Boston, April 1981.

Beckwith, L., & Cohen, S. Pre-term births: Hazardous obstetrical and postnatal events as related to caregiver-infant behavior. *Infant Behavior and Development*, 1978, *1*, 403-411.

Beckwith, L., Cohen, S., Kopp, C., Parmelee, A., & Marcy, J. Caregiver-infant interaction and early cognitive development in pre-term infants. *Child Development*, 1976, *47*, 579-587.

Bekoff, M., & Fox, M. Postnatal neural ontogeny: Environment dependent or environment expectant. *Developmental Psychobiology*, 1972, *5*, 323-341.

Bell, R. Q. A reinterpretation of the direction of effects in studies of socialization. *Psychological Review*, 1968, *75*, 81-95.

Bell, R. Q. Stimulus control of parent or caretaker behavior by offspring. *Developmental Psychology*, 1971, *4*, 63-72.

Bell, S. M. The development of the concept of object as related to infant-mother attachment. *Child Development*, 1970, *41*, 291-311.

Bell, S. M., & Ainsworth, M. D. S. Infant crying and maternal responsiveness. *Child Development*, 1972, *43*, 1171-1190.

Belmont, L., & Marolla, F. Birth order, family size and intelligence. *Science*, 1973, *182*, 1096-1101.

Belmont, L., Stein, Z., & Zybert, P. Child spacing and birth order. *Science*, 1978, *202*, 995-996.

Belsky, J. A family analysis of parental influence on infant exploratory competence. In F. Pedersen (Ed.), *The father-infant relationship*. New York: Praeger, 1980.

Belsky, J. Early human experience: A family perspective. *Developmental Psychology*, 1981, *17*, 3-23.

Belsky, J., & Steinberg, L. The effects of day care: A critical review. *Child Development*, 1978, *49*, 929–949.

Bernstein, B. A. A sociolinguistic approach to socialization: With some reference to educability. In F. Williams (Ed.), *Language and poverty: Perspectives on a theme*. Chicago: Markham, 1970, pp. 25–61.

Bettelheim, B. *Children of the dream: Communal childrearing and American education*. New York: Macmillan, 1969.

Biller, H. B. A multiaspect investigation of masculine development in kindergarten-age boys. *Genetic Psychology Monographs*, 1968, *76*, 89–139.

Biller, H. B. Father dominance and sex role development in kindergarten age boys. *Developmental Psychology*, 1969, *1*, 87–94.

Biller, H. B. Paternal deprivation, cognitive functioning, and the feminized classroom. In A. Davids (Ed.), *Child, personality and psychopathology: Current topics*. New York: Wiley, 1974.

Biller, H. B., & Bahm, R. M. Father absence, perceived maternal behavior, and masculinity of self-control among junior high school boys. *Developmental Psychology*, 1974, *4*, 178–181.

Bishop, D., & Chace, C. Parental conceptual systems, home play environment and potential creativity in children. *Journal of Experimental Child Psychology*, 1971, *12*, 318–338.

Blank, M. Some maternal influences on infants' rates of sensorimotor development. *Journal of the American Academy of Child Psychiatry*, 1964, *3*, 668–687.

Bleckman, E., & Nakamura, C. Mother's test anxiety and task selection and children's performance with mother or a stranger. *Child Development*, 1971, *42*, 1109–1118.

Blehar, M. I. Anxious attachment and defensive reactions associated with day care. *Child Development*, 1974, *45*, 683–692.

Blehar, M. C., Lieberman, A. F., & Ainsworth, M. D. S. Early face-to-face interaction and its relation to later infant–mother attachment. *Child Development*, 1977, *48*, 182–194.

Bloom, B. *Stability and change in human characteristics*. New York: Wiley, 1964.

Boehm, L. The development of independence: A comparative study. *Child Development*, 1957, *28*, 85–92.

Borgman, R. D. Maternal influences upon the development of moral reasoning in retarded children. *Dissertation Abstracts International*, September 1972, *33B*, 1280–1281.

Borke, H. Interpersonal perception of young children: Egocentrism or empathy? *Developmental Psychology*, 1971, *5*, 263–269.

Borke, H. The development of empathy in Chinese and American children between three and six years of age: A cross-cultural study. *Developmental Psychology*, 1973, *9*, 102–108.

Borke, H. Piaget's mountains revisited: Changes in the egocentric landscape. *Developmental Psychology*, 1975, *11*, 240–243.

Bowlby, J. Forty-four juvenile thieves: Their characters and home life. *International Journal of Psychoanalysis*, 1944, *25*, 107–128.

Bowlby, J. The nature of a child's tie to his mother. *International Journal of Psychoanalysis*, 1958, *39*, 350–373.

Bowlby, J. *Attachment and loss*. Vol. 1. *Attachment*. New York: Basic Books, 1969.

Bowlby, J., Ainsworth, M. D. S., Boston, M., & Rosenbluth, D. The effects of mother–child separation: A follow-up study. *British Journal of Medical Psychology*, 1956, *29*, 211–247.

Bradley, R., & Caldwell, B. Early home environment and changes in mental test performance in children from 6–36 months. *Developmental Psychology*, 1976, *12*, 93–97. (a)

Bradley, R., & Caldwell, B. The relation of infants' home environment to mental test performance at 54 months: A follow-up study. *Child Development*, 1976, *47*, 1172–1174. (b)

Bradley, R., & Caldwell, B. The relation of home environment, cognitive competence, and IQ among males and females. *Child Development*, 1980, *51*, 1140–1148.

Bradley, R., & Caldwell, B. *The stability of the home environment and its relation to child development*. Paper presented to the International Society for the Study of Behavioral Development, Toronto, August 1981.

Bradley, R., Caldwell, B., & Elardo, R. Home environment, social status and mental test performance. *Journal of Educational Psychology*, 1977, *69*, 697–701.

Bradley, R., Caldwell, B., & Elardo, R. Home environment and cognitive development in the first two years: A cross-lagged panel analysis. *Developmental Psychology*, 1979, *15*, 246–250.

Bradshaw, C. Relationship between maternal behavior and infant performance in environmentally disadvantaged homes. *Dissertation Abstracts*, 1969, *30*, 163–164A.

Brazelton, T. B. Implications of infant development among the Mayan Indians of Mexico. *Human Development*, 1972, *15*, 90–111.

Brazelton, T. B., Koslowski, B., and Main, M. The origins of reciprocity: Early mother–infant interaction. In M. Lewis & L. Rosenblum (Eds.), *The origins of behavior*. New York: Wiley, 1974.

Brazelton, T. B., Tronick, E., Adamson, L., Als, H., & Wise, S. Early mother–infant reciprocity. In M. A. Hofer (Ed.), *Parent–infant interaction*. London: CIBA, 1975.

Bretherton, I., & Ainsworth, M. D. S. Responses of one-year-olds to a stranger in a strange situation. In M. Lewis & L. A. Rosenblum (Eds.), *The origins of behavior*. New York: Wiley, 1974.

Brim, O. G. Family structure and sex role learning by children. *Sociometry*, 1958, *21*, 1–16.

Brittain, C. F. Adolescent choices and parent–peer cross-pressures. *American Sociology Review*, 1963, *28*, 358–391.

Brody, G. Relationships between maternal attitudes and behaviors. *Journal of Personality and Social Psychology*, 1965, *2*, 317–323.

Broman, S., Nichols, P., & Kennedy, W. *Pre-school IQ: Prenatal and early development correlates*. New York: Wiley, 1975.

Bronfenbrenner, U. Response to pressure from peers versus adults among Soviet and American school children. *International Journal of Psychology*, 1967, *2*, 199–207.

Bronfenbrenner, U. When is infant stimulation effective? In D. Glass (Ed.), *Environmental influences*. New York: Rockefeller Press, 1968.

Bronfenbrenner, U. *Two worlds of childhood: U.S. and U.S.S.R.* New York: Russell Sage Foundation, 1970.

Bronfenbrenner, U. *Is early intervention effective?* Department of Health, Education, and Welfare Publication #(OHD)76-30025. Washington, D.C., 1974.

Bronfenbrenner, U. Toward an experimental ecology of human development. *American Psychologist*, 1977, *32*, 513-531.

Bronson, W. C. The growth of competence: Issues of conceptualization and measurement. In H. E. Schaffer (Ed.), *The origins of human social relations*. New York: Academic Press, 1971.

Bronson, W. C. Competence and the growth of personality. In K. J. Connolly & J. S. Bruner (Eds.), *The growth of competence*. New York: Academic Press, 1974.

Bronson, W. C. Development in behavior with age-mates during the second year of life. In M. Lewis & L. A. Rosenblum (Eds.), *Friendship and peer relations*. New York: Wiley, 1975.

Brossard, M., & Decarie, T. The effects of 3 kinds of perceptual-social stimulation on the development of institutionalized infants. *Early Child Development and Care*, 1971, *1*, 111-130.

Brozek, J. Nutrition, malnutrition and behavior. *Annual Review of Psychology*, 1978, *29*, 157-178.

Bruner, J. Organization of early skilled action. *Child Development*, 1973, *44*, 1-11.

Bruner, J. The ontogenesis of speech acts. *Journal of Child Language*, 1975, *2*, 1-19.

Burchinal, P., & Farran, D. *How important is early mother–infant interaction for development during infancy*. Paper presented to the International Conference for Infant Studies. New Haven Conn., 1980.

Burton, R. V., & Whiting, J. W. M. The absent father and cross-sex identity. *Merrill–Palmer Quarterly*, 1961, 7, 85-95.

Busse, T., Ree, M., Gutride, M., Alexander, T., & Powell, L. Environmentally enriched classrooms and the cognitive and perceptual development of Negro preschool children. *Journal of Educational Psychology*, 1972, *63*, 15-21.

Cairns, R. B. *Social development: The origins and plasticity of interchanges*. San Francisco: Freeman, 1979.

Caldwell, B. The usefulness of the critical period hypothesis in the study of filiative behavior. *Merrill–Palmer Quarterly*, 1962, *8*, 229-242.

Caldwell, B. The effect of psychosocial deprivation on human development in infancy. *Merrill–Palmer Quarterly*, 1970, *16*, 260-277.

Caldwell, B., & Richmond, J. The Children's Center in Syracuse, New York. In C. Chandler, R. Laurie, & A. Peters (Eds.), *Early child care*. New York: Atherton, 1968.

Caldwell, B., Bradley, R., & Elardo, R. Early stimulation. In J. Wortis (Ed.), *Mental retardation and developmental disabilities*. New York: Bruner/Mazel, 1973.

Calhoun, J. Population density and social pathology. *Scientific American*, 1962, *206*, 139-150.

Carey, S. Cognitive competence. In K. Connolly & J. Bruner, *The growth of competence*. New York: Academic Press, 1974.

Carpenter, G. Mother's face and the newborn. In R. Lewis (Ed.), *Child alive*. London: Temple Smith, 1974.

Casler, L. Maternal deprivation: A critical review of the literature. *Monographs of the Society for Research in Child Development*, 1961, *26*, No. 2.

Casler, L. The effects of extra tactile stimulation on a group of institutionalized infants. *Genetic Psychology Monographs*, 1965, *71*, 137-175. (a)

Casler, L. The effects of supplementary verbal stimulation on a group of institution-alized infants. *Journal of Child Psychology and Psychiatry*, 1965, *6*, 19–27. (b)

Casler, L. Perceptual deprivation in institutional settings. In G. Newton & S. Levine (Eds.), *Early experience and behavior*. New York: Springer, 1967.

Casler, L. Supplementary auditory and vestibular stimulation effects on in-stitutionalized infants. *Journal of Exceptional Child Psychology*, 1975, *19*, 456–463.

Caspari, E. Genetic endowment and environment in the determination of human behavior: A biological viewpoint. *American Educational Research Journal*, 1968, *5*, 43–55.

Charlesworth, R., & Hartup, W. W. Positive social reinforcement in the nursery school peer group. *Child Development*, 1967, *38*, 993–1002.

Chazan, S. Development of object permanence as a correlate of dimensions of mater-nal care. *Developmental Psychology*, 1981, 17, 79–81.

Cherry, L., & Lewis, M. Mothers and two year olds: A study of sex differentiated aspects of verbal interaction. *Developmental Psychology*, 1976, *12*, 278–282.

Clarke, A., & Clarke, A. The formative years. In A. Clarke & A. Clarke (Eds.), *Early experience: Myth and evidence*. London: Open Books, 1976.

Clarke, A., & Clarke, A. Early experience: Its limited effect upon late development. In D. Shaffer & J. Dunn (Eds.), *The first year of life*. New York: Wiley, 1979.

Clarke, A. D. Predicting human development. *Bulletin of the British Psychological Soci-ety*, 1978, *31*, 249–258.

Clarke-Stewart, K. A. Interactions between mothers and their young children: Characteristics and consequences. *SRCD Monographs*, 1973, *38*.

Clarke-Stewart, K. A. *The father's impact on mother and child*. Paper presented to the Society for Research in Child Development, New Orleans, 1977.

Clarke-Stewart, K. A. And daddy makes three: The father's impact on mother and young child. *Child Development*, 1978, *49*, 446–478.

Clarke-Stewart, K. A. *Assessing social development*. Paper presented at the biennial meeting of the Society for Research in Child Development, San Francisco, March 1979.

Clarke-Stewart, K. A., Vanderstoep, L., & Killian, G. Analysis and replication of mother–infant relations at 1 year of age. *Child Development*, 1979, *50*, 777–793.

Clarke-Stewart, K. A., Umeh, B., Snow, M., & Pedersen, J. Development and prediction of children's sociability from one to two and one-half years. *Develop-mental Psychology*, 1980, *16*, 290–302.

Clement, P. W., & Milne, D. C. Group play therapy and tangible reinforcers used to modify the behavior of 8-year-old boys. *Behavioral Research and Therapy*, 1967, *5*, 301–302.

Cohen, S., & Beckwith, L. Caregiving behaviors and early cognitive development as related to ordinal position in pre-term infants. *Child Development*, 1977, *48*, 152–157.

Cohen, S., & Beckwith, L. Pre-term infant interaction with the caregiver in the first year of life and competence at age 2. *Child Development*, 1979, *50*, 767–776.

Cohen, S., Glass, D., & Singer, J. Apartment noise, auditory discrimination and reading ability in children. *Journal of Experimental Social Psychology*, 1973, *9*, 407–422.

Combs, M. L., & Slaby, D. A. Social skills training with children. In B. Lakey & A. Kazdin (Eds.), *Advances in clinical child psychology* (Vol. 1). New York: Plenum Press, 1971.

Comrey, A. L. *A first course in factor analysis*. New York: Academic Press, 1973.

Cooke, T. P., & Apolloni, T. Developing positive social-emotional behaviors: A study of training and generalization effects. *Journal of Applied Behavior Analysis*, 1976, *9*, 65-78.

Coopersmith, S. *The antecedents of self-esteem*. San Francisco: Freeman, 1967.

Cornell, E., & Gottfried, A. Intervention with premature human infants. *Child Development*, 1976, *47*, 32-39.

Corter, C., Zucker, K., & Galligan, R. Patterns in the infant's search for mother during brief separation. *Developmental Psychology*, 1980, *16*, 62-69.

Cowan, P. A. *The link between cognitive structure and social structures in two-child verbal interaction*. Paper presented at the Society for Research in Child Development, Santa Monica, 1967.

Cowen, E. L., Pedersen, A., Babigan, H., Izzo, L. D., & Trost, M. A. Long-term follow-up of early detected vulnerable children. *Journal of Consulting and Clinical Psychology*, 1973, *41*, 438-446.

Crandall, V., & Preston, A. Pattern and levels of maternal behavior. *Child Development*, 1955, *26*, 267-277.

Cronbach, L. The two disciplines of scientific psychology. In D. Jackson & S. Messnick (Eds.), *Problems in human assessment*. New York: McGraw–Hill, 1967.

Cummings, E. Caregiver stability and daycare. *Developmental Psychology*, 1980, *16*, 31-37.

Darlington, R., Royce, J., Snipper, A., Murray, H., & Lazar, I. Preschool programs and later school competence of children from low income families. *Science*, 1980, *208*, 202-204.

Das, J. P. Cultural deprivation and cognitive competence. In N. Ellis, *International review of research in mental retardation VI*. New York: Academic Press, 1973.

Davids, A., Holden, R., & Gray, G. Maternal anxiety during pregnancy and adequacy of mother and child adjustment eight months following child's birth. *Child Development*, 1963, *34*, 993-1002.

Dember, W., & Earl, R. Analysis of exploratory, manipulative and curiosity behaviors. *Psychological Review*, 1957, *64*, 91-96.

Denenberg, V., & Zarrow, N. Effects of handling in infancy upon adrenocortical reactivity. In D. Welcher & D. Peters (Eds.), *Early childhood: The development of self regulatory mechanisms*. New York: Academic Press, 1971.

Dennis, W. Does culture appreciably affect patterns of infant behavior? *Journal of Social Psychology*, 1940, *12*, 305-317.

Deschner, J. The influence of mother–child interaction on early manifestations of competence. *Dissertation Abstracts*, 1973, *33*, 4485B.

Deutsch, C. Auditory discrimination and learning. *Merrill–Palmer Quarterly*, 1964, *10*, 277-296.

Deutsch, C. Social class and child development. In B. Caldwell & H. Ricciuti, *Review of child development research: III*. Chicago: University of Chicago Press, 1973.

Deutsch, F. Female preschoolers' perceptions of affective responses and interpersonal behavior in videotaped episodes. *Developmental Psychology*, 1974, *11*, 733-743.

Devereaux, E. L., Shouval, R., Bronfenbrenner, U., Rodgers, R. R., KavVenaki, S., Kiely, E., & Karson, E. Socialization practices of parents, teachers, and peers in Israel: The kibbutz versus the city. *Child Development*, 1974, *45*, 269-281.

DeVries, R. The development of role-taking as reflected by the behavior of bright, average, and retarded children in a social guessing game. *Child Development*, 1970, *41*, 759–770.

Dickie, J. R., & Gerber, S. C. Training in social competence: The effects on mothers, fathers, and infants. *Child Development*, 1980, *51*, 1248–1251.

Dickson, L., Hess, R., Miyake, N., & Azuma, H. Referential communication accuracy between mother and child as a predictor of cognitive development in the United States and Japan. *Child Development*, 1979, *50*, 53–59.

Distler, L. S. *Patterns of parental identification: An examination of three theories.* Unpublished doctoral dissertation, University of California, Berkeley, 1964.

Dlugokinski, E. L., & Firestone, I. J. Other centeredness and susceptibility to charitable appeals: Effects of perceived discipline. *Developmental Psychology*, 1974, *10*, 21–28.

Donovan, W., & Leavitt, L. Early cognitive development and its relation to maternal physiologic and behavioral responses. *Child Development*, 1978, *49*, 1251–1254.

Douglas, J. W. B., Lawson, A., & Cooper, J. E. Family interaction and the activities of young children. *Journal of Child Psychology and Psychiatry*, 1968, *9*, 157–171.

Doyle, A., Connolly, J., & Rivest, L. The effect of playmate familiarity on the social interactions of young children. *Child Development*, 1980, *51*, 217–223.

Dunn, J. B., & Richards, M. P. M. *Observations on the developing relationship between mother and baby in the neonatal period.* Unpublished paper, University of Cambridge, 1974.

Durham, M., & Black, K. The test performance of 16–21 month olds in homes and laboratory settings. *Infant Behavior and Development*, 1978, *1*, 216–223.

Easterbrooks, M. A., & Lamb, M. E. The relationship between quality of infant–mother attachment and infant competence in initial encounters with peers. *Child Development*, 1979, *50*, 380–387.

Elardo, R., Bradley, R., & Caldwell, B. The relationship of infant's home environment to mental test performance from 6–36 months: A longitudinal analysis. *Child Development*, 1975, *46*, 71–76.

Elardo, R., Bradley, R., & Caldwell, B. A longitudinal study of the relation of infant home environment to language development at age 3. *Child Development*, 1977, *48*, 595–603.

Elkind, D. Piagetian and psychometric conceptions of intelligence. *Harvard Educational Review*, 1969, *39*, 319–337.

Emmerich, W. Stability and development of personal-social behaviors in economically disadvantaged preschool children. *Genetic Psychology Monographs*, 1977, *95*, 191–245.

Emmerich, W., Cocking, R., & Sigel, I. Relationships between cognitive and social functioning in preschool children. *Developmental Psychology*, 1979, *15*, 495–504.

Endler, N. S., Boulter, L. R., & Osser, H. *Contemporary issues in developmental psychology.* New York: Holt, Rinehart & Winston, 1968.

Engelmann, S. The effectiveness of direct instruction on IQ performance and achievement in reading and arithmetic. In J. Hellmuth (Ed.), *Disadvantaged child III.* New York: Bruner/Mazel, 1970.

Epstein, H. Phrenoblysis: Special brain and mind growth periods. I. Human brain and skull development. *Developmental Psychobiology*, 1974, *7*, 207–216. (a)

Epstein, H. Phrenoblysis: Special Brain and mind growth periods. II. Human mental development. *Developmental Psychobiology*, 1974, *7*, 217–224. (b)

Epstein, S. Comment on Dr. Bandura's paper. In M. Jones (Ed.), *Nebraska Symposium on motivation*. Lincoln, Neb.: University of Nebraska Press, 1962.

Escalona, S., & Corman, H. The impact of mother presence upon behavior: The first year. *Human Development*, 1971, *14*, 2–15.

Evers, W. L., & Schwartz, J. C. Modifying social withdrawal in preschoolers: The effects of filmed modeling and teacher praise. *Journal of Abnormal Child Psychology*, 1973, *1*, 248–256.

Falender, C., & Heber, R. Mother–child interaction and participation in a longitudinal intervention program. *Developmental Psychology*, 1975, *6*, 830–836.

Fantz, R. L. The origin of form perception. *Scientific American*, 1961, *204*, 66–72.

Farran, D., & Haskins, R. Reciprocal influence in the social interactions of mothers and three year old children from different socioeconomic backgrounds. *Child Development*, 1980, *51*, 780–791.

Farran, D., & Ramey, C., Social class differences in dyadic involvement during infancy. *Child Development*, 1980, *51*, 254–257.

Farran, D., Ramey, C., & Campbell, F. *Social interactions of mothers and young children*. Paper presented to the Society of Research in Child Development, New Orleans, April 1977.

Faust, O. A., Jackson, K., Cermak, E. G., Burtt, M. M., & Winkley, R. *Reducing emotional trauma in hospitalized children*. Albany, N.Y.: Albany Research Project, Albany Medical College, 1952.

Fawl, C. Disturbances experienced by children in their natural habitat. In R. Barker (Ed.), *The stream of behavior*. New York: Appleton–Century, 1963.

Feffer, M. The cognitive implications of role-taking behavior. *Journal of Personality*, 1959, *27*, 152–168.

Feshbach, N., & Feshbach, S. The relationship between empathy and aggression in two age groups. *Developmental Psychology*, 1969, *1*, 102–107.

Feshbach, N., & Roe, K. Empathy in six and seven year olds. *Child Development*, 1968, *39*, 133–145.

Field, T. Infant arousal, attention, and affect during early interactions. In L. Lipsitt (Ed.), *Advances in infant behavior and development*. Hillsdale, N.J.: Erlbaum Associates, in press.

Field, T., Hallock, N., Ting, G., Dempsey, J., Dabira, C., & Shuman, H. A first year follow-up of high-risk infants in formulating a cumulative risk index. *Child Development*, 1978, *49*, 119–131.

Filler, J. Modifying maternal teaching style: Effects of task arrangement on the match to sample performance of retarded school age children. *American Journal of Mental Deficiency*, 1976, *80*, 602–612. (a)

Filler, J., & Bricker, W. Teaching style of mothers and the match to sample performance of their retarded children. *American Journal of Mental Deficiency*, 1976, *80*, 504–511. (b)

Finkelstein, N., & Ramey, C. Learning to control the environment in infancy. *Child Development*, 1977, *48*, 806–814.

Finkelstein, N., Gallagher, J., & Farran, D. Attentiveness and responsiveness to auditory stimulation of children at risk for mental retardation. *American Journal of Mental Deficiency*, 1980, *85*, 135–144.

Fishbein, H. D., Lewis, S., & Keiffer, K. Children's understanding of spatial relations: Coordination of perspectives. *Developmental Psychology*, 1972, 7, 21–33.

Flavell, J. H. *The development of role-taking and communication skills in children.* New York: Wiley, 1968.

Flavell, J. H. The development of inferences about others. In T. Mischel (Ed.), *Understanding other persons.* Oxford, England: Blackwell, Basil, & Mott, 1974.

Floeter, N., & Greenough, W. Cerebellar plasticity: Modification of purkinje cell structure by differential rearing in monkeys. *Science*, 1979, *206*, 227–229.

Fowler, W. Cognitive learning in infancy and early childhood. *Psychological Bulletin*, 1962, *59*, 116–152.

Fowler, W. Structural dimensions of the learning process in early reading. *Child Development*, 1964, *35*, 1093–1104.

Fowler, W. The effects of early stimulation: The problem of focus in developmental stimulation. *Merrill–Palmer Quarterly*, 1969, *15*, 157–170.

Fox, N. Attachment of kibbutz infants to mother and metapelet. *Child Development*, 1977, *48*, 1228–1239.

Fraiberg, S. The development of human attachments in infants blind from birth. *Merrill–Palmer Quarterly*, 1975, *11*(5), 589–601.

Fredrickson, W., & Brown, J. Posture as a determinant of visual behavior on newborns. *Child Development*, 1975, *46*, 579–582.

Freeberg, N., & Payne, D. Parental influence on cognitive development in early childhood: A review. *Child Development*, 1967, *38*, 65–87.

Freedman, D. G. Hereditary control of early social behavior. In B. M. Foss (Ed.), *Determinants of infant behavior* (Vol. 3). London: Methuen, 1965.

Freud, A. *Normality and pathology in childhood.* New York: International Universities Press, 1966.

Freud, A., & Burlingham, D. T. *Infants without families.* New York: International Universities Press, 1944.

Freud, A., & Dann, S. An experiment in group upbringing. In R. Eisler *et al.*, (Eds.), *The psychoanalytic study of the child.* New York: International Universities Press, 1951.

Freud, S. *An outline of psychoanalysis.* New York: Norton, 1940.

Friedman, J., Maarten, S., Streisel, I., & Sinnamon, H. Sensory restriction and isolation experiences in children with phenylketonuria. *Journal of Abnormal Psychology*, 1968, *73*, 294–303.

Friedrich, L. K., & Stein, A. H. Aggressive and prosocial television programs and the natural behavior of preschool children. *Monographs of the Society for Research in Child Development*, 1973, *38*, (4, Serial No. 151).

Furman, W., Rahe, D., & Hartup, W. W. Rehabilitation of socially withdrawn preschool children through mixed-age and same-age socialization. *Child Development*, 1979, *50*, 915–922.

Furrow, D., Nelson, K., & Benedict, K. Mothers' speech to children and syntactic development. *Journal of Child Lanauge*, 1979, *6*, 423–442.

Gaiter, J. *Cognitive play experiences and 13 month old infant performance with objects.* Symposium presentation, Southeastern Conference on Human Development, Nashville, Tenn., April 1976.

Garms, R. *Preference and accelerating perceptual development in the human infant.* Unpublished doctoral dissertation, Purdue University, 1974.

Geber, M. Development psycho-moteur des petits Baganda de la naissance a six ans. *Schweizerische Zeitschrift für psychologie and ihre anwendungen*, 1961, *20*, 345-357.

George, C., & Main, M. Social interactions of young abused children: Approach, avoidance, and aggression. *Child Development*, 1979, *50*, 306-318.

Gewirtz, J. Levels of conceptual analysis in environment–infant interaction research. *Merrill-Palmer Quarterly*, 1969, *15*, 7-48.

Gibson, E. Development of perception. In J. Wright (Ed.), Basic cognitive processes in children. *Monographs of the Society for Research in Child Development*, 1963, *28*.

Glenn, L., Nerbonne, G., & Tolhurst, G. Environmental noise in a residential institution for mentally retarded persons. *American Journal of Mental Deficiency*, 1978, *82*, 594-597.

Globus, A. Brain morphology as a function of presynaptic morphology and activity. In A. Reisen (Ed.), *The developmental neuropsychology of sensory deprivation*. New York: Academic Press, 1975.

Glucksberg, S., Krauss, R., & Weisberg, R. Referential communication in nursery school children: Method and some preliminary findings. *Journal of Experimental Child Psychology*, 1966, *3*, 332-342.

Glueck, S., & Glueck, E. *Unraveling juvenile delinquency*. New York: Commonwealth Fund, 1950.

Glueck, S., & Glueck, E. *Physique and delinquency*. New York: Harper, 1956.

Glueck, S., & Glueck, E. *Predicting delinquency and crime*. Cambridge Mass.: Harvard University Press, 1959.

Goldberg, S. Infant care and growth in urban Zambia. *Human Development*, 1972, *15*, 77-89.

Goldberg, S. Infant development and mother–infant interaction in urban Zambia. In P. Leiderman, S. Tulkin, & A. Rosenfeld (Eds.), *Culture and infancy*. New York: Academic Press, 1977. (a)

Goldberg, S. Social competence in infancy: A model of parent–infant interaction. *Merrill-Palmer Quarterly*, 1977, *23*, 163-178. (b)

Golden, M., & Birns, B. Social class and infant intelligence. In M. Lewis (Ed.), *Origins of intelligence*. New York: Plenum Press, 1976.

Goldfarb, W. The effects of early institutional care on adolescent personality. *Journal of Experimental Education*, 1943, *12*, 106-129.

Goldfarb, W. Effects of early institutional care on adolescent personality: Rorschach data. *American Journal of Orthopsychiatry*, 1944, *14*, 441-447.

Goldfarb, W. Psychological privation in infancy and subsequent adjustment. *American Journal of Orthopsychiatry*, 1945, *15*, 247-255.

Gottfried, A., & Gottfried, A. *Home environment and mental development in middle class infants in the first two years*. Paper presented to the Society for Research in Child Development, Boston, April 1981.

Gottman, J. M. Toward a definition of social isolation in children. *Child Development*, 1977, *48*, 513-157.

Gottman, J. M., Gonso, J., & Rasmussen, B. Friendships in children. *Child Development*, 1975, *46*, 709-718.

Gray, M. D., Tracy, R. L., & Lindberg, C. L. Effects of maternal interference on the attachment and exploratory behaviors of one-year-olds. *Child Development*, 1979, *50*, 1211-1214.

Gray, S., & Klaus, R. The early training project and its general rationale. In R. Hess & R. Bear (Eds.), *Early education*. Chicago: Aldine, 1968.

Gray, S., & Klaus, R. The early training project: A seventh year report. *Child Development*, 1970, *41*, 909–924.

Gray, S., & Miller, J. Early experience in relation to cognitive development. *Review of Educational Research*, 1967, *37*, 475–493.

Green, J. A. *A developmental analysis of mother–infant interactions: Changes in infant behavior and capabilities*. Unpublished master's thesis, University of North Carolina at Chapel Hill, 1977.

Greenbaum, C. Comment on Kagan *et al*. *Monographs of the society for research in child development*, 1979, *44*.

Greenbaum, C., & Landau, R. Mothers' speech and the early development of vocal behavior. In A. Liederman, S. Tulkin, & A. Rosenfeld (Eds.), *Culture and infancy*. New York: Academic Press, 1977.

Greenberg, D. Accelerating visual complexity levels in the human infant. *Child Development*, 1971, *42*, 905–918.

Greenburg, N. Developmental effect of stimulation during early infancy: Some conceptual and methodological considerations. *Annals of the New York Academy of Sciences*, 1965, *118*, 831–859.

Greenough, W., & Juraska, J. Experience-induced changes in brain fine structure: Their behavioral implications. In M. Hahn, C. Jensen, & B. Dudek (Eds.), *Development and evolution of brain size: Behavioral implications*. New York: Academic Press, 1979.

Gregory, J. Anterospective data following childhood loss of a parent. I. Delinquency and high school drop out. *Archives of General Psychiatry*, 1965, *13*, 99–109.

Grotevant, H., Scarr, S., & Weinberg, R. Intellectual development in family constellations with adopted and natural children. *Child Development*, 1977, *48*, 1699–1703.

Grusec, J., & Kuczynski, L. Direction of affect and socialization: A comparison of the parents versus the child's behavior as determinants of disciplinary techniques. *Developmental Psychology*, 1980, *16*, 1–9.

Gump, P., & Kounin, J. Issues raised by ecological and classical research efforts. *Merrill–Palmer Quarterly*, 1960, *6*, 145–152.

Gunnar, M. Control, warning signals and distress in infancy. *Developmental Psychology*, 1980, *16*, 281–289.

Haith, M. M., Bergman, T., & Moore, M. J. *Eye contact and fact scanning in early infancy*. Unpublished manuscript, University of Denver, 1977.

Hambrick-Dickson, P. *The effects of subway extraneous noise on children's psychomotor, cognitive and perceptual performance*. Symposium presentation, Acoustical Society of America, Los Angeles, 1980.

Hanks, C. The role of mother–infant interaction in cognitive development of 7 month old infants. *Dissertation Abstracts*, 1972, *33*, 1764B.

Hanson, R. Consistency and stability of home environmental measures related to IQ. *Child Development*, 1975, *46*, 470–480.

Harlow, M. K. Nuclear family apparatus. *Behavioral Research Method and Instrumentation*, 1971, 301–304.

Hart, B. M., Reynolds, N. J., Baer, D. M., Browley, E. R., & Harris, F. R. Effect of contingent and non-contingent social reinforcement on the cooperative play of a preschool child. *Journal of Applied Behavior Analysis*, 1968, *1*, 73–76.

Hartup, W. W. Friendship status and the effectiveness of peers as reinforcing agents. *Journal of Experimental Child Psychology*, 1964, *1*, 154–162.

Hartup, W. W. Peer interaction and social organization. In P. H. Mussen (Ed.), *Carmichael's manual of child psychology*. New York: Wiley, 1970.

Hartup, W. W. Peers, play and pathology: A new look at the social behavior of children. *Newsletter*, Society for Research in Child Development, Fall 1977.

Hartup, W. W., & Coates, B. Imitation of a peer as a function of reinforcement from the peer group and rewardingness of the model. *Child Development*, 1967, *38*, 1003–1016.

Hartup, W. W., & Keller, E. D. Nurturance in preschool children and its relation to dependency. *Child Development*, 1960, *31*, 681–689.

Haskins, R., Ramey, C., Stedman, D., Dixon, J., & Pierce, J. Effect of repeated assessment on standardized test performance by infants. *American Journal of Mental Deficiency*, 1978, *83*, 233–239.

Haywood, H., & Tapp, J. Experience and the development of adaptive behavior. In N. Ellis (Ed.), *International review of research in mental retardation*. New York: Academic Press, 1966.

Hebb, D. *Organization of behavior*. New York: Wiley, 1949.

Heilbrun, A. B. An empirical test of the modeling theory of sex role learning. *Child Development*, 1965, *36*, 789–799.

Herman, S. The relationship between maternal variable scores and infant performance in a Negro experimental stimulation training program. *Dissertation Abstracts*, 1971, *32*, 239–240A.

Hess, R., & Shipman, V. Early experience and the socialization of cognitive modes in children. *Child Development*, 1965, *36*, 869–886.

Hess, R., & Shipman, V. Cognitive elements in maternal behavior. In J. Hill (Ed.), *Minnesota symposium on child psychology*. Minneapolis: University of Minnesota Press, 1967.

Hess, R., & Shipman, V. Maternal influences upon early learning. In R. Hess & R. Bear, *Early education*. Chicago: Aldine, 1968.

Hess, R., Shipman, V., Brophy, J., & Bear, R. Mother–child interaction. In I. Gordon (Ed.), *Readings in research in developmental psychology*. Glenview, Ill.: Scott Foresman, 1971.

Hetherington, E. M. A developmental study of the effects of sex of the dominant parent on sex role preference, identification, and imitation in children. *Journal of Personality and Social Psychology*, 1965, *2*, 188–194.

Hetherington, E. M. Effects of paternal absence on sex-typed behaviors in Negro and white preadolescent males. *Journal of Personality and Social Psychology*, 1966, *4*, 87–91.

Hetherington, E. M. The effects of familial variables on sex typing, on parent-child similarity, and on imitation in children. In J. P. Hill (Ed.), *Minnesota symposium on child psychology I*. Minneapolis: University of Minnesota Press, 1967.

Hetherington, E. M. Effects of father-absence on personality development in adolescent daughters. *Developmental Psychology*, 1972, *7*, 313–326.

Hetherington, E. M., & Parke, R. D. *Child psychology: A contemporary viewpoint* (2nd ed.). New York: McGraw–Hill, 1979.

Hill, W. F. Learning theory and the acquisition of values. *Psychological Review*, 1960, *67*, 317–331.

Hoffman, L. W. The father's role in the family and the child's peer group adjustment. *Merrill–Palmer Quarterly*, 1961, 7, 97–105.

Hoffman, M. L. Parent discipline and the child's consideration for others. *Child Development*, 1963, *34*, 573–588.

Hoffman, M. L. Moral development. In P. H. Mussen (Ed.), *Carmichael's manual of child psychology*. New York: Wiley, 1970.

Hoffman, M. L. Moral internalization, parental power, and the nature of parent–child interaction. *Developmental Psychology*, 1975, *11*(2), 228–239.

Hoffman, M. L., & Saltzstein, H. D. Parent practices and the development of children's moral orientations. In W. E. Martin (Chair), *Parent behavior and children's personality development: Current project research*. Symposium presented at the meetings of the American Psychological Association, Chicago, September 1960.

Hoffman, M. L., & Saltzstein, H. D. Parent discipline and the child's moral development. *Journal of Personality and Social Psychology*, 1967, *5*, 45–57.

Hollenbeck, A. Problems of reliability in observational research. In G. Sackett (Ed.), *Observing behavior II*. Baltimore: University Park Press, 1978.

Hollos, M., & Cowan, P. A. Social isolation and cognitive development: Logical operations and role-taking abilities in three Norwegian social settings. *Child Development*, 1973, *44*, 630–641.

Holstein, C. B. *Parental consensus and interaction in relation to the child's moral development*. Unpublished doctoral dissertation, University of California, Berkeley, 1969.

Honig, A. S. The developmental needs of infants: How can they be met in a day care setting? In R. Elardo & B. Pagan (Eds.), *Perspectives on infant day care*. Little Rock, Ark.: Southern Association in Children under Six, 1976.

Honig, A. S., Caldwell, B., & Tannenbaum, J. Patterns of information processing used by and with young children in a nursery school setting. *Child Development*, 1970, *41*, 1045–1065.

Honzik, M. Environmental correlates of mental growth: Predictions from the family setting at 21 months. *Child Development*, 1967, *38*, 337–364. (a)

Honzik, M. Prediction of differential abilities at age 18 from the early family environment. *APA Proceedings*, 1967, *2*, 151–152. (b)

Horowitz, F., & Paden, L. The effectiveness of environmental enrichment programs. In B. Caldwell & H. Riccutti (Eds.), *Review of child development research*. Chicago: University of Chicago Press, 1975.

Horowitz, F., Linn, P., Smith, C., & Buddin, B. *Paternal responsivity in relation to developmental outcome*. Paper presented to the Society for Research in Child Development, Boston, April 1981.

Horton, C., & Crump, E. Growth and development: Descriptive analysis of the backgrounds of 76 Negro children whose scores were above or below average on the Merrill–Palmer Scale of Mental Tests at 3 years of age. *Journal of Genetic Psychology*, 1962, *100*, 255–265.

Hoy, E. A. Measurement of egocentrism in children's communication. *Developmental Psychology*, 1975, *11* (3), 392.

Hudson, L. M. On the coherence of role-taking abilities: An alternative to correlational analysis. *Child Development*, 1978, *49*, 223–227.

Hunt, J. McV. *Intelligence and experience*. New York: Ronald Press, 1961.

Hunt, J. McV. Intrinsic motivation and its role in psychological development. In M. Levine (Ed.), *Nebraska Symposium on motivation*. Lincoln, Neb.: University of Nebraska Press, 1965, 189–287.

Hunt, J. McV. How children develop intellectually. In W. Bernard & W. Hucking (Eds.), *Readings in human development*. Boston: Allyn & Bacon, 1967.

Hunt, J. McV. Reflections on a decade of early education. *Journal of Abnormal Child Psychology*, 1975, *3*, 275–330.

Hunt, J. McV. Personal communication, 1976.

Hunt, J. McV. *Specificity in early development and experience*. O'Neill Invited Lecture, Meyer Children's Rehabilitation Institute, University of Nebraska Medical Center, 1977.

Hunt, J. McV. Psychological development: Early experience. In M. Rosenzweig & L. Porter (Eds.), *Annual Review of Psychology*. 1979, *30*, 103–143.

Hunt, J. McV., Mohandessi, K., Ghodssi, M., & Akizama, M. The psychological development of orphanage reared infants: Interventions with outcomes. *Genetic Psychology Monographs*, 1976, *94*, 177–226.

Hutt, C. Specific and diversive exploration. In H. Reese & L. Lipsitt (Eds.), *Advances in child development and behavior V*. New York: Academic Press, 1970.

Hutt, C. Sex differences in human development. *Human Development*, 1972, *15*, 153–170.

Hutt, S., & Hutt, C. *Direct observation and measurement of behavior*. Springfield, Ill.: Charles C. Thomas, 1970.

Huttenlocher, J., & Presson, C. C. Mental rotation and the perspective problem. *Cognitive Psychology*, 1973, *4*, 277–299.

Itard, J. *The wild boy of Aveyron*. New York: Appleton–Century, 1962.

Jacob, T. Family interaction in disturbed and normal families. *Psychological Bulletin*, 1975, *82*, 33–65.

Jacobs, B., & Moss, H. Birth order and sex of siblings as determinants of mother–infant interaction. *Child development*, 1976, *47*, 315–322.

Jacobson, L., Berger, S., Bergman, R., Millham, J., & Greeson, L. Effect of age, sex, systematic conceptual learning, acquisition of learning sets and programmed social interaction on the intellectual and conceptual development of preschool children from poverty backgrounds. *Child Development*, 1971, *42*, 1399–1415.

Jason, L., Gesten, E., & Yock, J. Relational and behavioral interventions with economically disadvantaged toddlers. *American Journal of Orthopsychiatry*, 1976, *46*, 270–278.

Johnson, D. W. Affective perspective-taking and cooperative predisposition. *Developmental Psychology*, 1975, *11*, 869–870.

Johnson, M. M. Sex role learning in the nuclear family. *Child Development*, 1963, *34*, 315–337.

Jones, D., Rickel, A., & Smith, R. Maternal child rearing practices and social problem-solving strategies among preschoolers. *Developmental Psychology*, 1980, *16*, 241–242.

Jordan, T. Influences on vocabulary attainment: A 5 year prospective study. *Child Development*, 1978, *49*, 1096–1106.

Jordan, T., & Daner, S. Biological and ecological influences on development at 12 months of age. *Human Development*, 1970, *13*, 178–181.

Jordan, T., & Spooner, S. Biological and ecological influences on development at 24 and 36 months of age. *Psychological Reports*, 1972, *31*, 319–322.

Jordan, T., Radin, N., & Epstein, A. Paternal behavior and intellectual functioning in preschool boys and girls. *Developmental Psychology*, 1975, *11*, 407–408.

Kaffman, M., & Elizar, E. Infants who become enuretics: A longitudinal study of 161 kibbutz children. *Monographs of the Society for Research in Child Development*, 1977, *170*.

Kagan, J. On the need for relativism. *American Psychologist*, 1967, *22*, 131–142.

Kagan, J. Continuity in cognitive development during the first year. *Merrill–Palmer Quarterly*, 1969, *15*, 101–119.

Kagan, J., & Freeman, M. Relation of childhood intelligence, maternal behaviors and social class to behavior during adolescence. *Child Development*, 1963, *34*, 899–911.

Kagan, J., & Klein, R. Cross-cultural perspectives on early development, *American Psychologist*, 1973, *28*, 947–961.

Kagan, J., & Moss, H. A. *Birth to maturity: The Fels study of psychological development*. New York: Wiley, 1962.

Kagan, J., Henker, B., Hen-Tov, A., Levine, J., & Lewis, M. Infants' differential reactions to familiar and distorted faces. *Child Development*, 1966, *37*, 519–532.

Kagan, J., Kearsley, R. B., & Zelazo, P. R. The effects of infant day care on psychological development. *Educational Quarterly*, 1977, *1*, 109–142.

Kagan, J., Kearsley, R. B., & Zelazo, P. R. *Infancy: Its place in human development*. Cambridge, Mass.: Harvard University Press, 1978.

Kagan, J., Klein, R., Finley, G., Rogoff, B., & Nolan, E. A cross-cultural study of cognitive development. *Monographs of the Society for Research in Child Development*, 1979, *44*.

Kagan, S., & Madsen, M. C. Cooperation and competition of Mexican, Mexican-American, and Anglo-American children of two ages under four instructional sets. *Developmental Psychology*, 1971, *5*, 32–39.

Kagan, S., & Madsen, M. C. Experimental analyses of cooperation and competition of Anglo-American and Mexican children. *Developmental Psychology*, 1972, *6*, 49–59.

Kahn, J. *Cognitive and language training with profoundly retarded children*. Paper presented to the International Society for the Study of Behavioral Development, Toronto, August 1981.

Kamin, L. Sex differences in susceptibility of IQ to environmental influence. *Child Development*, 1978, *49*, 517–518.

Katz, V. Auditory stimulation and developmental behavior of the premature infant. *Nursing Research*, 1971, *20*, 196–201.

Keller, M. E., & Carlson, P. M. The use of symbolic modeling to promote social skills in preschool children with low-levels of social responsiveness. *Child Development*, 1974, *45*, 912–919.

Kennedy, C., & Wachs, T. D. *Environmental factors related to children's preference for visual complexity*. Paper presented to the Midwestern Psychological Association, Chicago, May 1975.

Kenny, D. *Correlation and causality*. New York: Wiley, 1979.

Kent, N., & Davis, R. Discipline in the home and intellectual development. *British Journal of Medical Psychology*, 1957, *30*, 27–33.

Kierscht, M., & Vietze, P. *Multivariate model of infant competence*. Paper presented to the Society for Research in Child Development, New Orleans, 1977.

King, J. Parameters relevant to determining the effect of early experience upon the adult behavior of animals. *Psychological Bulletin*, 1958, *55*, 46–58.

Klaus, R., & Gray, S. The early training project for disadvantaged children. *Monographs of the Society for Research in Child Development*, 1968, *33*.

Klein, R., Lasky, R., Yarbrough, C., Habicht, I., & Seller, M. Relationship of infant/caretaker interaction, social class, and nutritional status to developmental test performance among Guatemalan infants. In P. Leiderman, S. Tulkin, & A. Rosenfeld (Eds.), *Culture and infancy*. New York: Academic Press, 1977.

Kohlberg, L. Early education: A cognitive development view. *Child Development*, 1968, *39*, 1013–1062.

Konner, M. Infancy among the Kalahari Desert San. In P. Leiderman, S. Tulkin, & A. Rosenfeld (Eds.), *Culture and infancy*. New York: Academic Press, 1977.

Kopp, C., & Shaperman, J. Cognitive development in the absence of object manipulation during infancy. *Developmental Psychology*, 1973, *9*, 430.

Korner, A. Individual differences at birth: Implications for early experience and later development. *American Journal of Orthopsychiatry*, 1971, *41*, 608–619.

Korner, A. State as variable, as obstacle, and as mediator of stimulation in infant research. *Merrill–Palmer Quarterly*, 1972, *18*, 77–94.

Korner, A. Early stimulation and maternal care as related to infant capabilities and individual differences. *Early Child Development and Care*, 1973, *2*, 307–327.

Korner, A. The effect of the infant state, level of arousal, sex, and ontogenetic stage on the caregiver. In M. Lewis & L. Rosenblum (Eds.), *The effect of the infant on its caregiver*. New York: Wiley, 1974.

Korner, A., & Grobstein, R. Visual alertness as related to soothing in neonates. *Child Development*, 1966, *37*, 867–877.

Korner, A., & Thoman, E. Visual alertness as evoked by maternal care. *Journal of Experimental Child Psychology*, 1970, *10*, 67–78.

Kotelchuck, M. *The nature of a child's tie to his father*. Unpublished doctoral dissertation, Harvard University, 1972.

Kotelchuck, M. The infants relationship to the father: Experimental evidence. In M. E. Lamb (Ed.), *The role of the father in child development*. New York: Wiley, 1976.

Lacey, J. Somatic response patterning and stress. In M. Appley, & R. Trumbell, *Psychological stress*. New York: Appleton-Century, 1967.

Lagerspetz, K., Nygard, M., & Strondvik, C. The effects of training in crawling on the motor and mental development of infants. *Scandanavian Journal of Psychology*, 1971, *12*, 192–197.

Lamb, M. E. Interactions between two year olds and their mothers and fathers. *Psychological Reports*, 1976, *38*, 447–450. (a)

Lamb, M. E. *The role of the father in child development*. New York: Wiley, 1976. (b)

Lamb, M. E. Father–infant and mother–infant interaction in the first year of life. *Child Development*, 1977, *48*, 167–181.

Landau, R. Extent that the mother represents the social stimulation to which the infant is exposed: Findings from a cross-cultural study. *Developmental Psychology*, 1976, *12*, 399–405.

Laosa, L. Maternal teaching strategies in Chicano families of varied educational and socioeconomic levels. *Child Development*, 1978, *49*, 1129-1135.

Laosa, L. Maternal teaching strategies in Chicano and Anglo-American families. *Child Development*, 1980, *51*, 759-765.

Lawson, A., & Ingleby, J. Daily routine of pre-school children: Effect of age, birth order, sex and social class and developmental correlates. *Psychological Medicine*, 1974, *4*, 399-415.

Lee, L. C. Toward a cognitive theory of interpersonal development: Importance of peers. In M. Lewis and L. Rosenblum (Eds.), *Friendship and peer relations*. New York: John Wiley & Sons, 1975.

Leiderman, P., & Leiderman, G. Affective and cognitive consequences of polymatric infant care in the east African highlands. In A. Pick, *Minnesota Symposium in Child Psychology*, (Vol. 8). Minneapolis: University of Minnesota Press, 1974.

Leiderman, P., Tulkin, S., & Rosenfeld, A. (Eds.). *Culture and infancy*. New York: Academic Press, 1977.

Levenstein, P. Cognitive growth in pre-schoolers through verbal interaction with mothers. *American Journal of Orthopsychiatry*, 1970, *40*, 426-432.

Levine, L. E., & Hoffman, M. L. Empathy and cooperation in 4 year olds. *Developmental Psychology*, 1975, *11*, 533-534.

Lewis, M. State as an infant-environment interaction: An analysis of mother-infant interaction as a function of sex. *Merrill-Palmer Quarterly*, 1972, *18*, 95-122.

Lewis, M., & Brooks-Gunn, J. *Self, other and fear: The reaction of infants to people*. Paper presented at the meeting of the Eastern Psychological Association, Boston, April 1972.

Lewis, M., & Coates, D. Mother-infant interaction and cognitive development in twelve week old infants. *Infant Behavior and Development*, 1980, *3*, 95-105.

Lewis, M., & Goldberg, S. Perceptual cognitive development in infancy: A generalized expectancy model as a function of the mother-infant interaction. *Merrill-Palmer Quarterly*, 1969, *15*, 87-100.

Lewis, M., & Lee-Painter, S. An interactional approach to the mother-infant dyad. In M. Lewis & L. Rosenblum (Eds.), *The effect of the infant on its caregiver*. New York: Wiley, 1974.

Lewis, M., & Wilson, C. Infant development in lower class American families. *Human Development*, 1972, *15*, 112.

Lewis, M., Young, G., Brooks, J., & Michalson, L. The beginning of friendship. In M. Lewis & L. A. Rosenblum (Eds.), *Friendship and peer relations*. New York: Wiley, 1975.

Lichtenberg, P., & Norton, D. *Cognitive and mental development in the first 5 years of life*. National Institute of Mental Health Report. Washington, D.C., 1970.

Lieberman, A. F. Preschoolers' competence with a peer: Relations with attachment and peer experience. *Child Development*, 1977, *48*, 1277-1287.

Lifshitz, M. Internal-external locus of control dimension as a function of age and the socialization milieu. *Child Development*, 1973, *44*, 538-546.

Littenberg, R., Tulkin, S., & Kagan, J. Cognitive components of separation anxiety. *Developmental Psychology*, 1971, *4*, 387-388.

Long, B. H., Henderson, E. H., & Platt, L. Self-other orientations of Israeli adolescents reared in kibbutzim and moshavim. *Developmental Psychology*, 1973, *8*, 300-308.

Lougee, M. D., Grueneich, R., & Hartup, W. W. Social interaction in same- and mixed-age dyads of preschool children. *Child Development*, 1977, *48*, 1353–1361.

Lovell, K. A follow-up study of some aspects of the work of Piaget and Inhelder on the child's conception of space. *British Journal of Educational Psychology*, 1959, *29*, 104–117.

Lusk, D., & Lewis, M. Mother–infant interaction and infant development among the Wolof of Senegal. *Human Development*, 1972, *15*, 58–69.

Lynn, D. B., & Sawrey, W. L. The effects of father absence on Norwegian boys and girls. *Journal of Abnormal and Social Psychology*, 1959, *59*, 258–262.

Lytton, H. Observation studies of parent–child interaction: A methodological review. *Child Development*, 1971, *42*, 651–684.

Lytton, H. Three approaches to the study of parent–child interaction: Ethological, interview, and experimental. *Journal of Child Psychology and Psychiatry*, 1973, *14*, 1–17.

Maccoby, E. E., & Feldman, S. S. Mother-attachment and stranger-reactions in the third year of life. *Monographs of the Society for Research in Child Development*, 1972, *37*, Serial No. 146.

Maccoby, E. E., & Jacklin, L. N. *The psychology of sex differences*. Stanford, Calif.: Stanford University Press, 1974.

Macrae, J., & Jackson, E. Are behavioral effects of infant day care program specific? *Developmental Psychology*, 1976, *12*, 269–270.

Madden, J., Levenstein, P., & Levenstein, P. Longitudinal IQ outcomes of the mother child home program. *Child Development*, 1976, *47*, 1015–1025.

Maier, S., Seligman, M. E., & Solomon, R. L. Fear conditioning and learned helplessness. In R. Church & B. Campbell (Eds.), *Punishment and aversive behavior*. New York: Appleton–Century–Crofts, 1970.

Main, M. *Exploration, play, and level of cognitive functioning as related to child–mother attachment*. Unpublished doctoral dissertation, Johns Hopkins University, 1973.

Masangkay, Z. S., McCluskey, K. A., McIntyre, C. W., Sims-Knight, J., Vaughn, B. E., & Flavell, J. H. The early development of inferences about the visual percepts of others. *Child Development*, 1974, *45*, 357–366.

Mash, E., & Makohonuk, G. The effects of prior information and behavioral predictability on observer accuracy. *Child Development*, 1975, *46*, 513–519.

Mash, E., & McElwee, J. Situational effects on observer accuracy. *Child Development*, 1974, *45*, 367–377.

Matas, L., Arend, R. A., & Sroufe, L. A. Continuity of adaptation in the second year of life: The relationship between quality of attachment and later competence. *Child Development*, 1978, *49*(3), 547–556.

McCall, R. The use of multivariate procedures in developmental psychology. In P. Mussen (Ed.), *Carmichael's manual of child psychology*. New York: Wiley, 1970.

McCall, R. Challenge to a science of developmental psychology. *Child Development*, 1977, *48*, 333–344.

McCall, R., Appelbaum, M., & Hogarty, P. Developmental change in mental performance. *Monographs of the Society for Research in Child Development*, 1973, *38*.

McCall, R., Hogarty, P., & Hurlburt, N. Transitions in infant sensorimotor development and predictions of childhood IQ. *American Psychologist*, 1972, 27, 728–748.

McCall, R., Eichorn, D., & Hogarty, P. Transitions in early mental development. *Monographs of the Society for Research in Child Development*, 1977, *42*.

McCall, R. B., & Kagan, J. Stimulus schema discrepancy and attention in the infant. *Journal of Experimental Child Psychology*, 1967, *5*, 381–390.

McCord, J., & McCord, J. Cultural stereotypes and the validity of interview for research in child development. *Child Development*, 1961, *32*, 171–185.

McCord, W., McCord, J., & Howard, A. Familial correlates of aggression in non-delinquent male children. *Journal of Abnormal and Social Psychology*, 1961, *62*, 79–93.

McCord, W., McCord, J., & Howard, A. Family interaction as antecedent to the direction of male aggressiveness. *Journal of Abnormal and Social Psychology*, 1963, *66*, 239–242.

McDowell, E. Comparison of time sampling and continuous recording techniques for observing developmental changes in caretaker and infant behavior. *Journal of Genetic Psychology*, 1973, *123*, 99–105.

McGrew, W. I. *An ethological study of children's behavior*. New York: Academic Press, 1972.

McQuiston, S., & Wachs, T. D. *Developmental changes in the nature of infants exploratory behavior*. Paper presented to the biennial meeting of the Society for Research in Child Development, San Francisco, March 1979.

Medinnus, G. N. Delinquents' perception of their parents. *Journal of Consulting Psychology*, 1965, *29*, 5–19.

Manzel, E. Naturalistic and experimental approaches to primate behavior. In E. Willems & H. Raush (Eds.), *Naturalistic viewpoints in psychological research*. New York, 1969.

Millar, W. A study of operant conditioning under delayed reinforcement in early infancy. *Monographs of the Society for Research in Child Development*, 1972, *37*.

Millar, W., & Watson, J. The effect of delayed feedback on infant learning re-examined. *Child Development*, 1979, *50*, 747–751.

Miller, L., & Dyer, J. Four preschool programs: Their dimensions and effects. *Monographs of the Society for Research in Child Development*, 1975, *40*.

Moerk, E. Relationships between parental input frequencies and children's language acquisition. *Journal of Child Language*, 1980, 7, 105–118.

Money, J., Hampson, J. G., & Hampson, J. L. Imprinting and the establishment of gender role. *American Medical Association, Archives of Neurological Psychiatry*, 1957, 77, 333–336.

Moore, T. Language and intelligence: A longitudinal study of the first eight years. *Human Development*, 1968, *11*, 1–24.

Mora, J. Personal communication, 1979.

Morgan, G. A., & Ricciuti, H. N. Infants' responses to strangers during the first year. In B. M. Foss (Ed.), *Determinants of infant behavior IV*. New York: Wiley, 1969.

Moss, H. Methodological issues in studying mother–infant interactions. *American Journal of Orthopsychiatry*, 1965, *35*, 482–486.

Moss, H. Early sex differences and mother–infant interactions. In R. Friedman, R. Richart, & R. Wiele (Eds.), *Sex differences in behavior*. New York: Wiley, 1974.

Moss, H., & Kagan, J. Maternal influences on early IQ scores. *Psychological Reports*, 1958, *4*, 655–661.

Moss, H. A., & Robson, K. S. *The role of protest behavior in the development of mother–infant attachement*. Paper presented at the American Psychological Association, San Francisco, 1968.

Moulten, D. W., Burnstein, E., Liberty, D., & Altucher, N. The patterning of parental affection and dominance as a determinant of guilt and sex-typing. *Journal of Personality and Social Psychology*, 1966, *4*, 363–365.

Mueller, E., & Lucas, T. A developmental analysis of peer interaction among toddlers. In M. Lewis & L. A. Rosenblum (Eds.), *Friendship and peer relations*. New York: Wiley, 1975.

Murphy, L. B. *Social behavior and child personality: An exploratory study of some roots of sympathy*. New York: Columbia University Press, 1937.

Mussen, P. H. Some antecedents and consequences of masculine sex-typing in adolescent boys. *Psychological Monographs*, 1961, *75* (Whole No. 506).

Mussen, P. H., & Distler, L. Masculinity, identification, and father/son relationships. *Journal of Abnormal and Social Psychology*, 1959, *59*, 350–356.

Mussen, P. H., & Distler, L. Child-rearing antecedents of masculine identification in kindergarten boys. *Child Development*, 1960, *31*, 89–100.

Mussen, P. H., & Eisenberg-Berg, N. *Roots of caring, sharing, and helping: The development of prosocial behavior in children*. San Francisco: Freeman, 1977.

Mussen, P. H., & Rutherford, E. Parent–child relations and parental personality in relation to young children's sex-role preferences. *Child Development*, 1963, *34*, 589–607.

Nelson, K. Structure and strategy in learning to talk. *Monographs of the Society for Research in Child Development*, 1973, *38*, Nos. 1–2.

Nelson, K. Individual differences in language development. *Developmental Psychology*, 1981, *17*, 170–187.

Newman, B. M., & Newman, P. R. *Infancy and childhood: Development and its contexts*. New York: Wiley, 1978.

Ninio, A. The naive theory of the infant and other maternal attitudes in two subgroups in Israel. *Child Development*, 1979, *50*, 976–980.

O'Connor, R. D. Modification of social withdrawal through symbolic modeling. *Journal of Applied Behavioral Analysis*, 1969, *2*, 15–22.

O'Connor, R. D. The relative efficacy of modeling shaping and the combined procedure for the modification of social withdrawal. *Journal of Abnormal Psychology*, 1972, *79*, 327–334.

Ogston, K. *The comparative effects of language and gross motor stimulation on infant cognitive development*. Paper presented to the Society for Research in Child Development, Boston, April 1981.

Olson, S., Bates, J., Pettit, G., & Bayles, K. *Antecedents of individual differences in children's cognitive and language competence at age two*. Paper presented to the Society for Research in Child Development, Boston, April 1981.

O'Rourke, J. F. Field and laboratory: The decision-making behavior of family groups in two experimental conditions. *Sociometry*, 1963, *26*, 422–435.

Osofsky, J., & Connors, K. Mother–infant interaction: An integrative view of a complex system. In J. Osofsky (Ed.), *Handbook of infant development*. New York: Wiley, 1979.

Osofsky, J., & Danzger, B. Relationship between neonatal characteristics and mother–infant interaction. *Developmental Psychology*, 1974, *10*, 124–130.

Palmer, R. C. Behavior problems of children in navy officers' families. *Social Casework*, 1960, *41*, 177–184.

Papousek, H. *Elaborations of conditioned head turning*. Paper presented to the 19th International Congress of Psychology, London, 1969.

Paraskevopoulos, J., & Hunt, J. McV. Object construction and imitation under differing conditions of rearing. *Journal of Genetic Psychology*, 1971, *119*, 301–321.

Parke, R. Perspectives on father–infant interaction. In J. Osofsky (Ed.), *Handbook of infant development*. New York: Wiley, 1979.

Parker, R. The preschool in action. In E. Schaefer & M. Aaronson (Eds.), *Infant education research project: Implementation and applications of a home tutoring program*. Boston: Allyn, Bacon, 1972.

Parmelee, A., & Sigman, M. Development of visual behavior and neurological organization in pre-term and full-term infants. In A. Pick (Ed.), *Minnesota symposium on child psychology*. Minneapolis: University of Minnesota Press, 1976.

Patterson, G. R., & Reid, J. B. *Reciprocity and coercion: Two factors of social systems*. Unpublished manuscript, Oregon Research Institute, University of Oregon, 1969.

Pavenstedt, E. A comparison of the child-rearing environment of upper-lower and very low-lower class families. *American Journal of Orthopsychiatry*, 1965, *35*, 89–98.

Pedersen, F. *Mother, father and infant as an interactive system*, Symposium paper, American Psychological Association, Chicago, 1975.

Pedersen, F. A., & Robson, K. S. Father participation in infancy. *American Journal of Orthopsychiatry*, 1969, *39*, 466–472.

Pedersen, F. A., Rubenstein, J. L., & Yarrow, L. J. Infant development in father-absent families. *The Journal of Genetic Psychology*, 1979, *135*, 51–61.

Pedersen, F., Yarrow, L. J. Anderson, B., & Cain, R. Conceptualization of father influences in the infancy period. In M. Lewis (Ed.), *The child and its family: Genesis of behavior II*. New York: Plenum Press, 1979.

Pettigrew, T. F. *A profile of the Negro American*. Princeton, N.J.: Van Nostrand, 1964.

Piaget, J. *The origins of intelligence in children*. New York: International Universities Press, 1952.

Piaget, J. *Play dreams and imitation in childhood*. New York: Norton, 1962.

Piaget, J. *The moral judgment of the child*. New York: Free Press, 1965. (Original translation, London: Kegan Paul, 1932.)

Piaget, J. Piaget's theory. In P. H. Mussen (Ed.), *Carmichael's manual of child psychology* (Vol. 1). New York: Wiley, 1970.

Piaget, J., & Inhelder, B. *The child's conception of space*. London: Routledge & Kegan Paul, 1956.

Piaget, J., & Inhelder, B. *The psychology of the child*. New York: Basic Boosk, 1969.

Piper, M., & Ramsay, M. Effects of home environment on the mental development of Down's syndrome infants. *American Journal of Mental Deficiency*, 1980, *85*, 39–44.

Plomin, R., & DeFries, J. *Environmental influences salient to behavioral development in infancy*. Paper presented to the International Conference of Infant Studies, New Haven, Conn., April 1980.

Pontius, A. Neuro-ethics of walking in the newborn. *Perceptual and Motor Skills*, 1973, *37*, 235–245.

Portnoy, F.,& Simmons, C. Day care and attachment. *Child Development*, 1978, *49*, 239–242.

Powell, L. The effect of extra stimulation and maternal involvement on the development of low-birth weight infants and on maternal behavior. *Child Development*, 1974, *65*, 106–113.

Prescott, J. Early somatosensory deprivation as an ontogenetic process in the abnormal development of the brain and behavior. In I. Goldsmith & J. Moor-Jankowski, *Medical primatology 1970*. Basel: Kazer, 1971.

Provence, S., & Lipton, R. *Infants in institutions*. New York: International Universities Press, 1962.

Prugh, D. G., Staub, E., Sands, H., Kirschbaum, R., & Lenihan, E. A study of the emotional reactions of children and families to hospitalization and illness. *American Journal of Orthopsychiatry*, 1953, *23*, 70–106.

Radin, N. Maternal warmth, achievement motivation and cognitive functioning in lower class pre-school children. *Child Development*, 1971, *42*, 1560–1565.

Radin, N. Father–child interaction and the intellectual functioning of four-year-old boys. *Developmental Psychology*, 1972, *6*, 353–361. (a)

Radin, N. Three degrees of maternal involvement in a pre-school program: Impact on mothers and children. *Child Development*, 1972, *43*, 1355–1364. (b)

Radin, N. Observed paternal behaviors as antecedents of intellectual functioning in young boys. *Developmental Psychology*, 1973, *8*, 369–376.

Radin, N. The role of the father in cognitive, academic and intellectual development. In M. Lamb (Ed.), *The role of the father in child development*. New York: Wiley, 1976.

Ramey, C. T., & Finkelstein, N. Contingent stimulation and infant competence. *Journal of Pediatric Psychology*, 1978, *3*, 89–96.

Ramey, C. T., Campbell, F. A., & Nicholson, J. E. The predictive power of the Bayley Scales of Infant Development and the Stanford–Binet Intelligence Test in a relatively constant environment. *Child Development*, 1973, *44*, 790–795.

Ramey, C., Starr, S., Pallas, T., Whitten, C., & Reed, V. Nutrition and response contingent stimulation and the maternal deprivation syndrome: Results of an early intervention program. *Merrill–Palmer Quarterly*, 1975, *4*, 48–53.

Ramey, C., Farran, D., & Campbell, F. Predicting IQ from mother–infant interaction. *Child Development*, 1979, *50*, 804–814.

Randall, T. *An analysis of observer influence on sex and social class differences in mother–infant interaction*. Paper presented to the biennial meeting of the Society for Research in Child Development, Denver, 1975.

Reid, J. Reliability assessment of observation data. *Child Development*, 1970, *41*, 1143–1150.

Reisen, A. *The developmental neuropsychology of sensory deprivation*. New York: Academic Press, 1975.

Rheingold, H. Mental and social development of infants in relation to the number of other infants in the boarding home. *American Journal of Orthopsychiatry*, 1943, *13*, 41–44.

Rheingold, H. The modification of social responsiveness in institutional babies. *Monographs of the Society for Research in Child Development*, 1956, *21*.

Rheingold, H. L. The effect of environmental stimulation upon social and exploratory behavior in the human infant. In B. M. Foss (Ed.), *Determinants of infant behavior*. New York: Wiley, 1961.

Rheingold, H. L., & Eckerman, C. O. Fear of the stranger: A critical examination. In H. W. Reese (Ed.), *Advances in child development and behavior*. New York: Academic Press, 1973.

Riksen-Walraven, J. *Infant development, environmental variables and social class*. Unpublished paper, 1974.

Riksen-Walraven, J. Effects of caregiver behavior on habituation rate and self-efficacy in infants. *International Journal of Behavioral Development*, 1978, *1*, 105–130.

Ringle, N., Trause, M., Klaus, M., & Kennell, J. The effects of extra-postpartum contact and maternal speech patterns on children's IQ, speech, and language comprehension at 5. *Child Development*, 1978, *49*, 862–865.

Robbins, L. The accuracy of parental recall of aspects of child development and of child rearing practices. *Journal of Abnormal and Social Psychology*, 1963, *66*, 261–270.

Roberts, C., & Rowley, J. A study of the association between quality of maternal care and infant development. *Psychological Medicine*, 1972, *2*, 42–49.

Robinson, C., & Robinson, J. Sensory motor functions and cognitive development. In M. Snell (Ed.), *Systematic instruction of the moderately and severely handicapped*. Columbus, Ohio: Merrill, 1978.

Robinson, H., & Robinson, N. The problem of timing in preschool education. In R. Hess & R. Bear (Eds.), *Early education*. Chicago: Aldine, 1968.

Roff, M. A factorial study of the Fels Parent Behavior Scale. *Child Development*, 1949, *20*, 29–45.

Roff, M., Sells, B., & Golden, M. *Social adjustment and personality development in children*. Minneapolis: University of Minnesota Press, 1972.

Rogosa, D. A critique of cross-lagged correlation. *Psychological Bulletin*, 1980, *88*, 245–258.

Rohrer, J. H., & Edmondsen, M. S. (Eds.). *The eighth generation*. New York: Harper, 1960.

Rohrer, W., Ammons, P., & Cramer, P. *Understanding intellectual development*. Hinsdale, Ill.: Dryden Press, 1974.

Rose, S. Enhancing visual recognition memory in pre-term infants. *Developmental Psychology*, 1980, *16*, 85–92.

Rose, S., Blank, M., & Spatler, I. Situational specificity of behavior in young children. *Child Development*, 1975, *46*, 464–469.

Rosenberg, B. G., & Sutton-Smith, B. Ordinal position and sex role identification. *Genetic Psychology Monographs*, 1964, *20*, 297–328.

Rosenberg, M. *Society and the adolescent self-image*. Princeton, N.J.: Princeton University Press, 1965.

Rosenzweig, M., & Bennett, E. Effects of environmental enrichment or impoverishment on learning and on brain values in rodents. In A. Oliverio (Ed.), *Genetics, environment and intelligence*. Amsterdam: North Holland, 1977.

Ross, H. S. The effects of increasing familiarity on infants' reactions to adult strangers. *Journal of Experimental Child Psychology*, 1975, *20*(2), 226–236.

Rotter, J. B. Generalized expectancies for internal versus external control of reinforcement. *Psychological Monographs*, 1966, *80* (Whole No. 609).

Rubenstein, J., Pedersen, F., & Yarrow, L. What happens when Mother is away: A comparison of mother and substitute caregivers. *Developmental Psychology*, 1977, *13*, 529–530.

Rubin, K. H., & Maioni, T. L. Play preference and its relationship to egocentrism, popularity and classification skills in preschoolers. *Merrill–Palmer Quarterly*, 1975, *21*, 171–179.

Rubin, K. H., & Schneider, F. W. The relationship between moral judgment, egocentrism, and altruistic behavior. *Child Development*, 1973, *44*, 661–665.

Rutherford, E., & Mussen, P. Generosity in nursery school boys. *Child Development*, 1968, *39*, 755–765.

Rutter, M. Parent–child separation: Psychological effects on the children. *Journal of Child Psychology and Psychiatry*, 1971, *12*, 233–260.

Rutter, M. Maternal deprivation, 1972–1978: New findings, new concepts, new approaches. *Child Development*, 1979, *50*, 283–305.

Rynders, J., & Horrobin, J. Project Edge. In D. Friedlander, G. Sterritt, & G. Kirk (Eds.), *Exceptional Infant 3*. New York: Bruner/Mazel, 1975.

Sackett, G. P. *Observing behavior II*. Baltimore: University Park Press, 1978.

Sackett, G. P., Holm, R., Ruppenthal, G., & Fahrenbruch, C. The effects of total social isolation rearing on behavior of rhesus and pigtail macaques. In R. Walsh & W. Greenough (Eds.), *Environments as therapy for brain disfunction*. New York: Plenum Press, 1976.

Sackett, G. P., Ruppenthal, G., & Gluck, J. An overview of methodological and statistical problems in observational research. In G. Sackett (Ed.), *Observing behavior II*. Baltimore: University Park Press, 1978.

Saltz, R. Effects of part time "mothering" on IQ and SQ of young institutionalized children. *Child Development*, 1973, *9*, 166–170.

Sameroff, A. Can conditioned responses be established in the newborn infant? *Developmental Psychology*, 1971, *5*, 1–2.

Sameroff, A., & Cavanaugh, P. Learning in infancy. In J. Osofsky (Ed.), *Handbook of infant development*. New York: Wiley, 1979.

Sameroff, A., & Chandler, M. Reproductive risk and the continuum of caretaking casualty. In F. Horowitz (Ed.), *Review of child development research IV*. Chicago: University of Chicago Press, 1975.

Santrock, J. W. Paternal absence, sex typing, and identification. *Developmental Psychology*, 1970, *2*, 264–272.

Sayegh, Y., & Dennis, W. The effect of supplementary experiences upon the development of infants in institutions. *Child Development*, 1965, *36*, 81–90.

Scarr-Salapatek, S. Genetics and the development of intelligence. In F. Horowitz (Ed.), *Review of child development research IV*. Chicago: University of Chicago Press, 1975.

Scarr-Salapatek, S., & Weinberg, R. IQ test performance of black children adopted by white families. *American Psychologist*, 1976, *31*, 726–739.

Scarr-Salapatek, S., & Williams, M. The effects of early stimulation on low birth weight infants. *Child Development*, 1973, *44*, 94–101.

Schaefer, E. S. A circumplex model for maternal behavior. *Journal of Abnormal and Social Psychology*, 1959, *59*, 226–235.

Schaefer, E. S. Converging conceptual models for maternal behavior and for child behavior. In J. C. Glidewell (Ed.), *Parental attitudes and child behavior*. Springfield, Ill.: Charles C Thomas, 1961.

Schaefer, E. S. Children's report of parental behavior: An inventory. *Child Development*, 1965, *36*, 413–424.

Schaffer, H. R. Objective observations of personality development in early infancy. *British Journal of Medical Psychology*, 1958, *32*, 174–183.

Schaffer, H. R. Activity level as a constitutional determinant of infantile reaction to deprivation. *Child Development*, 1966, *37*, 595–602. (a)

Schaffer, H. R. The onset of fear of strangers and the incongruity hypothesis. *Journal of Child Psychology and Psychiatry*, 1966, *1*, 95–106. (b)

Schaffer, H. R. *Studies in mother–infant interaction.* London: Academic Press, 1977.

Schaffer, H. R., & Callender, W. M. Psychologic effects of hospitalization in infancy. *Pediatrics,* 1959, *24,* 528–539.

Schaffer, H. R., & Emerson, P. E. The development of social attachments in infancy. *Monographs of the Society for Research in Child Development,* 1964, *29* (Whole No. 94). (a)

Schaffer, H. R., & Emerson, P. Patterns of responsivity to physical contact in early human development. *Journal of Child Psychology and Psychiatry,* 1964, *5,* 1–13. (b)

Schaffer, H., & Emerson, P. The effects of experimentally administered stimulation on developmental quotients of infants. *British Journal of Social and Clinical Psychology,* 1968, *7,* 61–67.

Schoggen, M., & Schoggen, P. Environmental focus in the home lives of three year old children and three population subgroups. *Darcee Papers and Reports,* *5,* 1971.

Scott, J. P. *Early experience and the organization of behavior.* Belmont, Calif.: Brooks Cole, 1968.

Scott, K. Learning theory, intelligence, and mental development. *American Journal of Mental Deficiency,* 1978, *82,* 325–336.

Scott, R., & Kobes, D. The influence of family size on learning readiness patterns of socioeconomically disadvantaged preschool blacks. *Journal of Clinical Psychology,* 1975, *31,* 85–88.

Sears, R. R. Relation of early socialization experiences to self-concepts and gender role in middle childhood. *Child Development,* 1970, *41,* 267–289.

Sears, R. R., Maccoby, E., & Levin, H. *Patterns of child rearing.* Evanston, Ill.: Row, Peterson, 1957.

Sears, R. R., Rau, L., & Alpert, R. *Identification and child rearing.* Stanford, Calif.: Stanford University Press, 1965.

Seegmiller, B., & King, W. Relations between behavioral characteristics of infants, their mothers' behavior and performance on the Bayley Mental and Motor Scales. *Journal of Psychology,* 1975, *90,* 99–111.

Selman, R. L. The relation of role-taking to the development of moral judgment in children. *Child Development,* 1971, *42,* 79–91. (a)

Selman, R. L. Taking another's perspective: Role-taking development in early childhood. *Child Development,* 1971, *42,* 1721–1734. (b)

Selman, R. L., & Byrne, D. F. A structural-developmental analysis of levels of role-taking in middle childhood. *Child Development,* 1974, *45,* 803–806.

Shantz, C. U. The development of social cognition. In E. M Hetherington (Ed.), *Review of child development research* (Vol. 5). Chicago: University of Chicago Press, 1975,

Shapiro, A., & Madsen, M. C. Between and within group cooperation and competition among kibbutz and nonkibbutz children. *Developmental Psychology,* 1974, *10,* 140–145.

Shipman, V. *Stability and change in family status: Situational and process variables and their relation to children's performance.* Paper presented to the Society for Research in Child Development, New Orleans, 1977.

Shure, M., Spivack, G., & Jaeger, M. Problem-solving, thinking, and adjustment among disadvantaged preschool children. *Child Development,* 1971, *42,* 1791–1803.

Siegel, L. Infant perceptual, cognitive and motor behaviors as predictors of subsequent cognitive and language development. *Canadian Journal of Psychology*, 1979, *33*, 382–395.

Siegel, L. *Home environmental influences on cognitive and language development in the first three years.* paper presented at the Society for Research in Child Development, Boston, April 1981.

Siegman, A. W. Father-absence during childhood and antisocial behavior. *Journal of Abnormal Psychology*, 1966, *71*, 71–74.

Sigel, I. Developmental theory, its place and relevance in early intervention programs. *Young Children*, 1972, 27, 364–372.

Sigel, I., & Olmstead, P. Modification of cognitive skills among lower class black children. In J. Hellmuth (Ed.), *Disadvantaged child III*. New York: Bruner/Mazel, 1970.

Simon, H. A., & Newell, A. Human problem-solving: The state of the theory in 1970. *American Psychologist*, 1971, *26*, 145–159.

Simons, C., & McCluskey, K. *Early cognitive development and its relationship with infant and maternal sensitivity.* Paper presented to the International Society for the Study of Behavioral Development, Toronto, August 1981.

Singh, A. Urban monkeys. *Scientific American*, 1969, *221*, 108.

Siqueland, E. Biological and experiential determinants of exploration in infancy. In L. Stone, H. Smith, & L. Murphy (Ed.), *The competent infant*. New York: Basic Books, 1973.

Skeels, H. M. Adult status of children with contrasting early life experiences. *Monographs of the Society for Research in Child Development*, 1966, *31*(3), 1–65.

Slovin-Ela, S., & Kohen-Raz, P. Developmental differences in primary reaching response of young infants from varying social backgrounds. *Child Development*, 1978, *49*, 132–140.

Smart, M. S., & Smart, R. C. *Children: Development and relationships.* (3rd ed.). New York: Macmillan, 1977.

Solkoff, N., & Matuszak, D. Tactile stimulation and behavioral development among low birthweight infants. *Child Psychiatry and Human Development*, 1975, *6*, 33–37.

Solkoff, N., Sumner, Y., Weintraub, D., & Blase, B. Effects of handling on the subsequent development of premature infants. *Developmental Psychology*, 1969, *1*, 765–768.

Sontag, L., Baker, C., & Nelson, V. Parental growth and personality development. *Monographs of the Society for Research in Child Development*, 1958, *23*.

Spiro, M. E. Is the family universal? *American Anthropologist*, 1954, *56*, 840–846.

Spitz, R. A. The smiling response: A contribution to the ontogenesis of social relations. *Genetic Psychology Monographs*, 1946, *34*, 67–125.

Spitz, R. A. Anxiety in infancy: A study of its manifestations in the first year of life. *International Journal of Psycho-Analysis*, 1950, *31*, 138–143.

Spitz, R. A., & Wolf, K. M. Anaclitic depression. *Psychoanalytic Study of the Child*, 1946, *2*, 313–342.

Spivack, G., & Shure, M. *The social adjustment of young children*. San Francisco: Jossey-Bass, 1974.

Sroufe, L. A. Attachment and the roots of competence. *Human Nature*, 1978, *1*, 50–59.

Sroufe, L. A. Socio-emotional development, In J. Osofsky (Ed.), *Handbook of infant development*. New York: Wiley, 1979.

Sroufe, L. A., & Waters, E. Attachment as an organizational construct. *Child Development*, 1977, *48*, 1184-1999.

Sroufe, L. A., Waters, E., & Matas, L. Contextual determinants of infant affectional response. In M. Lewis & L. Rosenblum (Eds.), *Origins of fear*. New York: Wiley, 1974.

Staub, E. The use of role playing and induction in children's learning of helping and sharing behavior. *Child Development*, 1971, *42*, 805-816.

Stayton, D. J., Hogan, R., & Ainsworth, M. D. S. Infant obedience and maternal behavior: The origins of socialization reconsidered. *Child Development*, 1971, *42*, 1057-1069.

Stephens, W. N. Judgment by social workers on boys and mothers in fatherless families. *Journal of Genetic Psychology*, 1961, *99*, 59-64.

Stern, D. The goal and structure of mother-infant play. *Journal of the American Academy of Child Psychiatry*, 1974, *13*, 408-421. (a)

Stern, D. Mother and infant at play: The dyadic interaction involving facial, vocal and gaze behaviors. In M. Lewis & L. Rosenblum (Eds.), *The effect of the infant on its caregiver*. New York: Wiley, 1974. (b)

Stern, G., Caldwell, B., Hersher, L., Lipton, E., & Richmond, J. A factor analytic study of the mother-infant dyad. *Child Development*, 1969, *40*, 163-182.

Stevenson, H., Parker, T., Wilkinson, A., Bonnevaux, B., & Gonzalez, M. Schooling, environment and cognitive development: A cross-cultural study. *Monographs of the Society for Research in Child Development*, 1978, *175*.

Stevenson, M. B., & Lamb, M. E. Effect of infant sociability and the caretaking environment on infant cognitive performance. *Child Development*, 1979, *50*, 340-349.

Stewart, R., & Burgess, R. *Parent-child interaction in home and laboratory settings*. Paper presented to the International Conference on Infant Studies, New Haven, Conn., 1980.

Streissguth, A., & Bee, H. Mother-child interactions and cognitive development in children. In W. Hartup (Ed.), *The young child: Reviews of Research* (Vol. 2). Washington, D.C.: National Association for the Education of Young Children, 1972.

Sullivan, E. V., & Hunt, D. E. Interpersonal and objective decentering as a function of age and social class. *Journal of Genetic Psychology*, 1967, *110*, 199-210.

Suomi, S. J., Harlow, H. F., & McKinney, W. T. Monkey psychiatrists. *American Journal of Psychiatry*, 1972, *128*, 41-46.

Sutton-Smith, B., & Rosenberg, B. G. Age changes in the effects of ordinal position on sex role identification. *Journal of Genetic Psychology*, 1965, *107*, 61-73.

Taplin, P., & Reid, P. Effects of instructional set and experimenter influence on observer reliability. *Child Development*, 1973, *44*, 547-554.

Thomas, A., & Chess, S. Behavioral individuality in childhood. In L. Aronson, E. Tobach, D. Lehrman, & J. Rosenblatt (Eds.), *Development and evolution of behavior*. San Francisco: Freeman, 1976.

Thomas, H. Discrepancy hypothesis: Methodological and theoretical considerations. *Psychological Review*, 1971, *78*, 249-259.

Thompson, W. Storage mechanisms in early experience. In A. Pick (Ed.), *Minnesota symposium in child psychology VI*. Minneapolis: University of Minnesota Press, 1972.

Thompson, W., & Grusec, W. Studies of early experience. In P. H. Mussen (Ed.), *Carmichael's manual of child psychology*. New York: Plenum Press, 1970.

Tiller, P. O. Father-absence and personality development of children in sailor families. *Nordisk Psyckologis Monograph Series*, 1958, *9*, 1–48.

Tiller, P. O. *Father separation and adolescence*. Oslo: Institute for Social Research, 1961.

Tinbergen, N. Ethology and stress diseases. *Science*, 1974, *185*, 20–26.

Titkin, S., & Hartup, W. W. Sociometric status and the reinforcing effectiveness of chilren's peers. *Journal of Experimental Child Psychology*, 1965, *2*, 306–315.

Tizard, B., & Rees, J. A comparison of the effects of adoption, restoration to the natural mother and continued institutionalization on the cognitive development of 4 year old children. In A. Clarke & A. Clarke (Eds.), *Early experience: Myth and evidence*. London: Open Books, 1976.

Tizard, B., & Hodges, J. The effect of early institutional rearing on the development of eight year old children. *Journal of Child Psychology and Psychiatry*, 1978, *19*, 99–118.

Tizard, B., Copperman, O., Joseph, P., & Tizard, J. Environmental effects on language development: A study of young children in long stay residential nurseries. *Child Development*, 1972, *43*, 337–358.

Tulkin, S., & Cohler, B. Child rearing attitudes and mother–child interaction in the first year of life. *Merrill–Palmer Quarterly*, 1973, *19*, 91–106.

Tulkin, S., & Covitz, F. *Mother–infant interaction and intellectual functioning at age 6*. Paper presented to the biennial meeting of the Society for Research in Child Development, Denver, 1975.

Tulkin, S., & Kagan, J. Mother–child interaction in the first year of life. *Child Development*, 1972, *43*, 31.

Ullman, C. A. Teachers, peers and tests as predictors of adjustment. *Journal of Educational Psychology*, 1957, *48*, 257–267.

Ulvund, S. E. Cognition and motivation in early infancy: An interactionistic approach. *Human Development*, 1980, *23*(1), 17–32.

Uzgiris, I. Patterns of cognitive development in infancy. *Merrill–Palmer Quarterly*, 1973, *19*, 181.

Uzgiris, I. Organization of sensorimotor intelligence. In M. Lewis (Ed.), *Origins of intelligence*. New York: Plenum Press, 1976.

Uzgiris, I. *Changing patterns of infant environment interaction at various stages of development*. Paper presented to symposium on biosocial factors and the infant who is at high risk for developmental disabilities, University of Massachusetts Medical School, Worcester, Mass., May 1980.

Uzgiris, I., & Hunt, J. McV. *Assessment in infancy*. Urbana, Ill.: University of Illinois Press, 1975.

Van Alstyne, D. *The environment of 3 year old children*. Doctoral dissertation, Columbia University, New York, 1929.

Van Lieshout, C. F., Leckie, G., & Smits-Van Sonsbeek, B. *The effect of a social perspective-taking training on empathy and role-taking ability of preschool children*. Paper presented at the International Society for the Study of Behavioral Development, Ann Arbor, Mich., 1973.

Vaughn, B., Egeland, B., Sroufe, L., & Waters, E. Individual differences in infant–mother attachment at 12 and 18 months: Stability and change in families under stress *Child Development*, 1979, *50*, 971–975.

Vaughn, B., Gove, F., & Egeland, B. The relationship between out of home care and the quality of infant–mother attachment in an economically disadvantaged population. *Child Development*, 1980, *51*, 1203–1214.

Wachs, T. D. Similarity in developmental profile among related pairs of human infants. *Science*, 1972, *178*, 1005–1006.

Wachs, T. D. The measurement of early intelligence: Contributions from developmental psychology. In E. Meyers, R. Eymon, & G. Tarjan, Sociobehavioral studies in mental retardation. *American Association of Mental Deficiency Monographs*, Washington, D.C., 1973. (a)

Wachs, T. D. Reinstatement of early experience and later learning: An animal analogue for human development. *Developmental Psychobiology*, 1973, *6*, 437–444. (b)

Wachs, T. D. The optimal stimulation hypothesis and early development. In I. Uzgiris & F. Weizmann (Eds.), *The structuring of experience*. New York: Plenum Press, 1977.

Wachs, T. D. The relationship of infants' physical environment to their Binet performance at 2½ years. *International Journal of Behavioral Development*, 1978, *1*, 51–65.

Wachs, T. D. Proximal experience and early cognitive-intellectual development: The physical environment. *Merrill–Palmer Quarterly*, 1979, *25*, 3–41.

Wachs, T. D. *Noise in the nursery: Background stimulation and infant cognitive development*. Paper presented to the Acoustical Society of America, Los Angeles, November 1980.

Wachs, T. D. Early experience and early cognitive development: The search for specificity. In I. Uzgiris & J. McV. Hunt (Ed.), *Research with scales of psychological development in infancy*. Urbana, Ill.: University of Illinois Press, in press.

Wachs, T. D., & Gandour, N. J. *Temperament, environment and six month cognitive-intellectual development*. Paper presented to the Society for Research in Child Development, Boston, 1981.

Wachs, T. D., & Hubert, N. Changes in the structure of cognitive-intellectual performance during the second year of life. *Infant Behavior and Development*, 1981, *4*, 151–162.

Wachs, T. D., & Mariotto, M. Criteria for the assessment of organism–environment correlation in human developmental studies. *Human Development*, 1978, *21*, 268–288.

Wachs, T. D., & Peters-Martin, P. Temperament, environment and twelve month sensorimotor development. Paper presented to the International Society for the Study of Behavioral Development, Toronto, August 1981.

Wachs, T. D., Uzgiris, I., & Hunt, J. McV. Cognitive development in infants of different age levels and from different environmental backgrounds. *Merrill–Palmer Quarterly*, 1971, *17*, 283–317.

Wachs, T. D., Francis, J., & McQuiston, S. Psychological dimensions of the infant's physical environment. *Infant Behavior and Development*, 1979, *2*, 155–161.

Waddington, C. *New patterns in genetics and development*. New York: Columbia University Press, 1962.

Waters, E. The reliability and stability of individual differences in infant–mother attachment. *Child Development*, 1978, *49*, 483–494.

Watson, J. S. Memory and "contingency analysis" in infant learning. *Merrill–Palmer Quarterly*, 1967, *13*, 55–76.

Watson, J. S. Smiling, cooing, and "the game." *Merrill–Palmer Quarterly*, 1972, *18*, 323–340.

Watson, J. S., & Ramey, C. T. *Reactions to responsive contingent stimulation in early infancy.* Paper presented at the biennial meeting of the society for Research in Child Development, Santa Monica, Calif., March 1969.

Watson, J. S., & Ramey, C. T. Reactions to response-contingent stimulation in early infancy. *Merrill–Palmer Quarterly*, 1972, *18*, 219–228.

Waxler, C. Z., Yarrow, M. R., & Smith, J. B. Perspective taking and prosocial behavior. *Developmental Psychology*, 1977, *13*, 87–88.

Weick, K. Systematic observational methods. In G. Lindzey & F. Aronson (Eds.), *Handbook of social psychology* (2nd ed.). Reading, Mass.: Addison–Wesley, 1968.

Weinraub, M., & Lewis, M. The determinants of children's responses to separation. *Monographs of the Society for Research in Child Development*, 1977, *172*.

Weisbender, L. A four year follow-up of educationally disadvantaged preschool children analyzing home environment variables facilitating achievement. *Dissertation Abstracts*, 1969, *30*, 1447A.

Weizmann, F. Correlational statistics and the nature–nurture problem. *Science*, 1971, *171*, 589.

Weizmann, F., Cohen, L., & Pratt, J. Novelty, familiarity and the development of infant attention. *Developmental Psychology*, 1971, *4*, 149–154.

Wenar, C. Executive competence in toddlers: A prospective observational study. *Genetic Psychology Monographs*, 1976, *93*, 189–285.

Werner, E. Sex differences in correlations between children's IQs and measures of parental ability and environmental ratings. *Developmental Psychology*, 1969, *1*, 280–285.

White, B. Child development research: An edifice without a foundation. *Merrill–Palmer Quarterly*, 1969, *15*, 49–80.

White, B. *Human infants: Experience and psychological development.* Englewood Cliffs, N.J.: Prentice–Hall, 1971.

White, B. Critical influences in the origins of competence. *Merrill–Palmer Quarterly*, 1975, *21*, 243–266.

White, B., & Held, R. Plasticity of sensorimotor development in the human infant. In J. Rosenbluth & T. Allensmith (Eds.), *The causes of behavior* (2nd ed.). Boston: Allyn & Bacon, 1966.

White, B., & Watts, J. *Experience and environment.* Englewood Cliffs, N.J.: Prentice–Hall, 1973.

White, B., Kaban, B., Shapiro, B., & Attanucci, J. Competence and experience. In I. C. Uzgiris & F. Weizmann (Eds.), *The structuring of experience.* New York: Plenum Press, 1977.

Whiting, B. B., & Whiting, J. W. M. *Children of six cultures: A psychocultural analysis.* Cambridge, Mass.: Harvard University Press, 1975.

Widmayer, G., & Field, T. Effects of Brazelton demonstrations on early interaction of pre-term infants and their teenage mothers. *Infant Behavior and Development*, 1980, *3*, 79–89.

Wildman, B., Erickson, M., & Kent, R. The effect of two training procedures on observer agreement and variability of behavior ratings. *Child Development*, 1975, *46*, 520–524.

Willems, E. Planning a rationale for naturalistic research. In E. Willems & H. Raush, *Naturalistic viewpoints in psychological research*. New York: Holt, Rinehart & Winston, 1969.

Willems, E., & Raush, H. *Naturalistic viewpoints in psychological research*. New York: Holt, Rinehart & Winston, 1969.

Williams, J., & Scott, R. Growth and development of Negro infants IV. Motor development and its relationship to child rearing practices in two groups of Negro infants. *Child Development*, 1953, *24*, 103–121.

Williams, M., & Scarr, S. Effects of short term intervention of performance in low birth weight disadvantaged infants. *Pediatrics*, 1971, *47*, 289–298.

Williams, T. Infant development and supplemental care: A comparative review of basic and applied research. *Human Development*, 1977, *20*, 1–30.

Wilson, R. Twins: Early mental development. *Science*, 1972, *175*, 914–917.

Winick, M. Changes in nucleic acid and protein content of the human brain during growth. *Pediatric Research*, 1968, *2*, 352–355.

Winick, M., Meyer, K., & Harris, R. Malnutrition and environmental enrichment by early adoption. *Science*, 1975, *190*, 1173–1175.

Wohlford, P., Santrock, J. W., Berger, S. E., & Liberman, D. Older brothers' influence on sex-typed, aggressive, and dependent behavior in father-absent children. *Developmental Psychology*, 1971, *4*, 124–134.

Wohlwill, J. *The study of behavioral development*. New York: Academic Press, 1973. (a)

Wohlwill, J. The concept of experience: S or R. *Human Development*, 1973, *16*, 90–107. (b)

Wohlwill, J. *Environmental stimulation and the development of the child: How much and what kind*. Paper presented to the Conference on Environment and Cognitive Development, Arad, Israel, 1974.

Wohlwill, J. Stability and change in cognitive development. In O. Brim & J. Kagan (Eds.), *Constancy and change in human development*. Cambridge, Mass.: Harvard University Press, 1980.

Wohlwill, J., & Heft, H. *Environments fit for the developing child*. Paper presented to the International Society for the Study of Behavioral Development, Guildford, England, 1975.

Wolff, P. H. Observations on the early development of smiling. In B. M. Foss (Ed.), *Determinants of infant behavior II*. London: Methuen, 1963.

Wright, H. *Recording and analyzing child behavior*. New York: Harper & Row, 1967.

Wulbert, M., Ingles, S., Kriegsmann, F., & Mills, B. Language delay and associated mother–child interaction. *Developmental Psychology*, 1975, *11*, 61–70.

Yakovlev, P., & RochLecours, A. The myelogenetic cycles of regional maturation of the brain. In A. Minkowski (Ed.), *Regional development of the brain in early life*. Philadelphia: F. A. Davis, 1967.

Yarrow, L. J. Research in dimensions of early maternal care. *Merrill–Palmer Quarterly*, 1963, *9*, 101–114.

Yarrow, L. J. Separation from parents during early childhood. In M. Hoffman & L. Hoffman (Eds.), *Review of child development research* (Vol. 1). New York: Russell Sage Foundation, 1964.

Yarrow, L. J. The crucial nature of early experience. In D. Glass (Ed.), *Environmental influences: Biology and behavior series*. New York: Rockefeller University Press & Russell Sage Foundation, 1968.

Yarrow, L. J., & Klein, R. Environmental discontinuity associated with transition from foster to adoptive homes. *International Journal of Behavioral Development*, 1980, *3*, 311–322.

Yarrow, L. J., & Pedersen, F. A. The interplay between cognitive and motivation in infancy. In M. Lewis (Ed.), *Origins of intelligence: Infancy and early childhood*. London: Wiley, 1976.

Yarrow, L. J., Goodwin, M. S., Mannheimer, H., & Milowe, I. D. *Infancy experiences and cognitive and personality development at ten years*. Paper presented at the annual meeting of the American Orthopsychiatric Association, Washington, D.C., March 1971.

Yarrow, L. J., Goodwin, M., Mannheimer, H., & Milowe, I. Infancy experience and cognitive and personality development at 10 years. In J. Stone, H. Smith, & L. Murphy (Eds.). *The competent infant*. New York: Basic Books, 1973.

Yarrow, L. J., Rubenstein, J., & Pedersen, F. *Infant and environment*. New York: Wiley, 1975.

Yarrow, M. Problems of methods in parent–child research. *Child Development*, 1963, *34*, 214–226.

Yarrow, M. R. Personal communication, August 1981.

Yarrow, M. R., & Waxler, C. Z. *The emergence and functions of prosocial behaviors in young children*. Paper presented at the meeting of the Society for Research in Child Development, Denver, 1975.

Yarrow, M. R., & Waxler, C. Z. Dimensions and correlates of prosocial behavior in young children. *Child Development*, 1976, *47*, 118–125.

Yarrow, M. R., Campbell, J., & Burton, R. Recollections of childhood: A study of the retrospective method. *Monographs of the Society for Research in Child Development*, 1970, *35*.

Yogman, M. J., Dixon, S., Tronick, E., Als, H., & Brazelton, T. B. *The goals and structure of face-to-face interaction between infants and fathers*. Paper presented at the biennial meeting of the Society for Research in Child Development, New Orleans, March 1977.

Youniss, J. Another perspective on social cognition. In A. Pick (Ed.), *Minnesota Symposia on Child Psychology* (Vol. 9). Minneapolis: University of Minnesota Press, 1975, pp. 173–193.

Zahn-Waxler, L., Radke-Yarrow, M., & King, R. A. Childrearing and children's prosocial initiations toward victims of distress. *Child Development*, 1979, *50*, 319–330.

Zajonc, R. Family configuration and intelligence. *Science*, 1976, *192*, 227–236.

Zegiob, L., Arnold, S., & Forehand, R. An examination of observer effects in parent–child interactions. *Child Development*, 1975, *46*, 509–512.

Zeskind, P., & Ramey, C. Fetal malnutrition: An experimental study of its consequences on infant development in 2 caregiving environments. *Child Development*, 1978, *49*, 1115–1162.

Zigler, E., & Butterfield, E. Motivational aspects of changes in IQ test performance of culturally deprived nursery school children. *Child Development*, 1968, *39*, 1–14.

Zunich, M. Relationship between maternal behavior and attitude toward children. *Journal of Genetic Psychology*, 1962, *100*, 155–165.

Zunich, M. Child behavior and parental attitudes. *Journal of Psychology*, 1966, *62*, 41–46.

Author Index

Subject Index